Kant on History and Religion

Kant

on History and Religion

with a translation of Kant's 'On the failure
of all attempted philosophical theodicies'

by Michel Despland

McGill – Queen's University Press   Montreal and London 1973

© McGill-Queen's University Press 1973
ISBN 0 7735 0125 8
Library of Congress Catalog Number 73 79094
Legal Deposit Fourth Quarter 1973

This book has been published with the help of a grant from the
Humanities Research Council of Canada, using funds provided by the
Canada Council.

Design by Richard Hendel
Printed in Canada by T. H. Best Printing Company Ltd.

Regis College Library

Contents

Introduction

The ultimate aim of this study is a reinterpretation of Kant's views on religion and especially of *Religion within the Limits of Reason Alone*. The interpretation I am offering is a fresh one, I believe, because Kant's writings on religion are brought into the wider context of Kantian thought, not by reference exclusively to his writings on ethics, but rather by reference to his writings on history. I hope to bring out the full meaning of Kant's philosophy of religion not primarily through the study of his views on morality and on the source of the moral law, but rather through the study of his views on the philosophy of history and on the problems of theodicy. His writings on history, being little known and often little understood, are necessarily an important part of this study.

An intrinsic contention of this study therefore is that the approach through his writings on history provides a better interpretative key to Kant's difficult[1] writings on religion than the traditional approach which starts with the results of his philosophical ethics. This is the maximal form, so to speak, of my contention. The minimal form is that the interpretation of his philosophy of religion through his philosophy of history should be placed alongside the interpretation through the results of his ethics.

That the "traditional" approach to Kant's philosophy of religion is a well-established one is not to be doubted. It has a basis in *Religion within the Limits of Reason Alone*, where it is made clear that the limits set upon religious conviction and religious activity are those determined by morality. To conclude from this that Kant offered a strictly moral interpretation of religion and that the *Critique of Practical Reason* was the book that would shed light on his views of religion were easy steps, and many have taken them. One widely used paperback introduction to Kant treats Kant's views on religion at the end of a chapter on the possibility of moral experience and implies that religion has no other significant content except the rational faith, or moral act of faith.[2] The only major work in English on Kant's philosophy of religion is probably responsible for this kind of statement. C. C. J. Webb stated in 1926 that "it is the distinctive feature of his philosophy of religion that it teaches us to seek in our moral consciousness and there alone the essence of religion."[3] To go further back, a whole nineteenth century tradition, focused in Matthew Arnold's famous and catchy phrase "religion is morality touched with emotion,"[4] identified the genuine concerns of religion with those of morality and always claimed, not without reason, Kant as their master in these matters.

These traditional views seem to me unnecessarily extreme and suspiciously lacking in nuances. (Remember Webb's "and there alone.") More importantly, I believe I can show that since 1926 Kantian studies have progressed in such a way as to make imperative a review and revision of such traditional views.

Numerous are the developments in Kantian studies since the publication of Webb's book that give us a solid basis for a reevaluation. One must first mention the ongoing publications of Kant's manuscripts, of the lectures on metaphysics, on history of religion, of the notes written during the preparation of *Religion within the Limits of Reason Alone*, and of numerous other reflections. This material, of course, is to be used very carefully: the lectures are edited for the most part on the basis of students' notes, and whatever was written while Kant prepared a book and did not find its way into the published work is perhaps to be considered as suspect (although this point should not be pushed too far). But even with these reservations it remains true that the material of Kant on religion is now quite vast, and is such as to show him defining problems in a wide range of issues, groping with difficulties, rather than expounding a doctrine. Thus there can be more breadth and more depth to contemporary studies of Kant on religion, which may go beyond the material published by Kant during his lifetime and which form the almost exclusive basis of Webb's study.

Furthermore, German scholarship focusing on Kant's theory of religion achieved some important results since that time. At the beginning of the century, with the studies of E. Troeltsch and A. Schweitzer, the view was firmly established that Kant's own piety and religious views were of the "enlightened" type, with a strong presence of the characteristic traits of deism. Troeltsch focused on the relationship established by Kant between religion and history and, after deciding that Kantian talk of revelation and forgiveness is prudential, concluded that, while Kant inaugurated a philosophical interest for the investigation of the history of religion, he remained philosophically entirely with the deistic position according to which history serves only as an illustration.[5] A. Schweitzer saw in Kant's philosophy of religion a tension between the results of critical idealism and those of practical philosophy, but in any case made religion instrumental to a rationally derived civilizational endeavour.[6] In 1929 however, Schmalenbach, under the impact of Otto's book *The Idea of the Holy* (1923), inquired afresh into Kant's personal religiousness and his presentation and understanding of what religiousness is like.[7] Schmalenbach, who did not really examine Kant's elaborated theology or his philosophy of religion, concluded after an imposing gathering of evidence that Kant's awe before infinity, his respect for the moral law, and his religious sense of the *deus absconditus* are both deep and central and are a well-developed and well-characterized sense of the holy which sees the holy primarily as righteous. On this point (and on others) Schmalenbach's *Kant's Religion* also documented the kinship of Kant's piety with that of the Old Testament and of Calvinism. Bohatec called the study revolutionary: it established that Kant's personal religiousness is not rooted in the Enlightenment.[8] Nothing has since come to refute the main body of Schmalenbach's conclusions.

German investigations have also revised the dossier on Kant and Protestantism. In 1899 Friedrich Paulsen's *Kant, der Philosoph des Protestantismus* defined an ideological conflict between the Catholic principle and the Protestant principle, between Aquinas and Kant. Kant is identified with Protestantism, or rather perhaps *Kultur-protestantismus* is identified with Kant, his principle of autonomy of reason and conscience, and his objection to dogmatism. In 1917 in a writing with the same title, Julius Kaftan summarized the results of the whole Ritschlean school: Kant's is the Protestant philosophy on account of the self-critical limits he placed upon our knowledge, and on account of the primacy of the ethical (and, within that, of duty over eudaemonism). The culture of Protestantism is said to have found its philosophical expression in Kant. Further minor articles draw parallels between Kant and Luther, occasionally somewhat laboriously. Since those days however, Werner Schultz's study *Kant, als Philosoph des Protestantismus* (1960) has dealt with these oversimplifications. One might quarrel with Schultz's Troeltsch-like understanding of the problem of the "essence of" something, and with his presentation of the essence of Protestantism as a dialectical neo-orthodoxy, but Schultz's book must be accepted as a remarkably balanced account of the similarities and differences between Kant and classical Protestantism on such matters as faith, freedom, law, love, and grace. Schultz proposed giving up labelling Kant the philosopher of Protestantism.

To this we must add Bohatec's definitive investigation of the sources of *Religion within the Limits of Reason Alone*, a study published in 1938. The book also contains an esteemable interpretation of the main themes of Kant's only book specifically devoted to the philosophy of religion. And, finally, one should not neglect the revival of metaphysical interest in Kant, heralded by Max Wundt's *Kant als Metaphysiker* (1924), a development which gave us Heimsoeth, Heidegger, M. Krüger, and G. Martin.[9]

Besides these developments in Kantian studies there have also been developments in the questions philosophers ask about religion. Kant stated that man learns from nature not like the pupil from the teacher, but like the judge from the witness. The inquirer formulates the questions.[10] The history in this century of the *Forschung* in Kant's philosophy of religion shows that the same happens with inquiries into the thought of major thinkers. Developments in philosophy of religion since the twenties led interpreters to ask different questions of Kant and new nuances of meaning appeared in the master's answers. I have already referred to the impact of Otto's book, *The Idea of the Holy*. The confluence of the streams of Christian theology, philosophy of religion, and history of religions is producing different perspectives with which to approach the Kantian corpus on religion. Likewise, developments in the debate on "morality and beyond" and the whole field of theology of culture (consider the impact of Tillich's work, for instance) prepare us to ask fresh questions about the whole issue of the relationship between morality and religion in Kant. On these grounds too the time has come for a reopening of the dossier on Kant and religion.

The reader may grant that a fresh look at Kant's philosophy of religion is needed, but why, he may ask, should this be done in the light of his philosophy of history?

I believe a prima facie case for this kind of a fresh approach can be made by referring to elements internal to the Kantian corpus. The case rests first of all—but not mainly—on a negative point: Kant's ethical philosophy presents many problems, both in interpretation and, more importantly, in evaluation. Convergent criticisms charge it with formalism, legalism, and a less than adequate attention to the emotional dynamisms of man's ethical life. As we shall see, many of these criticisms are unfounded, but there remains nevertheless a suspicion that the kind of ethical outlook Kant had did not predispose him to the best and fairest awareness of the real dynamics of man's religious life. Thus the question is raised whether Kant's ethics does provide the most satisfactory starting point for any interpretation of religion. And indirectly the question is also raised as to whether his ethical philosophy is the only context in which Kant developed his interpretation of religion and the only part of his philosophical authorship that can function as the gate to an understanding of his philosophy of religion.

The case for attempting to see Kant's writings on history and on religion in a single glance rests also on positive considerations. During the eighteenth century a very close connection existed between philosophy of history and the labours of theologians.[11] Theologians dealt with history constantly and the first philosophers of history were passionately involved with religious issues. First of all theologians gave the initial impetus for the development of techniques of historical criticism, and believers and unbelievers soon crossed swords over the principles of historical criticism and over the interpretation of documents. This need not concern us here, for when Kant thought about history he was not especially interested in the methods and skills of the professional historian. As Weyand pointed out, for instance, he made no clear distinction between *Geschichte* and *Historie*.[12] (Later German historians, not to mention philosophers and theologians, would be left quite speechless if they did not have that distinction to dwell upon!) Secondly and more importantly, the grand philosophy of history created by Augustine (or Lactantius?) long remained the peculiar province of theologians: the interpretation of the overall course of human history, the statement of its purpose, and the timid beginnings of reflection on the significance of man's historical predicament were developed by theologians with religious and occasionally apologetic concerns in mind. Think of Bossuet, for instance, whose statement towers in lonely grandeur and was constantly restated or used as a foil. The eighteenth century anti-theologians gladly accepted to join battle with the believers on this chosen field of philosophy of history. Voltaire, for instance, deemed it essential to develop a non-Christian philosophy of history, or a philosophy of history that would refute the claims of orthodox Christianity. The names of Vico, Bayle, Montesquieu, Leibniz, Lessing, Herder, Hume, and Gibbon all confirm the intimate connection between the first modern philosophies of history and theological debates. Both sides of the argument joined in the belief that the true philosophy of history would firmly establish faith in Providence or definitively discredit the Christian faith. This very agreement among the most bitter adversaries makes it clear that in the eighteenth century the philosophy of history was a burning religious question. The solid hold upon minds gained by the philosophy of progress during the second half of the century indicates the depth and the scope of the intellectual energies devoted to the question. There can be no doubt then that in this century philosophical problems in interpretation of history and theological problems were closely connected and examined together. This connection was at least as close as, if not closer than, the connections seen between morality and religion. Unbelievers were at least as fond of saying that religion stifled progress as of saying that it discouraged virtue.

The desirability—and the feasibility—of a study devoted to Kant's views on both history and religion is ultimately based on a look at the content of Kant's writings in these two areas.[13] Often the two kinds of writings come to deal with the same problems.

On at least four points Kant's writings on history deal with problems which have been traditionally theological problems, since they naturally arise out of key tenets of Christian theism. These four points are: How did evil arise in the world? (see *Conjectural Beginnings of Human History*); Why does God tolerate moral evil and especially the sufferings of the innocent? (see *On the Failure of All Attempted Philosophical Theodicies*); How will history end? (see *The End of All Things*); and Can evil be overcome, or is there moral progress? (see *Perpetual Peace* and the second part of *The Strife of Faculties*). Each one of these questions reappears in one form or another in *Religion within the Limits of Reason Alone*.[14]

It is apparent therefore that Kant's writings on history as they examine the idea of a development of the human race express many theological concerns and often overlap in their content with his writings on religion. Most of them attempt to give some kind of justification of the purposes of the will or agency that lies behind the course of all things and the destinies of men. The problem of theodicy therefore lies at the heart of his attempts at constructing a philosophy of history. Reflections on the nature of moral purposefulness, on the scope of evil in the world, and on the possible empirical evidences of moral purposefulness in history are found also in his writings on religion. This common concern of both sets of writings makes it very difficult to decide for instance whether the essay *On the Failure of All Attempted Philosophical Theodicies* should be classified with his writings on history or with his writings on religion. (Incidentally this essay is so important for this study that I include my translation of it in an appendix. In it Kant profoundly renewed the worn out problem of theodicy, and I trust that the availability of its translation will provide clear evidence for the intellectual forcefulness which Kant brought to problems in philosophy of history and of religion and of the connection which he saw between the two disciplines.)

That Kant approached philosophy of history with religious concerns and especially with the problems of theodicy in mind, is made clear by his use of a peculiar concept of Nature, a use found only in his writings on history.[15] Nature there is not used in the pastoral–poetic sense (country with arresting vistas or scenes of animal life with moral lessons), and not in the scientific, critical sense of Newtonian nature (the system of causal relations empirically known). We hear there of a Nature which is Providence, the mother of mankind, the mainspring of progress, and the guarantee of order. (I shall always capitalize the word when used with that meaning.)[16] Succinctly, we hear of the Nature of the classical metaphysicians. That Kant should use there such a weighty metaphysical concept—and use at first sight rather uncritically—is enough to give considerable philosophical importance to his writings on history. More importantly for my argument now, it establishes a further connection between Kant's views on history and his religious faith that the universe is, ultimately, firmly in wise moral hands. As I hope to show, the use of this concept is also closely related to his conception of a moral faith and his own personal expressions of a philosophic faith in reason.

Finally I may add that Kant's philosophy of history is also concerned with the nature of the Kingdom of God and the significance of the teaching of Jesus. I feel justified, therefore, in concluding that the contents themselves of Kant's writings on history and on religion confirm the suitability of a common study examining both in the light of each other.

But to claim to find a key to Kant's philosophy of religion in his writings on history entails two sizeable problems. The philosophy of history has been a neglected part of Kantian scholarship (although there are signs that a different trend is coming).[17] And this claim of ours means that we will find our meat in Kant's shorter or minor writings, which many tend to consider as being far away on the periphery of Kantian philosophical authorship and as having little relation to the three Critiques,[18] the masterpieces of the critical philosopher (unless one altogether refuses to give them genuine philosophical significance, on grounds of their not being "critical"). On these two points some kind of defense of my position seems to be necessary.

How can one account for the fact that the philosophy of history has not yet imposed itself as a significant or important part of the Kantian whole? Körner and Copleston for instance do not devote a single paragraph to it. As Fackenheim put it: "Many expositors treat Kant's philosophy of history; but few treat it seriously. Many treat it, for it is popular and attractive; few treat it seriously, for it seems unconnected, and indeed incompatible with the main body of his thought."[19] It was once commonly accepted that the eighteenth century was shallow in historical matters[20] and this may have something to do with the little amount of serious interest Kant's philosophy of history received at the hands of Kantian scholarship. And its lack of immediately apparent connection with the monumental Critiques must also have been a factor. The major revivals of Kantian scholarship and thought in the nineteenth century were all led by thinkers who, not particularly concerned about history, were in reaction against post-Kantian "speculation" (and philosophy of history was a large part of Hegelian "speculation"), and found their lodestar in either one of the first two Critiques. (I am thinking mainly of the Heidelberg and Marburg schools respectively.) Dilthey, Troeltsch, Medicus, and Delbos were exceptions in that respect.[21] But, however important these authors were, they have hardly been the dominating influences in Kantian scholarship, particularly in that of the English-speaking world. And when their impact was felt it was more in schools of theology than among the philosophers. Vorländer devoted himself to Kant's shorter writings and went so far as to call the philosophy of history "Kant's favourite topic."[22] (With Weyand I believe this is going a bit too far.) Vorländer's influence however was again limited.

Finally Kant's writings on history have suffered from suspicions arising out of their literary quality. His writings on history have an obvious quality of persuasiveness. They transparently express a rare quality of intellectual concern. (On these two counts only a few pages of the major Critiques can compete with them. Think, for instance, of the prefaces to the *Critique of Pure Reason* and of the opening pages of the section on the transcendental doctrine of method in that same Critique.)[23] Their brilliance, however, may appear to be boldness, and their eloquence may seem to imply lack of philosophic care.

This very literary quality brings us to the second problem. Just how important are Kant's shorter writings in comparison with the three Critiques, these major philosophical achievements? Can one take seriously Kant's thoughts expressed in short occasional essays meant for a wide reading public? Kant's shorter writings on history may have the same force and originality as the Critiques (and I believe they do), but they certainly do not have the same technical thoroughness. To this one should reply that the quick yet well-written essay may be—and often is—more readily expressive of a thinker's deep intellectual concerns than the vast monuments using all the technical philosophical machinery prevalent in the schools of that day. It just may be that we will have to turn to the "minor writings" to find an inkling of the profound intellectual commitments that led Kant to the fastidious and complex work of the Critiques. At any rate to dismiss them as philosophically insignificant strikes me as an insult to their writer.[24]

For those who doubt that the writings on history bear any relation to the standpoint of the Critiques, I shall point out the following facts. Although Kant's pen was quick when it came to letters and essays, the gestation of the Critiques was slow, laborious, and came late in his life. It took him twelve years to write the *Critique of Pure Reason* and he was 57 when he published it. The *Critique of Judgement* was more quickly written (and shows it, for it does not exhibit the same care and throroughness in analysis, and limits itself to two kinds of judgements: the aesthetic and the natural teleological one, with a brief treatment of the moral teleological one), but it appeared in 1790 when Kant was 66. The picture of a Kant growing old, feeling the need to express himself quickly on subjects dear to his heart and mind, resorting to the style of the essay and taking a short cut from the professional drudgery of writing a philosophical monument, is credible indeed.[25]

The earliest of Kant's important writings on history *The Idea* appeared in 1784 (he was then 60) and the last appeared in 1798 in *The Strife of Faculties* and is thus found among the very last texts he prepared for the publisher. When Kant wrote his shorter writings on history he was in full possession of his mature critical standpoint. His works in this field are not essays of his youth, nor of his long pre-critical middle age. And if they are the work of an older man who feels the onrush of age, they are not yet works of senility. The very chronological simultaneity between the writings on history and the publication of the three Critiques forces one to look seriously for a relationship between them.

Moreover, I cannot imagine in Kant's mind a dichotomy between salon polite conversation and philosophical endeavour, the kind of dichotomy, for instance, that some writings of Hume seem to suggest. Kant saw his philosophy of history as working out the problem of a "moral teleology,"[26] namely a teleological process that strives toward the highest good and strives in conformity with the laws of freedom. This puts it right in conjunction with the *Critique of Judgement* and its analysis of the possibility of teleological judgements and with the *Critique of Practical Reason* and its statement of the moral ends men must set before themselves. The force of Fackenheim's statement becomes inevitable: we are obliged to take Kant's philosophy of history seriously, that is, "to treat it as a systematic whole, and a systematic part of a larger systematic whole—the Kantian system."[27]

To accept this view is not to contend that Kant's philosophy of history is a piece of work that is as carefully constructed and as thoroughly worked out as the critical philosophy found in the three Critiques. No serious interpreter will dream of asserting that Kant created a philosophy of history as he created criticism. Kant from time to time simply took up various problems in philosophy of history, all problems which were discussed by his contemporaries, and treated them in the form of essays. What I do contend is that these various essays add up to the outline of a philosophy of history, namely, that they are a consistent whole, and that each piece and their sum exhibit the Kantian philosophical genius at work, and thereby produce a specifically Kantian approach to problems of philosophy of history.

Kant's philosophy of history therefore must and may be squared with the results of the critical philosophy, although this is a task Kant did not pursue himself in detail. The compatibility of the two will be shown later. All we need now is to trust that Kant was intelligent enough to be consistent with himself. As a working hypothesis therefore, I am prepared to take over L. W. Beck's judgement that: "Kant's mature interpretation of history is his application of the principal theses of his critical philosophy to (the) widespread beliefs of his time. None of them he originated. Most of them he accepted when young and modified when old, all of them he illuminated."[28]

I therefore feel no qualms in taking Kant's philosophy of history as philosophically important and as a part of a coherent Kantian whole, even though it came to expression only in "minor writings," nor in turning to it to provide the content for the interpretation of Kant's philosophy of religion, and especially of *Religion within the Limits of Reason Alone.*

In fact, a demonstration of the philosophical significance of the writings on history may be necessary to help the reader see the writings on religion (as a corpus distinct from the philosophical discussion of the theistic proofs) as a significant part of the Kantian whole. To accept Kant's shorter writings as philosophically substantial pieces is a necessary pre-condition of any serious study devoted to Kant's writings on religion. Because, after all, Kant's writings on religion are "minor writings" too. *Religion within the Limits of Reason Alone* is not a fourth Critique, and literarily belongs to the shorter writings, although it is the longest, most elaborate, and obviously most thought out of them.[29] (That Kant's writings on religion and those on history belong both to the same literary category, and were composed during the same period, are further indications of the suitability of a common study devoted to both.)

Furthermore, the very fact that Kant's shorter writings on history do amount to a philosophy of history strengthens the credibility of the view which holds that his writings on religion also amount to a philosophy of religion even though they were never embodied in a "major" work with Critique in its title, and even though they are not immediately and apparently connected to the systematic whole formed by the three Critiques.[30]

That we find in Kant a philosophy of religion is not universally granted, far from it. Many have turned to Kant's writings on religion out of curiosity for the "religious opinions" of such a great man. A few quotations from *Religion within the Limits of Reason Alone* are placed next to testimonies from his friends regarding his practice of church attendance and the question is left at that. In a slightly more sophisticated way, some have turned to Kant's positive utterances on God and to his writings on religion to find out what is left after one has denied the possibility of proofs of the existence of God.

But this is not the kind of interest that I bring to my study nor the kind of study that I propose to offer. My study of Kant "on religion" entails the claim that I find in Kant not just religious views (who does not have those?), not just some conclusions on God (most philosophers have that), but also a thought-out philosophy of religion that can be of use today to anyone concerned with a responsible philosophical and systematic treatment of the problems raised by the notion of "religion." I voiced my dissatisfaction with a tradition of interpretation which, having found a system in the *Critique of Practical Reason*, proceeds to find nothing in *Religion within the Limits of Reason Alone* except a confirmation of the theses of that system, thereby flattening out, so to speak, and treating as a mere appendage, two hundred pages of Kantian effort. Rather I shall contend that there exists in Kant the elements of a self-subsisting philosophy of religion, part of a larger systematic whole to be sure, but nevertheless a coherent intellectual effort, pursued in its own right, following methods of its own, and dealing with problems of its own. I believe that Kant's writings on religion will more readily appear in this light if placed alongside a serious consideration of his writings on history and thereby removed somewhat from the overwhelming intellectual domination of the three Critiques.

Furthermore, I shall contend that there exists in Kant's writings on religion not only a coherent body of thought, but an important transition in the history of Western philosophical efforts regarding religious issues. Until Kant's time, religious philosophy meant primarily metaphysics, first philosophy, or ontology. The concept of God is the major and often the only locus of such a discipline. It is readily granted that Kant effected a shift from "philosophical theism" to "moral theism" and his treatment of the proofs of the existence of God is evidence enough of that. I believe, however, that Kant's writings on religion are important for a further reason. In them Kant effected a transition from a tradition of religious philosophy preoccupied with the doctrine of our knowledge of God to a modern outlook that offers also and perhaps primarily a philosophical interpretation of the nature of religion, of man's religiousness, and of man's religious symbols and institutions. In other words, Kant appears as one of the founders of philosophy of religion in the modern sense of the word. To put it briefly, the philosophical problem of God is religionized and is placed in the broader context of a philosophical consideration of man's religious nature and of man's historical religious communities. A full treatment of Kant on religion must let this philosophy of religion appear beside—or in relationship with—his moral theism. This is one more reason for placing Kant's writings on religion in the context of his philosophy of history. For in Kant's writings on history we find his examination of what man has revealed about himself and his communities throughout his history.

The focusing of attention on Kant's shorter writings on religion does not entail permanently setting aside the philosophical achievements of the three Critiques. The relationship between the critical philosophy as found in the three Critiques on the one hand and the philosophy of religion on the other, will be constantly assumed and clearly shown when relevant, just as I said that the results of the philosophy of history can be squared with those of the critical philosophy. I will thus not fail to illumine Kant's views on religion by reference to the conclusions of the three Critiques.

Thus for the purpose of the interpretation of Kant's philosophy of religion (which is after all my ultimate goal), I do not question at all the relevance and crucial importance of the three Critiques, but I question the value of the tradition that begins and ends with the Critiques (and commonly only with the first two) to interpret Kant's views on religion (how often has Kant's philosophy of religion been summarized by saying that there cannot be any theoretical proof of the existence of God, but there can be a moral one, and that the religious man accepted the imperatives of the moral law as coming from God himself and does not need to go to church?). The quarrel is really with a question of order. It may be that Kant's philosophy of religion has been a neglected part of Kantian scholarship because it has not yet yielded all its meaning on account of the established custom of interpreting it in the light of a few *loci classici* of the critical philosophy. At any rate, by placing it first in the context of the shorter writings on history, the one to which it naturally belongs, I hope to be able to show its full meaning and to present all its implications with greater accuracy and greater depth. I do not believe that the statement will emerge that Kant's philosophy of religion is not at all a moral one. But I do hope to circumscribe more exactly and with greater nuances the sense in which it can be said that Kant offered a moral interpretation of religion.

One last point needs to be made. It takes us beyond Beck's judgement quoted earlier. I shall also suggest that a new avenue for the understanding of the three Critiques can perhaps be found if the

Critiques are set in the context of the writings on history and religion. The critical philosophy was not for Kant a *philosophia perennis* but a historical event. Kant presented it as a new stage growing out of the previous ones. Kant's very concept of criticism is ultimately related to his philosophy of history and to his kind of belief in God, and the critical philosophy can be inscribed within the framework provided by his philosophy of history and that of religion. To show that, however, would be a huge task far beyond the already not too modest scope of this study.

It will have to remain my general contention therefore that there is an organic relationship between the philosophy of history and religion on the one hand and the critical philosophy on the other. Although vastly differing in style, each of the two sets of writings is conditioned by the other and each must be illumined by the other. In the discussion of Kant's philosophy of history and of his philosophy of religion I will include chapters drawing upon the three Critiques to illumine the philosophical issues encountered in his doctrine of history and of religion. What reassessment, if any, of his entire philosophy may follow from the results of this investigation into his philosophy of history and his philosophy of religion remains to be seen. Whatever is the worth of my suggestions in this area, to contribute to a better grasp of a part of Kant's philosophy would be reward enough for me:

I. The Philosophy of History

Chapter 1

The Context of Kant's Philosophy of History: The Omnipresence of Teleological Statements

Kant's philosophy of history wrestles with the idea of progress and with the notion of development of the human race. More specifically, natural and historical teleology (or the idea of steady development in nature and history, aiming towards the realization of a good goal or a desirable purpose) is a theme frequent in Kant's writings on history. They will also be found in his writings on religion.

Kant's proneness to teleological thinking is a trait which is characteristic of the eighteenth century. Such assumptions as: the world is progressing towards a greater perfection; mankind is heading towards a goal; there is a wise and intelligent Creator who ordered the "course of things"; man has a chief end to which all his purposes may be subordinated, hierarchically organized in a coherent whole; or, man has a goal towards which all his impulses lead him; man's chief end is union with God (or an end willed and set by God)—may no longer be common in our age but in some form or other were accepted in the deistic atmosphere of eighteenth century philosophy. (They were of course taken for granted and refurbished by Christian theologians.) Teleology was seen in a more or less religious light, arguments from teleology in nature were thought to be the best to lead human minds to a contemplation of God, and God was seen as the Author of a plan (even though his active providential role in the carrying out of the plan came under increasing attack in deistic circles). If authors remained shy of the rather theistic affirmation of a divine purpose freely chosen by God out of love, they often only compensated by speaking more abundantly and more uncritically of a plan of Nature automatically unfolding.[1]

As we shall see, in Kant's case the critical philosophy was brought to bear incisively on the problem of teleological language. Here too Kant was Kant, namely proved himself the philosopher who came to see the sterility of the philosophical opposition of schools in his age (as is well known for matters of epistemology, metaphysics, and theology), transcended the alternatives between the teleological and mechanical schools and opened a fresh path of thought. In the case of teleology Kant began with conservative opinions, with a firm belief in purposefulness in the natural world and in history.[2] Furthermore a religious faith in purpose in Nature or in divine purpose remained with Kant throughout his life, although the reality of doubt and the fear of meaninglessness in human developments came to press Kant for a close examination of the meaning of this faith and led to a clarification and qualification of it. Teleological statements being so crucial for the constitution of Kant's philosophy of history (and being even for him a condition *sine qua non* of the discovery of meaning in history), it becomes very important to trace exactly the Kantian expressions of beliefs in purposiveness in the universe and to try to discern in what ways his mind evolved on that subject. Thus we shall see at the outset both the positive substance at the heart of the content of his philosophy of history and the problematic elements that made it into a philosophy rather than an unexamined set of notions and beliefs.

The earliest of Kant's teleological statements is found in 1755 in his first publication *The General History of Nature and Theory of the Heavens*. The whole of the cosmos is seen as teleologically organized as well as operating according to mechanical laws. Aristotelian finality is used thoroughly. To what ridiculous extremes Kant was prepared to go in the name of teleology is shown by a short piece of the same year on earthquakes which explains the benefits of such apparent calamities. Even the famous Lisbon earthquake (1 November 1755) cannot have been unadulterated evil since it occasioned the appearance of health-giving mineral springs in East Prussia! The *Theory of the Heavens* firmly affirms the goodness of the Supreme Purpose which rules everything in the world, states that ours is the best of all possible worlds, that all evils contribute in the production of the highest perfection. The contemplation of this perfection of Nature gives rational creatures their highest satisfaction:

> All nature, which involves a universal harmonious relation to the self-satisfaction of the Deity, cannot but fill the rational creature with an everlasting satisfaction, when it finds itself united with this Primary Source of all perfection. Nature, seen from this centre, will show on all sides utter security, complete adaptation.

The changeful scenes of the natural world will not be able to disturb the restful happiness of a spirit which has once been raised to such a height. And while it already tastes beforehand this blessed state with a sweet hopefulness, it may at the same time utter itself in those songs of praise with which all eternity shall yet respond.[3]

Kant at this stage showed no sign whatsoever of wishing to make any dent in the Leibnitian conviction about the perfection of this world, even less of being tempted to make a frontal attack upon this conviction in the manner of Voltaire's *Candide* (1759). One qualifying point however is made: man is among all living beings the one who least reaches the end of his existence. This announces Kant's further probings. The problematic nature of human teleological development is hinted at at this early stage, but this is not allowed to qualify the general statement of religious and complete optimism, since it is assumed that the human race, if not the individual, will surely reach its end.[4] Kant remained firmly embedded in the philosophical tradition of the day.

In 1759 when he published the program outline of a course under the title *An Attempt at Some Considerations on Optimism*, he remained the faithful disciple of Leibniz and Wolff. The world is under a "benevolent necessity"[5] which makes us feel secure and gives rise only to what is best. "The whole is for the best, and everything is good in relationship to the whole."[6] We live under "the most perfect of all possible plans which could be conceived by the best of all beings."[7] In 1764, in his *Observations on the Sense of the Beautiful and the Sublime* he drew attention to the fact that Providence "placed within us as supplements to virtue assisting drives."[8] Our impulses help us towards our moral goal when our will is weak.

In 1764, however, something new appeared and there were signs of a turning point. In remarks written in an interleaved copy of the *Observations* Kant credited two authors for having shown to him that destiny and God are "justified."[9] In the light of his previous writings one would assume that Leibniz was the one who had done just that but instead of him we find the names of Newton and Rousseau.

That Newton dealt severe blows to the Aristotelian theory of causality, and especially to final causes, by setting forward a mechanical picture of the universe of nature is well-known and Newtonian science did frequent yeoman's service in all the polemical onslaught against the Leibnitian system.[10] Rousseau was presented by Kant as having "strange and irrational opinions which are so contrary to what is generally practised." Yet he is said to have "set me right." "I learned to honour men." "Rousseau was the first who discovered underneath the manifoldness of the forms assumed by man his deeply hidden nature and the concealed law according to which destiny is justified by his observations."[11] A specific parallel is drawn between the discovery made by Rousseau and that of Newton who opened up understanding of the natural world.

The interpretation of these references to Newton and Rousseau is delicate. References linking the name of Rousseau to the "dignity of human nature" are numerous at that time. That "a change of heart" occurred is maintained by Schilpp[12] and Rousseau is said by him to have been "the inspirer of Kant in one of his most fruitful periods of intellectual development."[13] It is not my task here to evaluate the significance of Kantian development at this time for his ethical theory[14] but I believe that something important happened at that time for the place of teleological thinking in Kant. That the integrated teleological world view of Leibniz gave way to admiration for Newton and Rousseau means the disruption of a whole and the replacement of it by the lineaments of a two world theory: the mechanical world of nature and causality on the one hand (later the phenomenal world) and the moral world of man, where the notions of human freedom and human destiny assume a central place (later the noumenal world, or that of practical reason). The uniquely problematic nature of the pursuit of ends in the case of man is allowed to stand out better since it is made to hang upon human freedom and morality. The problem of evil arose as one that could not receive a Leibnitian solution and that shattered any simple view of unhindered development in history. This means that from this time on teleological thinking in Kant was in need of re-examination and reconstruction. Kant's thinking about purpose had to be started freshly: an original philosophy of history and nature may have henceforth been in the making.

The next appearance of teleological statements is entirely congruent with this interpretation. Teleological beliefs reappeared with a very limited but clear meaning and scope in the important essay *On the Different Races of Men* (1775, revised 1777). The essay is concerned with demonstrating the biological unity of the human race and the usefulness of the diversity of races within this unity of the race. Biological unity is accompanied by a variety of species to allow adaptation to a variety of climates.[15]

"All men on the whole earth belong to one and the same race, because they can produce children with each other." And, "Man was destined for all climates and all kinds of lands."[16] There had to be in him therefore different "germs" and "natural dispositions" which could develop or be held back as the case may be, so that man could adapt everywhere to his habitat and appear "as if he were made for it." Kant's concern here was to demonstrate that the unity of the human race is dynamic and flexible, and that it is compatible with diversity of traits and characteristics. As Kant laid the biological basis for his anthropology, he used teleological modes of thought: the various kinds of men are produced by an intelligent cause which pursues a final end —the unity of mankind and the occupation of the entire planet. As Vlachos put it, "The biological unity has a purpose and anticipates the ideal community of ends which is prescribed by morality."[17] Mankind is one and cosmopolitan by nature and destiny (and that both in the physical—biological and geographical—sense and in the political sense).

To see mankind as teleologically organized, aiming from biological unity towards political (or moral) unity is a considerable restriction in comparison with the previous plethora of teleological statements.[18] Teleological statements, however, remain extremely important. Natural teleology (the biological unity of mankind under the differentiation of races) is the necessary condition for the possibility of a striving after political (or moral) unity, even though it does not guarantee the development of mankind into a cosmopolitan whole. Thus teleology in biological organization and teleology in human affairs may not be confused.

The minister from Gielsdorf, Schulz, was told so in no uncertain terms when Kant reviewed in *Raisonnirendes Bücherverzeichnis* in 1783[19] his *Essay on an Ethics for All Men without Distinction of Religion*. Schulz had argued for an exact continuity between natural necessity and the operations of the will. In his case, as in that of many others, the Leibnitian teleology under the impact of Newtonian science without the impact of Rousseau had become moral Newtonianism or moral determinism. This transforms human behaviour into a "puppet show," noted Kant, and "destroys entirely the concept of obligation." "Duty or the imperative which distinguishes the practical law from the moral law places us also in idea completely outside the chain of nature." I may not be able to answer how it came that I am a free being, but as I ask myself what I must do now, "freedom is a necessary practical supposition."[20] Even the fatalist acts on the assumption that he is free. It is clear that Kant cannot conceive human civilization and culture as gradually, naturally, appearing effects of the development of Nature. Any philosophy of history will have to deal with problems of teleology in the light of the specifically Kantian concept of freedom and with the idea of discontinuity between the worlds of which Newton and Rousseau speak.

Kant attempted just such a reconciliation between the idea of human freedom and the idea of an intelligent cause orienting the development of the human race in a decisive essay of 1784, *Idea for a Universal History from a Cosmopolitan Point of View*. (The year saw also the publication of the essay *What is Enlightenment?* in which Kant entered rather decisively the eighteenth century debate on history.) The *Idea* gives us the core of his philosophy of history. It presents itself as a possible outline for narrating a history of mankind which "should not displace the work of practising empirical historians" but is "only a suggestion of what a philosophical mind (which would have to be well-versed in history) could essay from another point of view."[21] The outline uses teleological concepts by attributing to Nature an end: the development of all natural capacities of man. This outline also affirms that man, being free, must be the cause of his own cultural development. The main task of the essay is to establish the links and distinctions between the end pursued by Nature and the fact that men choose the ends they set before themselves.

The essay begins with a definition of history, which is said to be concerned with narrating human actions, and a presentation of the problem which the philosopher sees in history, namely, Can we discern in history a regular movement? or Can "what seems complex and chaotic in the single individual" be seen, "from the standpoint of the human race as a whole, to be a steady and progressive though slow evolution of its original endowment"?[22] (Note that here Kant sought no higher standpoint than that of the human race as a whole. In the essay on earthquakes he had chided man's conceit in regarding himself as the sole purpose of Nature. Now he seems to have taken for granted that man is, to use a phrase he was to use later, "the ultimate end of Nature.") The question to Kant was a poignant one. "One cannot suppress a certain indignation when one sees men's actions on the great world stage and finds, beside the wisdom that appears here and there among individuals, everything in the large woven together from folly, childish vanity, even from childish malice and destructiveness."[23] Since men do not seem to be pursuing wise purposes, the only hope seems to lie in whether one "can discover a natural purpose in this idiotic course of things human."[24]

The essay proceeds by means of nine theses with comments. For present purposes, citation of the first three will suffice.

1. All natural capacities of a creature are destined to evolve completely to their natural end.

2. In man (as the only rational creature on earth) those natural capacities which are directed to the use of his reason are to be fully developed only in the race, not in the individual.

3. Nature has willed that man should, by himself, produce everything that goes beyond the mechanical ordering of his animal existence, and that he should partake of no other happiness or perfection than that which he himself, independently of instinct, has created by his own reason.[25]

The next year in 1785, besides commenting on Herder's philosophy of history, and thus confirming his stake in the field, Kant returned to what seems to have been one of the persistent sources of his interest in teleology after his critical awakening out of dogmatism, namely, biological anthropology and the notion of adaptability of the human race. While the essay on *The Concept of Race* seeks greater scientific accuracy than the essay of 1775-77 on the same subject, it adds nothing new but restates that man had to be able to occupy all the earth.[26] What is more interesting about this essay is the response it occasioned. Georg Forster in the *Deutsche Merkur*,[27] among other criticisms blamed Kant for using teleological concepts in his anthropology and denied that such principles were of any use in scientific investigation. (Is there any room to pause in the fact that Kant's use of the concept of purpose in biology brought controversy, while that of purpose in history did not?) Kant replied in 1788 with the essay *On the Use of Teleological Principles in Philosophy.*

The essay argues that there are two ways open to study the natural world: the theoretical one (that is the task of physics) and the teleological one (this runs into metaphysical problems). Reason is not perfectly satisfied by the former but must exercise extreme caution in the latter: it may speak only of the ends determined a priori by pure practical reason[28] (for instance to speak of a plan of Nature establishing the biological unity of the human race for moral purposes is legitimate since the moral unity of the human race is dictated by pure practical reason). Reason may use *only* the ends dictated by pure

reason but it *must* use them to be guided in its investigations. Thus
there is nothing wrong in having anthropological observation guided
by morally important concepts. Kant allowed that the right to use the
teleological principle in the study of the natural world is not yet set in
perfect light (his *Critique of Judgement* did just that two years later)
and he insisted that priority in the study of nature must always be
given to empirical research. Thus the scientist must forbear the use of
so-called "fundamental forces" that are too convenient to explain
everything.[29] There is no return to Aristotelian science after Newton.
Caution also dictates the avoidance of confusion between teleological
and theological language: the frontiers of each mode of knowledge
must remain scrupulously delineated. (Here again the third Critique
subsequently set things straight.)

To sum up, we have seen Kant speak loosely of purposefulness in
many things, thus sharing in a proneness of his century. With Newton
however, a mechanistic world view replaced a teleological one and
science undertook to know nature through material causes exclusively
and not through final causes. With Rousseau Kant discovered the
unique dignity of man and a discontinuity between human beings and
mechanically understood nature. Teleological thinking remained a
live option for him for biology (the adaptability of organisms in particular) and history and he continued to think teleologically in these
cases. What then is the proper place for teleological thinking? This
philosophical deadline is met partly in 1781 in the *Critique of Pure
Reason*, in the pages on the idea of purpose in Nature, and more fully
in 1790 with the *Critique of Judgement* which teaches the proper use of
the concept of purpose. Two parts of the third Critique examine the
use of teleological thinking in aesthetics and biology and prescribe
rules in each case. A long appendix summarizes the mature form of
Kant's philosophy of history by relating teleology of nature and teleology of history and showing their common roots in the purpose of a
wise and good God. Thus rules for the use of concept of purpose are
one of the tripartite critical achievements of Kant.[30] Statements of
purpose survived his awakening from dogmatic slumber.

I believe I shall show that the attention which Kant paid to the
problem of evil in the years which immediately followed the publication of the *Critique of Judgement* represents a further challenge to the
permanence and vigour of teleological thinking in Kant.[31] He came to
see evil as radical and such a perception did threaten to clash with the
underlying theme of teleological organization for a good end. But
even after this second earthquake Kant returned to teleological state-

ments to state his convictions. In 1793 in the essay *That May Be True in Theory But Does Not Hold Good in Practice* he refuted Mendelssohn's statement that the human race does not progress in the name of Nature and Providence, which instilled in us a self-love that leads to progress.[32] *Perpetual Peace* in 1795 states that Nature saw to it that wood would drift to the Arctic where it does not grow. Here again it is affirmed that Nature wanted men to spread everywhere and to force them to lawful relations.[33] *Anthropology* (1798, reprinted 1800) reaffirms in a compact form Kant's statements on the purpose of Nature. Providence educates man according to a clear purpose, which only the race reaches.[34]

While this survey, for the sake of simplicity, focused on concrete examples of teleological thinking in Kant and passed over lightly the technical discussions of the Critiques on ends and purposes, the importance of these discussions should not be overlooked. The crux of the entire matter, it seems, is to be found in Kant's wrestling with the concept of Nature, after the impact of Newton was felt. And the serious discussion of the problem of the conception of Nature (and the related problem of the idea of the world) is found in the Critiques, especially in the first one. How must I think of the natural world? In what sense, if any, can it be said to exhibit purposeful organization? These are the critical questions confronting Kant over his concept of Nature, after Newton.

Newtonian science, Kant saw, was metaphysically important because it led to a redefinition of the meaning of nature. The whole of nature may now be seen on the model of a machine, as a connection of simple and one-sided causal relations.[35] Yet the Newtonian meaning of nature did not exhaust Kant's thinking on Nature. The pages on the idea of the world, the second of the three Ideas of Reason in the *Critique of Pure Reason*, are of extreme interest in this connection. We find there a series of rational demonstrations which prove both thesis and antithesis in a series of antinomies.[36] (The world has a beginning in time and is limited in space; everything is made up of simple parts, or there are no simple parts; there is only one causality, that according to laws of nature, or there is also a causality of freedom; there belongs to the world, either as its part or as its cause an absolutely necessary being, or there is no absolutely necessary being.) F. Alquié was probably right when he emphasized that it is this series of antinomies which above all else awoke Kant from what he called his "dogmatic slumber."[37] At any rate the solution Kant gave to these antinomies (they all carry the presumption of treating of things-in-themselves as well as make the impossible claim of knowing the totality of an infinite series) has a very clear import: the Newtonian mechanical world-view cannot claim to give us knowledge of the world as a whole. As Alquié put it: "Kant criticized a very rational cosmology in order to fight the pretention of eighteenth century science to usurp the place of a defunct metaphysic and establish itself a sufficient system of reality."[38]

Since knowledge fails us in this domain a metaphysical consideration of Nature is still possible, and Newtonian science does not fill the space destined to it. Such metaphysical consideration of Nature is what we find in the philosophy of history where we hear of a Nature which is good and wise and has a plan (and which I consistently capitalize). Another metaphysical consideration of Nature is found in the critical philosophy, in the consideration of the existing natural world that does not follow Newtonian principles but rather uses teleological ones and speaks of purposeful organization of Nature. For Kant saw in the problem of teleology not only a problem of method but also a problem of philosophy of nature. In this sense Kant did not rest his case either with the Enlightenment mechanical world view (with or without a mechanic to put the machine together at the beginning) or with the mere methodological employment of a heuristic idea of an end-pursuing Nature. *The Metaphysical Elements of Natural Science* (1786) shows the strength of this interest of Kant's. He remained convinced about the possibility and necessity of a teleological philosophy of Nature. The literary activity of his very last years (besides the publications of his lectures on anthropology and pedagogy and the completion of a *Metaphysic of Morals* [1797]) returned to problems of metaphysics of Nature. Unlike the romantic school, however, which began with Herder and culminated in Hegel's philosophy of nature, Kant remained extremely cautious about overabundant statements of final causes that are not related to the purposes dictated to us by practical reason.

We must leave aside, however, the problems of Kant's philosophy of nature which are quite complex. (The reworking of the metaphysical elements of natural science was never completed precisely because Kant ran into problems when he tried to figure the passage between physics or transcendental philosophy on the one hand to the metaphysics of Nature he tried to constitute on the other.) Such problems are quite beyond the scope of this inquiry. We must return to the problems of teleology in general to emphasize that Kant's unique strength is to be found in the control which his moral philosophy exercised over his teleological thinking. Here again the tasks of meta-physics are built upon pure practical reason. Thus Kant formulated an original position on teleological statements. He tolerated only those teleological beliefs which were required by and strengthened moral imperatives, namely those teleological affirmations which affirmed the destiny of the human race to cosmopolitanism. This is why he retained the statement about the wisdom of Providence sending wood to the Arctic while he rejected without any apparent regret all the statements about ermine tails being meant to enable the little animals to see each other on the Siberian snow plains.[39]

Chapter 2

The Content of the Writings on History

As we saw in the previous chapter Kant brought to his philosophy of history a general readiness to make teleological statements about processes in nature and history, and thus a concern for discerning purpose in the development of human affairs. A radical questioning however arose due to scientific knowledge of nature which proceeds very well with an exclusion of all causes except those which Aristotle called material causes, and due to a view of man, strengthened by Rousseau, which affirms that man, whatever he is, is not very good at following the apparent purposes dictated to him by his nature. To this situation we owe the fact that Kant developed a philosophy of history that is critical rather than naive, original rather than a restatement of current beliefs.

Much of Kant's philosophy of history is to be found in essays already referred to: the two essays of 1784: *What is Enlightenment?* and the *Idea for a Universal History from a Cosmopolitan Point of View*, and the two reviews of Herder published in 1785. To this Kant added in 1786 the *Conjectural Beginnings of Human History* and, at the very end of his career, *An Old Question Raised Again: Is the Human Race Constantly Progressing?* (1798). To these essays should be added a variety of other related essays for a variety of reasons. *What does it Mean to Orient Oneself in Thought?* (1786) contains interesting remarks on the becoming of reason and the progress of philosophy. *Perpetual Peace* (1795) elaborates the important connection between the philosophy of history and political philosophy. *On the Failure of All Attempted Philosophical Theodicies* (1791) and *The End of All Things* (1794) deal with themes relevant to both the philosophy of history and the philosophy of religion. Finally the Appendix to the *Critique of Judgement* (1790) contains in summary form a mature systematic statement of the philosophy of history and is perhaps the best single source to which the reader should be referred.

I plan to proceed with the exposition of the Kantian philosophy of history not by using the order in which the various essays were written, but by means of a systematic division between the interpretation of the past, that of the present, and that of the future, or a division between what the plan of Nature was in the past (and how it worked), where it has taken us now, and where it may take us in the future. The relevance of such division to the Kantian philosophy is that it will set in clear focus the live core of this philosophy of history, namely our moral duty to effect a certain kind of transition between present and future. Furthermore this division will also bring to light Kant's views on our attitude towards the future (an area of his thought where the concerns of his philosophy of history and those of his philosophy of religion overlap). Thus in Kant's writings on history I shall discern three basic elements of a doctrine: an account of the origins of man's historical predicament (how Nature forced us out of the state of nature into a state of conflict and culture); a statement of what it means today to be a historical being (namely to live in a state of conflict, arbitrated by a civil community, or State, and under the discipline of the civil law as well as of the moral law); and finally an outline of what should be one's attitude toward the future, and a statement of what man may hope (to work for the League of Nations and hope for the perfect moral community).[1] This order will also enable me to touch upon what Beck called the three fundamental Ideas of Kant's historical writings: Nature as a theoretical Idea (which is thought to take us from one state to another with an end in view), the State, and a League of Nations, as practical Ideas (which embody ends we have and must have before ourselves).[2]

The Past: The Origins of Man's Historical Predicament; From Nature to Culture

A short essay of 1786, *Conjectures on the Beginnings of Human History* gives a conjectural account of how historical experience began. To describe the prehistorical state, Kant postulated a couple of human beings, led by instinct, by "this voice of God." (His picture coincides with *Genesis* and his essay continues to use the biblical narrative as a guiding thread.)[3] "As long as man obeyed the call of Nature, all was well within him. But soon reason began to stir,"[4] and it introduced representations distinct from those given by instinct. "One of the properties of reason consists in the capacity with the help of imagination to create desires artificially."[5] Creating new images of man, conceptions of new goals for man's behaviour, reason suddenly entered for the first time in conflict with the voice of Nature and thus gave to man the first opportunity of a free choice and broke his innocent simplicity. In other words man left the state of nature to enter the state of culture. (Culture incidentally is defined dynamically by Kant as "the production in a rational being of an aptitude for any ends whatever of his own choosing, consequently of the aptitude of a being in his freedom.")[6]

Man discovered in himself a power to choose for himself his own behaviour and not to be bound like other animals to one single course of action. To the satisfaction which must have been aroused in him by the discovery of this advantage, there must have succeeded immediately dread and restlessness (*Angst und Bangigkeit*): how would he deal with this newly discovered power, he who does not know latent properties and remote effects of everything? He was so to speak at the edge of a precipice, because besides the objects of desire which instinct indicated to him, an infinity of others were offered, among which he did not know how to choose. And after having known once this state of freedom it was impossible for him to fall again under the servitude of instinct.[7]

Nature expelled him from the existence of tranquil childish innocence as from a garden where he could find his subsistence without care, and precipitated him into the vast world, where so many cares, troubles and unknown woes await him. In the future, the difficulties of his life will often cause him to wish a return to a paradise, creation of his imagination, where he could in tranquil leisure and perpetual peace while away his existence in dream or play. But between him and this imaginary sojourn of delight, stands inexorable reason, which irresistibly pushes him to develop the faculties placed in him and does not allow him to return to the rustic and simple state from which it drew him.[8]

Men can be chagrined by this evolution: they entered into a state dominated by private pursuit, labour, inequality, and warfare; and there are no greater sorrows than those of wars.

The relationships between this Kantian view of the origins of the historical predicament of man and the eighteenth century debate centring on Rousseau are obvious. Kant, like Rousseau, knew that man no longer lives in the state of nature, but is now in a rather different kind of dispensation characterized by social rivalry, the presence of moral evil, and a variety of pressures to lead us to a vigorous exercise of all our faculties. He differed from Rousseau, or rather from the most common interpretations of Rousseau, in that he could not think of the transition from nature to culture as a decadence, and that even though he used the biblical narrative of the Fall to give an account of the transition.[9] The state of culture is the state in which human freedom has begun to be at work; human dignity is now achievable even though it may be rarely achieved and is a frequent victim of human evil-doing. The state of culture is an ambiguous state. It does not ensure happiness and does not guarantee the victory of good over evil. But, compared with simple innocence, ambiguity is a step ahead. Because in the state of culture (or war), man begins to develop his faculties, including those for rational thought, and even more importantly, develops them by himself, for purposes he chooses. Culture gives man the aptitude for freedom. The paradoxical nature of this "fall" or entry into culture and history is well expressed in a Kantian formula: Adam and Eve "abused reason in the very first use of reason." Indeed, but it was a first use of reason.[10]

The Present Historical Predicament: The Age of Legality and of Morality

Thus we have a picture of how man, through the awakening of imagination and desire, was precipitated into history, into a state of war and of striving after peace. This state of antagonism however is not without purpose: it corresponds to a plan of Nature. By precipitating men into war, Nature forces them to seek to "establish a lawful order among men," namely, to maintain a State. As the fourth thesis of the *Idea* puts it: "The means employed by Nature to bring about the development of all the capacities of men is their antagonism in society, so far as this is, in the end, the cause of a lawful order among men."[11]

By antagonism, added Kant, he means "anti-social sociability."[12] Man leans to association with others, but he is also anti-social because of his untutored desire to direct everything his own way. He therefore finds himself opposing others and opposed by them. This situation is the cause of an effort towards some ordering of society. It is opposition

> which awakens all his powers, brings him to conquer his inclination to laziness and, propelled by vainglory, lust for power, and avarice, to achieve a rank among his fellows whom he cannot tolerate but from whom he cannot withdraw. Thus are taken the first true steps from barbarism to culture, which consists in the social worth of man; thence gradually develop all talents, and taste is refined; through continued enlightenment the beginnings are laid for a way of thought which can in time convert the coarse, natural disposition for moral discrimination into definite, practical ethical principles, and thereby change a society of men driven together by their natural feelings into a moral whole.[13]

> Let us therefore thank Nature for this unconciliatory humour, for vanity rivalling in envy, for the insatiable appetite of possession or even of domination. Without this all the excellent natural dispositions of man would be stifled in eternal sleep. Man wants concord, but Nature knows better what is good for his species; she wants discord. He wants to live commodiously and at ease; but Nature wants him to be compelled to come out of his inertia and passive satisfaction, to throw himself into labour and toil, to find the means to liberate himself from it wisely. (All this) betrays the ordinance of a wise Creator.[14]

> All culture, art, which adorns mankind, and the most beautiful social order, are the fruits of insociability, which is forced by itself to discipline itself.[15]

Out of discord are born efforts towards, and relative achievement in, concord.

Kant apparently would have agreed with Heraclitus that "conflict is the father of all things."[16] The essay on *Perpetual Peace* reaffirms the idea that "the mechanism of human passions" forces men into civil arrangements to protect themselves against violence. The

Anthropology reduces these passions to five; two innate natural drives: the drive to freedom and the drive to reproduction; and three acquired passions born in the state of culture: the manias for honour, power, and possession (*Ehrsucht, Herrschsucht*, and *Habsucht*).[17] In the manner of Rousseau, the three passions inherited from culture come from a desire to have power over other human beings. Unlike Rousseau, however, Kant insisted that out of the paradox of anti-social sociability arise forms of relative justice and peace. The state of culture for Kant is characterized by public rules and social arrangements. What he contrasted to the state of nature is a civil state or a juridical condition. *The Metaphysical Elements of Justice* put it this way: "The state of nature is not to be contrasted to living in society, which might be called an artificial state of affairs: rather it is to be contrasted to civil society when society stands under distributive justice. Even in a state of nature there can be legitimate societies (conjugal etc.)."[18]

If Kant occasionally echoed Rousseau's themes to the effect that man becomes more skilled at artifice and deception as he becomes more civilized,[19] basically Kant was incapable of contrasting an innocent individual living in a state of nature with a corrupt man living in a state of society. The root of moral evil is and remains in the self and our current state is not just social but also civil. Thus we must emphasize that what characterizes the state of culture is not the need for social control, but civility, that is, organized public mechanisms to protect some rights and administer some justice.[20] The organization of the State is a sign of moral progress, not of moral decadence.

The organization of the civil state however leads inevitably to discussion of what are really rights and what is really justice. The consequences of non-moral behaviour in the age of culture force man to embark on the search for suitable moral conceptions. Morality therefore as well as legality characterizes our current historical predicament. Kant thus came to see two different paths toward peace. On the one hand conflicting men pursuing their desires and developing their faculties, will, out of sheer self-interest, come to some rules and some civil arrangements for the sheer sake of protecting themselves from the extreme forms of violence of others.[21] And subsequently they will come to seek the improvement of these rules and arrangements. This may be called the rise and growth of the legal process. At best it leads to an armistice, and that is not exactly peace. On the other hand undisciplined passions may come, not just under social and legal restraints, but also under personal self-discipline. This is the properly moral process and it was clear for Kant that it alone will lead to perfect peace (although the first kind of armistice may well arrive at a state of durability). The Kantian distinction between legality and morality is well known and ever present in his ethics. What is not so well known is that Kant found the processes of the law to be very significant for the cause of progress of morality even though they are not moral in nature. Thus Kant came to see a connection between the two processes.

Shall we see here two successive stages? Are we to believe that men are led to a state of legal discipline to which they submit for non-moral reasons and then, after that, rise to a state of moral, that is, autonomous, rational self-discipline? In support of this view we can mention that Kant made the life of reason dependent upon a civil constitution guaranteeing freedom of thought.[22] This might indicate that the second process grows out of and comes after the former.[23]

The appearance of an autonomous self-disciplining of reason is, however, a complex matter for Kant. This question, obviously crucial for him, received special treatment in an essay of 1786, *What Does It Mean to Orient Oneself in Thought?* (The essay deals with philosophical rather than legal conflict but the transpositions can easily be made.) Reason there is presented as an individualized dynamic capacity participating in all the predicaments of the human being in conflict with others. Reasons themselves are in conflict with each other. Reason is not science. It is a need. It is lack of knowledge passionately fighting for knowledge. (The traditional opposition faith-reason is undercut.) Reason participates in the individual's drive for self-development and self-realization, and thus clashes with the reason of others. Here Kant stated that it is by thinking aloud on their desires that reasons can orient themselves rationally. "Would we be thinking much, and would we think well, if we did not think in common with others, who make us partake of their thoughts, and to whom we communicate ours"?[24] The answer is obvious. We can be thinking and rational beings only by thinking in common, and we cannot think in common without perfect freedom of thought. Without it there is only authoritative decree and force, no reasoning and no reason. It is the end, not just of the Enlightenment, but of reason itself.[25] Kant could not more clearly say that the life of reason depends on the presence of some legal guarantees, or that the process of morality can arise only in the context of an already existing legal process. At the same time Kant makes it very clear that it is the same reason at work in both the legal and the moral processes.

I should conclude, therefore, that the question of the chronological sequence is not the most important one. The significant Kantian doctrine is that reason disciplines itself, or that man begins to become rational and moral, when man's need in war becomes intelligently self-conscious and when the administration of civil justice becomes conscious of the demands of all human beings. Man at this turning point assumes his duress and believes he has a right to see it answered, and really answered; that is, answered once and for all, in a manner fair to all, and not merely alleviated by social arrangements that check violence. Furthermore man at this stage comes to see his moral responsibility, namely that it is up to himself to decide on the path to follow, and enters into a dialogue with others as to the means whereby one can achieve the end common, by definition, to all: to maintain oneself as reason and as freedom. Such an end is the very foundation of our capacity of being in dialogue with others in a persuasive, non-coercive manner.

We thus cannot let the impression stand that the rational or moral stage of striving towards principled or genuine peace follows in simple chronological sequence the legal stage of accepting temporary or durable armistice arrangements. For one thing transitions and turning points are never so sudden in the Kantian doctrine of history which maintains a strong organic sense and prefers whenever possible to see stages overlap as well as grow naturally out of each other. Furthermore, Kant makes it very clear that our moral life is now lived in a context in which legal processes are not outdated. My topic in this paragraph is Kant's interpretation of our present historical predicament and there is no doubt that for him the legal and the moral processes are both simultaneously present realities. It may be that some men are more advanced in the moral process than others, but, in the light of the Kantian attention to the purity of motives of moral man, it would be hazardous to venture the opinion that for him some men are already beyond the stage of needing the controls of the law or its pragmatic counsels. Legality and morality are distinguished by Kant but not totally opposed. For instance, to pay lip service to the law is not to be moral but it is to show an inkling of morality.[26]

Finally it must be pointed out that besides leading us to the discovery of the concepts of socially imposed discipline and of rational self-discipline, the concept of anti-social sociability can also restore our faith in the wisdom of Nature or Providence. The more vigorously men pursue their own ends, the more opposition they will call forth, and the more urgent the need for discipline will become. Thus, "all conspire unknowingly to the design of Nature." This plan is to have all men develop all their capacities, and anti-social sociability is the means Nature uses to goad men towards this end.

With such a view of the crisis in man's current predicament and of man's current moral task, it follows that the most urgent historical task of the human race today is the realization of a civil society administering justice universally (Thesis five of the *Idea*). This task, dictated by natural teleology and by the moral law, is the most difficult of all and will be solved last, but it is the problem which reason will necessarily strive to solve (Thesis six). The establishment of a perfect civil constitution in any state is related with the establishment of regular relations between states (Thesis seven). The political bodies are at war with each other and thus are forced to strive towards a state of calm and security. In this way, the human species may "work its way out of the chaotic conditions of its international relations." (Here again, through wars, Nature drives men to do what reason would dictate to them in the first place: to enter into a league of nations, with a constitution in conformity with laws. "There shall be no war" was for Kant a clear moral imperative.)[27]

Thus Kant characterized the meaning of the present historical predicament by a plight, conflict, and a task, the rational mediation of conflict through legal and moral means. This being seen we can turn to the third aspect of the question: the prospects for the future.

The Future: Man and Hope

Kant's views on the past and the present historical predicament indicated that he held a theory of progress, or at least that he held a view according to which the human race had progressed from its origins until the present time. To enter into a state of culture, however high is the cost of war, to live in a civil state, however impure are the motivations of men in such a state, are elements of moral growth:

they lead to a state where the use of reason, moral autonomy, and dignity become possible. And current conditions show that man is well on his way towards such moral autonomy. We do not yet live in an enlightened age, but "we do live in an age of enlightenment" announced the first entry into philosophy of history.[28] Nature has uncovered from under its hard shell "the seed for which she most tenderly cares—the propensity and vocation to free thinking," and this "gradually works back upon the character of the people who thereby gradually become capable of managing freedom; finally it affects the principles of government, which finds it to its advantage to treat men, who are now more than machines, in accordance with their dignity."[29]

But Kant also asked questions which cast a shadow over this confidence in moral progress. Does progress in the past guarantee, promise, or even simply give a presumption of progress in the future? Has there really been progress in the past if mankind stays forever in its present woeful and morally ambiguous state? In the essays of 1784, Kant seems to have taken future progress for granted, or at least showed no anxiety over these questions. Buoyancy of spirit over the future, however frequent in the century, is nevertheless uncharacteristic of Kant. His century was not for him full of unambiguous signs of progress. And Kant also differed from his age in the source of his confidence in future progress. "What is the good of esteeming the majesty and wisdom of Creation in the realm of brute nature and of recommending that we contemplate it, if that part of the great stage of supreme wisdom which contains all the others—the history of mankind—must remain an unceasing reproach to it"?[30]

The question is rhetorical. History must have an end, the charted course of progress must reach its goal, or else we are the most miserable of all creatures. If Kant ever instinctively believed in favourable future prospects for the human race, he did it entirely on moral grounds—even on religious grounds—or out of moral need. It is because "Nature, or, better, Providence" must be justified.

Against this background of profound faith in Providence coupled with dark forebodings about the course of the human race, Kant undertook a specific and critical detailed investigation of the idea of progress.

In 1798, one section of *The Strife of the Faculties* (that dealing with the relationship between the faculties of law and of philosophy) broaches the discussion of future prospects by means of the specific question: "Is the human race in constant progress towards the better?"[31] What one wants when this question is asked is a prophetic history, which divines or announces the future. But, "How is an a priori history possible? Answer: if the diviner himself creates and contrives the events which he predicts in advance."[32]

Three answers are possible to the question, each having its difficulties. (1) The race goes from bad to worse until total annihilation: moral terrorism. (2) The race progresses: eudaemonism or chiliasm. (This seems impossible since "effects cannot go beyond the power of the active cause":[33] so, since man is mixed, there will always be a mixture of good and evil.) (3) An eternal alteration of good and evil: abderitism. The rock of Sisyphus is rolled up and rolls down again.[34] The activities of men are ultimately futile. The fact that men when compared to animals devote more intelligence to the task (and have more hopes while doing it) apparently does not give any more worth or guarantee any more success to their efforts.

The problem is further complicated, because even if it is shown that men progressed in the past, this does not establish that they will continue, "For we deal with beings who act freely, to whom one can *dictate* ahead of time what they *must do*, but of whom one cannot *predict* what they *will do*."[35]

To foresee free action is the point of view of Providence, and it is beyond man.

It still remains true that we know with certainty where man's duty lies. And this provides the first part of Kant's answer to the question of the prospect of progress: we have the task to work for the cultural and moral improvement of mankind. The third chapter of *On Theory and Practice* (1793) directed against Mendelssohn makes this clear. Moses Mendelssohn in his *Jerusalem, oder über religiöse Macht und Judenthum* (1783) had written against his friend Lessing's hypothesis of a divine education of the human race to affirm that mankind "maintains at all periods the same level of morality, and the same proportion of religion and irreligion, of virtue and vice, of happiness and misery."[36] Kant fully agreed with the statement of the mixed record of mankind but the one fulcrum on which he could rest his belief in progress was "the innate duty of every member of every generation to see to it that posterity does not cease to improve."[37] Practical reason orders us to act on the hypothesis that the world as a whole is progressing.[38] To state that there is no evidence of such progress so far is not a real obstacle. "The claim that what has not succeeded so far will never succeed, is no ground to give up a pragmatic or technical endeavour (for example, travel through the air in flying machines) and even less to give up a moral endeavour which becomes a duty as long as the impossibility of its realization is not demonstrated."[39]

Furthermore there is a second fulcrum on which the belief in progress can lean. And this is nothing other than a simple faith in Nature and Providence.[40] Success in the task of progress

> depends less on what *we* do (for instance on the education we give to youth) and on the method which *we* follow in order to reach it, than on what human *nature* will do in us and with us to constrain us to follow a path which we would not have broken on our own without difficulties. For it is only from Nature or rather from *Providence* (for a superior wisdom is necessary to achieve this end) that we can expect a success concerning a whole.[41]

The Strife of the Faculties (1798) finds one more ground for feeling somewhat confident about the future of man. It suggests we can find in history or experience one event which indicates in that race a disposition or an aptitude to be the cause of progress and the artisan of it, an historical sign demonstrating the tendency of humanity as a whole.[42] The Enlightenment and the French Revolution, or rather the response to it among all men, the sympathy for it, "bordering on enthusiasm," is such an event. In spite of all the evils the Revolution brought—Kant had heard of the Terror when he wrote—the event proved two things: the Enlightenment is bearing fruit and men are determined to fight for giving to themselves the constitution they deem appropriate, and they believe that such a constitution is in conformity with right and the moral good only if it is meant to avoid in principle offensive war.[43]

As the *Opus Postumum* put it, "The signs of these times reveal in the whole of humanity, among antagonistic societies, a moral disposition, never before observed to such degree, to abolish the greater obstacle to progress, war, and establish for that purpose a constitution incompatible with that purpose."[44]

So one can predict that man will reach his goal in history and that his march forward will never totally regress. The spread of the Enlightenment and the French Revolution are decisive. "Such phenomenon in the history of mankind *cannot be forgotten* because it reveals in human nature a disposition and capacity for improvement."[45]

But what gains exactly do we expect from such a superior political constitution? Not a growth of morality, but an augmentation of acts in conformity to duty. "Little by little, the powerful will use less violence." In other words, the exercise of power will be more and more checked by law. In his discussion of world law in *The Metaphysical Elements of Justice*, Kant states: "The rational Idea of a peaceful, even if not friendly, universal community of all nations on earth . . . is not a philanthropic (ethical) principle, but a juridical one."[46] One can hope for refinements of self-interest and more peaceful social relations, and even a League of Nations, or a "federation of free states" which will "like individual men," "give up their savage (lawless) freedom" and "adjust themselves to the constraints of public law."[47] But even such a tremendous political progress does not mean automatically progress in morality. The League of Nations is not yet the perfect moral community where all discipline is autonomous and based on mutual respect and good will. E. Fackenheim identified the problem exactly. "Even the most law-abiding society is mere glittering misery; no society can legislate a good will."[48] To avoid war is not to change hearts and give peace.[49] Cultural and legal progress is not necessarily moral progress.

I must add finally that Kant's faith in progress (legal or moral) was always expressed against a steadily dark background. The essay on *Perpetual Peace* (1795) begins by mentioning that such was the inscription on a Dutch innkeeper's sign "upon which a burial ground was painted" and this start gives to the whole work the tone of a man who has no illusions. To the essay on progress in *The Strife of Faculties*, after the confession of his faith, the examination of the evidence, and the conclusion that continuous progress "is tenable in the strictest theory," Kant gave a concluding remark telling of a sick man, who, comforted by all his physicians, still tells his friend: "I am positively dying with improvement!" Nations are still at war, *"Sero sapiunt Phryges!"* In the light of all that, Kant can only believe in the possibility of progress, hope for it (and this hope is held in full knowledge of all that denies it; it is a *spes contra spem*), and exhort mankind to orient itself in that direction. The essay on *The End of All Things* (1794) conceives of the possibility of a catastrophic end of history brought about by man's stupidity.[50]

One must insist therefore that besides the imperative we find the confession of a reasonable hope, not a claim to knowledge of what will happen. The emphasis is on the mapping out of man's moral and political duties and on arguing that the prospects of success are encouraging. Repeatedly, we find in Kant such a balance between pietist pessimism (its sense of the seriousness of life and the radicality of evil) and Enlightenment optimism (its confidence in the ongoing progress of reason). The essay of 1791 *On The Failure of All Attempted Philosophical Theodicies* concludes: "No theodicy held its promise until now; none managed to justify divine wisdom in the government of the world against the doubts concerning it which our experience of the world inspires us."[51]

So theodicy, or any doctrine stating that the world is wisely governed and is heading towards a desirable goal, "is much more an affair of faith than of science."[52] Kant had such faith. But he never misled his reader by suggesting that he had any sure knowledge in this matter.

Summary and Conclusion: The Problem of Purpose in History

The overview of the process of human history as presented by Kant lends itself quite easily to an outline of five stages.

1. *The pre-political life or life of instinct.* Man is one with nature and has no representation of future possibilities lying ahead of him and available to his choice. Reason is not awakened. History has not started yet.

2. *The state of cultural freedom.*[53] The imagination develops and men become aware of their capacity to pursue ends which they represent to themselves as desirable. Freedom has appeared. Man has "a capacity for setting before himself ends of his deliberate choice."[54] Men pursue ends defined by their natural inclination and fancies, more or less curbed by fear of others (or heteronomous discipline). This is the stage of war, both literal war and cultural war. Weapons and mental constructs clash. This state cannot last at all. It is really more a transition than a state.

3. *The civil state.* A growth in mutual discipline, motivated by self-interest, enables the appearance of a social organization built upon laws. The State now exists. There is "a constitution so regulating the mutual relations of men that the abuse by individuals striving one against another is opposed by a lawful authority centred in a whole, called a *civil community*."[55] The task of maintaining and im-

proving legality has begun. Besides the checks coming from the civil state, individual inclinations are also progressively made subservient to rational self-discipline and men begin to approximate the ideal of pursuing only rationally defined ends. Fine arts and the sciences, products of the civil state, "do much to overcome the tyrannical propensities of sense, and so prepare man for a sovereignty in which reason alone shall have sway."[56]

> The evils visited upon us, now by nature, now by the egoism of man, evoke the energies of the soul, and give it strength and courage to submit to no such force, and at the same time quicken in us a sense that in the depths of our nature there is an aptitude for higher end.[57]

In this age discipline begins to be autonomous. This is the age of Enlightenment, of the Critique, when men have come of age[58] and begin the transition from the state of war to that of peace. It is the present age.

4. *The state of the cosmopolitan republic.*

> If on the part of men war is a thoughtless undertaking, being stirred up by unbridled passions, it is nevertheless a deep-seated, maybe far-seeing, attempt on the part of supreme wisdom, if not to found, yet to prepare the way for a rule of law governing the freedom of states, and thus bring about their unity in a system established on a moral basis.[59]

Durable peace is to be achieved through a League of Nations. All human relations and all relations between states have come under civil legislation. No man or group of men is allowed to be a threat to any other man, or at least no author of injustice remains unpunished.

5. *The moral commonwealth.* Perfect peace is now achieved. The idea is no longer approximated (as in *3*) or realized exteriorily—and thereby imperfectly—through legislation and its enforcement (as in *4*), but it is now genuinely and internally achieved. The human race is morally unified. No man is a threat to any other man. The ends of no one are incompatible with the ends of any other. This stage is already anticipated in the lives of moral men who act out of pure respect for the law, but it will not be fully realized until that time in the future when all men shall act out of rational motives, or when all citizens of the Kingdom of God shall finally enter into their realm.[60]

To summarize Kant's philosophy of history by the presentation of the five stages could be very misleading if the reader were to place

Kant in continuity with the antique tradition that speaks of consecutive ages. Kant was very much, and perhaps primarily, concerned with problems of development. In each stage we hear of Nature pursuing its purposes. What interested him are not so much the characteristics of each age as the seeds in each for the transition or growth towards the next one. Specifically he strove to discern the laws that govern the transition from each stage to the next: Is such a transition inevitable or probable? Does the transition stem machine-like from instincts and social forces? Does it stem from human purposefulness, or from divine purpose? The attention he paid to the processes of imagination and desire in the case of Adam, to the processes arising from fear and anti-social sociability, and to the processes of the law and of moral education, all indicates his interest in philosophy of history not as a speculative or imaginative presentation of subsequent stages (a speculation which can be optimistic or pessimistic), but as an analysis and interpretation of human becoming and of human self-realization through an orientated process. Here is the strongest evidence for attributing to Kant, in spite of the sketchy nature of his philosophy of history and the apparent ease with which it can be reduced to a mere picture of a series of ages, a genuinely modern historical consciousness which makes of man an essentially temporal creature.[61] In any case it must be emphasized that Kant, like most eighteenth century authors of conjectural histories, was offering more than a picture of successive stages but a theory of social evolution. What proved durable in such attempts is not so much the set of patterns but the premises on which they consciously rest: namely the notion of man as passing through an evolution energized by the tension between his nature and his free will.[62]

We may now turn to the major question raised by such philosophy of history: the question of purpose. What purpose or purposes are there in history and whose purposes are they?

First of all it should be emphasized that Kant rejected the view that sees history as a simple "evolution" following "natural" principles (either mechanical or organic ones). As Delbos emphasized, "the constitutive concept of the philosophy of history is for Kant the concept of freedom."[63] The realm of history is here as an area of investigation distinct from the area of nature because human freedom is at work in it. Furthermore the realm of history can be constructed as a development going from an origin to a telos through stages only by using this very concept of freedom as the running thread of the whole account. The Kantian philosophy of history may be translated into a history of freedom, possibly into a history of the education of freedom.[64] The transition from the life of instinct to the state of cultural freedom witnesses the birth of freedom. Further stages witness the progressive orientation and disciplining of freedom until the last stage when freedom takes itself as its own content and comes to full realization and enjoyment of itself.

As Delbos put it: "By showing that history is the progress of freedom, Kant prepared himself to conceive that freedom could take itself as its own content."[65]

Reason thus is at work in history insofar as men orient their freedom towards the realization of an end: civil union of all men, which makes of each man a cosmopolitan citizen. The moral and political impacts of such a philosophy are obvious and Delbos showed that the practical philosophy of Kant arose out of this key aspect of his philosophy of history. What must be emphasized here is that there is reason in history for Kant only insofar as there is purposefulness in historical development.

But whose purpose is it? Certainly not history's. Unlike many nineteenth century minds Kant never hypostasized history. Most eighteenth century minds did not hesitate to answer that "Nature" pursues a plan which is progressively worked out in history. But this answer was not quite satisfactory to Kant who saw in history a legal and moral rather than a merely natural process. Nature for him does not contain the destiny of man. Nature's role is first of all limited to the task of bringing man to the point where he can and must assert his independence from her. Nature holds instinctual man as a link in its chain of causes. But man wrests himself free from her and becomes the originator of new causal series. It all happens as if Nature forces him to be free. This idea lies at the core of Kant's philosophy of history. The plan of Nature is to make man a self-governing being.

As Fackenheim rightly saw, there is a paradox here. Either freedom is independent of teleological or mechanical necessity and there is no connection between the two, and it is nonsense to speak of a plan of Nature working towards freedom; or freedom is necessitated and hence is not freedom. How can man be forced to be free? Fackenheim answered quite correctly:

This is possible because Nature confines herself to posing the problem to be solved; she does not solve it. Man himself both must and can give the solution. He must give it because Nature does not give it, and because the problem unless solved will destroy him. He can give it, because already free in the choice of means, he can free himself from the despotism of natural ends.[66]

This is consonant with Kant's voluntaristic convictions. Nature may begin the education of man; she cannot finish it. A free man can only be self-educated. A rational man is a man divorced from nature. In a rational ethics the attention of the moral philosopher will bear upon what man originates and the imperatives will tell him what to do with his predicament.

Nature has willed that man should by himself produce everything that goes beyond the mechanical ordering of his animal existence, and that he should partake of no other happiness or perfection than that which he himself independently of instinct, has created by his own reason.[67]

Moreover Nature has acted

just as if she willed that, if man ever did advance from the lowest barbarity to the highest skill and mental perfection, and thereby worked himself up to happiness (so far as it is possible on earth), he alone should have the credit and should have only himself to thank—exactly as if she aimed more at his rational self-esteem than at his well-being. For along this march of human affairs, there was a host of troubles awaiting him. But it seems not to have concerned her that he should live well, but only that he should work himself upward so as to make himself, through his own actions, worthy of life and of well-being.[68]

Kant never failed to call attention to the limited validity of the idea of a plan of Nature. The idea cannot ever be used to forecast what future events will be, since they are unknown and the task of our will. In the last analysis, therefore, it is the reality of human freedom and the practical interests of reason which limit the validity of the idea of a plan of Nature. Eternal peace will turn out to be a dangerous idea and a futile hope unless it is accepted today as a practical task. Thus when Kant argued for the relative usefulness of such an idea as a plan of Nature, he did it for moral considerations. The idea is a guiding thread for our action. It can also open a comforting prospect upon the future.[69]

So future history must be shaped by men according to the demands of morality. Thus history must be made by us subservient to morality and it follows that philosophy of history must in the last analysis be made subservient to ethics.[70]

To sum up, Nature and Nature's plan do not dictate our future. Only our own moral reason does it and it dictates to us clear purposes of its own (to affirm ourselves and all men as free, rational end-setting beings). So there is in Kant a discontinuity between Nature and freedom. Nature's only purpose is to force us to become purposeful beings who set themselves their own purposes and are responsible for them.

But this last sentence qualifies the discontinuity between Nature and freedom. Nature does have a purpose after all, liminal though it is, and more importantly Kant did not hesitate to see Nature as having a morally sound purpose: to make free men. Kant attributed no moral indifference to this Nature. Its purposes are morally wise and they are good for us men (inasmuch as the realization of these purposes— the appearance of free men—is a necessary precondition of the appearance of good wills). Furthermore, Kant asserted that Nature, besides taking us to the threshold of freedom, also teaches us free beings to make a rational use of our freedom (and that makes a second, even more crucial qualification to the idea of discontinuity between Nature and freedom). The instincts she planted in us (anti-social sociability), the conflict she precipitates us into, the pragmatic arrangements she teaches us to make, all force us to develop our faculties, take stock of ourselves, and learn the rational use of our faculties. Nature may use crude means to achieve her ends. "Need forces men, so enamoured otherwise of their boundless freedom, into (the) state of constraint."[71] But crude though the mechanisms of human passions may be, they nevertheless lead to the fulfilment by man of Nature's plan, the discovery by man of civic union and the search for the common good. So it seems that Nature (or Providence)[72] also has the purpose to force and to help (or to guide) men on the path on which they will learn to find what are their true purposes and learn to achieve them. Let us not forget what we saw about the guarantee of a morally sound human future. Perpetual peace is guaranteed by two factors, the plan of Providence "which predetermines the course of nature and directs it to the objective final end of the human race"[73] (and will achieve it admittedly only if we make its efforts our own) and the moral law which commands us unconditionally to work for it. (The two seem so

intimately related that each appears to be powerless without the other.)
Thus the opposition between Nature and freedom hardly appears as a
sharp and final one.

Cast in this light then, the philosophy of history begins to appear
as one of the Kantian efforts, the most notorious of which is the
Critique of Judgement, to reunite what the first two Critiques had so
energetically separated, or to rebuild bridges between the noumenal
and the phenomenal worlds. And sure enough, judgements of purpose
are presented in the third Critique as precisely that bridge. As Friedrich's elegant formula puts it:

> Palpably the world of history is the story of the men who, whether
> or not filled by the wonder at the world within and without them,
> are the bridge between the two orders which Kant considers the
> prime data of man's experience.[74]

George Vlachos, the French scholar whose work on the political
thought of Kant should be placed right among the few major monuments of Kantian scholarship, would probably have stated that the
determination to build bridges ran deeper in Kant than the care to
differentiate the two shores. In the context of a discussion of natural
teleology and progress he writes—giving in a nutshell Kant's view on
the relationship between nature and freedom—that "freedom does
not rise over against nature but is born in nature."[75]

A brief excursion into Kant's political thought will clarify the
meaning of this statement as well as indicate something of the wealth
of documentation that Vlachos brought to support it. Vlachos saw in
the eighteenth century a considerable series of efforts to bring reason
and history in connection with each other.[76] Three solutions appear
and each leads to a particular dialectic between nature and freedom
and to a particular political philosophy. In the end each leads also to a
different evaluation of the French Revolution.[77]

1. There is first of all the conservative school which emphasizes
organic development of societies and sees reason manifested in tradition and its fruits. Edmund Burke and, in Germany, Rehberg represent this tendency. Traditional metaphysical rationalism and Lutheran
orthodoxy side with this school in political matters. Nature and tradition are said to know what is best in social arrangements; whereas the
rational plans of individual minds for alterations of society are suspect
mainly because they are thought to overestimate the scope of freedom,
and to ignore the power of inertia, habit, and above all, evil in human

affairs. Individuals are educated by traditions and their slow growth. The French Revolution is the criminal result of pride.

2. The radical school of thought, embodied in Rousseau and in his followers, begins by accepting the *tabula rasa* in epistemology, goes on to emphasize the hostility between society and the few men who are moral, rational, and free, and ends up by producing plans for a radical rearrangement of social relations. It enjoys writing new constitutions and sees future rational society as a construct of rational men. Traditions are to be reshaped by gifted individuals.

3. The third position, or the reformist one, is that which Kant finally took and defended. In spite of the impact of Rousseau in moral matters, Kant refused to follow him in legal and political ones and defended the idea of organic continuities between nature and culture, between nature and freedom, and between historical tradition and reason. One quote clearly indicates the reformist's opposition to Rousseau who was seen by Kant as a radical and a utopian. "Rousseau is right to criticize historical institutions, but they are the germs of future good ones."[78]

Thus we can conclude that reflection on the processes of law, government, reform, and revolution led Kant to see freedom as an innovative human power embodied in Nature's own plan, and which is wisely exercised only when exercised vigorously and in accordance with Nature's underlying teleology. Slow organic evolution and urgent practical imperatives of reform are reconciled (the human race is biologically one and must become politically one). Kantian moral idealism appears in his political philosophy as the doctrine according to which freedom has the duty and the power to modify the sensible world in the light of the intelligent world, and according to which freedom's efforts must be measured by the knowledge of the actual potentialities which are teleologically inscribed in nature and human nature, and by the knowledge of the determinisms which a scientific study of society as part of the phenomenal world reveals. Machiavellians and utopians are sent away back to back. Historically Kant came to this position from a background of political conformity under the impact of Rousseau, but after having criticized the utopian elements of Rousseau's constructs.

But enough for the excursus. What we have seen is that Kant's thinking on politics and on history opens up a whole field of Kantian philosophy: the pragmatic field (illustrated in his anthropology, for instance)[79] where freedom is seen as a real power born out of Nature and exercised within the limitations prescribed by Nature. The multiplicity of history is thus seen as being "destined to being ordered by reason and as a medium of both birth and liberation of pure reason."[80] The phrase is Troeltsch's and he does not hesitate to see in Kant an anticipation of Hegel's philosophy of reason and history. More correctly perhaps, Delbos maintained a clearer tension between reason and history by stating, "For Kant, reason travels through history as a militant faculty, which must conquer its empire over sensible nature."[81] Delbos then contrasts Kant with Herder for whom reason naturally and without break of continuity arises out of Nature, and for whom all development in the natural world ceaselessly tends towards reason (Hegel, for Delbos, operates the fusion between Kant and Herder).

Such are the affirmations of the Kantian philosophy of history. Nature pursues a purposeful activity and so do all men. When men become rational and moral their purposeful activity cooperates with that of Nature and builds upon it. A moral teleology is at this stage brought into being and it harmonizes with the natural teleology. One question remains: how naive ultimately are these affirmations? Have they in any way gone through the rigour of the critical philosophical processes which Kant exhibits, say, in his epistemology, or in his critique of metaphysics? Will it turn out in the end to be full of non-explicit metaphysical affirmations which seek to explain what one does not understand by having recourse to what one understands even less?

A test of this may be found in Kant's own writings. Kant did vigorously criticize a non-critical philosophy of history in his two reviews of Herder's *Ideas for a Philosophy of the History of Mankind*. Kant characterized Herder's work as showing "a fleeting, sweeping view, an adroitness in unearthing analogies in the wielding of which he shows a bold imagination."[82] It is clear however that, for Kant, Herder got carried away by his poetic imagination.

> To be sure, this attempt is bold but still natural to the scientific bent of our reason, and it should not pass uncommended despite an execution that is only partially successful. All the more is it to be wished, therefore, that our gifted author in continuing his work, where there is solid ground before him, should constrain his lively genius. It is to be hoped that philosophy, whose concern consists more in the pruning than the sprouting of superfluous growth, may guide him to the consummation of his enterprise, not with hints, but precise concepts, not through supposed, but

through observed laws, not through the intervention of flighty imagination, whether metaphysical or sentimental, but rather through the exercise of careful reason in the execution of his bold project.[83]

Do these strictures hold against Kant's own bold design of the history of freedom? Can freedom be reconciled with the design of Nature? Was Kant perhaps less careful in his own philosophy of history (which is, once again, found only in short articles) than elsewhere in his philosophical opus? To state that, "This, then, is the truth of the matter: Nature inexorably *wills* that the right should finally triumph"[84] is to make an interesting affirmation, possibly an impressive or a touching one. But how permissible is such language? Is it in any sense true?

Admittedly a philosophy of history (as Kant understood the task) is full of conjectures and tentative ideas, because it seeks to speak of what we do not know. As Kant offered an idea for history from a cosmopolitan point of view, he was aware that "it seems that with an idea only a romance could be written."[85] So Kant knew that a philosophy of history has to be adventurous and bold. He granted that to Herder. But does this adventurousness lead rational men astray?

In an uncharted desert a thinker, like a traveller, must be free to choose his route at discretion. We should attend to how he succeeds; and if, after he has reached his goal, he returns home again to the domicile of reason, safe and sound at the correct hour, he can even anticipate having followers.[86]

Let us say that Kant in his philosophy of history charted a bold route in a desert. Did he succeed where Herder failed and bring us back to the domicile of reason? For an answer to this question we must turn to the three Critiques.

Chapter 3

Clarifications of Philosophical Issues in the Light of the Three Critiques

The Limits of Knowledge and the Ideas of Pure Reason

Nature (or Providence) has a plan, which she is slowly pursuing throughout history, and which so far has led men to the point where they can knowingly or unknowingly make Nature's final goal their own goal, where they are free to cooperate autonomously in the pursuit of the final goal. This goal is the creation of a commonwealth in which all men are united. Nature (or Providence) will go on pursuing this plan and prodding men into cooperation with it, although whether or not the goal will in fact be reached depends upon the moral choices of mankind. Such is the core of Kant's philosophy of history. It is an affirmation of divine purpose in history, a divine purpose fully consonant with the rational purposes which men, as free beings who set ends for themselves, strive after.

This philosophy of history, I wish to argue, was elaborated just as carefully—although more quickly—as the rest of Kant's philosophical work. In fact the philosophy of history is to a large extent an application of the theses of the critical philosophy to problems in the interpretation of history that were debated in his century. "Application" should be taken to mean that the Critiques provide us with a theoretical core, a set of critically established rules on the use of reason which are then applied to a specific subject matter. "Application" should not be taken to mean that with the Critiques written Kant proceeded merely to apply mechanically what he had found. Interest in the philosophy of history antedates the 70s, when the *Critique of Pure Reason* was in gestation. The *Idea* which contains in a nutshell the main elements of the philosophy of history was published in 1784, three years after the first Critique, four before the *Critique of Practical Reason*, and six before the *Critique of Judgement*. It is thus more accurate to say that the critical system and the thinking on history were developed simultaneously. It is chronologically correct. It fits the Kantian concern to learn to think in order to solve real problems. This being said, it still remains true that the Critiques provide us with the theory of philosophy and the philosophy of history with an application of it, and that the actual writing of the key-documents of the philosophy of history followed the publication of the first Critique.

While holding the view that the philosophy of history is an application, I believe that Kant, dealing with problems in the interpretation of history, arrived at solutions which in some important respects, if not actually depart from the results of the Critique, at least open new perspectives and amount to what we shall call a strain in Kantian philosophy which is somewhat in tension with the critical philosophy. I shall also argue later that Kant, dealing with problems in the interpretation of religion, also came to solutions which are not those which a strict application of the critical system would lead one to expect. It is therefore important to establish at this stage that "application" did not mean for Kant the end of creative philosophical endeavour and that, while the guiding thread of the critical system remained, the lessons of experience and the demands of specific intellectual problems could press themselves upon an open mind and lead to distinct solutions. While the neatness of the system may suffer, the author's reputation for intellectual vigour can only profit from the unearthing of such evidence.

My plan for this chapter therefore is to show by reference to each of the three Critiques how the philosophy of history is an application. I shall then at the end of each section list those open questions that indicate elements of tension between the philosophy of history and the critical system.

The Conditions of Knowledge and the Ideas of Reason

One of the positive results of the *Critique of Pure Reason* is the definition of valid knowledge as knowledge of objects of experience structured through the forms of sensibility and the categories of the understanding. One of the categories is causality and we see Kant in his philosophy of history concerned to extend our knowledge of the discernible empirical causes of human behaviour considered as an empirical phenomenon, or as appearance. He noted for instance that though free will has an obvious influence upon marriages, births, and deaths, yet these events obey definite, stable statistical laws.[1] So Kant's interest in final causes did not still his curiosity for material ones. (We should not forget that the Kant who rehabilitated teleological thinking as philosophically valid also outnewtonized Newton by showing how the planetary system could have come about mechanically.)[2] As a lecturer in philosophy Kant was concerned to teach the empirical kind of history to his students. Witness his announcement of the program of his lectures for the winter semester of 1765-66. Besides metaphysics, logic, and ethics he said he would teach geography (this turned out to include physical geography—the history of the earth—and moral and political geography—the history of commerce, of man, and of relations between states). The impact of Montesquieu on Kant is obvious: physical geography is the foundation for all study of history.[3] The announcement states:

> At the beginning of my academic career, when I noticed that a grave negligence of young students consists in their wanting to learn to *reason* without having sufficient historical knowledge (which alone can replace *experience*) I conceived the idea of making a convenient summary of the history of the actual state of the earth, or of geography in the widest possible sense.[4]

Kant's geography looks a good deal more like our history. (Remember that the eighteenth century German university did not offer much of a program in history[5] and that Kant, unlike Hume, Gibbon, Voltaire, or the French abbés who wrote histories, had to make his living as a teacher.) So I do not believe one can charge Kant with lack of interest for recorded history, nor with having the impudence of trying a philosophy of history without being something of a practising historian himself (or without having some sense of what historians do).

Therefore when Kant said that the philosophy of history was not claiming to be empirical knowledge nor seeking to displace it, and when he said that it actually required empirical knowledge, there is every ground to believe that he meant exactly what he said. But then what is the status of this "Idea" for a philosophy of history?

The answer to this question lies in the doctrine found in the *Critique of Pure Reason* concerning "Ideas" of reason (the term is capitalized when used in its specific technical sense) and their use. There are three such Ideas in the first Critique: the soul, the world, and God. After the transcendental dialectic which denounces the illusion that sees in these ideas concepts that yield knowledge of real objects, a long appendix on "the regulative employment of the Ideas of pure reason" shows that these Ideas have their usefulness yet. They "never allow of any constitutive employment" (that is, never lead to knowledge of any definite real object) but "on the other hand, they have an excellent, and indeed indispensably necessary, regulative employment."[6] The rest of the appendix proceeds to show how such regulative employment serves as a guide to direct our search for knowledge and leads to "the greatest possible unity combined with the greatest possible extension" in our knowledge.[7] The most important of the fruits of such speculative employment is the idea of the "purposive unity of things."

> The *speculative* interest of reason makes it necessary to regard all order in the world as if it had originated in the purpose of a supreme reason. Such principle opens out to our reason, as applied in the field of experience, altogether new views as to how the things of the world may be connected according to teleological laws, and so enables it to arrive at their greatest systematic unity. The assumption of a supreme intelligence, as the one and only cause of the universe, though in the idea alone, can therefore always benefit reason and can never injure it.[8]

The qualification "in the idea alone" is crucial. We cannot regard God as a real object "to which we may proceed to ascribe the ground of the systematic order of the world."[9] This could be to fall into a constitutive use of the idea and to return to all the errors of dogmatic rationalistic metaphysics.

The key ideas of the philosophy of history, however, are not directly the famous transcendental Ideas of the *Critique of Pure Reason*. They are derivations, namely they are analogous, similarly useful Ideas derived from and formed on the model of these transcendental Ideas. The Nature which pursues a plan in history, the State which establishes the rule of civil law and which we must seek to reform so that it will approximate its ideal, the League of Nations which establishes international law, are likewise regulative concepts.[10] Of each it can be said, in the words of the first Critique, that "it goes far beyond what experience or observation can verify; and though not itself determining anything yet serves to mark out the path towards systematic unity."[11] The Nature which pursues a plan (to focus on the Idea most important for our purposes) was thus for Kant a useful heuristic principle which will guide our empirical observations and will lead us to discern facts in history, and find meaning in it by enhancing our grasp of its systematic unity. It will thus regulate the activity of our mind and not constitute objects of knowledge. To "overlook this restriction of the Idea to a merely regulative use" is to be "led away into mistaken paths." Kant emphasized two errors in particular: the lazy mind which appeals "directly to the unsearchable decree of Supreme Wisdom," "instead of looking for causes in the universal law of material mechanism," and the perverse mind, which imposes ends upon nature, "forcibly and dictatorially" instead of seeking constantly to verify the suggestion made by the Idea in empirical fashion.[12] The philosophy of history at every turn complies with these rules and avoids these pitfalls.

To conclude, the *Critique of Pure Reason* and the philosophy of history both teach that we may and naturally must "assume a wise and omnipotent author of the world" but that by so doing we do not "extend our knowledge beyond the field of possible experience."[13] Furthermore I may "proceed to regard seemingly purposive arrangements as purposes and so derive them from the divine will."[14] However, since such an Idea is regulative and not constitutive it does not speak of any definite object nor give us any knowledge of it, but merely serves as a heuristic idea to guide our investigation of the world by assuming it to be a coherent whole likely to reward efforts at knowledge. Thus "it must be a matter of complete indifference to us, when we perceive such unity, whether we say that God in his wisdom has willed it to be so, or that Nature has wisely arranged it thus."[15] It becomes manifest now that the oscillation in philosophy of history between talk of a plan of Nature and talk of Providence at this stage of Kant's authorship (1781) was not the result of carelessness in expression but a calculated ambiguity. We do not know the ground of order in the world (if such a thing can be said to be).[16] We must assume that there is a purposive unity and must assume an author of it but cannot presume to know anything of him or it.

Thus the metaphysical idea of Nature was rehabilitated by Kant, who found it permissible to speak of a Nature which is purposefully active and of a Ground of all things. If Kant abandoned Leibnitian metaphysics and its affirmation that the world *is* perfect, or rather the best of all possible, he did not set aside all rational cosmology, or all metaphysical thinking on the world and on nature, but prescribed new rules to such thinking. Perfection or teleological arrangement in the order of the world—or of history—is something we think, not something we know; ultimately the necessity for thinking it comes from practical as well as from theoretical reason; we have the task to work for a better home for man in the world,[17] and we will inevitably be encouraged to pursue this purpose if we can conceive the world as being adapted for it, or suited to the pursuit of such purpose.

Thus rests the case for seeing in the philosophy of history an application of the results of the *Critique of Pure Reason* concerning the nature of knowledge and regulative use of Ideas. The case for the appearance of a new strain is based first of all on an important article by E. Troeltsch. In his 1904 article, "The Historical Element in Kant's Philosophy of Religion," a piece of writing which did perhaps more than any other piece of *Kanstudien* to open the field of inquiry of this book, E. Troeltsch spoke of a tension within the Kantian corpus between the standpoint of criticism which gives itself as timeless (and makes of time a form of our sensibility and denies its absolute reality) and the standpoint to which Kant arrived in his philosophy of history and philosophy of religion, a standpoint in which the becoming of man, and even the historical development of reason, become central concepts. Troeltsch noted how the reserve with which Kant approached the psychological and historical elements in religion stems from the deepest core of the method of transcendental criticism which keeps focusing on a priori conditions of possibility of experience and not on historical conditions.[18] (He did add that such reserve towards the historical is not exclusion or ignorance.)

It is indeed significant that when using an illustration of the use of regulative Ideas, the *Critique of Pure Reason* talks of the systematic unity of nature and takes its examples from morphology. The field of knowledge is not seen as undergoing historical change. There is much logical parallelism between the statements on unity of nature (or on order in the world) from the non-historical point of view, and the statements on order in history as an ongoing teleological process. In both cases the Idea has heuristic and systematic value. In neither case is the unity known and verified. But in the second case the unity may be in the process of being made (or not made at all), for the history of which Kant writes a philosophy includes the future. The League of Nations, for instance, may or may not be a fact of experience in the future, but whether it is or not depends on a fact, on whether it happens, and not on whether we succeed to extend further the theoretical use of our reason (although it does depend on whether we succeed to extend further the practical use of our reason). Enough is said thereby to indicate the problem. Our knowledge of nature, helped by regulative Ideas, is seen as an ongoing process: but the substratum for that knowledge is not seen as an ongoing process (or the question as to whether the substratum, or, better, the things in themselves are in the process of becoming is not raised because it cannot be raised in the context of the Kantian system.) Such is not entirely the case with history.[19] We make what we subsequently come to know (or at least participate in the making of it), and that we make it is morally very important. The critical philosophy answers the problem partly by saying that our rational relationship to the future is that of practical reason: we know what imperatives to obey. But the philosophy of history finds that to be only a partial solution: it wishes to talk about the future in order to communicate hope and not just moral imperatives.

Whether reason can know history as it knows nature is, however, not my topic so I cannot do more than merely raise the problem. Kant himself remained silent on the very existence of the problem, let alone on its solution. Yet the problem is there in his work and the application of the principle of regulative employment of Ideas of reason to the problem of history cannot be a simple transposition of what the application was in the case of the philosophy of nature. Here again the discontinuity between natural teleology and moral teleology must be emphasized. The former can be disproved by experience and knowledge any time. The latter can be proved or disproved by our future action only.

The Imperatives and Postulates of Practical Reason

To move from the *Critique of Pure Reason* to the *Critique of Practical Reason* is to move from a consideration of the idea of purposive order in the world (and of God as the Author of it) from the theoretical point of view, to a consideration of similar ideas as they arise from a consideration of practical problems, or, more precisely, as they arise from a consideration of the problems inherent in the practical use of our reason. The focus now moves to the active kind of ordering of their world which men in fact make through the practical use of their reason (namely through their action and the pursuit of their own purposes) to the conditions of possibility and the a priori norms of such ordering. We move from natural to moral teleology, from the system of purposes we believe we can discern prior to the action of man to the purposes we in fact pursue and the system of purposes we must pursue.

> Teleology views nature as a Kingdom of ends; ethics views a possible Kingdom of ends as a Kingdom of nature. In the first case the Kingdom of ends is a theoretical Idea used to explain what exists. In the second case it is a practical Idea used to bring into existence what does not exist but can be made actual by our own conduct—and indeed to bring it into existence in conformity with this Idea.[20]

Thus Kantian ethics presents human action as having to be oriented towards the realization of an ultimate goal: the *summum bonum* (to use the expression found in the second Critique) or the Kingdom of ends (a moral unity among end-setting beings or what we called above the moral commonwealth) realized under the conditions of this world. All the maxims of our action ought to harmonize with such a possible Kingdom.[21] The ultimate goal (the moral commonwealth), which is presented in the philosophy of history as the possible future which the plan of Nature has in store for us (if only we work for it), appears in the ethics as our own certain and immediate moral task. This shows right away the intimate connection between Kant's ethics and his philosophy of history; both put the same goal before man, the former prescribes it, the latter presents it as guaranteed by the plan of Nature.[22] The opening pages of the *Foundations of the Metaphysics of Morals* make this connection perfectly explicit when they present Kant's view of the function of reason. Kant there repeated that Nature did not have man's happiness or his welfare as her real purpose or she would have left man in a condition such that he remains guided by his instincts alone. No, Nature imparted reason to man and a reason that would "strike out into a practical use." From then on, man has been guided by his will, which may or may not be good. And this state of affairs takes us away from a condition where simple contentment is possible.[23]

H. J. Paton therefore was entirely correct when he emphasized that Kant's application of moral principles is based on a teleological view of man and of the universe.[24] This may seem to diminish Kant's title to originality in ethics (a title incidentally which he never claimed for his work in ethics as he did for his work on metaphysics) and may seem to clash with some interpretations of Kantian ethics which make it circle around the concept of duty exclusively. On this last point Paton did not hesitate to place Kant squarely within the grand tradition of Western philosophical ethics and affirm that for Kant "obligation is derivative and goodness original."[25] Surprising though it may be, Kant even quoted with approval the old scholastic formula *"nihil appetimus, nisi sub ratione boni"* (although he did find it ambiguous since *bonum* can be taken to mean either *das Gute* or *das Wohl*).[26] Where Kant was original was in his emphasis that we finite men cannot at the outset form a definite concept of the good (hence his constant polemics against the fallacies and ambiguities of the various forms of eudaemonism). Furthermore, frail and fallible that we are, we do not necessarily desire the good and must be constrained to seek it. This is why duty is the first and "only form in which the good appears to beings like man."[27] Hence a paradox of method in a critical examination of practical reason. "The paradox is that the concept of the good and evil is not defined prior to the moral law, to which, it would seem, the former would have to serve as foundation; rather the concept of good and evil must be defined after and by means of the law."[28]

To show that Kantian ethics presupposes a teleological view of man and nature and that it leads to a hierarchically organized system of ends with the good as the object of practical reason (that is, "an object as an effect possible through freedom")[29] is to show that Kant's ethics and the philosophy of history form a compatible whole (and let us not forget that there was a dialectical relationship between the elaboration of the two). It does not show in any way that the philosophical ethics in general and the *Critique of Practical Reason* in particular can function as a critical sieve through which whatever may be too simple in the philosophy of history could be sifted by us now or has been sifted by Kant himself.

Without embarking upon a critical examination of the *Critique of Practical Reason* or even a summary of it (two tasks which would be beyond the scope and purpose of this book), I can draw attention to passages in the second Critique which will bring further evidence to support my thesis that the key affirmations of the philosophy of history were not made lightly but are as close to the core of Kant's philosophical endeavour as any other affirmations of his.

We find such passages in the *Dialectic of Pure Practical Reason*, especially in the famous definition of the concept of the highest good (*summum bonum*).[30] The highest good is defined as the union of virtue and happiness. It is "the supreme end which united all other ends. Without it there could be no system of ends." Such a realization on earth, in history, of a state of affairs in which happiness is apportioned in proportion to virtue (or worthiness to happiness)—obviously a state of affairs which can be found only in the future—must be possible.[31] If it were to be impossible, "the moral law which commands that it be furthered must be fantastic, directed to empty imaginary ends, and consequently inherently false."[32] Thus the doctrine of the *summum bonum* affirms that moral man must be able to believe that the physical world is constituted in such a way that it is not hostile to the realization of moral purposes in it through human moral efforts, and that the moral law is constituted in such a way that it does not propose to us impossible goals. Ultimately only the idea of God as Author of both the world and of the moral law can provide us with such a guarantee. On this moral basis, the existence of God must be affirmed as a necessary postulate of the possibility of the *summum bonum*.

> Through the practical law which requires the existence of the highest good possible in the world, there is postulated the possibility of those objects of pure speculative reason whose objective reality could not be assured by speculative reason. By this, then, the theoretical knowledge of pure reason does obtain an accession, but it consists only in this—that those concepts which for it are otherwise problematical (merely thinkable) are now described assertorically as actually having objects, because practical reason inexorably requires the existence of these objects for the possibility of its practically and absolutely necessary object, the highest good. Theoretical reason is, therefore, justified in assuming them.[33]

Problems arise however where Kant tried to say *why* this highest good must be realizable. (A brief look at these problems will help to shed some light on why it was important to Kant to have a philosophy of history as well as an ethics.) To know that our goal is within reach is, of course, a great incentive for doing our duty to strive after it, but such an answer, although supplying the psychological incentives we finite men need, is no answer at all, since it contradicts the clear Kantian principle that moral men act motivated by duty alone and not by their own desire of any material end (however worthy) they may have set their hearts on. To affirm the need for the possibility of the highest good should not lead us—and it did not lead Kant—back to a heteronomous ethic based on the individual's desire for happiness. Since any re-introduction of the inclinations of finite men (which Kant also called pathological desires) is out of the question, we might come to agree with Beck's conclusion that the *summum bonum* has no practical consequences whatsoever. The idea of its possibility would then not be necessary to our moral or practical life—duty suffices for that—but would be important for the "architectonic purpose of reason in uniting under one idea the two legislations of reason, the theoretical and the practical."[34] We would thus remain with the results of the *Critique of Pure Reason*, where the Idea of God, Author of purposeful unity in the sensible world and in the intelligible world, and Author of an ultimate unity between the two worlds, is presented as a speculatively necessary Idea.[35] Thus Beck concluded "we must not allow ourselves to be deceived, as I believe Kant was, into thinking its possibility is directly necessary to morality."[36]

The difficulty with this conclusion, as Beck himself pointed out, is that it is not the one Kant drew in the *Critique of Practical Reason*. Repeatedly, and especially in his essay on *Theory and Practice*, Kant stated that it could not possibly be a duty to work for something which is impossible (and I am not prepared to suggest that Kant here was referring exclusively to a theoretical rather than a practical kind of impossibility). As is shown by the earlier fragment from the "moral proof" of the existence of God, Kant specifically claimed that the moral point of view adds something to the theoretical point of view,[37] and that the interests of pure practical reason have a supremacy over those of pure theoretical reason. The existence of God is thus no longer affirmed as a possible, useful, permissible, and necessary idea (necessary for the speculative employment of our reason) but is affirmed as "objective reality." It thus seems that in the practical employment of reason this idea is more necessary (whatever that means) or has a necessity of a more forcible nature. And this for Kant did seem to make an "existential" difference or a difference which can hardly be irrelevant to the nature and quality of the moral life (even though it does remain irrelevant to the content of the moral law and the determination of our duty). Or, to put it briefly, the existence of God (or the possibility of the highest good) though not necessary to the definition of duty appeared to Kant to be necessary to the moral disposition broadly interpreted.

A quote from Paton might put us on the way to an accurate solution of the problem created by the disagreement between Kant and his most distinguished American interpreter.

> The metaphysical beliefs about God and immortality which Kant justifies on the basis of his ethics lie beyond the scope of the present work. They do not alter the content of his ethics, nor can they add either to the supreme value of the moral will or to the binding nature of the categorical imperative. Nevertheless, as Kant recognizes, it is a great stimulus to moral effort and a strong support to the human spirit, if man can believe that the moral life is something more than a mortal enterprise in which he can join with his fellow men against the background of a blind and indifferent universe until he and the human race are blotted out for ever. Man cannot be indifferent to the possibility that his puny efforts towards moral perfection may, in spite of appearances, be in accord with the purpose of the universe, and that he may be taking part in an eternal enterprise under a divine leader.[38]

Paton spoke here of "support of the human spirit" rather than of psychological needs. Such admittedly vague language opens up a whole area of concerns important to Kant and to moral man. Indicative of these concerns are such questions as: What is moral character? Why do moral dispositions differ in strength? What is the importance of hope? To state that moral man needs—for his disposition, not for his incentives—to hope for the realization of his highest purpose is to shift the debate to an area not covered by the discussion of the imperatives of pure practical reason or by the discussion of our pathologically determined desires for happiness. (It is also to move into an area where as we shall see the Kantian philosophy of religion makes significant additions to and possible corrections of his ethics. *Religion within the Limits of Reason Alone* is the only place where Kant seriously wrestled with the continuous aspects of personality and will—namely with character—and tried to shed light upon the notion of disposition.) It is to open an area where we encounter what we could label as existential needs rather than psychological needs. To use the Kantian phrase it is to move into the area where one sees the "interests" of reason and —as Beck rightly saw—the interests of practical reason are distinct from and have priority over the interests of theoretical reason.[39] Thus when Beck spoke of the "need of reason to believe in the existence of a highest good and to postulate the existence of its conditions" as a "need of the all too human reason,"[40] it should be emphasized that we do not have an individual or even a universal psychological need of finite embodied men but "an absolutely necessary need"[41] which is part of the fabric of man's very finite humanity and a correlate of moral responsibility. In other words, what is necessary to the "moral disposition" should not be translated into what psychological incentives may be needed by weak and pathologically affected men; it is part and parcel of the moral condition of responsible men. Moral man, by heeding the voice of duty, makes a brave affirmation. Courage, however, is not acquired once and for all. It needs strength over a period of time, and, in time, its strength may be confirmed or weakened. There is thus nothing sub-moral—and no return to pathological desires— in affirming the need for sources of strength for one's moral disposition. The *Critique of Judgement* takes pains to show that the need for a moral intelligent Author of the world comes from "the purest moral sentiment" such as gratitude, obedience, and humiliation—and not at all from mercenary or self-interested motives. Through such noble sentiments our morality "gains in strength" and is even "at least on the side of our representation," "given a new object for its exercise."[42] Thus Kant, I suggest, would not have rejected Paton's notion that the human spirit needs support and would even have claimed to know where support of a noble kind may be found.[43]

We may conclude therefore that the boldest affirmation of the philosophy of history, namely the legitimacy of hope in the future realization on earth of the moral commonwealth, hope grounded upon the convergence between the plan of nature and the moral imperative, is also found in the *Critique of Practical Reason* in the conclusion of its Dialectic. The moral phenomenon, as analysed by Kant, requires a designer who assures that in the end happiness will be granted to the virtuous. Such an affirmation of what Kant called a rational faith is an

intrinsic part of the affirmation made by the moral man who undertakes to heed the imperatives of pure practical reason. As the *Progress
in Metaphysics* puts it in a statement that clearly expresses that there
is more in the Kantian moral proof of the existence of God than a
postulate, as commonly understood, would entail:

> It does not properly speaking absolutely (*simpliciter*) prove the
> existence of God, but proves it only from a certain point of view
> (*secundum quid*), i.e. relatively to the ultimate end which moral
> man has and must have; to *admit* this proof is simply to con-
> form oneself to reason as soon as one admits that man has the
> right to grant an influence upon decisions to an idea which he
> formed for himself in conformity with moral principles, and that
> this right is just as valid as if he had drawn this idea from a given
> object.[44]

The *Critique of Practical Reason*, however, presents God more as
the ultimate guarantee of the meaning of moral effort than as the
designer of a teleological system according to which such moral effort
is destined to reach it goal. The teleological element so crucial to the
philosophy of history is present in the *Critique of Practical Reason* but,
in the pages on the *summum bonum*, is allowed to recede before the
problematics of virtue and happiness.[45] This teleological element comes
to the fore again, and this time very conspicuously and self-consciously,
in the *Critique of Judgement* to which we shall now turn. So further
clarification is still to come and it is there that the crux of the matter
will be reached. It is, however, clear so far that Kant's statement on
the hope that lies before us as moral men who undertake to follow the
imperatives of duty is made squarely as a statement of faith, albeit a
rational faith. The ethics provide a basis for affirming that the bold
faith in the wisdom of the divine governance of the world is a faith
which stems from the very imperatives of duty and is thus a rational
faith and not a mere—however worthy—opinion. The metaphysical
boldness of the philosophy of history is matched by the metaphysical
boldness of the *Critique of Practical Reason* which finally rests upon a
typically Kantian confession of stubborn moral faith, which, however
much it may sound to twentieth century ears like a will to believe, is
proposed to us by Kant as an act of reason:

> I will that there be a God, that my existence in this world be also
> an existence in a pure world of the understanding outside the

system of natural connections, and finally that my duration be endless. I stand by this and will not give up this belief, for this is the only case where my interest inevitably determines my judgment because I will not yield anything of this *interest*; I do so without any attention to sophistries, however little I am able to answer them or oppose them with others more plausible.[46]

We now need to have a look at what we called the signs of tension between the Critiques on the one hand and the philosophy of history on the other. The second Critique speaks only of the Kingdom of ends where the philosophy of history spoke of both the prospects for the League of Nations and of those for the moral commonwealth as distinct goals. This however need not concern us. Bordering as it does so often upon the political and legal philosophies, the philosophy of history is concerned about what is politically and morally most urgent: the reform of the State and the League of Nations as the most immediate tasks, while the *Critique of Practical Reason*, which borders upon philosophical theology and develops a concept of rational faith, takes the longer view and focuses upon the Kingdom of ends as the ultimate goal to which God destines mankind. It is more important, however, to note that reason, autonomy, and morality are presented in the philosophy of history as arising within a process, whereas the laws of the practical employment of reason, or the laws of morality, are deduced transcendentally in the second Critique and are found a priori; it is thereby implied that they are above the time process and are "eternally valid." The second Critique ends with a "Methodology of Pure Practical Reason" and seeks to find "the way in which we can secure to the laws of pure practical reason access to the human mind and an influence on its maxims."[47] The Critique thus addresses itself to problems of education of youth and of making "objectively practical reason also subjectively practical." The philosophy of history, however, by seeing the whole of the human race as undergoing or having undergone a moral education undermines the distinction between objectively practical and subjectively practical. The philosophy of history shows how the "objective" moral law was "subjectively" learned by the race, or by some in it, only at some point in the process of history. We may be grateful to the philosophy of history for its undermining of some aspects of Kantian dualism (nature versus freedom, natural versus moral teleology), for such a new standpoint lays the basis for insights into moral character and into dispositions (and

moral courage as well) which are virtues and as such are moral realities which are lived in time, grow and develop in time (and are neither
a priori laws nor sensuously affected feelings). (And I repeat that the
second Critique tends to stumble when it comes to these problems
which *Religion within the Limits of Reason Alone* handles far more
subtly.) But this standpoint in the philosophy of history makes of
morality something embedded in the historical process, related to, say,
historical experience (to distinguish it from experience of natural
phenomena) and this cannot but appear to be in tension with the
rather timeless standpoint of the *Critique of Practical Reason*. Again I
shall have to leave this matter at that.

The *Critique of Judgement* and the Conditions of Possibility of Judgements of Purpose

As we saw, it is only in 1790, in the *Critique of Judgement*, that
Kant finally brought all his critical powers and all the results of the
philosophy of criticism to bear upon the problems raised by affirmations of purpose and purposeful organization. A consideration of this
Critique will enable us, therefore, to make the final determination of
just how much the philosophy of history is a part of the Kantian philosophical corpus and what grounds it has for affirming the ultimate cooperation between the purposes pursued by the Creator, those towards
which immoral men are driven willy-nilly through the operations of
their nature, and those finally which free rational men prescribe to
themselves by their autonomous moral legislation. The cruciality of
the *Critique of Judgement* for an examination of the philosophy of
history was ably stated by Delbos when he wrote that in the *Critique
of Judgement* the philosophy of history sheds its metaphysical form to
put on that of criticism and becomes subordinated to the practical
philosophy to the development of which it contributed so vigorously.[48]

The *Critique of Judgement* however raises problems of its own
and the story of its genesis seems to have been unusually tortuous.[49]
Kant discarded a first introduction to it and wrote a second, shorter
one.[50] Then, the smooth simplicity of the whole work (which has no
blind alleys, no difficult technical discussions, no painful footnotes)

can turn out to be deceptive. At least four quite diverse undertakings can be discerned in the work.

First of all the *Critique of Judgement* (which Kant was far from thinking of when he completed the second Critique) represents another one of the fresh starts we have discerned in the Kantian corpus: this time the problems of art and biology (both problems in which Kant had shown interest in his pre-critical period) are those which are formally examined and which cause the methods of criticism to be put to work again. (Note, therefore, that all the instances of purposeful organization and possible intelligent planning indicated in the Analytic and Dialectic books of the two parts of the Critique are taken from aesthetic experience, from the study of natural organisms, and from Kant's apparently favourite non-philosophical subject, geography. No consideration of purposefulness in history is present in those sections of the third Critique.)[51]

A second undertaking is indicated especially clearly in the second version of the introduction; namely, to build a bridge across the great gulf apparently drawn by the first two Critiques between the sensible world as known by natural science and the realm of freedom or the intelligible realm to which we have access through the practical use of our reason. An investigation of that bridge is all the more urgent since "the concept of freedom is meant to actualize in the sensible world the end proposed by its own laws."[52] (Note that the reunion of the two worlds is to be achieved by a process of moral activity, namely, by a process of historical development.) Here the third Critique clearly returns to concerns expressed in the second and in the philosophy of history.

Thirdly, as pointed out in the preface, the third Critique is said to bring "the entire critical undertaking to a close" and to leave only the doctrinal part to be done (the metaphysics of nature and of morals). Kant added that he would hasten to this task "in order as far as possible to snatch from my advancing years what time may yet be favourable to the task."[53] The third Critique can claim to be such a last panel of a triptych because it adds to the examination of the faculties of cognition and desire the examination of the third and last of the faculties of the human mind, that of feelings of pleasure and displeasure. (To the sceptic who will point out that Kant previously thought twice that the critical endeavour was completed, we can answer that Kant had, at this point, a systematic reason for deeming the whole critical endeavour complete.) In keeping with the idea of continuity between the third Critique and the first two, it is of little surprise that the whole work is moulded within the usual critical structure of Analytic, Dialectic, and Methodology and even comprises antinomies.

Fourthly, and finally, a long appendix on the method of applying the teleological judgement becomes opportunity for restating the philosophy of history, for developing a concept of Creation, for presenting moral man as its final end, for reworking the moral proof for the existence of God, mapping the task of theology, and defining religion. In short this appendix, with teleology as the common thread, handles all the major Kantian metaphysical problems. That these four undertakings could be carried out in an elegantly composed work gives a measure of the systematizing power of Kant's mind at this late stage of his life.

Thus teleological thinking, a kind of thinking which led the eighteenth century to make some of its most stupid statements, and which came under the justly famous attack of *Candide*, ends up receiving the consecration of being the final unifying concept in Kantian philosophy. That, however, was not to be done without severely examining the nature of teleological judgement, limiting the scope of its use and validity, and qualifying its capacity to be a final unifying concept. This could be done by Kant because the concept of teleology, or of organization of physical relations for the sake of an end, offered a bridge between a natural world where everything is mechanically determined and a moral world where everyone is free to strive after ends of his own choosing.

The results of the critique of judgement of purpose[54] may be briefly summarized as follows: the examination of living organisms leads us to the conclusion that some things in nature exist as physical ends (that is are both cause and effect of themselves). Some vaster natural phenomena lead us also to believe we can discern purposes in nature. This raises the possibility of considering nature as a whole as a system of ends with man himself as the final end of the system. This conclusion however clashes with the idea of mechanical causality on which natural science operates and we are thus led to an antinomy: either "all production of material things must be estimated as possible on mere mechanical laws" or "some products of material nature cannot be estimated as possible on mere mechanical laws."[55]

This antinomy is solved by pointing out that teleological judgement is a reflective, not a determinant judgement. Its use is regulative not constitutive. It does not tell us what are the real relations in phenomenal nature (or nature as known)—this only the categories of the understanding can do, and (Newtonian) causality is one of them—but it tells us how we must look at nature or guide our reflecting upon it. Thus when we use such slogans of natural teleology as "nature takes the shortest way,"[56] we are not told what happens, or how we judge when we know nature scientifically, but how we ought to judge when we reflect upon nature and upon our knowledge of it. Thus to accept teleological judgement in no way restricts or conflicts with the task of natural science and its search for the causal network of phenomena.[57] But the very fact that we can know natural phenomena according to the rules of our understanding is a sign of teleological organization: it all happens as if nature proceeds according to an Idea: the Idea of being knowable by us as an empirical system of causes.[58]

Once we admit that we may and must think of some natural phenomena as being organized towards an end, a further question raises: namely, Is such finality designed or not? Is it intentional?[59] Thus we move from an immanent use of judgements of purpose (a heuristic principle for the investigation of nature) to a transcendent use (a reflective principle to guide our thinking about the supersensible).[60] The idealisms of finality (the systems of Democritus or Spinoza) state that all finality on the part of nature is undesigned (is accidental or fatal). The realism of finality states that all finality is designed, and proposes either hylozoism or theism to account for the intentional design. All these four systems make objective assertions and claim to know something of the cause of Nature. All use concepts beyond the limits of experience (transcendentally) and thus all are victims of the famous transcendental illusion denounced once and for all by the first Critique. So we must reject them all and "weigh our judgement critically";[61] that is, we must reject the dogmatic use of these ideas and consider the regulative use of them. This means we must ask the question: which idea will best guide our reason in its attempts to think about the supersensible? To ask the question in this reflective way is to rule out the idealism of finality. Hylozoism has the disadvantage of involving self-contradiction and of yielding quickly to dogmatic assertions, namely to a claim of knowing nature as it is in itself. So a preference will be expressed for theism, which by assuming an unknowable Author of nature who is beyond nature, a cause which could not possibly be known in experience, will be warned against dogmatic statements about objective nature, or about what nature really is in itself.[62] Theism, for instance, will most quickly make its peace with the fact that we cannot know the supersensible substratum of nature,[63] or that there will never be a Newton who can explain a blade of grass. Thus, theism, of all four possibilities, is most able to keep the reflective judgements reflective and least prone to tranform them into dogmatic ones.

Thus the *Critique of Judgement* brings us back to the *Critique of Pure Reason*. Some ideas are rationally necessary and heuristically useful (for guiding our investigation of nature and our thinking on the super-sensible) even though they do not yield any knowledge of any specific object directly.[64] All judgements of purpose thus function in our mental activity in a way comparable to the ideas of reason. What the *Critique of Judgement* adds is a set of particularly brilliant illustrations of this principle, drawn from the realms of art and biology. (Remember that the *Critique of Judgement* lies at the basis of many subsequent aesthetics and did create the concept of organism; it dealt a blow to Descartes' animal machines from which they never quite recovered.)

The judgements of purpose made in the philosophy of history thus have to abide by the rules set for all judgements of purpose in the *Critique of Judgement* and they in fact do. This demonstration needs not to be done by us since Kant himself made the point in that famous, long appendix to which I drew attention earlier. This "Theory of the Method of Applying the Teleological Judgement" is a unique recapitulation of the various elements of Kantian thought that draw upon the idea of purpose. Paragraphs 83 and 84 restate his philosophy of history; paragraph 87 is a reworking of the postulates of pure practical reason as given in the second Critique; paragraph 91 is a summary of the section in the first Critique on "Opining, Knowing and Believing"; and the final general remark is Kant's best handling of the relationship between theology and religion. It is probably the metaphysical weight of this conclusion that led Troeltsch to state that the *Critique of Judgement* is a critical camouflage of a position that is in fact a metaphysical one.[65]

Here is, in summary form, the general picture of purposefulness in the universe that emerges from this appendix. To the timeless statement made in the critical standpoint to the effect that we must consider nature as constituted in such a way as to be knowable by man as an empirical system and to be amendable to the realization in it of human rational purposes, can be paralleled to the statement made by the philosophy of history that Nature acts in such a way as to educate man or, critically put, that we must think of Nature acting in such a way as to educate man. Man is Nature's ultimate end and all in it conspires to make man possible. Nature however does not aim at making man happy[66] (man receives no favourite treatment in the hands of Nature) but at making him a cultured being; that is Nature aims at making of man a being who sets his own ends. So like in the philosophy of history, we hear of the power of the imagination and of the reality of war to spur man into "developing to the highest pitch all talents that minister to culture."[67] But, interestingly enough, "Nature strives on purposive lines to give us that education that opens the door to higher ends than it can itself afford."[68] Nature trains us to make ourselves free from it. Thus if man is Nature's ultimate end, and since man's final end is moral and not natural, "To find the end of the real existence of nature itself, we must look beyond nature,"[69] namely we must look to God as Author of Creation.

Unlike in the *Critique of Pure Reason* or the early writings on history, Kant was here led to make a clear distinction between Nature and Providence. The point of this distinction is best expressed by saying that Nature and divine Providence are two teleological systems which pursue distinct though related ends. Nature's own ultimate end is man as an end-setting being, that is as an end in himself. Nature cannot dictate ends to such an autonomous man. Such man, when moral, chooses ends compatible with the rational moral law and thereby pursues another end higher than that of Nature. This other end is called by Kant man's final end (to distinguish it from the ultimate end pursued by Nature).[70] This final end or system of moral ends is the one divine Providence was aiming at (and which Nature alone was powerless to produce.) "It is only as a moral being that man can be the final end of Creation."[71] Nature's ends therefore have only a penultimate authority and Nature while pursuing her ends serves yet higher ends which are those of God as the Creator of the system of Nature. It appears now clearly that God pursues two sets of ends, those pursued through Nature's plan (man as end-setting being) and those pursued through his moral Providence (moral man). In this context it becomes clear that by calling God Creator or Author of Creation Kant attributes to him a creative scope vaster than that exhibited by Nature and her plan. Creation encompasses moral man and his moral ends. The teleological processes of Nature, one should add, go on no matter what man does. The moral teleological processes however are furthered only if man "has the intelligence and the will" to further them.[72]

On this basis Kant turned to this theology. Whereas the attempts of physical teleology to produce a physico-theology by trying to infer a cause of Nature and its attributes from the ends of Nature are doomed to fail (primarily because it cannot find attributes for the cause of

Nature nor an idea of what final purpose it has in mind), moral teleology can lead to an ethical theology which, on the basis of our a
priori knowledge of the final end of rational beings, can produce a
valid concept of God with proper attributes, as Intelligence legislating for Nature and as Sovereign Head legislating the moral law in a
Kingdom of ends. We are then treated to a restatement of the moral
proof of the existence of God based upon the familiar necessity of the
possibility of a *summum bonum*. (It is only in this text that Kant actually
called his argument "the moral proof of the existence of God.") But
this time, as in the first Critique and unlike the second, Kant did not
draw upon the need to join happiness to virtue, but upon the need to
be able to reach the purpose of moral teleology in a world which we
can at best assume embodies a physical teleology.[73] Thus the theme
of a teleological ordering of the world as a Creation of God present in
the first Critique, gloriously (and ambiguously) exploited in the philosophy of history (by temporalizing the principle), and neglected in the
second Critique, comes to a final statement in the third Critique.

I would like to be able to prefer the form of the moral proof that
draws upon physical and moral teleology to that which draws upon the
need to harmonize virtue and happiness and state that Kant was not
in his best form when he wrote the Dialectic of Pure Reason of the
second Critique. The argument in the third Critique has the merit of
distinguishing between natural and moral teleology and thus integrat-
ing the perspectives offered by the philosophy of history and of law
and of those which will be developed in *Religion within the Limits of
Reason Alone*, a work which, as we shall see, is also historically conscious. Furthermore, this formulation of the proof also opens fuller
ontological and metaphysical perspectives. It leads to a more characterized theology and even introduces the idea of the world as creation
within the scope of philosophical thinking.[74] The discussion of
Kantian theology, however, will come later.

For the time being, let us be content with stating that the *Critique
of Judgement*, at the end of its survey of all judgements of purpose,
restates in a critical form what the philosophy of history and the
Critique of Pure Reason shyly speaking of Nature had stated, namely:
"The ultimate intention of Nature in her wise provision for us had
indeed, in the constitution of our reason been directed to moral interests alone."[75] Neither Nature nor history hold man as an organism
integrated in their system of ends. Both conspire to bring man to a
threshold where, with his faculties developed, he must make use of his
freedom and choose his own ends. And when man chooses moral ends,

he has freed himself from Nature and transcends it. He then works towards ends which are the imperatives of his autonomous reason and are not dictated by Nature or history, although they must be thought to be the ends intended by the supersensible Author of Nature and Lord of history. At this point man has created, under the imperatives of reason, his own culture and strives to bring into being a moral teleology culminating in the moral commonwealth to be hopefully realized in the conditions of this world.

What we called signs of tension between the Critiques and the philosophy of history are harder to find when it comes to the third Critique. After all, for the first time the actual content of the philosophy of history finds its way into a Critique (albeit in an appendix) and the *Critique of Judgement* explicitly brings out the problem of building a bridge between the noumenal world and the phenomenal world, thus putting its finger on the very area of philosophical concern where the philosophy of history (dealing with the relationship between freedom and observable history) busies itself. On the other hand, the *Critique of Judgement* does not deal with judgements of purpose illustrated by temporal processes: its examples of purposefulness are taken from aesthetics and natural science, two topics that were not historicized for Kant, and, significantly, the philosophy of history finds room in an appendix. So here again we find that the philosophy of history deals with a subject matter which the critical system is ill-equipped to handle because of its ahistorical standpoint. (A similar tension appears in the philosophy of religion, since religion for Kant was partly historicized.)

Kant's notion of "sign," brought out in the third Critique, is perhaps also worth a pause. Aesthetic experience and teleological organization of Nature give us signs that the world is such as to have "meaning," or such as to be a home where human beings can strive towards moral goals without being doomed to absurdity. As such these signs are welcome to strengthen the human spirit and its moral dispositions. The philosophy of history likewise is seen by Kant as bringing comfort to a moral disposition that needs to be strengthened and confirmed. The *Idea for a Universal History* can serve, claimed Kant, to "offer a consoling view of the future."[76] The philosophy of history differs from the third Critique in that it offers us pages where Kant seems more poignantly to reveal his own existential need for signs that the human moral endeavour is not in vain. The display of human stupidity and perversity offered by human history is the worst challenge to Kant's rational faith and the philosophy of history is expected to lay the demon of nihilism to rest. Consider for instance the beginning of the "Concluding Remark" in the *Conjectual Beginnings*:

> A thoughtful person is acquainted with a kind of distress which threatens his moral fibre, a kind of distress of which the thoughtless know nothing: discontent with Providence which governs the course of this world. This distress he is apt to feel when he considers the evils which oppress the human species so heavily and, apparently, so hopelessly. It is true that Providence has assigned to us a toilsome road on earth. But it is of the utmost importance that we should nevertheless be content, partly in order that we should not lose sight of our own failings. These are perhaps the cause of all the evils which befall us, and we might seek help against them by improving ourselves. But this we should fail to do, if we blamed all these evils on fate.[77]

This text can serve to show the moral usefulness of the philosophy of history, but it also illustrates Kant's moral need for a philosophy of history and for a confidence in Providence. We do not find in the philosophy of nature or in aesthetics quite this tone of intense personal concern. The philosophy of history like the philosophy of religion gives us a glimpse into the moral fibre, or better, into the moral dispositions of Kant. We should not be surprised that issues of intense personal and religious convictions are at stake in the philosophy of history to an extent not found in aesthetics or philosophy of nature. Kant, after all, was a very moral person and the fate of the human race concerned him intensely. We should note, however that such pages in the philosophy of history show in Kant a disposition which is not merely made of awe before duty and determination, but which is also made of confidence and faith in Providence, moral feelings which have a distinctively religious colouring.

The Historic Position of the Kantian Philosophy of History

The three previous sections have shown that Kant's philosophy of history is almost entirely a derivation from the results of the three Critiques.[78] And they have indicated, in my opinion, that this history-conscious second strain in Kantian authorship has developed in constant dialectical interrelationship with the major strain, that embodied in the philosophy of criticism. Each strain contributed problems and elements of solution to the other and each spurred and nurtured the other's development. Thus I do not hesitate to conclude that Kant's philosophy of history while not fully developed and often expressed only in germs, bears the same imprint of philosophical labours as the rest of his authorship and lies close to the core of his philosophizing.

But there is more than this. First of all the philosophy of history offers us a promise that nothing else in Kant offered previously: in the future, man will perhaps escape the present limitations of his knowledge and the current burden of his obligations (not to mention the existential strain of being a creature who hopes). As B. Rousset put it: "Everything that we willed, postulated, looked for, and subjectively thought in morality and for the sake of morality, we can grasp it at work in the becoming of mankind."[79] Freedom is said in the third Critique to substantiate its own reality as a matter of fact in the world of action.[80] Man whose reason is so constituted as to be limited to what is given to him through his senses and to what obligations he places upon himself through the moral law, can entertain the hope of seeing the famous objects of reason realized in the world, in the future, and can entertain the belief that he observes the realization of this hope in the course of history. In other words the postulates, now objects of a practical faith, could perhaps some day be objects of knowledge. In this case *per hypothesin* the proof of the objective existence of these objects could be made theoretically, the *summum bonum* having become real through the development of history. Could it be that Kant is telling us the historical future may—or will—give us what only eternity was usually thought to give? Is the bridge that Kant built between the two worlds so solid and so wide that in the end, after much historical achievement (or after much traffic on the bridge), man on earth might cease to live torn between two worlds? Ultimately I believe Kant's answer to this would have to have been no. But prospects have been opened. Hegel clearly went beyond Kant's meaning but Kant had given him some cause. (Note especially that Kant's epistemology cannot say in what sense the *summum bonum* could be said to be real in the future. Its reality would certainly not be either that of the objects of sense or that of the moral law, the only two kinds of objective reality we know of now.)

The philosophy of history modifies the results of criticism, or, more correctly, opens new prospects on a second point: freedom is now presented to us as having a becoming, a history, and furthermore as being an acquisition of the being capable of reason which was made relatively late in his progress. While the *Critique of Practical Reason* in the methodology seeks the "method of founding and cultivating genuine moral dispositions"[81] in the individual and of awakening the pupil's attention "to the consciousness of his freedom,"[82] the philosophy of history shows the whole human race as having become free and conscious of its freedom through a long process of education.[83] Freedom no longer appears as a characteristic that always belongs to any rational being. This gives rise to a new meaning of freedom, a new aspect of it, and new problems in the examination of its destiny.[84]

This relationship of the philosophy of history to that of criticism enables us to situate the historic position of the Kantian philosophy of history, on the one hand as having to the ideology of the eighteenth century philosophes the same relationship that the philosophy of criticism has, and on the other as opening the possibility of developments beyond criticism in the history of European philosophy.[85] At first sight there is a considerable similarity between Kant's writings on history and the common Enlightenment theory of history. We find in both the idea of a plan (almost indifferently held to be a plan of Nature or of Providence) prescribing a progressive development of human faculties. In both cases the eighteenth century is felt to be a decisive turning point, the nature of which allows hopes for a greater amount of rationality and happiness in the future. But any close look at the texts reveals that, although Kant took elements from the familiar picture of an education of the human race which has just happily reached a well-auguring stage, he nevertheless constructed out of this material a rather different view of the human predicament. Three elements in the doctrine show Kant's distance from the philosophes on history.

First of all, Kant used the concept of education of the human race as an Idea in the specific technical sense of his philosophy. It is not a dogma, or a proven view, but a hypothesis meant to guide investigation and to help our understanding of the facts. The contingent facts have the last word in matters of knowledge, and the hypothesis gains only the status of a regulative idea; it has made sense of many facts so far, is necessary to bring a manifold of experience to some unity, and has proved its usefulness.

Secondly, the present stage is not applauded as an age of wisdom. It is merely an age in which the lights of reason begin to have a chance and in which men can begin to act rationally. It is the age of tasks begun and of practical reason. The destiny has not been reached yet but man can now work towards it rationally, if he chooses to. It is therefore eminently the age of responsibility.[86]

Finally, Kant did not allow his idea of progressive education to dictate to him a necessitarian view of the future. That the step just made was a progress does not mean that progress henceforth is inevitable. Unlike many of his contemporaries, Kant was very cautious in his predictions and never ceased to insist that the future will be what men will make it. Natural teleological development cannot serve as a guarantee of moral teleological development. As he pondered the prospects the mood was always one of a hope ready to be disillusioned.

Thus Kant differed from the philosophy of history then held by "enlightened" eighteenth century minds in that the cognitive status and the moral implications of his idea of a teleological plan of nature and a teleological history of freedom are clearly indicated in all their limits.[87] Two of the essays in which Kant returned to the problems of history after the publication in 1790 of the "final" statement in the *Critique of Judgement* strove to make this once again perfectly clear. In the words of *The Strife of Faculties* (1798) the realization on earth of the perfect State is a "sweet dream"; the possibility of a closer and closer approximation of it is "a thought" which can be conceived (or a regulative idea that has theoretical and practical necessity); and to work for it is a "duty."[88] Likewise when the essay on *The End of All Things* (1794) examines the various conceptions of the end of the world, it comes to the conclusion that this is a problem of which we have no rational cognition. To make "a dogma" out of universal or partial salvation for instance is "to overstep the speculative capacity of human reason."[89] Such ideas of reason must be absolutely limited to the "conditions of practical use." Representations of the historical end of the world are mere ideas, which the mind created and with which it plays. They have no cognitive value, since they are out of historical reach. But such ideas have value from the practical point of view.[90] If we cannot know what will happen, we can know what should happen, and towards which end we should work; we can know what would be the wrong, perverted end of the world (namely the reign of Antichrist, a tyrannical society where only fear and self-interest restrain a latent state of war).

To sum up, we have no knowledge of our future. Our rational relationship to the ideal future is only practical, not theoretical (as is our rational relationship to the super-sensible world—and the two are different aspects of the same thing).

These differences between Kant's philosophy of history and common enlightenment views are not superficial differences of opinions. They have profound roots in Kant's philosophy. At least three factors can account for both the originality and strength of the Kantian philosophy of history (and the three Critiques) as distinct from the thought of the Enlightenment.

First of all Kant was ontologically sophisticated and had the makings of a good metaphysician (among these we count Plato, Aristotle, Aquinas, and Leibniz, not Diderot, Condorcet, Voltaire, and Lessing) and that was a rather rare endowment in a century where men of letters called themselves philosophers and where many were prone to thinking that Newtonian science made any further inquiry into the nature of being unnecessary. Far from denying the importance of Newton, Kant rather proceeds with the matter of finding out results for metaphysics from these scientific discoveries. I do not mean to claim that Kant restated the old metaphysics this time on a practical basis as some commentators do, for such judgement is erroneous, but I do state that Kant reopened metaphysical investigation. Consider for instance how the problems of his moral philosophy led him to the question of the *summum bonum* and thus to ask questions about the being of the self (noumenal and phenomenal), the being of God, the being of Nature, and the being of Creation as a whole. Consider, for instance, the pains that he took to establish the objective reality of the postulates of pure practical reason (Kant was no believer in useful fictions) without infringing in any way upon the results of the *Critique of Pure Reason* and making them into definite objects. The result is the doctrine of the Ideas of pure reason, Ideas which are not ontologically empty and insignificant even though they do not yield any knowledge. Thus Kant was forced to find his way among the problems of the oldest ontological doctrine, that of the modes of being.[91] To put it briefly and negatively, Kant fully knew that the statement "God is the Author of Creation" says an analogous but not an identical thing to the statement "Lenôtre is the author of the gardens of Versailles," or Kant fully knew that God does not plan history in the way Marlborough planned the battle of Blenheim. But rare were the eighteenth century minds who had a doctrine of analogy.[92]

Secondly, Kant was morally sensitive and had a moral sensitivity that was modern insofar as it thought that the moral life was the life of a free being or was not moral at all, and that was Christian in that it thought that evil was a real but not undefeatable obstacle.[93] Unlike the proponents of the philosophy of automatic progress, Kant fully knew that the *summum bonum* might perhaps not be realized, either because the efforts of good men would be defeated by the works of evil men, or because good men themselves would never completely defeat the evil inclinations in themselves.[94] Thus for him the moral teleology cannot be built upon or run concurrently with the natural teleology without a break of continuity. That God transcends Nature, that man is free, and that evil is not yet defeated, all this is of a piece and led Kant to see the philosophy of history ultimately as a moral teleology that has not yet reached its goal and not as a natural teleology steadily advancing towards its end.

Nothing illustrates this better than the first essay published after the *Critique of Judgement, On the Failure of All Attempted Philosophical Theodicies* (1791), a work which is the logical Kantian sequence of the achievements of the third Critique. God having been "proved" and said to be the Author of a wise Plan, Nature and history having been "shown" to follow a natural teleology and to lead to a moral one, it might be thought to be only one step to a sound trouncing of the impiety and scepticism of a Candide.[95] Such is not the case. With Kant, unlike Leibniz (or what most interpreters believe Leibniz to have said), metaphysical achievements do not overreach themselves into moral pride and insensitivity. The presence of evil makes any doctrinal theodicy impossible. Moral evil constantly threatens to check, arrest, and divert any teleological development.[96] Such evil is a dreadful fact indeed and the question of knowing whether the radical nature of evil makes the realization of the *summum bonum* impossible is one of the questions that led Kant to reopen his whole inquiry into human destiny in *Religion within the Limits of Reason Alone* in 1793 and make yet another fresh start in a major work. But leaving aside the positive threat caused by evil, and what that does to hope, evil in another aspect is just the other side of human freedom. The very possibility of evil, inherent in human freedom, makes any guarantee of ending up with the best of all possible worlds impossible. A world with necessary developments and a guaranteed happy end is a world without moral tasks and moral men. It is a world with an imperious God and slavish men. Pagans and positivists may think they live in such a world. Kant did not.[97]

Finally Kant was a rationalist who did not yield to the enthusiasms of rationalism. He was a cautious, even pedestrian, rationalist, not a doctrinaire one. In his own words he rejected the dogmatism of reason as well as the evidences which geniuses put forward, and affirmed a self-critical rationalism. If this marks the distance between his own grand design and that of most of his contemporaries who developed a grand philosophy of history, it also differentiates him sharply from the romantics who in their philosophy of history followed in their way the path opened by Kant, and who claimed to be second to none in their insight into the nature of being or the demands of morality, but, alas, got bewitched by their own language. Thus Kant's philosophy of history is distinct from any doctrinaire rationalist one or any romantic enthusiastic one. One of Kant's last essays *On a Lordly Tone* (1796) berates the appearance in philosophy of the ancient lordly tone of wise men who reveal secrets to ordinary mortals. Listening to an inner oracle, such philosophers do not feel the need to embark upon philosophical work, since they claim that their means (or insights) are abundant enough, and thus can philosophize like rich lords and not like poor ordinary mortals. What philosophizing is that? Who can reason with such sentiments? Such questions for Kant were rhetorical; philosophy writes prose and the invitation to write poetry is the death of philosophy itself. Should one object that Kant's own philosophy of history occasionally smacks more of poetry than of prose—and as a matter of fact he himself said it—the simple answer is that Kant was no Monsieur Jourdain and knew when he was talking prose and when he was not.[98]

Thus we can now solve the apparent antinomy between Delbos who saw the *Critique of Judgement* as transforming the philosophy of history from the metaphysical form into a critical one and Troeltsch who saw in the third Critique metaphysics dressed up as criticism. Both are right. There is nowhere in the mature Kant metaphysics that is not critically refined and tested, and the Critique, while remaining short of delivering to Kant a finished metaphysics, encouraged Kant to pursue his courting. "We shall always return to metaphysics as to a beloved one with whom we have had a quarrel."[99] Couples and metaphysics alike no longer live in Eden. Yet both have been critically awakened and can learn how to find their way under their present conditions.

Finally I should point out that, if Kant's philosophy of history is neither that of the Enlightenment nor that of the Romantics who came after him, it is also not what contemporary philosophers want in a philosophy of history. Major problems have to be raised now about Kant's philosophy of history. There are issues which have come to be seen in an inescapable light and which he either did not see or did not focus on. For instance, Kant did not really examine the science—or art—of historiography. He did not examine those conditions of historical knowledge that avail in the work of the "empirical historian." He did not examine in depth the problems of historical causation. (That, however, presupposes the existence of the social sciences and they were hardly constituted during his lifetime. What did exist of the methods of the social sciences, Montesquieu's theories, for example, he knew and made full use of.) He did offer us an a priori approach to the philosophy of history, and while I believe I have shown that his a priori approach does bring us, after "conjectures" and "bold representations" back home again "to the domicile of reason," there is much more that is needed in a philosophy of history. For instance, I would like to see what interrelationships can be drawn between the philosophy of history (as *cognitio ex principiis*) and historical knowledge (as *cognitio ex datis*). Finally Kant did not develop a critique of historical reason as Dilthey and Troeltsch came to try building upon bases in Kant himself. Between the Enlightenment and contemporary philosophy, Kant's philosophy of history occupies the same place as that occupied by criticism, with the sole exception that with its incipient historicization of reason itself, it points more to future developments. I believe, therefore, that following the examples of post-Kantians such as Dilthey and Troeltsch, as Raymond Aron did, for instance, a full contemporary philosophy of history can be developed on an ultimately Kantian basis.[100] This, however, is an altogether different undertaking from that I have attempted as a sympathetic interpreter of what Kant said.

Chapter 4

The Results of the Philosophy of History

The Meaning of the Kantian Faith in Nature and Culture

Kant's philosophy of history, constituted after the loss of the early position that this was the best of all possible worlds, is periodically threatened by pessimism, "abderitism," cynicism, scepticism, the sense of the absurdity of life, and the general feeling that the human race is made up of a group of fools headed towards disaster.[1] (Moral pessimism was a larger threat to Kant than the sentiment of the brutal senselessness of the physical world. He would have agreed with Leibniz that "one Nero has caused more evil than an earthquake,"[2] and might have felt that a recurrence of Neros is as inevitable as a recurrence of earthquakes.) But the insights given by a hard look at the hardships of existence and the wicked cruelties of man were never allowed to penetrate the very core of Kant's faith in the wisdom of God and in the meaning of history.

Thus there is a theistic faith at the basis of Kant's philosophy of history and this theistic basis is what led Kant towards confidence both in God who governs the world and in human reason which has the power to guide men to wise self-government. This confidence is rooted in what was to Kant a rational faith of moral men. It also bears the characteristics of a religious faith. Like Leibniz again, Kant echoed the statement by Horace that divine justice, although lame and not always terribly swift, rarely fails to enforce its sentence.

> *Raro antecedentem scelestum*
> *Deseruit pede poena claudo*[3]

The ramifications of this theistic basis are best shown by drawing attention to the concept of Creation.[4] This concept appears in Kant's philosophic discourse in a long appendix of the *Critique of Judgement*.[5] The world as Creation is the theatre[6] in which God's plan works itself out, and it is the theatre in which Nature and freedom come to harmonize with each other. From this concept of Creation which includes moral teleology (since it harmonizes it with natural teleology), a "natural theology" can be drawn, which Kant calls ethico-theology, whereas from Nature alone, the only "natural theology" that becomes available, physico-theology, is not a theology at all, but rather simply a teleology. Whereas Nature (teleologically considered) could not any more than could (phenomenal) nature mechanically considered provide man with an answer to the question of what he must do, the contemplation of Creation does indicate where man's destiny lies, since Creation, unlike Nature, is a concept which synthesizes the moral law with the natural one, or encompasses moral man and the final end of his practical reason as well as man *qua* the ultimate (or last) end of Nature. Thus human autonomy and divine plan, law of nature and moral law come to a mutual harmonized relationship in the concept of Creation. Human freedom is freedom in a world which lends itself to action, just as human knowledge is a knowledge of a nature and an understanding of a world of which we reflect that they seem to be made in such a way as to be knowable and understandable by man. Thanks to the ends which God had when he created the world one can speak of "an adequation of the world to man."[7] And "signs" are available to reassure man on this point. Being a child of Nature, a child of God, and a mature free man no longer appear as mutually exclusive self-interpretations.[8]

Finally the concept of Creation brings unity to the three different modes of being to which Kantian ontology arrives in its conclusions. God is Creator—and pure spontaneity. Man is creature and creator— he is at the same time receptivity and spontaneity.[9] The phenomena are creatures of man and pure receptivity. (The things in themselves are the creatures of God and we do not know them. Since they do affect our sensitivity some spontaneity must be granted to them. Phenomena are our creatures and we know them.)

This concept of Creation comes to the fore as one to which judgement is led after consideration of the teleological processes only in the *Critique of Judgement*. The *Critique of Pure Reason* does however conclude that:

the *speculative* interest of reason makes it necessary to regard all order in the world as if it had originated in the purpose of a supreme reason.[10]

Although we may succeed in discovering but little of this perfection of the world, it is nevertheless required by the legislation of our reason that we must always search for and surmise it.[11]

Again and again the legislation of reason (theoretical in the first Critique, practical in the second, and reflective in the third) asks us to affirm a rational faith in spite of the fact that many evidences go against it. What needs to be emphasized here is that such belief in the world as Creation led Kant to believe that reason and nature can coincide, and thus to reject all presentations of history and society based upon the Hobbesian tradition, and its total opposition between the impulses of nature and the requirements of reason, between the nature of the individual and the mechanics of society. In other words, for Kant, culture, or civilization, is possible as a process that will refine and develop the human being, and lead him to his true nature. Thus Kant was part of the older tradition that saw reason as the educator of man that will teach him where his true social nature lies and how to fulfil it. He thus did not yield to the Hobbesian view, which was then becoming common, according to which reason in the individual is the skill one may deploy in the pursuit of the object of one's passion, and reason in society is the mechanism of social control necessary for social utility.

Man for Kant has the right to create a cultural world. The entry into the stage of culture is legitimate. Man grows into such a world, and humanizes and moralizes himself as he does so. Civilization—or culture—is the context of man's construction of a moral life. It is not a fate into which man is thrown and in which he will be alienated from his true nature, controlled, or dehumanized. Culture and civilization for Kant are thus not condemned to being forever a hypocritical farce or a machinery of oppression. The State can be an instrument of morality.[12] There is a possibility of "wisdom" (as moral wisdom rather than pragmatic rule of survival) in social arrangements. There is also the possibility of observing and gathering wisdom through the contemplation of history. Past history is not a pure display of the absurd or the morally wrong. It is not just a collection of examples of foolishness and crimes. The wisest men are thus not those who divorce present-day theory from previous experience. Praxis must be informed by both, and there is historical wisdom available in the knowledge of what theories men could and could not put into practice in the past. Nothing perhaps is more typical of young Fichte's break from Kant than his conviction that the history of freedom has just begun, that the so-called wisdom of the ancients is made up of the fears of slaves or of the fears of tyrants, fears that should not hold back vigorous free men.[13]

Thus Kant's faith in Nature and Culture is a faith in the possibility of a progressive humanization of man and realization of his freedom through wise social arrangements and historic achievements. It stands opposed equally to the conservatism that sees no possible moral benefits in political reform and to the utopianism that sees no possible moral benefits made available through the political arrangements that history bequeathed to us. With his refusal of radical utopianism Kant parted company with Rousseau, but he did agree with Rousseau in that he was in search of a culture that would do justice to man's nature.[14] He was in search because there exists a conflict between man and culture as we know it. In one sense our culture is unnatural. But in another sense our culture is rooted in our nature. The search is possible, or the task of moral men is meaningful, because our culture does contain within itself the conditions of possibility of its philosophical reform.

The ultimate source of such a position may be found in Greek philosophy: philosophers may discuss intelligently the nature of things and the nature of man. Our culture—or the city, as the Greeks put it—is at odds with Nature, but through cognitive and moral effort can be redressed to fit with Nature's norms.

Kant however differed from Greek philosophy with his Christian theism, which sharpens the conflict between Nature, culture, and the moral law and sees man as transcending Nature. Thus while Kant was willing to consider the concept of human nature as valid and philosophically important, he was not prepared to derive the moral law from a consideration of human nature. His theism instructs man to obey a moral law which transcends the laws dictated by his nature but ultimately does not abolish them. Could one say that the laws of Nature are *aufgehoben?* At any rate not Nature but a larger Creation is man's home.

The implications of such disjunction between the laws of Nature and the moral laws are very important. For one thing Kant here parts company with all the eighteenth century naturalists or aesthetic moralists who invite us to participate in an ongoing teleological development and make our own the ends of a metaphysically interpreted Nature. (He would also, I believe, have warned us against all those nineteenth century historical activists who invite us to make history's purposes our own.) In refusing to give us an ethics based on some teleology, Kant resisted the whole deistic tradition, which had demoted God's will (and its authoritarian overtones) to promote God's design (and its activist and eudaemonistic overtones).[15] Our action for Kant is to be guided not by our notion of God's design (for that we do not know as objectively certain, although we can make reflective judgements on it) but by what we know of God's will, for of that we do have a sure knowledge through the moral law. Hegel's *Philosophy of Right* was to present this moral standpoint as one that must be transcended. Without the benefit of this work, Kant could not see any theoretical or speculative knowledge, or any inspired vision into ultimate ends that could serve as a rational basis for our moral action and had to make moral action stem from moral obedience. Kant thereby remained part of the classical Christian theological tradition which stated in a *locus classicus* that we must take our bearings for our action from God's law and not from his Providence, since the Providential order is not intelligible to us now, although it will be made manifest to us in the end (and we can derive comfort from knowing that).[16] Providence, in other words, should be trusted but cannot be imitated. Kant thus was striking a sound theological vein as well as a deep moral one when he stated that we must do our duty and denied that we can play at being little Providences of our own who can pursue grand designs and are masters of good and evil.

This of course is not to say that we should not worry or care about whether we will achieve any worthwhile purposes through our obedience to the moral law. We just saw that the moral man is inevitably concerned about the results of his action. We might even argue with Kant—and against his ridiculous case showing why we should never lie, not even to a murderer—that a degree of calculation of foreseeable consequences being pragmatically good cannot be entirely morally bad. But to be concerned about the consequences of one's action, and even calculating some of them, is not the same thing as claiming—let alone gaining—control of such consequences. The Kantian answer in these matters is unambiguous. Our duty is clear but this moral certainty does not enable us to transcend the limits of our finitude. We can achieve a good will (the *bonum supremum*). We cannot become masters of good and evil. We can hope to see the *summum bonum* realized; we must believe it to be possible, but we cannot bring it about. Moral men are lords of their wills only. Tyrants and fanatics claim to be lords of history.

The Theistic Basis of Kant's Philosophy of History and Its Relationship to the Christian Tradition

The doctrine of God which is at the basis of the view of the world as Creation (or to which this view leads) is a subject for the second part of this study. Before we turn to it however, we must examine the case made by those who interpret the ambiguous Kantian phrase found so often in the early writings on history "Nature or Providence" in the direction of naturalism and its immanent developments rather than in the direction of theism as I did by giving a crucial place to the appendix of the third Critique and its concept of Creation.[17]

It must be allowed at the outset that the philosophy of history does have an anti-theological aspect. For instance it rejects the usefulness of the idea of special divine interventions, and rejects the distinction between general and particular Providence.[18] So it can be argued that through the critical analysis of teleology, the philosophy of history and the investigation of its purposes are shifted away from an area where theology has authoritative answers, to open the way for a naturalistic understanding of historical becoming. It can also be argued that Kant firmly built human development upon the conflict of human drives and put a strong basis of biological finality under his moral cosmopolitanism. Thus, in history, man could be educated simply by the regularities of nature and the previous answers of the species. In this way natural and providential processes could ultimately be reduced to a naturalistic monism.

Besides the date of the passage in the *Critique of Judgement* (which comes after most of the basic essays in the philosophy of history and can be presented as the final position), the following arguments may be brought to bear against such an interpretation.

First of all, unlike many naturalistic philosophies of history, the Kantian one does not "abolish" history, does not in any way lead us to transcend our predicament of historical beings, but keeps history open and keeps us as beings with a historical task to be carried on in faith. This emphasis, which does not abolish the terror there is in the prospect that history could have an unnatural end, is one very hostile to naturalism and its immanent and ultimately irresistible developments.[19]

Secondly, unlike most proponents of naturalism, Kant was so convinced of the proved capacity of human nature to do the unnatural that he arrived at a central distinction and opposition between nature and freedom. That Creation is not hostile to man does not diminish in any way the actual tension between the nature of things and the nature of man on the one hand and human freedom on the other. The distinction remains; the nature of things is an obstacle to freedom; it also remains that in its conflict with the natural world, freedom has committed evil deeds and has run against Nature. (Such a statement does not deny that a reconciliation between freedom and Nature is possible when freedom becomes more rational.) Furthermore, after stating his faith in the guarantees given by Nature and by Providence, Kant always repeated that the actions of man can defeat the wise plan and that the observed actions of man are not such as to build our hopes.[20] Thus with Kant any moral hopes based upon natural teleology are always shattered by the knowledge of what men do, and teleological thinking gets a badly-needed second wind, so to speak, by the statement of the imperative moral duty to work for rational goals. How long that second wind will last depends upon the perseverance of moral man, that is, we do not know.[21]

Further evidence is found in the fact that the ethico-juridical strain which is so squarely at the centre of the Kantian philosophy of history has to be balanced in the total picture with the ethico-religious one.[22] The first one holds before man the hope of seeing a good civil commonwealth realized on earth. The second one, which is the only one of the two strains present in the *Critique of Practical Reason* and which reappears along with the former in *Religion within the Limits of Reason Alone*, holds before man the hope of immortality and the hope of reaching the Kingdom of Ends as an individual (rather than as a race) in a supersensible world. Thus, for this strain, the noumenal world in which we have a rational faith and which is the ground of our hope, is an eternal supersensible one and one can doubt that it will ever be approximated (let alone realized) in history. (This strain, more Platonic in origin, led Kant in the second Critique to reflect on the relationship between happiness and virtue rather than on teleological processes in the world and the concept of Creation.) The ethico-religious strain also makes a sharper distinction between legality and morality, whereas the ethico-juridical strain allows an ambiguity to remain in the matter of knowing whether the cosmopolitan civil commonwealth is a moral progression besides being an obvious political one. The ethico-religious strain unlike the ethico-juridical one has very strong other-worldly components and this is hardly a naturalistic theme.

The two strains, however, for Kant were compatible and did not involve him in self-contradiction. This is shown by the essay on *The End of All Things* (1794), a difficult and not too successful piece where the two strains are constantly blended. For instance the end can mean either the termination of the individual's life (death) or of the world (the end of the world) or the inner-historical goal towards which individual and race are heading; Kant constantly oscillated between the two meanings. Thinking on the end can lead men to representations of an atemporal existence in an eternity which is an abyss of which we can have only a negative concept (and which individuals enter at death or the race at an end of the world with universal salvation), or to representations of various historical states of affairs, one, for instance, where a tyranny that cannot be overthrown (the reign of anti-Christ) has come to power. The very unsatisfactoriness of this essay comes from the fact that Kant was incapable of giving the supremacy to the juridico-ethical strain and its this-worldly historical end or to the religio-ethical one and its other-worldly end. The intimate connection between these two strains, one of which cannot be other than theistic, gives us one more reason for seeing a theistic basis to the hope Kant held before men in his philosophy of history.

Thus I believe that the careful definition of Providence found in *Perpetual Peace* (1795, another late writing) is the final result in Kant (a result consistent with the early positions) and is the result of a theism that wants to present the Author of the course of the world as "a higher cause" and to protect its transcendence.[23] Philonenko made a particularly observant point here. Having pronounced himself for the humanization of man through formal morality or through the work of culture rather than through the obedience to nature and the cooperation with her ends, Kant could not find anywhere else than in God the metaphysical guarantee that culture is not a sham or is not doomed to a tragic failure.[24] Nature herself cannot provide a guarantee for something that transcends it, and this remains true no matter what metaphysical meaning is given to "Nature."

Ultimately the theistic basis of Kant's faith in Providence is best exhibited by the essay on theodicy.

In the sequence of Kant's intellectual activities this essay of 1791 makes the transition between the *Critique of Judgement* and *Religion within the Limits of Reason Alone*. Its sober noting of the scandal of evil and of our incapacity to understand much of what is evidenced in history as morally meaningful cools any undue enthusiasm that might arise from the results of the *Critique of Judgement* and prepares for the systematic confrontation with the problem of evil in *Religion within the Limits of Reason Alone*. Thus this essay must be placed alongside the *Critique of Judgement*—something the romantic admirers of the third Critique certainly did not do as they were seized by their vision of the world as a live organic beautiful whole—if one is to maintain the typically Kantian oscillation and balance between affirmations of faith and confessions of ignorance, between affirmations of hope in the future and utterances of disillusioned "realism."[25]

This essay reviews all the objections to the idea of a wise governing of the world by God. These objections are reduced to three types: those that rest their case upon moral evil (the purely scandalous, purposeless, meaningless evil), those who rest their case upon the presence of pain and hardship, and finally those who rest their case upon the absence of just deserts. Thus either the holiness, the goodness, or the justice of God is impugned. Kant surveyed the answers to each of these accusations and found that they can be reduced to three types: either one tries to show that the scandal adduced does not exist, or it is accepted as real but something or somebody else other than God is made responsible for it, or it is accepted as real and presented as something permitted by God for the sake of a higher purpose. Each one of these types of answers in turn are criticized and rejected. None, it turns out, is any answer at all. Thus one conclusion emerges: reason cannot show what relationship exists between the world as we know it through experience and the Supreme Divine Wisdom.[26] (Neither can we prove that reason is powerless in these matters and always will be.) We are at best capable of a negative wisdom; that is, "We can understand the necessary limits of our reflections on the subjects which are beyond our reach." The conclusions which follow are the same as those in the third Critique (only the tone has changed). We can conclude that there is an artistic wisdom manifested in the arrangement of the world (hence the physical teleology) but such wise artistry shows no trace of real moral wisdom such as has to be predicated of God (physical theology is no theology at all). We must postulate the unity of artistic wisdom and moral wisdom in the Creator of the world but we cannot understand it and even less prove it.

Thus no theodicy will ever be possible. Kant however was able to give some answer to the good man confronted by evil and thus concluded with an authentic theodicy (which is possible while the doctrinal one remains beyond our reach). What is the good man to do when he sees himself the victim of dire evil or when he sees other innocent victims? For his answer Kant found a model in Job:[27] the good intelligent man in such circumstances does not ratiocinate; he does not despair. In positive terms, he is honest and faithful. He does not get into mental confusion: he knows what he knows (his conscience does not reproach him and God is just) and he knows what he does not know (why this is happening to him now and what God thinks he is doing). He has faith in God's justice, and his honesty coupled to his faith led him to argue with God and even to argue with some temper. In the denouement God is shown to prefer Job (who discovered the authentic theodicy) to Job's friends who in their efforts to know what cannot be known and in their attempts to ignore what they really know busily kept weaving doctrinal theodicies and ended up lying for God. The essay thus goes on to a concluding remark on formal conscience and the necessity to keep one's head clear, namely to know what one believes and what one does not believe, a point on which no conscience can deceive itself unless it positively wants to.

If there were any doubts left, this essay takes the problems of purpose in Creation, of perfection in the world, and of wisdom in the course of history firmly out of the context of any naturalistic development, into the context of biblical theism where God is transcendent and hidden in clouds, where man transcends nature and questions the ways of the natural world, and where the relationship between man and the ground of everything that is is a covenant of faith conceived by analogy with the relationship between persons, with a minimum of natural mediations and direct evidences.

Besides concluding that Providence since 1790 must be interpreted as an attribute of a theistic God rather than the equivalent of a metaphysical interpretation of Nature, I want also to draw attention to the fact that Kant's philosophy evidences also indebtedness to the Christian tradition. (Such a distinction between theism on the one hand and a specific religious tradition on the other will be a basic one in the examination of Kant's philosophy of religion.) More specifically I want to underline the fact that Kant found his authentic theodicy not in a philosophical doctrine but in a biblical document, more precisely yet, not in a biblical verse or idea but in a biblical picture, that of Job sitting in the dust and covered with loathsome sores, deserted by his wife, and surrounded by pseudo-friends. Similarly Kant found his fundamental insight into the nature of freedom and its power for evil, not in Leibniz's doctrine of metaphysical evil and the ultimately Platonic connection it establishes between limitation and evil, but again in the biblical story of Adam and Eve idling in the garden, eating the forbidden fruit, and being expelled from Eden. In two crucial cases, Kantian philosophical thinking consciously finds its orgin in non-philosophical thought and develops itself by means of a reading of religious symbols found in biblical literature.

To the figures of Adam and Job we can add a new one that hardly appears in the philosophy of history but will be at the centre of the philosophy of religion, that of Jesus. A source where Kant found the moral law presented with all its force and all its purity is the Gospels and the teachings of Jesus.[28] As the *Critique of Practical Reason* states:

> We may, without hypocrisy, truly say of the moral teaching of the Gospel that, through the purity of its moral principle and at the same time through the suitability of its principle to the limitations of finite beings, it first brought all good conduct of man under the discipline of a duty clearly set before him, which does not permit him to indulge in fancies of moral perfections; and that it set bounds of humility (i.e., self-knowledge) to self-conceit as well as to self-love, both of which readily mistake their limits.[29]

Or, "Christian ethics" (of which Jesus is the Author for Kant):

> because it formulates its precept as pure and uncompromising (as befits a moral precept), destroyed man's confidence of being wholly adequate to it, at least in this life; but it re-established it by enabling us to hope that, if we act as well as lies in our power, what is not in our power will come to our aid from another source, whether we know in what way or not.[30]

Thus, besides teaching us the moral law, Jesus, before Kant, taught us the idea of the Kingdom of God and of divine redeeming Providence. It is important at this stage to emphasize that Kant, besides thinking about God also read his Bible (and showed curiosity for the literature of other religious traditions as well), where he found pictures about which we can say what Kant said of aesthetic ideas, namely that they "give much to think" without any concept or definite thought being adequate to it.[31]

II. The Philosophy of Religion

Kant on history focused on problems of theodicy and teleological development. He asked about the scope of human freedom and its direction, about the nature and probability of progress (with a sharp eye on moral progress), and about the role of evil impulses (such as greed and pride) in the political and moral development of human affairs. Finally he asked whether human exertion in history conforms to a pattern of some kind, whether one can hope it will in the future conform to a better pattern, and whether the better pattern can be seen to rise out of the poorer one, and can be seen to be guaranteed by a Providential God. All this places Kant in the context of the movement fostered by enlightened militant philosophes who want to prepare a better future for mankind, although Kant's unease with the notion of inevitable progress, his willingness to take seriously conservative political philosophers such as Rehberg, and his readiness to ponder a deep notion of Providence should force us, in matters of philosophy of history, to see in Kant a philosophe of a very unique kind.

Kant on religion, as I noted before, focused on a set of problems that are either similar or closely related to those that appear in the philosophy of history. Sometimes the same problems appear in a different light. Sometimes they are problems in a different sense and thus lead to very different solutions (such is the case with evil for instance). There is also a difference in that Kant on religion has more specifically German roots and less broadly European ones. The context for Kant on religion is to be found in the philosophical and religious travail and transformation of eighteenth century Germany. Pietism, cool and hot, orthodoxy and its links with royal power, deism and its links with royal power, rationalist theology and its seat in the universities, the various moral theologies, unbelief and the beginning of interest in anthropology and comparative theology, all these factors and their unique fermentation in Germany are the particular strains Kant had to work his way through before he could provide us with a reasoned philosophy of religion.[1]

Our investigation of Kant on religion must therefore begin by trying to follow Kant in the midst of all these German movements in order to discern what path he opened for his philosophy of religion. Thus when our inquiry turns to its second object, it must not only look at different material but also at a somewhat different background. The convergence of the two parts of the inquiry will become apparent again from Chapter 7 onward.

Chapter 5

The Constitutive Elements of Kant's Philosophy of Religion

Biographical Data

It has frequently been said that pietism was the single most important influence on Kant's religious thought and this is quite correct. But what needs to be brought into better light is that the pietism of Königsberg was quite different from the variety common in the South. The introduction of pietist ideas and practice in Königsberg was due to a layman, T. Gehr, a forestry official, who, searching for a more authentic Christian life, got in touch with Spener in 1693 and subsequently with Francke as well. Encouraged by this contact Gehr gathered pietist teachers for his children. Subsequently his friends wanted their own children to share in this kind of education and by 1698 a small private school was operating in Gehr's house. Besides the quality of its religious instruction, the school was first in the city to teach history, geography, and mathematics. The school, thanks to a director J.H. Lysius, recommended by Spener and familiarized with Francke's school at Halle, prospered steadily, gained royal recognition, hence its name *Fredericianum*, and it became a gymnasium.

Religious orthodoxy did not favour this development. And with the rise of Wolff's school at the university, the stage was set for ideological tension in the city. On the one hand, there were Lutheran orthodoxy and Wolffian rationalism, on the other hand the values associated with the pietist group, values which increasingly appeared to be those of tolerance and truthfulness. One man embodied the strength of the two schools and thus became the intellectual and spiritual giant in the community. Franz Albert Schultz, who arrived at Königsberg from Halle as minister in 1731, became director of the *Fredericianum*, and from then on slowly amassed royal and ecclesiastical honours. The scope of reason extended for him as for the rationalist school to natural theology, to the exposition of revealed theology, and to reasonableness in the running of ecclesiastical affairs. Because Schultz was very much respected by the local pietists, there was no opportunity for pietism in Königsberg to develop in the direction of mysticism or enthusiasm, and from that Northern city *Schwärmerei* appeared as a foreign aberration. The pietism of Schultz furthermore made of religion something that directs the will rather than something that grants or encourages contemplation. Morality, he emphasized, was the only sure evidence of faith. Many teachers felt strongly the influence of Schultz; Martin Knutzen who became Kant's favourite teacher in the university was among them.

Many were also the families that felt the impact of Schultz's intense pastoral activity. Kant's mother turned to him to supervise Immanuel's education. Of Kant's parents we know that they were people of simple piety and of remarkable integrity. Nothing indicates that we should doubt this piece of traditional knowledge, but nothing enables us to say much more. Borovski states that the father, a saddler, was hard working and hated lies, and that the mother was the more interested in sanctity of the two.[2] The reminiscences of Kant's contemporaries present Kant speaking movingly of his mother, of the education she gave him (including walks in the country to look at the beauties of nature and pious reflections on the omnipotence of God, his wisdom and his goodness).

> She engraved in my heart a deep respect for the Creator of all things. I will never forget my mother for she planted and nurtured in me the first germ of goodness; she opened my heart to impressions of nature; she aroused and extended my ideas and her teachings have had a permanent and healthy influence upon my life.[3]

Pietist influences remained strong in the *Fredericianum* when Kant attended it. If Kant did break with the practices of formal organized piety his praise of pietism remained apparently as unqualified as that of his mother's piety and moral sense.

> Whatever may be said about pietism, it is enough that those in whom it was an earnest belief were distinguished by their praiseworthy conduct. They possessed the highest good known to man,

that tranquillity, that joy, that inner peace, which no passion can disturb. No misery, no persecution dismayed them, no controversy was capable of provoking them to anger or enmity. In a word: even the mere onlooker was compelled to involuntary admiration.[4]

Many believe they can discern a Calvinistic strain in Kant and this, I believe, is quite correct. Some tried to "account" for it by calling upon the Scottish ancestry of his father. We could also draw attention to the Scots who sat at his table, which, as is well known, welcomed men of affairs and travellers more often than university professors.[5] It seems more reasonable, however, to emphasize that Schultz was no Zinzendorf and then to draw attention to Kant's sources for his writings on religion.

The investigation into Kant's theological readings has been painstakingly done by Bohatec who established a lengthy list of works known by Kant (including the *Dogmatik* of Michaelis) and definitively refuted the view that Kant knew only the Königsberg form of Christianity.[6] Kant knew and used the multivolume *Grundlegung zur wahren Religion* by the Swiss J.F. Stapfer (1708-75), a work of strong Calvinistic orientation. Gone are the days when we could assume that Kant wrote *Religion within the Limits of Reason Alone* out of the insights of a great mind and a hasty reading of the catechism of his youth. That Kant returned to that catechism in the 1790s is of course still true.[7]

Kant heard Schultz's lectures at the university as well as those of Knutzen and in his time came to lecture on various topics relating to religion. His lectures on geography to which I already referred, contain more discussion of Asian ethnography and religion than of practically anything else. He also lectured on natural religion and on philosophical theology, following, as was the custom, the textbook by Baumgarten.[8] One semester his lectures on rational theology were so poorly attended that he thought of abandoning the course. Learning that his audience consisted almost entirely of theological students, he went on delivering them. There is other evidence that he took very seriously his opportunity to teach future *Geistlichen*.[9]

I believe we can therefore accept prima facie and as a working hypothesis the view that Kant's philosophy of religion is an effort to understand his own religion, to clarify its meaning, and to come into a more mature possession of its basic insight. In other words I believe that his philosophy of religion had theological value for him and may have that value for us too. There is no reason to doubt, and there are many reasons to believe, that Kant was in his own way a religious man. That statement, however, should not be made without inquiring into what was precisely Kant's own way of being religious and into his understanding of what religion was all about.[10] Such inquiry is the object of the next section and will be the necessary prelude to the third section of this chapter in which I will try to show how Kant understood the specific task of the philosopher who confronts religion.

But before I turn to the inquiry into what Kant meant by religion I must in the end of this section provide a solution to one delicate problem: does Kant really let us know what "religion" was to him or in what sense he was religious, or does his natural reticence in religious matters coupled with a possible need to keep his thoughts to himself prevent us from seeing what his real attitude was? My statement that Kant was a religious man has been doubted and various kinds of evidence have been brought forward. It would be wise to examine the problem at this early stage of the inquiry.

The climate of opinion in eighteenth century Germany did not always readily lend itself to a free and open declaration of one's opinions in religious matters, and society certainly afforded circumstances where, to paraphrase an expression of Kant, it was safer to state one believed more than one really did. But this should not be overstated. After all the publication by Lessing of the Reimarus bombshell led only to a very heated controversy in print. This being said, it remains true that Kant did suffer the indignities of censorship. In April 1792 the official censors in Berlin acting on Wöllner's 1788 edict refused permission to publish Book Two of *Religion within the Limits of Reason Alone*. Subsequently Kant submitted the last three books to the philosophical faculty at Jena and secured their imprimatur. In 1794 the King asked him to refrain from giving offence by his writings. Kant pleaded his innocence and pledged he would entirely refrain from all public statements in matters of religion.[11] Furthermore, the University of Königsberg would certainly remember what happened to C. G. Fischer who in 1725 had declared himself a partisan to Wolff's philosophy shortly after Wolff himself had been forbidden to teach and was expelled from Prussia (1723). Fischer likewise received the order to leave Königsberg within 24 hours and Prussia within 48. Admittedly, such events did not take place under Frederick II; nevertheless they can be brought forward to suggest the idea that neither Kant's publications nor his lectures can be taken at face value as revealing what he really thought in religious matters. We might be getting access through them only to Kant's prudent official views and not to his real innermost convictions.

Troeltsch, for instance, defended the view that *Religion within the Limits of Reason Alone* contains many diplomatic statements or many concessions to orthodoxy that are there only for exoteric purposes. The affirmations of the possibility of revelation are especially identified as being the utterances of prudence.[12] Readers of Kant who are somewhat familiar with his ethics will be surprised by such allegations which seem to tarnish the character of a conscientious man who hated duplicity and praised the art of honest expressions of one's thought, and rigorously saw the need for principled action in all cases. To this one may retort that the only moral slip up one can find in Kant's life is precisely in a matter of censorship. Upon the death of Friedrich Wilhelm II, Kant resumed in 1797 public utterances on religion, in spite of his previous promise, on the ground that the phrase in his pledge "as your Majesty's most faithful servant" bound him only during the King's lifetime, thus having recourse to that abominable Jesuitical invention, the mental reservation.[13] To this one can add that even atheists are known to keep fond memories from their pious mothers. Atavism and political prudence can thus be construed as being responsible for Kant's ultimate personal position, namely a willingness to go along with the minimum of a profession of faith, something like a pale deism, transparently covering his real attitudes, which are expressed in his criticism of and abstention from religious observances, and by his attack upon belief in miracles, special providence, and so forth.

The suspicion of extreme prudence lingers in many authors who do discern that Kant did not speak or write like the average unbeliever or minimal deist and are thus tempted to believe that we may never really know what Kant really thought in these matters. In response to all this it should be stated, first of all, that Jachmann's protest against those contemporaries who assumed Kant believed more or less than he indicated in his writings or lectures seems the voice of common sense. Furthermore the two modern authors who most thoroughly investigated this matter, J. Collins and J.L. Bruch, both voiced their disagreement with Troeltsch and proceeded with the task of finding out what exactly Kant did write without forcing him into any battle line of an eighteenth century ideological confrontation.[14] Besides the unpleasantness involved in doubting the truthfulness of Kant, the following evidence can be amassed to defend the commonsensical view. First of all Kant's letters to his private correspondents compared to his public statements are nowhere more ruthless in their discussion of the church nor more hostile, and even occasionally contain some very crucial positive affirmations. Obviously one cannot oppose public professions with private belief in Kant. Secondly, Kant described himself as shy of stating his innermost religious conviction and specifically denied ever affirming what he did not believe: "Although I am absolutely convinced of many things that I shall never have the courage to say, I shall never say anything I do not believe."[15] Thirdly, the expressions of enthusiasm found in his published writings are not the proclamations of belief of a crusading ideologue (as is so often the case with the non-religious eighteenth century rationalistic minds), but are undoubtedly the expressions of a personal faith, the moral and religious dimensions of which are self-authenticating.

Three such passages may be evoked. I have already referred to the page in the second Critique in which Kant categorically affirmed his will to defend his interests, spiritually understood, without shame or restraint, since these interests spiritually understood are those of all men. We can add the two passages in which Kant has recourse to apostrophe. "Duty! Thou sublime and mighty name. . . . What origin is there worthy of thee . . . ?"[16] and "O Sincerity! Thou Astraea, that hast fled from earth to heaven, how mayst thou (the basis of conscience, and hence of all inner religion) be drawn down thence to us again?"[17] These passages pay no lip service to official dogma; they are expressions of a most deeply felt and thought-out personal conviction, and they have a moral and religious ring.

To affirm that there are authentic religious convictions behind Kant's affirmations in his philosophy of religion is of course not to make him an adherent of any orthodoxy whatsoever. Borovski was quite aware of this point. Kant, he said, resolved many doubts against positive religion (this is, as we shall see, true), but a few pages later he deplored the fact that Kant did not see in Jesus the Son of God sent from on high but a model of man.[18] The basic index of Kant's unorthodoxy is found in his personal attitude towards the rituals of the church. Borovski indicated that already in the *Fredericianum* he could not enter into or acquire a taste for the "Schema" of piety (or rather pseudopiety) which many of his fellow pupils accepted and got accustomed to.[19] It is better known that he did not attend church and even usually dropped out of the academic procession when it reached the door of the church. This distaste, however, which could perhaps prove much to an eighteenth century orthodox minister should hardly prove very much to us. After all, pietism criticized folk-religion from a Christian perspective, and, unlike his non-church-going contemporaries, Kant did not relish masonic rituals. His abhorrence then was clearly for public exercises and common demonstrations of piety. It seems to me to derive from an intense respect for the privacy of other consciences, of which he repeatedly stated that only God can fathom,[20] and a certain deeply engrained reticence and constant desire to have his own heart protected from preying minds.

Finally, although Kant criticized the pietist community which educated him, this in no way grew into animus; as a matter of fact he never departed from admiration for it. We find in him thus no parallel to those nineteenth century individuals who saw their religious childhood as a jail from which they had to break free for their moral or spiritual development. Kant there is even unlike Schleiermacher who was to look upon his pietist upbringing with a mixture of resentment and nostalgia. Therefore, we can agree with Collins that, while Kant saw many defects in the theism professed in his day, he "neither withdrew his assent from personal theism free from these defects, nor ceased to investigate the intellectual problems of religion."[21] I conclude, therefore, that we have no reason to try to investigate what Kant thought but did not say and can turn to the study of what he said without fear of being misled.

Problems of Definition: Religion, Pure and Applied

An inquiry into Kant's philosophy of religion must begin by an attempt to see what Kant meant by the word "religion."[22] What kind of definition of religion do we find in Kant? (And let us remember that what is at stake here philosophically is not so much whether the definition found will be true or false but whether it will turn out to be useful or misleading.) We should also note that when Kant writes "religion" he might be pointing to his own personal sense of religion, or religiousness, or again he might be speaking of something he does not particularly feel involved in but studies nevertheless. The results of the previous section indicate that, as a working hypothesis, we should assume that when we read "religion" in Kant, we come across something that will have something to do both with his own religiousness (about which he is so reticent) and with that exteriorized reality which he examines so carefully when he discusses religion philosophically.

Two quotes will enable us to grasp initially Kant's basic practice when it comes to the usage of the word. "Religion is the recognition of all duties as divine commands."[23] This definition is both well-known and in need of comment. To it we must add a lesser-known passage that is perhaps more illuminative.

> There is only *one* (true) religion; but there can be *faiths* of several kinds. We can say further that even in the various churches, severed from one another by reason of the diversity of their modes of belief, one and the same true religion can yet be found. It is therefore more fitting (as it is more customary in actual practice) to say: This man is of this or that *faith* (Jewish, Mohammedan, Christian, Catholic, Lutheran), than: He is of this or that religion. The second expression ought in justice never to be used in addressing the general public (in catechisms and sermons), for it is too learned and unintelligible for them; indeed, the more modern languages possess no word of equivalent meaning. The common man always takes it to mean his ecclesiastical faith, which appeals to his senses, whereas religion is hidden within and has to do with moral dispositions.[24]

In the light of these two texts which make a point frequently repeated in Kant we can state that when Kant speaks of *die Religion* the proper English translation in practically all cases is "religion" without any article, definite or indefinite. He is not speaking of a religion (a religious tradition with its own Scriptures, continuity of doctrines, and cultic practices). He is not speaking either of the religion, namely that of my fathers, of my tribe, or of my civilization, or that which I have just presented in a philosophical book and which is obviously the true one. Kant is miles away from the good conscience of Parson Thwackum who could see no difference between religion, the Christian religion, the Protestant religion, and the Church of England.[25] I suggest therefore that "religion" to Kant was first that inner personal quality, the presence or the absence of which enables us to say of a man that he is religious or not. Religion to Kant meant an attitude not a doctrine, and the first sign of Kant's originality in contrast to the deist exponents of natural religion is that to him "pure" religion, or religion simply considered, did not refer to a minimum of doctrine and practice but to an inner attitude of the heart. One version of the definition of religion specifically states that religion is "the heart's disposition to fulfil all human duties as divine command.[26] In other words, after centuries of Protestant–Catholic controversy and decades of Christian–deist debates which had pitted objectified systems of religious doctrine and practice against each other, Kant deobjectified the term "religion" and returned to something like the original Latin and Ciceronian meaning of *religio*. I believe I can show that this is part of the import of Kant's "moral" definition of religion. Where many saw doctrines and beliefs, Kant saw a disposition, a state of the inner being. (The individual system of doctrine and cultic practice Kant called "a faith." Faith, taken simply, is yet another thing again, as we shall see.) To call this state of the inner being a moral disposition is to emphasize that it is a personal and active (or action-oriented) state, not a sentimental state of repose and contemplation. (For this reason Kant would not in any way affirm religion to be a feeling.)[27]

This point was seen by Beck and Collins, neither of whom became hypnotized by the presence of this adjective "moral," and neither of whom allowed it to empty Kant's meaning of religion of all religiousness. Consider first Beck's interpretation:

> Religion, properly understood, is nothing but the recognition of the holiness of morals, to the defense of which the whole of his ethical work had been devoted from the beginning.[28]

Collins summarized Kant's view in this way:

> In its subjective or dispositional character, religion is an active relating of our moral freedom to God, viewed as the source of moral commands. Although the philosopher may not be able to specify the particular doctrinal content of religion in its full range, he can certainly determine the human religious attitude in which all theological doctrines must be rooted.[29]

The religious nature of this recognition of all duties as divine commands may be brought out by quoting the *Critique of Pure Reason*. "We shall not look upon actions as obligatory because they are the commands of God, but shall regard them as divine commands because we have an inward obligation to them."[30] Such a typical passage may seem to restrict the scope of religion by making it dependent upon morality and not the other way around. In fact, however, this position establishes the genuine originality of religion by defining it not as the acquisition of one more duty or set of duties (such as duty to God or his Church), not as the buttress of existing duties, but as a distinct way of viewing all our moral duties.[31]

Kant had numerous precedents for such a moral interpretation of religion. Stapfer (in his *Sittenlehre*) and, among the philosophers, Baumgarten and the whole school of Wolff, agreed to relate religion to morality.[32] But to relate religion and morality is not to identify them, and I believe Kant made a sharper distinction than is often seen between the good will, which is the fundamental moral attitude, and the attitude of "humble confidence," which is his most frequent characterization of the religious attitude.

I therefore do not agree with those commentators who claim that Kant's moral definition of religion evaporates all religiousness from religion, or leaves no room for a specifically religious feeling. What I prefer to call Kant's interpretation of religion is indeed moral but the meaning of this "moral" interpretation must be clearly delineated. There is no need to emphasize that Kant did not make of religion a moralistic affair overburdened by duties and prone to scrupulousness about exterior things. But I may need to show that his moral interpretation of religion establishes a relation between morality (obedience to duty, or recognition of the voice of reason in duty with a feeling of respect for the law and for man) and religion (as recognition of all duties as divine command with a feeling of awe and confidence *coram Deo*, as the Author of the moral law) that does not entail the disappearance of religion or religiousness as something distinct from morality. I shall argue for this view by looking at texts scattered throughout all periods of Kant's authorship where he is found discussing religion as an inner attitude and doing it in such a way as to express something of what this inner attitude was to him.

A clear presentation of a kind of religious feeling may be found in Kant's first publication, the *Theory of the Heavens*. I quoted above an expression found in this work of admiration for the beauty and harmony of the world.[33] But besides such an aesthetic and deistic version of the sublime type of religious sense we find in the same work a passage with a more typically Kantian ring.

The Universe, by its immeasurable greatness and the infinite variety and beauty that shine from it on all sides, fills us with silent wonder. If the presentation of all this perfection moves the imagination, the understanding is seized by another kind of rapture when, from another point of view, it considers how such magnificence and such greatness can flow from a single law, with an eternal and perfect order.[34]

A similar structure will be found in Kant's mature theory of religion; a movement of the imagination leads to silent wonder and becomes "another kind of rapture," or a higher feeling, when purified by reason.

The lectures on the philosophy of religion shed light on this higher, less aesthetic sense, by speaking of the experience of a deeply felt "contradiction between the path of nature and the path of morality."[35] The lectures on metaphysics state that the doctrine distinguishing between the intelligible world and the sensible world is among the oldest possessions of mankind and point to the ancient Egyptians.[36] Finally the lectures on geography work their way towards a definition of the essence of religion by affirming that the natural world around us is in sharp contrast to the ethical world which our thinking requires. All religions, they go on to say, attempted to restore the harmony between the two, or to overcome this deeply felt conflict.[37] This seems to be Kant's formula to discern "religion" in all religions. Religion everywhere and in all higher forms is said to be faith in a moral ordering of the world or in the fact that the world is somehow, ultimately ruled by a moral law, as well as being ruled by the physical laws of which we have so much evidence, and which seem so often to produce human situations incompatible with the demands of morality.[38]

This theme is echoed in the famous "confession" in the *Critique of Practical Reason* on the moral law within me and the starry heaven above me, the two things which "fill the mind (*Gemüt*) with ever new and increasing admiration and awe" and which I associate "directly with the consciousness of my own existence."[39] It is the keenly felt insight into these two worlds, one of which "annihilates as it were my importance," while the other "infinitely raises my worth,"[40] which, I submit, made Kant a religious man and sensitive to the expressions of religion in all religious traditions. (Hence the point of the well-known passage is not the two laws, but the contrast between them and the higher authority of the former.) Such confession of the sense of belonging to "another world" as well is not found only in the mature Kant. The early essay on earthquakes in a statement that directly contradicts the optimistic main thrust of the argument, namely the attempt to reconcile man with the ways of Providence in this world, denies that we really belong to "this" world, and affirms that much in life teaches that "the goods of this earth cannot offer any satisfaction to our longing for beatitude."[41]

Finally we find in *Religion within the Limits of Reason Alone* two texts which shed further light on the feeling content of the religious attitude.

> The contemplation of the profound wisdom of the divine creation in the smallest thing, and of its majesty in the great—which may indeed have already been recognized by men in the past, but in more recent times has grown into the highest wonder—this contemplation is a power which cannot only transport the mind into that sinking mood, called *adoration*, annihilating men, as it were, in their own eyes; it is also, in respect of its own moral determination, so soul-elevating a power that words, in comparison, even those of the royal suppliant David (who knew so little of all those marvels) must needs pass away as empty sound because the emotion arising from such a vision of the hand of God is inexpressible.[42]

It is interesting to note that in 1793 Kant still held to the belief found in his first writings that eighteenth century natural science was in a way doing great things for religion. More interesting, however, is the reappearance of a duality in the characterization of the religious feeling, a duality this time between the sinking mood and the soul-elevating one. Here again the religious feeling is presented as a higher one, higher than what we might call a cosmic feeling (or perhaps oceanic?), and higher because of the injection of the moral or rational point of view.

The definition of "the spirit of prayer" is a further indication that Kant was not indifferent to the emotional colouring of religion.

> A heart-felt wish to be well-pleasing to God in our every act and abstention, or in other words, the disposition, accompanying all our actions, to perform these as though they were being executed in the service of God, is the *spirit of prayer* which can, and should, be present in us without ceasing.[43]

The religious sense of conflict between the two worlds makes of Kant a courageous man of faith who affirms the ultimate authority of the world to which we belong through the moral law and the interior life. The last word belongs to the soul-elevating feeling, not to the sinking mood. Thus the religious disposition shades over into the moral disposition, and both the religious sense and the moral feeling affirm man to be a courageous fighter for ideal ends in a world where such ends meet with difficulties. And both the religious sense and moral faith affirm these ends to be rooted in another world of unconditional and ultimate authority. To recognize duty as divine command means therefore to discern in it a truthful promise; the moral authority of the Author of the moral law will ultimately prevail. Man can trust, humbly, that the moral law does not direct him towards illusions and impossibilities. The moral confident resolve, deep though it is, does not allow the sense of conflict between the two worlds to disappear. No worldly philosophy will ever "solve" the conflict in which the moral man finds himself and which Kant's moral man bears with religious faith and hope. The feeling of the insolubility of the conflict led Kant, for instance, to write the essay on theodicy which is a good door into Kant's innermost religious mind and an eloquent witness to the seriousness of it.

The fact that Kant's religious sense is built upon a sense of conflict between two irreconcilable worlds or orders and occasionally takes on a tragic colouring does not, however, rule out the possibility of the emergence in Kant either of a sense of the ultimate reconcilability of these two worlds both made by God the Creator, or of a sense of their actual reconciliation in the sense of the order of the whole of Creation, a sense that finds expression also in the feeling of the sublime. The two worlds can be reconciled by affirming the sovereignty of God as Moral Ruler over both, in other words, by affirming that the "lower" world, that which "annihilates" us and tries us, is ultimately subject to the higher world where morality reigns supreme. The sense of the conflict of the two worlds may be a permanent existential reality in the life of finite man, but ontologically, one world has a higher status of reality. The former is the world of the conditioned and penultimate. The other is the world in which the Unconditional and Ultimate is to be found. This means of course that the religious sense qua soul-elevating feeling is not a sublime defiance thrown by moral man to the face of an indifferent universe, but is a deeply felt confidence in the Creator of all.

An examination of the feeling of the sublime is useful because it confirms that there are feeling–states in which the authority of the higher world is driven home to the heart of man. But it is also particularly useful to refute those commentators who state that Kant "reduced" religion to morality and deny that Kant had any sense of religious feeling. For the examination of the feeling of the sublime led Kant to a very satisfactory discussion of religious feeling. The fact that this discussion is to be found in the *Critique of Judgement* (a work which has also the feeling of the beautiful among its topics) may be responsible for the lack of attention it received. (The absence of almost any trace of this discussion—save the text we quoted—in *Religion within the Limits of Reason Alone* is one of the major weaknesses of this work.) Religious feeling is presented in the third Critique in terms closely approaching those describing the feeling of the sublime.[44]

> Both the admiration for beauty and the emotion excited by the profuse variety of ends of Nature, which a reflective mind is able to feel prior to any clear representation of an intelligent author of the world, have something about them akin to a *religious* feeling.[45]

Such feeling "akin to a religious feeling" is distinct from the feeling of the sublime, in that the feeling of the sublime indistinctly points to the vastness of nature and its forces and simultaneously to the fact that man transcends them (the sublime is aptly characterized by Krüger as the terrible which is not dangerous),[46] whereas the religious feeling sees a moral Sovereign behind the might of Nature and leads us to "accept it with deep veneration—wholly different from any pathological fear,"[47] and leads us to bow down willingly before it. If the feeling of the sublime is a sense of the grandeur of man, the religious feeling roots all grandeur in a supreme moral Legislator. The discussion of religious feeling in the third Critique is also an opportunity to emphasize its distinction from superstitious feeling. The former is characterized by respect, the latter by terror; the former by "humility and reverence," the latter by "submission, prostration, and a feeling of utter helplessness."[48] The one characterizes a morally mature man; the other a morally primitive one.

In a sharp statement of the difference between religion and superstition, Kant affirms that religion fosters the courage to stand on one's feet.[49] Such discussions of religious feeling, however, are rare in Kant and the more frequently quoted passage in the *Critique of Judgement* speaks of moral feeling.

Imagine a man at the moment when his mind is disposed to moral feeling! If, amid beautiful natural surroundings, he is in calm and serene enjoyment of his existence, he feels within him a need —a need of being grateful for it to someone. Or, at another time, in the same frame of mind, he may find himself in the stress of duties which he can only perform and will perform by submitting to a voluntary sacrifice; then he feels within him a need—a need of having, in so doing, carried out some command and obeyed a Supreme Lord. Or he may in some thoughtless manner have diverged from the path of duty, though not so as to have made himself answerable to man; yet words of stern self-reproach will then fall upon an inward ear, and he will seem to hear the voice of a judge to whom he has to render account. In a word, he needs a moral Intelligence; because he exists for an end, and this end demands a Being that has formed both him and the world with that end in view. It is waste of labour to go burrowing behind these feelings for motives; for they are immediately connected with the purest moral sentiment: gratitude, obedience, and humiliation—that is, submission before a deserved chastisement —being special modes of a mental disposition towards duty.[50]

There is profound irony for this interpreter in the reading of a description of a moral feeling that leads us to the thoughts of God as Creator, Legislator, and Judge. We may well wonder whether what is here called moral feeling should not be called religious feeling. It is certainly a sense of the unity and order of all Creation. It is perhaps appropriate in this case to attribute prudence to Kant. A similar glowing description of religious feeling would have sounded to Kant as *Schwärmerei* and he must have been very afraid of encouraging such aberration in any of his readers. To speak of moral feeling may have appeared safer and more apt to convey his own meaning of the quality of religiousness.

A further index of the validity of our interpretation of the meaning of religion for Kant may be found in his numerous attempts to distinguish clearly between religion and theology. Unlike the sentimentalists who praise religious feeling and decry theology (but nevertheless have implicitly a theology of their own), and unlike the popular authors who in their intellectual confusion give the name of religion to their own natural theology and deplore theology as the haven of mediaeval superstition, Kant did not find theology to be an irreligious undertaking or sterile book-learning. He rather saw in religion the attitude, and in theology the rational reflection on this attitude and the development of suitable doctrine. "It seems that there cannot be any religion without a previous determined concept of God; it is the opposite, religion must precede and the determined concept of God is drawn out of it."[51] Thus to him there can be both good and bad theology (whereas there can be only good religion, bad religion being superstition). The point seems elementary but had to be made in a century when theology seemed embodied by committees of the Sorbonne or consistories and religion by enthusiastic conventicles or pietist "collegia" and lyrical poetry.

On the basis of the textual evidence thus gathered I believe I can summarize the meaning of religion for Kant in the following three points. (Remember that in my hypothesis "the meaning of religion for Kant" means both what he means by the word "religion" when this word is found under his philosophical pen, and his own personal religiousness or intimate sense of religion.)

1. Religion to Kant at one first and most fundamental level was a sense, an inner attitude, distinct from the moral feeling but closely akin to the feeling of the sublime, which is a sense of awe before the majesty of an ideal and moral order which stands in authority far above the natural order of things which is manifested in our daily experience. This sense may be characterized as one of "speechless wonder" or of "holy shudder."[52] There is a duality in Kant's thought at this level. The feeling may be one of harmony under the Creator. It may also be one of conflict in which the holy moral order is affirmed although it is contradicted in most of our experience.

This is the basis of all religion. This is what Kant was reticent about.

2. When clarified and purified by reason and when related to the growth of the moral consciousness, this "religion" becomes "the recognition of all duties as divine command," namely an internal attitude which is still distinct from the moral one (that is, which is more a matter of feeling than of practical self-determination or resolve), and which centres upon the sense of the holiness of the moral law of which God is the Author. If Kant's own characterization tended to become increasingly theocentric at this level there are still examples of relations established by him between moral earnestness and non-theocentric religion.

This "recognition of all duties as divine command" leads also to the creation in the heart of man of a basis of conscientiousness for all moral action, thereby creating another link between religion and morality.[53] It seems to lead to the conviction that we cannot cheat the moral law within us. At any rate the recognition of all duties as divine command is accompanied by an effort at self-knowledge aiming at the defeat of that within us which lures us away from such conscientious recognition.

> Religion is conscientiousness (*mihi hoc religioni*), the holiness and truthfulness of the saying according to which man must know himself. Know thyself. To have this does not require the concept of God, even less the postulate that there is a God.[54]

In this connection between religion and inner integrity (which very interestingly draws upon the archaic Latin usage of *religio*) religion is presented as the very foundation of all rational integrity and all honest knowledge. Conscience, in the *Metaphysic of Morals*, is defined as "consciousness of an *inner court* in man" ("before which his thoughts accuse or excuse one another") and is specifically related to the idea of an "ideal person," to "the authorized judge of conscience" who is a "scrutinizer of hearts."

> Since such an omnipotent moral being is called *God*, conscience must be conceived as a subjective principle of responsibility before God for our deeds. In fact the latter concept will always be contained (even if only in an obscure way) in the moral self-awareness of conscience.[55]

Of this religion, which is so linked to inner integrity, Kant was not shy, and was a tireless exponent. "Moral self-knowledge, which requires one to penetrate into the unfathomable depths and abyss of one's heart, is the beginning of all human wisdom."[56]

3. When further characterized, exteriorized, and shared, religion becomes faith. The philosopher finds basically two kinds of faith: the rational faith, or that faith which is postulated by pure practical reason, and historical faiths, or those faiths which are embodied in religious traditions, their symbols, rituals, Scriptures, and doctrines. (Only the second kind may properly be called a faith.) Faith of both kinds is doctrine, not feeling, although it is not doctrine to the point of being divorced from sense and conative will. This is made apparent by the definition of faith found in the third Critique, definition which comes directly from the "moral proof" of God in the second Critique:

> Faith (absolutely so called) is trust in the attainment of a design, the promotion of which is a duty, but the possibility of the fulfilment of which (and consequently also that of the only conditions of it thinkable by us) is not to be *comprehended* by us.[57]

This distinction between the two kinds of faith is what Kant believed to be his major contribution to the philosophical investigation of religion[58] and it makes the link between the ethics and the philosophy of religion. *Religion within the Limits of Reason Alone* is an inquiry into the meaning of a faith (the Christian one) and into faiths (by drawing parallels between all faiths). These faiths are of course critically evaluated in the light of pure rational faith as developed in the second Critique but, against those who see Kant's contribution to philosophy of religion merely in his notion of pure rational faith, it must be emphasized that Kant's philosophical inquiry shows equal interest for what he calls the historical faiths.

What Kant meant by historical faith will be looked at in the next chapter; what need to be emphasized at this stage are the numerous and radical implications of this fundamental distinction between religion as religiousness and "a" religion, as religious tradition. The clearest of these implications is that the distinction between natural and supernatural (or revealed) religion is undercut and may even be set aside. For when one begins by distinguishing between on the one hand an attitude at the heart of man and on the other an objective body of myths, texts, practices (or the totality of a historical, embodied, institutionalized religious tradition), one will be at pains to distinguish what is natural and what is supernatural in origin in either, or at least one will begin to lose confidence in the validity and worth of such attempts. In other words one has begun to consider religion from an anthropological and social point of view, and the doctrines of nature and supernature classically formulated in the thirteenth century will lose their relevance. (I do not want to imply that such an approach to religion from an anthropological point of view inevitably leads to atheism. In many cases it leads to a restatement of the theistic position.) A fragment from a discarded earlier version of the preface to *Religion within the Limits of Religion Alone* will show Kant's hesitations with the notions of natural versus revealed religion:

One usually divides religion into *natural* and *revealed* religion (or better, into religion of reason and religion of revelation); at the basis of the former lies a rational theology and a similar ethics, and at the basis of the latter lies a revealed theology (which is called *biblical* when a holy Scripture serves as its text) and a similar ethics.

This division is not precise enough to prevent all misunderstanding; because there can be no religion of revelation (and with it no biblical theology and ethics) in which one could not find also a religion of reason (and a similar theology and ethics), and this is so much the case that the latter will be conceived as existing by itself (a priori) and the former will be conceived as the practice (Ausübung) of the latter in concreto, adding to what it requires and completing it (if this were not the case, faith would be not religion but superstition). Therefore the division into *pure* and *applied* religion would prevent misunderstanding more successfully, especially concerning the borders between the two.[59]

This distinction also is not without antecedent. Many including Lessing had spoken of "learned religion" (in opposition to the natural one) and F. A. Schultz had introduced the expression "applied religion" in preference to *religio acquisita* (although he did not connect it particularly with morality).[60]

I conclude this section therefore by stating that Kant approached the task of a philosophy of religion with a definitional distinction best expressed as that between religion pure and religion applied. Admittedly, this distinction is not found frequently in these terms in Kant's writings. But these are the terms which, I believe, will be found most useful. Religion pure is inner, and easily secretive. It is a sense of relationship to God (or to the Ultimate and Unconditional, to be sensitive, as Kant was, to the possibility of non-theistic religion), or it is a sense of living one's moral life before God in awe and confidence. As such it is a sense of something mysterious which cannot be put into words. It is a sense which definitely transcends morality. "The sort of moral relationship that holds . . . between God and man surpasses completely the boundaries of ethics and is altogether inconceivable to us."[61] Religion applied is concretely exteriorized and can be observed. It is a historical and social, institutionalized reality. This new distinction between religion pure and religion applied raises the prospect of a philosophical discourse on religion that can be a unified discourse on religion in its totality, private and public, personal and social. Religion pure and religion applied together present us with the totality of religion as lived by men in history and with the live core, or norm, that may judge of all religions.

Since philosophy of religion thereby promises a theory of religion that will include a normative element, it may be said to become theological. At any rate it encounters theologians on its path and finds that they too have their notion of what "true religion" really is. This possibility of conflict between philosophers and theologians leads us into another set of definitional problems to which I shall turn in the next section.

Problems of Definition: Theology, Philosophical and Biblical

The program of Kant's philosophy of religion, we just saw, creates the possibility of a conflict between philosophy and theology. Specifically this prospect disturbs the balance of power, or rather the division of labour, between philosophers and theologians (and their respective faculties within the university) which had been established by the traditional distinction between natural and revealed theology, a distinction which had more or less kept the peace in German universities and had not too badly served the interests of the pursuit of knowledge. Kant, however, while he disliked the old division of labour, was not entirely satisfied with the idea of a unified intellectual approach to religion and wanted to preserve a distinction between philosophers and intellectually competent *Geistliche* or university professors of theology. That he wanted to preserve the distinction has been attributed to his desire to keep the peace with the theological establishment; thus he could be construed as offering to them a specific task for which he pronounced himself incompetent (and upon which jurisdiction he professed to be unwilling to trespass) as a merely political gesture. I believe, however, that this desire of his to preserve a distinction is genuine and furthermore is methodologically grounded in his philosophy in the distinction he made between the judge on the bench and the professor of law,[62] and in the thought-out theory of the university he developed in *The Strife of Faculties*. At any rate, the Kantian distinction was found to be satisfactory by Karl Barth, of all theologians the one who would perhaps most quickly take umbrage at any philosopher presuming to tell theologians what they should be doing.[63]

Kant most frequently expressed this distinction through the terms "biblical theologian" on the one hand and "philosopher" or "rational theologian" on the other.[64] The choice of the first expression may be surprising but the reasons for it are quite clear. At the beginning of the eighteenth century Protestant dogmatics as taught in the university was following largely a rationalistic scholastic method not too different from Thomism, with however a greater abundance of biblical verses as *dicta probantia*. A variety of factors in eighteenth century Germany came to place the centre of theological endeavour more and more in the biblical part. First of all, pietism resisted orthodoxy in the name of the Bible and requested a piety and a theology based on the Bible. Secondly, biblical investigation acquired its own autonomy, its own independence, and developed and used canons of historical criticism. It thus began to embark upon its modern developments. This movement began with the pietist Bengel and culminated with Semler and Michaelis for whom being a serious, scholarly, scientific university theologian meant investigating the text and meaning of the Bible critically. The historical rather than the philosophical method came to be the source of the scientific credentials of university theologians. Finally the rationalistic method fell under increasing discredit so that by the end of the century J. P. Gabler (*De iusto discrimine biblicae et dogmaticae*, 1787) could give ultimate authority to biblical over dogmatic theology. Kant's choice of "biblical theology" to designate the central work of the Christian theologian thus indicates both his pietist background and his expectation of scientific (historical, in this case) work on the part of university professors. Thus to him the task of the church theologian (there is no indication on his part that he thinks he is taking a particularly Protestant point of view) is ultimately that of a kind of talmudist; it is the investigation and exposition of a sacred Scripture: and Scripture, not the sixteenth century Protestant confessions, nor the "rational" doctrines of traditional scholastic theology, is the ultimate authority. The biblical theologian is thus properly called a theologian of revelation because he believes he has such a revelation in his Holy Scripture.

The "biblical theologian" acknowledges an easily identifiable authority and exercises an authority of his own as well. He lives and works in the world of religious positivity. He teaches the future official pastors who, as they take office, must swear not to depart from official doctrine, and he has the right to censure whatever departs from received biblical doctrine. He thus fully cooperates with the State and its official establishment of religion. He is among the office bearers in the State.

In contrast, the philosopher–theologian firmly ensconces himself in the safe establishment of the philosophical faculty which, unlike all other faculties, resigns all use of authority, and makes no claim to teach, lead, judge, or administer the population. In exchange, philosophers ask for the right to recognize no other authority but their reason. The philosopher of religion will not depart from the practice of all philosophers, and if his writings appear too bold, he may always claim that they are obscure (a generation ago the defense was that they were written in Latin) and are read only by a few scholars, and are not meant to have authority in church or state.

These broad lines of the Kantian solution are strongly reminiscent of Frederick's enlightened policy, "Argue all you want but obey." However its simplicity is deceptive. For one thing the biblical theologian, who must clarify and transmit the meaning of the fundamental scriptures of the religious tradition, is not entirely enslaved to the tradition or to the state church authority. He is after all a state official and a university professor. And as professor he is entitled to a degree of freedom of inquiry. This freedom appears on two points: as a historian investigating the Bible, he must be free to go wherever his discoveries lead him; as an interpreter he must be free to express the meaning of the Bible in terms that are meaningful to him and his readers. Neither the authentic nor the doctrinal meanings of the Bible can be totally subject to authority, each having an intellectual integrity of its own to respect.

> In the former case the interpretation must be literally (in the philological sense) in conformity with the meaning of the writer, but in the latter case, the scholar has the freedom to give to the passage (philosophically) the meaning it takes in an exegesis that has a practical moral end (for the edification of the disciple); for faith in a simply historical proposition is by itself dead.[65]

This second task of the biblical theologian, which is properly hermeneutic and as such must obey philosophical and moral principles, brings him into dialogue with the philosopher–theologian, or brings him inevitably—for after all he is no archaeologist but must edify, talk sense to honest contemporary minds—into a territory into which the philosopher-theologian has moved as well for reasons of his own and which are just as compelling. Thus the division of labour does not prevent cooperation, or heated argument either, in the overlapping area of hermeneutics or transmission of significant meaning.

The philosopher-theologian or rational theologian is interested in the edification of the people because following a sound Kantian principle he could not be interested in views saying what "religion" as such is (following the dictates of pure practical reason) that would be sound in theory but not in practice. Thus his first task, the identification of the distinction between religion and superstition, leads him to a second task, the look at the actual lived religions of people in general and of his society in particular. So while he will cautiously not presume to tell the biblical theologian what the Bible says, he will nevertheless take an interest in the real institutional religious life which develops under the authority of the biblical theologian. As the discarded preface to *Religion within the Limits of Reason Alone* puts it:

> The philosopher may very much abstain from dealing with the conceptions of a revealed faith and limit himself merely to the principles of pure reason, but he must nevertheless take into consideration the possibility of application of his ideas in experience, without which these ideas would necessarily be mere empty ideals, without practical reality.[66]

The major lines of debate between the two theologians can be characterized as follows. The biblical theologian may charge the philosopher or rational theologian with paying mere lip service to the idea that the biblical theologian responds to a revelation, while in fact deep down inside the philosopher really believes that the biblical theologian is a mere intellectual menial administering an institution according to established authoritative traditions. The biblical theologian may also charge the other with being an ivory-tower intellectual who has no feel for the real religious life of people. The philosopher-theologian on the other hand may accuse the biblical theologian with failing to make use of his intellect. The usual accusations of rational presumptuousness and theological obscurantism can still fly. However, by emphasizing that both must be concerned with the transmission and development of meaningful religious life to the people, an area of common religious (and not just theological) concern has been created and, with the increasing grasp of the hermeneutical problem, this area was to grow progressively.

Ultimately I believe Kant developed this distinction in good faith and wanted biblical theologians to pursue their specific task in their own way. Using Tillichian terms we would say that their responsibility was the orderly transmission of the substance of the religious tradition and the concern for ecclesiastical continuity. The philosopher-theologian is concerned with the form of religious conviction, or the characteristic manner in which it is to be held. Both are interested in fighting superstition and enhancing true religion. There will be conflict between both, but as *The Strife of Faculties* shows at length, this conflict is healthy and entirely legitimate as long as it respects the rules necessary for the promotion of science and the peace of the state (two objectives Kant believed compatible). In the final analysis such conflict seems necessary to ensure the vitality of a religious tradition, to protect it from its various pitfalls such as fanatic orthodoxy or heated enthusiasm on the one hand, or dry theorizing and rationalistic ideologies on the other.[67]

I shall not return to the task of the biblical theologian except to point out indirectly how Kant the philosopher-theologian expected them to perform their task, and how he counted on the results of their labours, even though Kant himself did not keep very much up to date with the results of their scholarship (with the exception of Michaelis). The task of the philosopher-theologian however needs further clarification before we turn to the second chapter.

The Two Parts of the Philosophy of Religion: The Doctrines of God and of Religion

To emphasize that Kant used the term religion in a de-objectifying way is not yet to show the full measure of his originality. Kant also played a creative part in the elaboration of philosophy of religion in the modern sense of the word, namely in the elaboration of philosophy of religion as a specific sub-discipline within the autonomous discipline of philosophy that sees religion, whatever it is, as a definite enough object to become an object of a systematic investigation. It is my contention that his contribution to this development is based upon the distinction between religion pure and applied and consists of the elaboration of a doctrine of God on a religious basis (on religion pure) and the elaboration of a doctrine of religion which seeks to elucidate all or most of the problems raised by the diverse phenomena of religion and different religious traditions (or by religion applied). The philosopher in him is interested both in developing a rational faith and in understanding the various historical faiths. As James Collins put it, Kant is one of the modern philosophers who insisted "that their inquiry into our knowledge of God was only part of a larger inquiry into the religious relationship between man and God" and is also one of these modern minds who "in a philosophical spirit which is not itself a minister to some theological purpose" sought "the properly human significance of religion as it can be grasped and lived cooperatively by all men."[68]

The originality of Kant's approach will be set in better light if one looks at what was done about "religion" by philosophy before Kant. (For the purpose of this study I shall mean by this European philosophy in the seventeenth and eighteenth centuries.) Troeltsch's summary, rough though it is, is perfectly adequate: before Kant, philosophy of religion was either a rational metaphysical doctrine arriving at a concept of God and of our duties towards Him (results which in the rule could be harmonized with those of revealed theology which also used a rationalistic method), or an empirical psychological approach which saw religion as an affect of the soul and sought to find its cause.[69] It is not surprising that in philosophy of religion also Kant would find dogmatism and empiricism equally unsatisfactory. By contrast, said Troeltsch, Kant offered a philosophy of religion containing two aspects: an inquiry into the relevant epistemological and metaphysical problems on the one hand, and an inquiry into history of religions on the other.[70]

Fair though it is, this interpretation does not seem to me to bring Kant's achievement into the most accurate light. It leaves in shadow a very significant aspect of Kant's approach, namely, to use Tillich's phrase, the conquest of the concept of religion.[71] In the period of Kant, Western philosophers became aware that the problem of religion is distinct from the problem of God, that the fact that man is religious raises philosophical problems (that is, must be inquired into and evaluated normatively), and that the fact that there are different religions also raises problems that must be grasped, analysed, and hopefully solved. (The old solution linked with the objectification of religion: my religion is true, the others are false, no longer seems self-evident.)

As Tillich put it, the dominance of the concept of religion becomes conscious[72] and the concept of religion must be conquered; that is, this suddenly visible and problematic religiousness of man and this suddenly discovered and puzzling richness of world religious phenomena (with their variety and bizarreness) must be somehow integrated in a total philosophical interpretation.[73] In a similar manner, Ernst Cassirer spoke of "the conquest of the historical world" in the eighteenth century. Suddenly the century learned much more about history, cared more about it, developed numerous philosophies of history, lost the old certainties about the divine plan and the simple outline of the course of the world, lost the old certainties about our place in the whole drama, and inquired into fundamental questions, such as the rules of historical evidence, the purpose of history (if any), and the condition of possibility of history itself.[74] So the world of religion also became a more richly documented one, a vaster and more varied one, and the scene of severely conflicting schools of interpretation. Philosophy had to conquer this newly seen territory to bring to it a measure of order. It seems to me therefore that it must be emphasized that Kant's contribution consisted both in "religionizing" the problem of God and in seeing the problems raised by what we know of the history of religions and of religious institutions as equally important religious problems.

For the sake of brevity I shall refer to the two parts of his philosophy of religion as the doctrine of God and the doctrine of religion, but the integral part played by religiousness in both will have to be always assumed. The doctrine of God is not a metaphysical endeavour that obeys only cognitive criteria and reaches only cognitive results. On the basis of such criteria no doctrine of God is possible at all. It employs what it calls "practical criteria" and this, as we shall see, ultimately means that the true doctrine of God is that which is most religious in the normative sense of the word. The true doctrine of God is that which is the correlate of rational faith, or pure moral faith. We should not of course speak of a religious doctrine of God, for this to most readers would oppose it to a philosophical doctrine and that in Kant's case would be a damaging and gravely misleading error. The term "doctrine of religion" creates fewer problems: while it does not make immediately apparent the full scope of the doctrine which examines religious doctrines, institutions, and practices, it has over the term "history of religions" the clear advantage of not hiding the fact that Kant continuously sought religion in the religions. Furthermore

Kant's doctrine of religion is normative philosophy, not a purely descriptive endeavour. It seeks to sort out the wheat from the chaff, and evaluates the faiths in the light of faith. In summary both the doctrine of religion and the doctrine of God have something to do with the Ultimate and Unconditional. The doctrine of religion turns to what men do, feel, and think when they turn to the Ultimate. The doctrine of God turns, in an intellectual way, to the Ultimate itself. Both doctrines are rooted in the religiousness found in the self, in pure religion, or in pure religious faith. The doctrine of God, as we shall see, must be religious in the sense that it must be such as to make it possible for a religious self to hold it. And the doctrine of religion must be such as to indicate how historical religious life ought to be in order to facilitate, or at least not to obstruct the religiousness of selves. The distinctions between religion pure and applied, between faith pure and ecclesiastical, and between the doctrine of God and the doctrine of religion are not allowed to become separations. The investigation into each is in dialectical relationship with the investigation into the other, and Kant saw the philosophical truth in matters of religion emerge only at the end of this kind of procedure.

To announce such wealth of philosophical enquiry in a Kant whose philosophy of religion is often thought to consist of a refutation of the proofs of the existence of God and of reduction of religion to morality may be surprising to some. (Of course the very fact that Kant was leaving aside an old approach and embarking upon a new one means that he had little positive to say about the old problems which are always those that interpreters are most familiar with.) The very bulk of Kant's writings on various aspects of the philosophy of religion however is here for all the sceptics to look at. The discussion of the doctrine of God, being in the three Critiques, is the most visible of course. To this we can add the lectures on metaphysics and those on the philosophical doctrine of religion. The doctrine of religion is found almost exclusively in the minor writings (see the list in note 13 of the introduction) to which we can add the lectures on the philosophical doctrine of religion and those on geography. *Religion within the Limits of Reason Alone* can conveniently be used as the core of the doctrine, to be supplemented from the other sources.[75]

My investigation of Kant's philosophy of religion shall thus be naturally divided into two chapters. I believe I can treat the former or the doctrine of God in a somewhat summary fashion since it is better known and since there is available excellent interpretative material.

The latter or the doctrine of religion however will be looked into in greater detail. In this context it may be useful to show why it is intrinsically necessary for Kant to add a doctrine of religion to his doctrine of God, or to add a historical kind of philosophical investigation of the religious in the religions to his philosophical investigation of the religious in the self.

We already saw that the basic Kantian abhorrence for the maxim "it may be true in theory but it is not in practice" generally led him to investigate the practical not only in its pure theoretical sense (that is to say, ethics) but also in its pragmatic sense (for instance, anthropology, politics, the practice of law, or of virtue). We find here at work the same tendency and interest that led Kant to investigate history and to speculate about it. Thus Collins was quite correct in his judgement that "religious theory itself require(s) further humanization by being considered within the experimental context of some historical mode of religion."[76] This should not surprise us from an author who said of himself, "My place is in the fruitful *bathos*, the bottom land, of experience."[77]

Note, however, that the philosophy of religion qua doctrine of religion did not for Kant in any way supplement the moral proof of the existence of God or extend our knowledge of God. There is no room in Kant for any proof out of religious phenomena or out of the history of religions. The doctrine of religion investigates religion in the religions and does not offer us a second or more privileged road to God after the moral one.[78] This of course happened with some subsequent authors who found in their doctrine of religion a "proof of God" unavailable anywhere else, while others found in their investigation of the phenomena of religion a basis for an atheistic metaphysic.

One more thing needs to be said. The doctrine of religion cannot be used to rescue a metaphysics that is in trouble, but it cannot for Kant be developed without a dialectical relationship with metaphysics. The development of philosophy of religion as a chapter in or subdiscipline of philosophy in general does not mean in Kant's case that it becomes a peripheral subparagraph, as might be the case if Kant's philosophy, for instance, were a reified metaphysical theism unaware of religion as personal quality, or an a-religious humanism that believes it must somewhere briefly "explain" religion. The philosophy of religion provides us an insight into Kant's philosophical position, which is a religious kind of humanism, a position which can be known apart from an investigation of his philosophy of religion (from his ethics, for instance, or from what he said about the results of criticism), but which becomes fully explicit only in his philosophy of religion. His philosophy of religion is of course a worldly philosophical enterprise in the sense that it is undertaken by a man come of age for whom the question "What is man?" represents the ultimate question of philosophy. But it is not an a-religious enterprise and it is developed by a philosopher who has given a rational basis to faith in God.

Collins was able to put the matter quite correctly.

> Kant is able to infuse his theory of religion with the spirit of his entire philosophy. Just as his theory of the world remains incomplete until it becomes integrated with a moral and religious humanism, so also in a reciprocal way his analysis of religious life must be in conformity with his general account of our scientific knowledge of the natural world.[79]

It is hard to say whether the worldly or the religious outlook has the last word in this ongoing reciprocal relationship. Here also Collins provided the answer, "Kant firmly rejects any opposition in principle between the worldly and the religious."[80]

Chapter 6

The Doctrine of God and Pure Moral Faith

The Persistence of Metaphysics

A degree of clarity about Kant's thoughts on the subject of metaphysics is a precondition of any serious consideration of Kant's doctrine of God (*Gotteslehre*). That Kant dealt a death blow to traditional metaphysics is a familiar thesis. Many interpreters however emphasize that Kant denounced the easy sequel to a rebuttal of metaphysical dogmatism, namely the move to scepticism or some variety of empiricism.

Since the thirties an important body of German and French interpreters, following an impulse that was originally given by a German reaction to the neo-Kantian school of the beginning of the century, investigated closely the positive ontological and metaphysical positions of Kant and came to speak of Kant as a metaphysician in the grand classical tradition.[1]

I should not venture beyond the confines of my subject but a summary outline of the state of the question as I see it will be useful to the argument. That the old metaphysics fell before the Kantian critique on epistemological grounds is the first thing to say but it is not the full story. As the *Prolegomena* put it, the "old metaphysics" was useful because it trained the mind, but

> this was all the good it did; service was subsequently effaced when it favoured conceit by venturesome assertions, sophistry by subtle distinctions and adornment, and shallowness by the ease with which it decided the most difficult problems by means of a little school-wisdom.[2]

The old metaphysics claimed to have knowledge where it had none and used concepts "illegally," beyond the limits of their epistemologically legitimate use. But as the text indicates, the old metaphysics had also shortcomings of a more moral nature: it was presumptuous and favoured conceit (there is here an echo from all the religious warnings against the pride of philosophers who try to scale the heavens or fathom the unfathomable—Kant always saw humility as a virtue becoming thinkers), and it was morally shallow as well. Consider the essay *On the Failure of All Attempted Philosophical Theodicies* and its attitude to the answers Job's friends gave to the most difficult of all problems; we see there what use Kant had for textbook wisdom as found in the classics of eighteenth century philosophy when they wrestled with the problem of theodicy. The old metaphysics, I conclude, lacked at the same time the sense of the limits of our reason and the sense of the precariousness of our wisdom.

Another point which is very clear is that Kant did not want to write another metaphysical system in the same traditional vein and that he did want to pave the way for a new metaphysics that could, as he says, present itself as a science. "The world is tired of metaphysical assertions" and does not want new points to definitions, new crutches for lame proofs, or "the adding to the crazy-quilt of metaphysics fresh patches" or the changing of its patterns. It wants "the possibility of the science."[3]

Kant never doubted that any robust mind would want to find such a path for metaphysical thinking (or reflection, or science). "Experience never satisfies reason fully."[4]

> Who can satisfy himself with mere empirical knowledge in all the cosmological questions of the duration and of the quantity of the world, of freedom or of necessity, since every answer given on principles of experience begets a fresh question, which likewise requires its answer and thereby clearly shows the insufficiency of all physical modes of explanation to satisfy reason?[5]

> Metaphysics, in its fundamental features, perhaps more than any other science, is placed in us by nature itself, and cannot be considered a production of an arbitrary choice or a casual enlargement in the progress of experience from which it is quite disparate.[6]

Thus Kant was not about to imitate Hume, who having cut his moorings from dogmatism "ran his ship ashore, for safety's sake, landing on scepticism, there to let it lie and rot," but wanted to find a pilot who, "provided with a complete chart and compass, may steer the ship safely."[7]

The ship, however, cannot be steered by empirical knowledge since precisely the lack of it is what leads man to metaphysical thinking. Metaphysics does move beyond the borders of empirical knowledge of objects, but, with Kant, does it knowingly, that is, in full knowledge of the problematic nature of the undertaking and of the need for a new pilot. Reason does not come to rest at that famous border (for as a crucial Kantian metaphor put it: all bounds point to something positive, namely that "beyond them there still lies something").[8] The pathfinder in this new land will be, as is well known, the practical rather than the theoretical use of our reason, namely the defense of our practical interests as free finite beings rather than the desire to extend our theoretical knowledge. "We are at liberty, indeed we are summoned, to take occupation of (this territory), if we can, by practical data of reason."[9]

This does not mean, as has often regrettably been suggested, that metaphysical thinking was replaced by morality. The criteria of morality were those used to discriminate among metaphysical conceptions but they did not force metaphysical conceptions entirely aside. The utterances of a judge when he passes sentence are not the only utterances in court proceedings nor are they the only meaningful ones.

Thus metaphysics became for Kant wedded to the defense of our interests as free and finite beings, and this means not only that it is based upon the dictates of our pure practical reason which alone has a sure grasp a priori of our rational human interests, but also that metaphysical thinking acquires a therapeutic character. Metaphysics is necessary not only to the full use of reason, but also to the defense of reason and the attack upon nonsense. And the abundance of false teachings tempt the frailty of human reason and its need for metaphysical orientations and answers. The demand for genuine metaphysics has an urgent tone. Charlatans abound because physicians do not know everything. The answer of course is for physicians to know all there is to know and to develop a superior wisdom when it comes to what cannot be known. "That the human mind will ever give up metaphysical research is as little to be expected as that we should prefer to give up breathing altogether, to avoid inhaling impure air."[10]

That the air carries many impurities is a fact Kant was much aware of, and the villains here are not the traditional metaphysicians, but the popular teachers of mankind, the foolish rhetoricians, to use the mediaeval description. The traditional metaphysicians are the villains here only so far that they did not manage to provide an answer once and for all to all the nonsense of those who mislead mankind. Kant believed he could provide the answer that would once and for all give reason a sure defense against all unreason.

> In our thinking age it is not to be supposed but that many deserving men would use any good opportunity of working for the common interest of the more and more enlightened reason, if there were only some hope of attaining the goal. Mathematics, natural science, laws, arts, even morality, etc., do not completely fill the soul; there is always a space left over, reserved for pure and speculative reason, the vacuity of which prompts us to seek in vagaries, buffooneries, and mysticism for what seems to be employment and entertainment, but what actually is mere pastime; in order to deaden the troublesome voice of reason, which in accordance with its nature requires something that can satisfy it, and not merely subserve other ends or the interests of our inclinations.[11]

The first positive result of Kantian metaphysics accordingly was to be the slaying of all metaphysical positions that are inimical to the rational interests of man, or as he occasionally put it, that are hostile to morality and religion. Materialism, naturalism, and fatalism are the first victims.[12] (This of course is exactly what most mediaeval metaphysicians claimed for their metaphysics.) The therapeutic effect of metaphysics was also apparent to Kant in that it protects religion from two of its most common enemies: speculative dogmatism (the most obvious of the products of the objectification of religion to which I referred) and the ravings of mysticism (*Schwärmerei*, and its anarchic sentimentality).[13]

We have seen so far what metaphysics will not do, and what errors it will combat, rather than what it will actually say. There are two reasons for this. First of all Kant, true to the adage *"nil actum reputans, si quid esset superesset agendum"*[14] spent more time working and reworking the foundations of the metaphysics for which he prepared the way than actually developing its doctrinal content. Most philosophers do so and most of us want them to do so. Secondly Kant, like Bacon, whom he quoted in the motto to the second edition of the *Critique of*

Pure Reason, preferred to be remembered for his work rather than for his opinions.[15] He brought this principle to unmistakeable clarity when he stated that "philosophy can never be learned, save only in historical fashion; as regards what concerns reason, we can at most learn to philosophize,"[16] or that "there is no simple book to which you can point as you do to Euclid, and say, 'this is metaphysics'."[17] Kant did not state here that each man must think his own thoughts and may think whatever he pleases. His view was that metaphysical thinking begins by autonomous thinking and goes on with rational discourse and verification. The task of metaphysics begins afresh with every mind, and the results of any other mind, some of which may be true and some of which may be false, must be critically examined. When G. Krüger characterized the basic affirmation of Kant's metaphysics as "the recognition, in an autonomous manner, of the world as a "state" created by God and to which the knower belongs as a free member"[18] he did not only give an apt summary of the content and results of Kant's metaphysics but also brought to light that to do metaphysics is a moral kind of act. It is not a "merely intellectual" search for "explanations" but it is a practical intention and turning towards wisdom. Thus what is called the Kantian grounding of metaphysics in morality may be the recapturing of what Socrates and Plato meant by *philosophia*: namely a conversion of the self. As we examine Kant's doctrine of God, which is the most important part of his doctrinal metaphysics, we will do well to remember that metaphysics is an *opus*, not an *opinio* and we will find fresh ramifications of this principle.

In this context we can understand the role Father Coreth gave to Kant in "the history of the concept of Metaphysics" with which he prefaced his *Metaphysics*: "Kant has demonstrated once and for all that metaphysics is impossible without a return to being."[19] This statement is not as bold as may at first appear. Wolff had defined metaphysics as "the science of all possible things, in so far as they are possible" and had thus made of it "a mere formal doctrine of axioms of principles ... no longer rooted in being."[20] Knutzen and Baumgarten, whose textbook Kant used, had followed in his path, making of metaphysics a study of essences. When Kant argued that the practical use of reason enables us to make assertoric judgements affirming the reality of the Ideas of reason, whereas the theoretical use of reason made only problematic judgements,[21] he moved beyond a metaphysics examining possibles to one returning to the reality of being and affirming a real relationship of the self to being. The theoretical mind makes no onto-logical judgement. The practical use of reason is an act of the human being orienting itself among being. The former discusses *opiniones*, the latter is involved in an *opus* (and philosophizes rather than studies philosophy). The former is an empty speculative game, the latter is morally serious, ontologically rooted metaphysical work. The subject may be involved in the former in an entirely second-hand manner (such are *opiniones*). It can do the latter only first-hand, as is the case with all work. This distinction between *opus* and *opiniones* is the important thing in my opinion, and once this is seen, whether one prefers to speak of a return to being, or of a metaphysics rooted in morality is secondary.

The Different Kinds of Theologies

Kant left in his papers a brief outline of a natural history of reli-gion (the term was used by Eberhard, whose textbook *Vorbereitung zur natürlichen Theologie* Kant used in his lectures)[22] which traces the slow appearance of rational theological thinking in the religious his-tory of mankind. At first mankind follows the ways of the imagination as they seek to represent that which lies beyond experience. The ways of the imagination produce representations of invisible or occasionally visible forces (Kant lists fetishes, Manitou, Talisman, and shadows of the dead, among those which are occasionally visible). The most primitive forms are labelled by Kant as superstition. (The processes give rise to enthusiastic fanaticism—*Schwärmerei*—only at a later state.) All these ways of the imagination see the gods as objects of nature, although as objects with greater power than is common. Such objects are at first seen as powerful beings without morality. The ways of reason appear when religious men begin to see their gods as following a law, and as authors of a law. This simultaneously leads to the shoving aside of the representation of gods in favour of that of God. Concern appears over the influence of religion upon morality. Among the ways of reason, Kant distinguished two stages, that of speculative proof and that of moral belief.[23] The latter is the last and highest. The former, however, has an important role to play in the establishing of the notion of the unity of God and his relationship to legality, thus in the overthrow of the conceptions of polytheism. In my own words, by rising to the notion of order, it prepares the transition to the notion of moral order.

The contrast which Kant established between religion as a practical bond with God and theology as orderly thinking about God, does not prevent him from giving to theology, qua work of reason, a positive role to play in the development of mankind out of primitive religiousness (rather to be called superstition) into mature or genuine religion (the only one to be properly worthy of the name "religion").

This, however, was possible to him only because Kant made some crucial distinctions between kinds of theologies.[24] First of all one must see the difference between archetypal theology, that is, God's own self-knowledge which lies entirely beyond our reach and belongs to the *intellectus archetypus* alone, and ectypal theology,[25] that is, human knowledge about God, which is derived, imperfect, not immediate, and is compatible with the discursive kind of mind characteristic of our own intellect, namely the *intellectus ectypus*. Kant, like Calvin, was quite convinced that our theology does not penetrate to the divine essence, which remains hidden.

In the ectypal theology one can go on distinguishing between empirical theology and rational theology. The former is the theology of revelation found in the religious community, the latter is the theology proper to the philosopher. This distinction between empirical and rational may create difficulties for the interpreter. Did Kant mean to say that the theology the philosopher-theologian finds in the church is a sheer manifold of experience in no way brought under the sway of reason? That position is hardly likely to help the cause of a legal peace between the church theologian and the philosopher-theologian. The terminology should of course not be interpreted to mean that the empirical theology being based on experience is valid scientific knowledge while the rational theology is a repetition of a rationalism victim of the transcendental illusion. The first kind of theology is rather the positive theology which has validity in the religious community and functions as matter (or as material a posteriori) to the form (or formal a priori) represented by "rational theology." But it has rationality, and itself functions as form to the matter of, say, the religious imagination of the faithful. The basic insight of Kantian criticism must be brought to bear upon—and does no violence to—this basic distinction between theologies: reason regulates but does not constitute experience and reason is not allowed theoretical scope beyond the limits of experience; or intuitions without concepts are blind, and concepts without intuitions are empty.[26]

Kant made further important distinctions within rational theology. James Collins summarized them ably in the following diagram.[27]

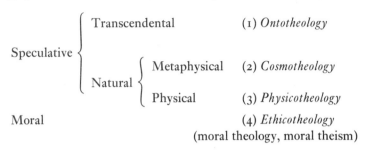

As the lectures on the philosophy of religion show particularly clearly, many of the discredited metaphysical doctrines find meaning and validity again when considered from the critical standpoint and restrained from that standpoint. A look at the content of each kind of theology will be useful before embarking on an examination of the kind of validity each has.

Transcendental theology or ontotheology[28] has three constitutive concepts of God as original being, highest being, and being of all beings (*ens originarium, ens summum, ens entium*). This theology further predicates of God that he is an *ens extramundum* who has no passivity in relationship to the world. Those who accept only the transcendental theology are called deists by Kant[29] and have the least determinate concept of God, that is, "the idea of something which is the ground of the highest and necessary unity of all empirical reality."[30] The lectures and the *Critique of Pure Reason* are both clear that there is no proof that such a being exists. All that speculative reason shows is that we must necessarily accept it as an hypothesis but cannot demonstrate it as apodictically certain.[31] The so-called ontological proof remains an important element in the development of the concept.

Cosmotheology[32] teaches us a theistic concept of God and makes him the highest intelligence which, with understanding and freedom, is the origin of all things. His relationship to nature is to be represented as Creation, not emanation, and the following attributes are predicated of him: skill, intelligence, and wisdom. God is no longer seen as a cause of the world (whether by freedom or necessity remaining undecided) but as the Author of the world. Thus cosmotheology teaches us the concept of a living God. The arguments *a contingentia mundi* while losing their quality of proof are used to determine this concept of God.

Physical theology[33] differs only slightly from cosmotheology. It further determines the concept of God in that it discerns a purposeful unity in the course of nature (or design) and relates it to the will of the Creator. The Creator is thus represented as pursuing in an orderly way a definite purpose and this representation makes the transition to the next kind of theology.

Finally moral theology[34] arises when speculation of God takes place in conjunction with the fundamental religious insight, namely "the conflict in the course of nature and morality."[35] The need arises now for a very distinct hypothesis about God: there must be a being who will in the future distribute happiness fairly. Of this moral concept of God three new perfections may be predicated: holiness (as legislator-author of the law), goodness (as Providential governor of the world), and justice (as fair judge in the end). And thus only morality arrives at a fully determinate concept of God.[36] There are no further attributes we can—or need to—predicate of God. God must be thought of now as having a three-fold divine function for which Kant found the basic analogy in political life: legislative, govermental, and judiciary.[37] It is only in this theology that the problem of theodicy proper arises (a key religious problem for Kant, as we saw), since opponents of theodicy attack or cast doubt upon God's holiness, goodness, or justice. Finally of this God we can see it is not just a necessary hypothesis but that we must affirm its existence, since the practical interests of our reason are at stake.

This Kantian structuring of the various kinds of theologies calls forth the following observations.

1. Each theology builds upon the previous one and predicates new attributes of God. The movement through these theologies is therefore a movement towards a greater definiteness of the thought of God.

2. In each theology the philosophical mind makes normative decisions: thus Kant was not merely involved in listing existing or possible theologies. In the ontotheology God is said to be extramundane rather

than intramundane. Likewise in cosmotheology both the systems of emanation and of creation were theoretically possible, but only the latter is accepted.

3. Each theology obeys those norms which make it compatible with the further attributes of the next theology in the progression. Thus all are ultimately dependent upon the moral theism which is the final norm of them all.

4. From the *Critique of Pure Reason* onward Kant remains basically consistent in his evaluation of the various theologies and in his system of them as mapped out in the first Critique and his lectures on philosophy of religion. (Glimpses of it appear, for instance, in *Religion within the Limits of Reason Alone* as well as in various articles.) The key statements in the other two Critiques are also based upon it.

5. Each one of these theologies, except the moral one, which is a special case, is ultimately legitimitized as exercise of theoretical reason by virtue of its being the object of a regulative rather than constitutive use of reason. Here again the results of the *Critique of Pure Reason* were never trespassed upon. Thus the regulative principle enables us to salvage the content of the speculative idea of God as being necessary for theoretical purposes. (The matter of practical and religious significance of the Idea of God is another thing again.) And these elements are deemed to be sound enough to enter into the moral and religious view of God. Thus, as Collins put it, "the speculative idea of God is useful not only for scientific explanation but also for the theory of religion."[38]

6. It seems that Kant was nowhere tempted to tamper with the results of the *Critique of Pure Reason*. Whereas some might assume that it is religiously or morally important to buttress up the shaky theoretical basis for the Idea of God as legitimate and necessary on the regulative basis, it all happens as if Kant thought it was morally and religiously important to leave the theoretical or speculative Idea of God just as it was.

7. Thus theistic conviction remains independent of any theoretical efforts at demonstrating God's existence, and will have a basis elsewhere.

Obviously the whole of Kant's position ultimately hangs upon the peculiar characteristics of moral theism which, although last in his progressive list, really functions as the ultimate basis of all our thinking about God. This point is so crucial to Kant's position that it will be examined in a section by itself which will look at the grounds of the distinctiveness and of the superiority of moral theism.

The Superiority of Moral Theism

We saw that Kant refused on epistemological grounds to integrate religion with a natural theology that claims to provide us with a proof of the existence of God and a theoretical metaphysical presentation of his attributes. He does it partly because of the negative results of his epistemology. Such a God is not an object of sense and cannot be known. The temptation to build a concept of him by the theoretical use of empty concepts must be resisted since it leads us into nothing but illusion. Kant thereby was merely paying heed to the results of his *Critique of Pure Reason* and the limits which his epistemology sets to what can be known. In other words, to use Collins's expression, he was at that point merely following "Hume's counsel" which was "that the religious mind cannot afford to remain epistemologically ignorant in the modern world."[39]

Natural theology in the sense of rational speculative (or theoretical) theology cannot thus lead us to religion, cannot be integrated with religion, and cannot be used to lead men to religion, or to buttress religion. A passage between natural theology and its concept of God and religion and its bond with God can be made, however, provided that one places in-between the moral interval which will turn out to be the crucial hinge in the matter. Collins spoke here, using a rather forbidding term, of a moral radication of religion: "Only after man's religious assent and action are thoroughly radicated in their practical context can the problem of . . . religion be meaningfully studied in the philosophy of religion."[40]

But where does that unique significance of the passage through the moral interpretation of religion and through ethical theology (or moral theism) lie?[41] Taking a cue from the famous "I have . . . found it necessary to deny *knowledge*, in order to make room for *faith*"[42] we suggest that the unique strength of moral theism is to be found in the mode of its affirmation of the existence of God, namely in the fact that it arrives at a first-hand statement of faith rather than at a categorical statement of the existence of an object. The affirmations of moral theism stem from an *opus*, not from a gathering of *opiniones* of an object. Moral theism not only does not trespass beyond the limits set by epistemology but also arrives at a conception of God which is rooted in an autonomous interior act and has thus roots of a religious nature. The "moral radication of religion" is done on religious as well as on epistemological grounds.

> No one, indeed, will be able to boast that he *knows* that there is a God, and a future life; . . . No my conviction is not *logical* but *moral* certainty; . . . I must not even say, "*It is* morally certain that there is a God, etc.," but "*I am* morally certain etc."[43]

It was quite important to Kant to emphasize that statements of rational faith are to be made in the first person singular. This reappears in a lesser known creed in three articles of the pure practical reason:

> I believe in one God, source of all good in the world, as the ultimate end of the world;

> I believe in the possibility, in so far as it lies in our power, of harmonizing this ultimate end with the highest good in the world;

> I believe in a future eternal life as the condition under which the world can unceasingly become nearer the highest good possible in it.[44]

As Kant himself stated immediately following this creed, the significance of such a first person statement is that it is a free faith, the only one that has any moral (or, we would want to add, religious) significance. Theoretical reason makes objectively necessary statements which are binding upon all minds. And this is true whether the statements are made in the regulative or in the constitutive use of reason. Likewise reason in its practical use issues imperatives which are equally inescapable. Faith does not talk the language of proofs or imperatives and any attempt to make it talk that language leads inevitably to insincere expressions of belief.[45] Thus moral theism has at least one ground to superiority over all the other ones, it talks the language of faith, which is that of personal, spiritual, free uncoerced affirmation. Furthermore it is the language of personal seriousness not of individual playfulness about possibles or of weighing of probable opinions. The uniqueness of the language of faith is easily understood when it is placed in the context of Kant's basic understanding of the essence of religion as a conflict between the world that is and the world that ought to be. This conflict is existentially felt; furthermore it is a conflict in which the self participates. After all is said and done about society and history, this conflict can begin to be overcome or conquered only within the self. Thus faith in God is religious only if it is a personal act. Moral theism is the only acceptable form of theism because it is the only one that does not let the religious tension between the two worlds and the two orders evaporate within the self, and the only one that actively involves the self in the struggle to overcome the tension.

In this perspective we can begin to see that to deny knowledge to make room for faith is a gain not a loss. Where there are speculative demonstrations, there is a matter of fact assent to objective truth. Likewise should God be proved on a theoretical basis, the personal nature of one's religious life and, if one is a theist, of one's religious bond to God is destroyed. As E. Weil points out, too good a proof of God plays into the hands of authoritarian religion by allowing the fundamental religious attitude to be distorted into that of the shaking slave who is lectured, threatened, and generally badgered until he assents to all that his master wants him to assent to.[46]

Kant was here proposing a fairly radical departure from the prevailing tradition of his time: he was offering the conclusion that the apologetic monuments proving the existence of God did no service whatsoever to the cause of religion (although they may have served the cause of a religion). He was quietly departing from the assumption common to John Locke and many undergraduates: "I should know whether God exists or not before I can rule whether I am (or am going to be) religious."

> The critically aware mind comes to view the entire theoretical approach to God as a development made out of a fundamental, moral and religious belief in Him, rather than the converse relationship.[47]

Kant here was part of a larger movement in the history of Western thought: this kind of step seems to be involved in every case of a transition from rational theology (deist or orthodox) to what is called the specifically modern philosophy of religion.

There is a second ground for the superiority of moral theism (besides that it speaks the language of personal faith), namely that it leads to a more suitable concept of God, and here by more suitable

I mean more exalted a conception of God, one more likely to elicit and be reinforced by religious feeling (or one which is more religiously available to use Whitehead's expression) Beck expresses the point with perfect clarity: "The moral argument, paradoxical though it may seem, leads to a less anthropomorphic conception of God than that of natural theology."[48]

Consider again Kant's views on the religious development of mankind: under superstition the gods are beings of nature with unusual power. With ontotheology appears the concept of God as being distinct from the world, but with a relationship to the world that is of a type found within the world, namely he is the "cause of the world" ("le Dieu de la chiquenaude"). With cosmotheology, the relationship between God and the world becomes more complex: God is now conceived as a being with an intelligence and a will. It is clear that the creation is voluntary and contingent. With moral theology, the relationship between God and the world becomes more complex yet, to the point of being mysterious and inconceivable, and it becomes impossible to conceive it on the model of the mechanic and the machine, or the artist and the creation. Remember that the God of moral theism is said to be holy, good, and just (holiness especially is an absolutely transcendent moral quality: there is none among us who is holy) and this God "created" the world as we know it, namely a world in which the fundamental religious sense of the moral wrongness of things is pervasive.

Moral theism therefore represents the last step in a progressive series that rises to a concept of God as transcendent and absolutely distinct from all beings in the world, both in his nature and in his relations. To make God into a cause, a mechanic, or an artist is to make him like us. To make him holy, good, and just is to make him unlike us. Kant thereby did not satisfy an abstract theoretical requirement but arrived at a conception of God (as he arrived at a conception of faith) which alone is religiously satisfactory. To see the conflict between the world as we know it and as it morally should be is to conceive the life of religion as a life lived in tension, conflict, courage, and drama, ultimately lived in faith as a personal act. The God of the deist does not hold his own in this drama, being too pale, too tired, and too unmysterious. At best it leads to a religious life of quiet smugness. Deism is "of no value" and "cannot serve as any foundation to religion or morals."[49] Only the moral God is capable of meeting the kind of dramatic problem of theodicy which Kant came to see, and to which he could give only a religious and moral answer, not a speculative theoretical one.

The personal nature of faith and the transcendence of God are both related to the Kantian enterprise of deobjectification of religion. Making good use of the concepts of reification, E. Weil found the metaphysical achievement of the *Critique of Pure Reason* to be its destruction of the reifications which hide being.[50] The understanding reifies and arrives at precise, definite, objectified objects. This is its merit and the basis of the achievement of science. But a metaphysics that follows this model in the work of theoretical reason, that is, a metaphysics that claims to be able to have a constitutive use of theoretical reason, effectively blocks our approach to an understanding of being. Kant does not want metaphysics to become naive again, that is, prone to think of God, world, and soul as objects more or less like the objects we know through our understanding and senses. A reified God is the most unacceptable outcome of such a metaphysics.[51] God remains a non-objectified object; that is, an object of faith, not of knowledge, only on the basis of being an object of thought as a postulate of pure practical reason.[52]

The whole thrust of my interpretation leads to one conclusion: the superiority of moral theism is to be found not in purely moral but in religious considerations as well. Its merit is not that it places our duties more clearly before our eyes (the categorical imperatives are as clear as can be). It is not that it helps us to become better men. (Any moral improvement based on non-moral motivations is not moral. Ethics for Kant remains autonomous.) Its merit lies in the fact that it gives a meaning to faith which makes of faith an act which is both rational and religious. Faith is a free and personal act of affirmation, which struggles against the split (inside the self and outside it) between what is and what ought to be. This act cannot be encompassed in a series of objectified psychological attitudes or a series of objectified beliefs. Moral theism also gives us a meaning for God which makes God into the only possible correlate of the religious act. God is a free transcendent being who cannot be reduced to an object that is known and analysed or knowable and analysable. That the religious disposition and the moral disposition have in common the characteristics of autonomy and maturity should not lead us to reduce one to the other. Kant himself made extremely clear that the moral attitude is distinct and pure. I think that the same can be said of his interpretation of the religious attitude. He gave it features of autonomy and maturity because these were to him essential to man but this was not an indirect way of affirming that it was the same as the moral one. Thus the moral radication of religion was Kant's way of taking religiousness away from the realm of understanding and of objectification and towards the realm of the personal which was to him the realm of reason and its defense of the interests of man as a rational and finite being. Such a step was inevitable to him as long as he wanted to say that God was approachable through interiority and not through the processes associated with exteriority (a rather incontrovertible position). It is rather important to remember here what sway Newtonian science had in his century. The model for theoretical intellectual activity was Newtonian science (and not prayer, meditation, poetry, or games theory) and thus the model was an objectifying one. In my view, Kant's moral theism may well remain the highest concept of God for Western man as long as natural science rather than meditation or contemplation remains the model for theoretical activity, for it alone will protect the quality of interiority that is necessary to any religious approach to God.

Having said all this, one point remains to be made. Kant's moral theism secures a subjective interior approach to our thinking about God and secures a transcendent, religiously available God. This does not mean that Kant opened the way for all the vagaries of subjective interpretations based on inner unverifiable feeling. Kant disapproved of subjectivistic sentimentality in religion just as much as of authoritarian objectifying orthodoxy. He believed he had found a non-objectifying rational approach to thinking about God. And his definition of religion as personal attitude, unlike that of many, does not mean that all thinking about rational norms is useless in this domain. We shall see in the next section the relevant norms in the use of symbols about God. The unique strength of criticism is that "rational" is not restricted in meaning to cognitive. The Ideas of reason can be thought rationally without being objectified into possible objects of knowledge. Kant in German could make a clear distinction between *wissen* (savoir) and *erkennen* (connaître)[53] whereas English usage tends to lend itself more readily to the general distinction between what one knows scientifically and the opinions one has in his head. There was for Kant a *wissen* which does not know but does think according to rational norms. The whole section on Opining, Knowing, and Believing in the *Critique of Pure Reason* is at pains to show that faith can be rational, namely can be distinct both from knowledge and from opinion and be held on the basis of rational criteria. The quality of certainty of faith is therefore an objectively necessary subjective certainty whereas the quality of certainty of strong opinions is merely subjective. The relationship between faith and reason (in its practical use) is best shown by a passage in the paragraph in the *Critique of Judgement* that reworks the basic ideas already found in the first Critique. As the text shows, the meaning of such usage of the term faith obeys severe norms and is sharply distinguished from the general willingness to assent to unproved propositions or even the cautious readiness to assert to probable ones, and it could be shown that religious as well as moral considerations go into the definition of this normative, rational kind of faith.

> Faith as *habitus*, not as *actus*, is the moral attitude of reason in its assurance of the truth of what is beyond the reach of theoretical knowledge. It is the steadfast principle of the mind, therefore, according to which the truth of what must necessarily be presupposed as the condition of the supreme final end being possible is assumed as true in consideration of the fact that we are under an obligation to pursue that end—and assumed notwithstanding that we have no insight into its possibility, though likewise none into its impossibility. Faith, in the plain acceptation of the term, is a confidence of attaining a purpose the furthering of which is a duty, but whose achievement is a thing of which we are unable to *perceive* the possibility—or, consequently, the possibility of what we can alone conceive to be its conditions. Thus the faith that has reference to particular objects is entirely a matter of morality, provided such objects are not objects of possible knowledge or opinion, in which latter case, and above all in matters of history, it must be called credulity and not faith. It is a free assurance, not of any matter for which dogmatic proofs can be found for the theoretical determinant judgement, nor of what we consider a matter of obligation, but of that which we assume in the interests of a purpose which we set before ourselves in accordance with laws of freedom. But this does not mean that it is adopted like an opinion formed on inadequate grounds. On the contrary it is something that has a foundation in reason (though only in relation to its practical employment), and *a foundation that satisfies the purpose of reason*.[54]

The norms of faith, those that enable us to make the distinction between the genuine and religious faith or pure rational faith on the one hand and mere historical belief and/or superstition on the other hand, belong to the doctrine of religion proper and a full discussion of them will be postponed until then, especially since the normative faith comes to clarity only in the context of the forms of faith which concrete religious communities propose to us.

Symbols and Our Conception of God

Kant's "knight of Faith" or his "moral believer" is in the last analysis a believer in the rational deployment and use of our faculties, and is committed to the "greatest possible extension" of our reason both in its practical and in its theoretical use.[55] Thus he affirms his faith in God because the Idea of God, as a regulative Idea, is an Idea necessary to guide our reason in its fullest empirical use and to guide our judgement in its fullest reflective scope. God, as rational object of faith, is also a postulate of the practical use of our reason, and faith in God is thus a correlate of any conscientious humanism. The affirmation of God which results jointly from the regulative use of Ideas of pure reason and postulates of practical reason is finally necessary to the development of a sound metaphysics that will put our reason on the sure path to the answers to the questions which experience cannot answer. It is worth noting that the one who is an unbeliever is in this case not a disobedient rebel but a lazy indifferentist who does not care to know as much as can be known and is not stirred by the fate of man.

It was very clear for Kant however that such affirmation of God should not lead to the irrational enthusiasms to which those who are stirred by the fate of man so easily yield. The norms for the kind of religious association and community that is the home of the genuine moral believer were discussed by Kant fully in his doctrine of religion and our discussion of it will accordingly be postponed until the next chapter. I want, however, at this stage to examine how the moral believer in his thinking about God, while not lacking in intellectual curiosity, nevertheless does not presume to know more than he does know.

Kant's doctrine of God proceeds to define quite a few divine attributes. The thought God of Kant is thought in quite a precise and determinate sense. This man who concluded one major piece of work by saying that we do not know God ends up thinking quite a lot about him. The solution to this state of affairs is to be found in the position according to which we know God symbolically. The *Critique of Judgement* puts it this way:

> Supposing the name of knowledge may be given to what only amounts to a mere mode of representation (which is quite permissible where this is not a principle of the theoretical determination of the object in respect of what it is in itself, but of the practical determination of what the idea of it ought to be for us and for its final employment), then all our knowledge of God is merely symbolic.[56]

To state that we know God symbolically, or, strictly, that we think of him by means of symbols, meant for Kant first of all that his divine nature itself remains completely unfathomable to us. "*Natura divina est imperscrutabilis.*"[57] We do not claim to know what God is in himself but speak only of his relation to us and to the world.[58] God's holiness, for instance, is defined negatively; it is the absence of moral conflict, or it is a goodness for which the good is not received as an imperative.[59] And secondly it means that when we affirm of God attributes of an anthropomorphic character[60] (as inevitably we must, for what do we know that is more unqualifiedly good than a good will?), we are practising a symbolic regulative anthropomorphism, not a dogmatic constitutive one.[61] We are stating "what the idea of it ought to be for us."

Kant's doctrine of symbolic anthropomorphism first arises out of the older doctrine of analogy.

> If I say that we are compelled to consider the world as if it were the work of a Supreme Understanding and Will, I really say nothing more than that a watch, a ship, a regiment, bears the same relation to the watchmaker, the shipbuilder, the commanding officer, as the world of sense (or whatever constitutes the substratum of this complex of appearances) does to the Unknown, which I do not hereby cognise as it is in itself, but as it is for me or in relation to the world, of which I am a part.
>
> Such a cognition is one of analogy, and does not signify (as is commonly understood) an imperfect similarity of two things, but a perfect similarity of relations between two quite dissimilar things.[62]

The last sentence is very important. Kant used the *analogia relationis* (as older metaphysicians did, while most readers tend to see the simpler *analogia proportionis*) and this kind of analogy does not enable us to say that God is like a watchmaker, shipbuilder, or commanding officer, but larger or more powerful (an analogy which claims to say what God is in himself), but only that his relationship to the world is like that of a watchmaker, etcetera. Kant found in symbolism the general answer to the problem of what language we can apply to the supersensible (beyond the mere affirmation of its objects as Ideas or as postulates). We cannot conceive the supersensible as we come to perceive objects of sense, but we can give it a symbolic determination, which is the indirect representation of the relations the supersensible has to us, relations which are not knowable in their objective reality. Thus symbols can show what we think (I mean of course rational thought).

Using a phrase that brought his doctrine on this point in contact with a basic doctrine in his epistemology, Kant referred also to this use of symbols as a schematism of analogy. His epistemology had arrived at a chasm between the categories of the understanding and that to which the categories are applied, namely the manifold given in sensation. The transcendental schema, or a representation issuing from "a universal procedure of imagination in providing an image for a concept,"[63] bridges just that gap and enables me to relate the sight of this black four-legged animal with whiskers to the concept of cat. The transcendental scheme is based upon rules for the forming of all possible mental images of cats.[64] The two schematisms have in common the fact that they result from the legitimate universal activity of the imagination. The schematism of analogy, however, unlike the schematism of objective determination, does not extend our knowledge (although it may serve to extend it in a heuristic way) but merely provides for an analogical interpretation of our condition in the world.[65]

The way of analogy enabled Kant both to purify our thinking about God from inner contradiction and, more important, from univocal attribution of attributes which would spell a return to naive objectifying metaphysics that claim to say what God is. On these points, however much he may have departed from eighteenth century rationalism (orthodox and deist) and its confident optimism when it came to saying who God is, Kant was returning to the older metaphysical tradition which had a religious sense of the mysteriousness of God, did not underestimate the difficulties inherent in the attempt to try to think God, knew of the different kinds of analogies, and was fully aware of the aporias into which the attempt to think analogically precipitates us.

Kant's conscious use of symbols to think about God is best illustrated by his frequent return to the thought of God as Creator, the correlate of the thought of the world as Creation.[66] To think of God as Creator is to accept the *systema liberae productionis* and this is the only adequate Idea of the origin of the world, since it roots this origin in a mysterious, free, moral act of a transcendent Author, and thereby provides us with a representation of God that affirms a discontinuity between God and world, preventing any direct knowledge of God from that which we know of the world. Deism provides us with too worldly a representation of God and does not offer a religiously valid notion of God. The statement of God as Creator is properly called symbolic, using a formulation of the *Critique of Judgement*, because "the concept is one which only reason can think, and to which no sensible intuition can be adequate."[67] It directs our imagination towards God as Idea of Reason, and not towards some super-mechanic (a concept to which sensible intuition can be adequate). This is probably the clearest illustration of the necessity of symbolic thinking in theological matters and of Kant's dissent from deism. The symbol of the Creator is also "a symbol for reflection"[68] in that it provides opportunity for enlarging our sense of the Majesty of God.

Where Kant was original is in his extending his insight about our analogical doctrine of God to the totality of our theological doctrines and our religious life. And thus his limited doctrine of analogy and symbolic knowledge of God moves into a general theory of symbols in religion and culture. We already saw Kant turn to "stories" and "pictures" to develop parts of his philosophy of history. I ventured to say that moral dispositions for Kant needed "signs" to grow in strength. Finally Kant came to see religious doctrine and ritual as symbolic. As we shall see in *Religion within the Limits of Reason Alone*,[69] numerous are the doctrines and rituals which can be criticized as being superstitious if they are taken literally or dogmatically but which are acceptable and even desirable if they are taken symbolically.

The determination of the religious world as being a world of symbols, or a world where truth is couched in symbols rather than literally verifiable statements, had already begun in eighteenth century Germany with Lessing who intervened in the polemics between the system of eternal punishment for the wicked and the system of ultimate universal salvation to reject the former as literal truth but state that it carried a deeper insight about the nature of evil than the latter (thus casting doubt upon the latter as literal truth as well).[70] This radicalization of the insight into the symbolic nature of religious language and behaviour places Kant squarely in the emerging camp of modern philosophy of religion, or in the camp of liberal Protestants (in the nineteenth century sense), the camp that was subsequently occupied by modernist Catholics as well, and takes him out of the camp of traditional Protestantism as well as out of that of traditional rationalistic metaphysics. As Troeltsch put it in a statement reminiscent of the debates of the beginnings of this century as to whether modernity began with Luther or with the Enlightenment, the idea of a symbolic anthropomorphism as the necessary form of every religious faith, and the idea of the task of purification and control of such symbolism as the task of the philosopher–theologian, is something that belongs to the modern world of thought, not to Reformation Protestantism.[71] As this is a new apprehension of the religious world, it is also the definition of a new task for philosophers encountering religion: the development of the theory of symbols, the analysis of live symbols, and the discrimination among them. In the passage of the essay *On a Lordly Tone* where Kant made the distinction between poetry and prose in philosophy, he gave to philosophy the clear mandate of controlling our aesthetic representations of God and of the supersensible and of not allowing the imagination to become overheated and yield to exaltation.[72]

Interpreters may have to conclude that in the final analysis Kant did not win through to, say, Coleridge's reevaluation of the imagination, and straightjacketed the use of schematism of analogy within the narrow confines of his rational moral theism. A conclusion on this point must however await the examination of the doctrine of religion. It will be useful nevertheless to draw attention at this point to an achievement of the *Critique of Judgement*, namely its analysis of "the faculties of the mind which constitute genius."[73] For the genius, or the poet who has the capacity to create soulful representations, has the capacity to produce aesthetic ideas. In the context of this discussion Kant underlined more the positive assets of this talent than the negative features and inherent perils. "By an aesthetic idea I mean that representation of the imagination which induces much thought,"[74] even though the abundance of thinking it elicits and suggests cannot find definite concepts to express itself. In this case the imagination displays a creative activity, animates the mind, opens for it prospects into fields of kindred representations, and thus stretches the mind beyond its accustomed representations and limited vision.[75] The examples Kant gave (taken from poetry) of such an effect may not be the most effective ones in our eyes and to our own taste, but it certainly would be unfair to charge Kant with insensitivity to the value of symbols and aesthetic language.

Summary and Conclusion

The life of religion for Kant, either in the life of the self or in that of the community, is not in any fundamental way dependent upon the results (positive or negative) of the speculative effort of knowledge of God. Kant was not saying thereby that we will be guided in religious matters by our passions and by custom no matter what our reason may say, for Kant, in contrast to Hume, believed that our reason is de jure and de facto supreme in matters of behaviour as well as in matters of thought (the practical power of reason was even of greater concern to him than its theoretical faculty). The independence of religion from speculative reason is therefore no denial of the power of reason to exercise a normative influence upon religion, far from it.

On one minimal point however, one result of speculative theology is necessary to the grounding of religion upon a sound rational basis: the minimum of theology (speculative theology of course) to which Kant referred in this way exercises a strictly negative control: my concept of God must not be intrinsically impossible, and it must not contradict the laws of the understanding.[76]

The doubts concerning the theoretical proofs of the existence of God and even the repudiation of these proofs do not undermine in any way the kind of affirmation of God which alone is morally and religiously significant, that is, faith in God.[77] It rather paves the way for another kind of rational theology, the moral theology and its proof of God, which will provide a rational basis for and a control upon religion that will not rob religion of its personal quality. Moral theology will not deprive religion of its religiousness as it purifies it from superstition, fanaticism, sentimentality, enthusiasm, and all other forms of immoral nonsense. It gives us certainty of the existence of God, and a certainty which is that of rational faith, which is rationally legitimated. It also gives us a definite concept of God as Creator of the world whose creation is done in accordance with moral laws. Finally "this theology also leads directly to *religion*," namely to "the recognition of our duties as divine commands"[78] or the personal attitude of humility and reverence before God that acknowledges a bond with him, the meaning of which is for us the dutiful obedience to the holy moral law of which God is the author and the confidence that such obedience will lead to the fulfilment of the whole of our humanity.

We need such a theology, Kant stated, not "for the extension or rectification of our knowledge of nature nor, in fact, for any theory whatever. We need theology solely on behalf of religion, that is to say, the practical or, in other words, moral requirement of our reason, and need it as a subjective requirement."[79] To this I would add that we need a theology made up of the postulates of practical reason and the ideas of pure reason for the sake of a metaphysical orientation, an orientation which is no "theory," but gives us rationally developed thinking about our place in the universe. The clearest evidence of the usefulness of moral theology to religion lies in the polemics it sustains against all forms of religion or rather all pseudo-religions which objectify God or precipitate man into—or encourage him to remain in—the slavish attitude of a superstitious being that seeks to please, bribe, or manipulate a despotic God. Theology bars the road to theosophy, and demonology, and all attempts to probe into and control God as if he were an object of nature, and thus prevents religion from turning into theurgy or idolatry.[80]

The consequences of Kant's position for subsequent religious thought are momentous. Tillich formulated a radical interpretation of these implications.

> First theology is not the science of one particular object, which we call God, among others; the *Critique of Reason* put an end to this kind of science. It also brought theology down from heaven to earth. Theology is a part of science of religion, namely the systematic and normative part. Second, theology is not a scientific presentation of a special complex of revelation. This interpretation presupposes a supernaturally authoritative revelation; but this concept has been overcome by the wave of religious–historical insights and the logical and religious criticism of the conception of supernaturalism.[81]

We shall see later in our discussion of the problem of revelation what to think of this second affirmation. The first one is substantially correct. For just as our thinking about God must be linked to a philosophical investigation of the religious dimension of our nature and the religious experience of mankind, so must a philosophy of lived religion (as object of study) develop a normative element that will seek to discriminate the genuine from the spurious among the religious attitudes, beliefs, and behaviours of man. To see religion as a peculiar cultural phenomenon whose symbols are to be investigated from the point of view of an autonomous man-centred rational philosophy, is not necessarily to deprive religion of any connection with the Unconditional and the true. As Tillich put it, when in religion the Unconditional becomes conditioned and is destroyed (as it inevitably will be, for who will say that religion has never been or will never become all too human or that symbols will never die?), then we can observe "the protest of religion against religion."[82] This breaking through of the Unconditional through the conditioned in religion is part of the object of the philosophy of religion and is the basis for its normative criteria. Along these lines (which he called those of a theonomous philosophy of religion) Tillich proposed to overcome the conflict between the worldly philosophy of religion and theology, which he so deeply felt at the beginning of the twentieth century.[83] Such results are indebted to Kant and can be used to shed light upon the distinctions Kant made between the doctrine of God and the doctrine of religion as the two parts of his philosophy of religion.

That Kant's investigation into "the Unconditional" is to be called a philosophy of religion rather than a theology is self-evident. It is part of a systematic investigation of the symbols to which men respond and it is that part which seeks to think normatively about symbols. Kant made a fresh start and creatively reoriented investigations of the religious problem under the impact of a strong, autonomous, worldly "enlightened" philosophy which made the question, "What is man?" (rather than "What is God?") its crucial inquiry. To this he added a major breakthrough, the elements of a radical discovery of man as a symbol-using animal. His contribution is a philosophical one above all, in that he sought to uncover those laws that govern our scientific knowledge and those laws which ought to govern our thinking on matters beyond the scope of science. It is his philosophical position that brought renovation to theology as well as fresh conquests to philosophy. This however should not obscure the fact that his philosophy can be considered as "theonomous," because it provides systematic norms for religion and for our knowledge of God that arise intrinsically out of the nature of religion itself and thus it ultimately becomes a theological discourse that attempts to speak responsibly of God.

Chapter 7

The Philosophical Problems with Which Kant Approached the Doctrine of Religion

The Relationship between *Religion* and the Three Critiques

Kant's doctrine of religion is distinct from his doctrine of God. The continuity, of course, is inescapable. Both doctrines have something to do with the Ultimate. The former turns to the Ultimate itself, the latter to what men do, think, and feel when they turn to the Ultimate. Both come to their solutions through an understanding of the role of symbols. Both doctrines are ultimately rooted in Kant's understanding of the religious as found in the self, namely in his doctrine of pure religious faith. The doctrine of God must be religious, and historical concrete religious life ought to be such as to facilitate the religiousness of selves.

This being said, the distinction nevertheless remains clear between a doctrine which examines the Idea of God and one which examines the various facets of various kinds of religious life, their doctrines, institutions, and rituals. The pages on God in the first and second Critiques and the pages on religion in *Religion within the Limits of Reason Alone*, the one work in which the doctrine of religion is to be found, differ in their subject matter. And it may bear repeating that Kant may be considered one of the founders of modern philosophy of religion precisely because of the pioneering work he did in *Religion*. But, just as importantly, *Religion* has some very weighty things to say about the predicament of moral man (his character, his dispositions, his propensity to evil) that were not said in the ethical writings. The doctrine of religion therefore is not only a complement to the doctrine of God but also a deepening and possible revision of the moral philosophy. Two factors thus lead Kant to press his inquiry in *Religion*: unfinished business in his mind about the nature of concrete historical religious life, and unfinished business in his mind about his ethics and man's moral life.

Kant undertook work on *Religion* with a very definite approach in his mind. He had specific philosophical problems to look at that arose out of the Critiques and were not satisfactorily treated there. The nature of these problems will appear in an inquiry into the relationship between the three Critiques (the third one dates of 1790) and *Religion* (1793).

Although I depart from a body of Kantian interpreters by stressing the philosophical importance of *Religion*, I should state at the outset that I do not see in it anything like a fourth Critique. There is every ground to believe that Kant thought his main philosophical endeavour to be completed with the *Critique of Judgement*.[1] The three Critiques have a systematic unity and completeness, and comprise a full theory of mental activity. When it comes to this subject there is no gap in the monuments of criticism to be filled by a subsequent major work.

We cannot find a place for *Religion* by including it among the doctrinal works, the *Metaphysics of Nature* and the *Metaphysic of Morals*, in which Kant worked out the implications of his critical system, for *Religion* is not merely a work in which Kant applied results of his philosophy. It is also a fresh inquiry into new problems, and an inquiry which he deemed important enough to delay further work on his *Metaphysic of Morals* (which appeared in 1797) even though he declared in 1790 that he was eager to do it soon since he was aware of his age.

To minimize the significance of *Religion* is of course one answer to our problem. This, however, contradicts the philosopher's own testimony since Kant himself gave a rather important place to the work in 1793 when he mailed a copy of it to C. F. Stäudlin.

. . . The plan I prescribed for myself a long time ago calls for an examination of the field of pure philosophy with a view to solving three problems: (1) What can I know? (metaphysics). (2) What ought I to do? (moral philosophy). (3) What may I hope? (philosophy of religion). A fourth question ought to follow, finally: What is man? (anthropology, a subject on which I have lectured for over twenty years). With the enclosed work, *Religion*, I have tried to complete the third part of my plan. In this book I have proceeded conscientiously and with genuine respect for the Christian religion but also with a befitting candor, concealing nothing but rather presenting openly the way in which I believe that a possible union of Christianity with the purest practical reason is possible.[2]

We are again confronted here with the lack of perfect coordination between the three (or four) questions and the three Critiques. No matter what we come to think of that, it still remains true that here Kant sees *Religion* as putting the finishing touch to his tripartite system, not the third Critique. Furthermore, we can emphasize that moral philosophy (as found in the second Critique and in the *Metaphysic of Morals*) finds its completion only in the doctrine of religion (just as morals find their completion only in religion) by Kant's own admission.

> Morals is not really the doctrine of how to make ourselves happy but of how we are to be *worthy* of happiness. Only if religion is added to it can the hope arise of someday participating in happiness in proportion as we endeavoured not to be unworthy of it.[3]

A. Schweitzer's interpretation may also be brought forward to show the distinctiveness and importance of *Religion*. Whereas the moral world in the second Critique was always the eternal intelligible world, in *Religion* it means the world of our inner moral dispositions, the world which is very much existing here and now in time and which may or may not change in the future.[4] Moral development, he adds, is now thought out as taking place and heading towards fulfilment on earth, and the thought of immortality is conspicuously absent.[5] (This is also true of the philosophy of history.)

Finally we find Goldmann's statement that *Religion* introduces a serious discussion of the theme of the relations between man and the human community, and that thereby we find ourselves at the centre "not only of Kant's thought but of all human philosophy."[6]

All this is to me evidence of the work-hypothesis I have assumed in this study, namely that we find in Kant's authorship a series of fresh starts in which his mind, a mind gifted with unusual systematizing power, takes up new problems and lets its thinking arise from a consideration of these problems. *Religion*, a late work, and the only major one which was completed after the Critiques, is another one of these fresh starts (the last one to lead to a perfected work), which takes up a new problem, re-examines problems previously investigated, and thus builds upon previous work but does it in such a way that different solutions emerge and that this work can be said to modify the previous results.[7] *Religion* is thus a vast, new and vigorous undertaking which draws upon new sources and is prompted by a new problem.

But what then is the new problem that occasioned such vigorous intellectual activity and led to such momentous results? I suggest that this new factor which prompted Kant to undertake a fresh inquiry in his late sixties is a series of problems which arise from the temporality (or historicity) of our existence, problems which had not been investigated in the three Critiques, and could not because of the use of the transcendental method, or the search for a priori conditions of possibility. When Kant, in a dependent clause in a footnote, stated that the "existence of a temporal being as such" is characterized by the failure "ever wholly to be what we have in mind to become,"[8] he not only makes an interesting observation paralleling Lessing's famous humble request to be given what is in God's left hand, but he becomes aware of the problems proper to the existence of a temporal being as such, none of which had seriously entered into the discourse of the three Critiques.[9]

The problems of time-bound man which Kant came to see can be summarized under three headings: those arising from the very notion of a progressive realization of freedom, those arising from the specific task of evaluating freedom's actual power to realize itself (what we shall call the inquiry into the existential predicament of freedom, or the investigation into the current limits of freedom's power), and those arising from the problem of evil (as the one obstacle that stands in the way of a progressive realization of freedom). An examination of each one of these three problems will accordingly show what was there that prompted Kant to reopen his inquiries, this time into the phenomena of religious life, what issues he had in mind as he probed into the nature of religious life, and the solutions to what problems he was trying to discover in the facts of religious life. In this way the specific philosophical results of *Religion* will be brought to light.

All these problems are ultimately investigations into the fate of freedom, or into its destiny and its prospects. They all naturally and inevitably arise out of a moral theory that focuses on the concept of man as a finite and free being and that presents the moral law which human beings qua free beings must obey. The moral theory had argued that moral men, while their action should be determined by duty, must exhibit a positive concern for the establishment of goodness in the world. A fresh question thereby arises: What are the prospects of such establishment of goodness? Thus the philosophical transition to the problems of religion is specifically a transition from the results of Kantian ethics. The question will be: What does religion add to ethics? What does the religious life have that the moral life does not have? Not that Kant's ethical theory has gaps that must somehow be filled by some other doctrine. His ethics answer perfectly and completely the question it set out to deal with, namely: What must I do? But that the ethical theory is complete in this way does not mean that there are no further problems, distinct and different. In particular the ethical theory had not dealt with the question of what may be hoped to follow —in the world—from the practice of duty. The three questions we have begun to formulate became Kant's way to handle the large but natural existential issue of concern for the moral quality of the human future: What will come to pass if I do my duty? How much power do I have to transform the world of men by actions done from duty alone? How much of an obstacle is moral evil itself, in myself and in others? An elucidation of these three questions will bring to light the philosophical transition between the Critiques and *Religion*.

The first of these problems (the progressive realization of freedom) is the problem which lies at the basis of Kant's philosophy of history. The second one, that about the actual power of freedom, is present in the philosophy of history and in the political thought, in their affirmation of reformism as opposed to conservatism and utopianism. The last one, that of evil, really comes to a head and a radical discussion only in the philosophy of religion. We have here further evidence of the hypothesis I have been developing and testing concerning the intimate relationship between the philosophy of history and the philosophy of religion and a validation of my claim that the full scope and originality of the philosophy of religion will be brought to light when set in the context of the philosophy of history. For both have in common the usually hidden suspicion that time is more than a form of our sensitivity and both begin to depart from the doctrines that the temporal man is phenomenal man and that man as a thing in himself—or as a noumenon—does not participate in time. As both give crucial existential significance to the problems arising from the temporality or historicity of man's essence, together they constitute that second historically conscious strain in Kant's philosophy which is in conflct and creative tension with the first and which found expression only in the so-called minor writings.

This interpretation gives us the answer to the lack of parallelism between the work of the three Critiques and the famous three interrogations. By adding to the questions, What can I know? and, What must I do? the question, What may I hope? Kant included in his philosophy the question which is closest to the heart of the essentially historical man.[10] (Note that hope is indicated as precisely that which religion adds to morality in the quote given above from the *Critique of Practical Reason*.) This list of the three questions thus represents a confluence of the two strains in Kant, and in its last question opens prospects, which the three Critiques, the major and dominant strain, could not possibly handle, and which had to be left to the philosophy of history and that of religion. Thus while it is not correct to hold, as Lacroix seemed to do, that *Religion* is the synthesis and crown of the three Critiques,[11] it is correct to hold that it is the completion of the answers to the three questions.

The Results of the Ethical Theory and the Two Meanings of Freedom

Kant's ethical theory, defining man as a responsible being, finite and rational, is an interpretation of man as a freely striving being. Kant's ethics puts before us and argues for an image of active man as the end of Creation. He quoted with approval the letter of a young man, C. A. Willmanns, thanking him for speaking against the view of man as an element of the world and calling man to "a thoroughly active existence in the world."[12]

Problematic man, man who is a question to himself, cannot start from what he is; this is precisely what is ambiguous and under radical questioning—he must make himself into whatever he ought to be. Naturalism, thus, is not a live option. Man cannot work towards the restoration of a state of nature, a state of well-being resulting from happy coordination with the facts of nature, because man's "own nature is not so constituted as to rest or be satisfied in any possession or enjoyment whatever."[13] Problematic man is involved in contradiction; his nature coerces him to go beyond his nature. Happiness, or the concord of natural tendencies, cannot be the end of man. The end is to be a moral being, living in a state of culture, namely a being consciously working towards ends of his own. Value in life will be found not in what we enjoy but in what we do. "Man himself must make or have made himself into whatever in a moral sense, whether good or evil, he is or is to become."[14]

This attitude challenges classical rationalism and undoubtedly shows a touch of the pietistic background which emphasized the wisdom of the heart, the goodness of the inner attitude of free persons of kindly disposition responding freely and humanly to everyday situations, rather than a codification of rules of behaviour or a description of instrinsic goods to be reached. But it is more important to see that this follows from Kant's basic conception of the problematic character of man inherent in his finitude. Man is not the truth and he is not infallible. The very best he can do is to be conscientious, that is, to mean well and try hard.

This is again strongly reminiscent of Lessing who humbly chose God's left hand and wrote that the dignity of man lies not in the possession of truth but in the endless striving after it (and slyly added that it is better to hold a false doctrine with conviction and good intention than to hold the truest one but with prejudice and contempt for those who disagree).[15] Man cannot hope to be God to be holy. To be of good will is the only absolute valid for finite man. But it is always valid. Conscience cannot be violated in any circumstances. By the very nature of his rationality man cannot partake of any good unless he partakes of it by his own judgement and by his own activity. And he can always know what his own judgement is.

If man on earth can only achieve conscientiousness, this achievement is by itself a noble one. Assuming the burden of responsibility and judging himself responsible of all ends, man knows himself to be the final end. This knowledge is the *bonum supremum* (the highest good possible now) because it is accompanied by a feeling of one's worth and of that of all fellow-men.

The rigour of this distinction between conscientiousness and perfection (which is a radicalization of the metaphor that makes of human life an unceasing pilgrimage) committed Kant to an approach which always distinguishes between form and content in the moral life, or between the method of decision-making and the attainable results.[16]

The method of decision-making is Kant's formal principle: there is only one such principle: the law of human freedom or worth. This principle, as formulated in the categorical imperative, has permanent validity; it defines nothing except the form of humanity:

1. The right to cultivate ends of one's own choosing, so long as they are compossible with the ends of others.

> No one may force anyone to be happy according to his manner of imagining the well-being of other men; instead, everyone may seek his happiness in the way that seems good to him as long as he does not infringe on the freedom of others to pursue a similar purpose, when such freedom may coexist with the freedom of every other man according to a possible and general law.[17]

2. The right to refuse to accept anything as one's own end unless one has approved of it in one's own mind.

> Enlightenment is man's release from his self-incurred tutelage. Tutelage is man's inability to make use of his understanding without understanding, without direction from another... *Sapere aude!* Have courage to use your own reason.[18]

3. The duty to heed reason's demand for universality. These are "the maxims of common human understanding": "a) To think for oneself; b) to think from the standpoint of everyone else; c) always to think consistently."[19]

Kant's formal ethics, by telling us how to decide not what to strive after, opens the door to historical development. It sees man as a dynamic being whose material goals are not predetermined and who is always capable of achieving new goals.[20] This, however, leads beyond ethical theory to another question, existentially equally important, namely that of the attainable results. The question is inevitably raised about a progressive realization of freedom. Which one of its morally selected goals can man really achieve in history? Can freedom create a society which bears its mark and where it will encounter fewer obstacles? Freedom for Kant in one sense participates in the finitude which characterizes our humanity. Our freedom is absolute in the sense that it can make or unmake our humanity. Whether we are freely striving or not is always an open question which can always be answered by an internal fiat. But freedom is finite and relative in that it cannot make man into whatever man pleases (it is no amoral divine creativity). There are the limitations of our finitude, the limit which our neighbour is, and the limitations caused by the strength of our moral dispositions.

So for the thinker inspired by Kant, there emerges a twofold meaning of freedom, the absolute and the relative. A remark from the *Opus Postumum* will help make my meaning clear.

> *Honeste vive.* Do not act in contradiction to the duty innate in you. Do not act in contradiction with the humanity in your person. Do not reduce yourself to a mere means. . . . . Freedom is that innate right on which all other rights are founded and with which they finally are all confounded. For all injustice consists in a violation of this freedom, which is compatible with the freedom of everyone. By nature every one has the (negative) right to be treated as an honest man, which does not mean an honorable man.[21]

Every man must be considered as a man who knows what he is doing, and is open to dialogue as to the meaning of what he does. Every man must be treated as a man who rightfully means to assert his own freedom, and who rightfully insists on yielding only to rational persuasion. But this does not mean that every man asserts his freedom in the right way; some assert it in a way which destroys the freedom of others and thereby immediately (not in the long run!) destroy their own. In one sense freedom is absolute; every man means to be free and it is every man's right. Each act must rightfully be imputed to its doer and responsible agent. This freedom is inalienable. No previous voluntary act determines the present ones, though it creates a predisposition to them.

In another sense, freedom is relative. It expresses itself more or less; it penetrates concrete reality in our lives more or less. It becomes more or less a historical reality; it is more or less denied or incarnated in our habits. It overcomes sloth, duplicity, and all the forms of moral evil in us more or less. This freedom may be enslaved, lost, or alienated. In his absolute freedom, fallible man acquires habits or patterns of relative freedom or enslavement, and thereby succeeds or fails in the progressive realization of his freedom.

The person or self is born when the individual assumes his own absolute freedom and considers himself responsible. The genesis of the person as historical phenomenon open to development begins when this self acquires a moral disposition, or the habit of the expression of his freedom in dialogue with the expressions of the freedom of others. Birth and genesis cannot be separated, yet two distinct terms are necessary. In the birth of the person, the self gains the vision of a community of selves living in free cooperation (and not competing through the exercise of power), living in perpetual peace, and free from the antagonisms of war and from mutual coercion. In the genesis of the person, the self begins to practise such human life in earthly reality, progressively gains habits of such personal exchange and dialogue between free men, acquires in this life a relative freedom which approximates the absolute freedom to which he has a birthright. Man-who-strives unites both absolute and relative freedom: absolute freedom since he strives after a goal which his own reason defines; relative freedom since he is not there yet and finds many obstacles.

The ethical theory translates the notion of man as finite and rational into the notion of the two meanings of freedom. The categorical imperative is the only possible formulation of the moral law because we are free in an absolute sense. We receive it as an imperative because we are free only in a relative sense. The moral law is rooted in our freedom in its absolute sense, but the moral life is lived in a context in which our freedom is only relative. The second Critique focuses on the critical question of freedom in an absolute sense, but Kant showed equal interest—though elsewhere—in the problems related to the relative sense of our freedom. Character, dispositions, virtue, are all notions related to the relative power of our freedom to realize itself in the world and Kant examined them in his *Metaphysic of Morals* and in *Religion*. Only freedom in its absolute sense is the topic in a critical investigation of the conditions of possibility of our moral life, but the relative sense of freedom is of equal concern to the moralist.[22] A person can be held accountable for his acts, because a person is neither merely an absolute freedom nor an unrelated series of mental states, that is, because a person is also a relative freedom, which shapes a moral character through which its absolute freedom seeks to express itself in time and from which all moral acts issue. Besides the imperative to have all our maxims determined by duty, we must also promote the highest good with all our strength, and that is a task for our freedom in its relative sense. Our duties may be divided between those that are perfect and narrow (a duty to attain an end) and those that are imperfect and wide (a duty to strive after an end). The former bring to light our freedom in its absolute sense: we must be conscientious, and to fail there is to be guilty. The latter bring to light our freedom in its relative sense. We must strive to cultivate virtue and strive after the establishment of goodness in the world, and to fail there is to be weak.[23] One of the objectives of *Religion*, considered as an extension of the previous moral writings, is to open up some problems about our freedom in its relative sense. And our concrete religious life will be found to have much to say that is relevant.

The Existential Predicament of the Will

Kant's thought did not come to rest with the results of the ethical theory reached and outlined above. For the theme of hope had been introduced, hope to realize the objectives of freedom, moral perfection, or the moral commonwealth. Kant then sought to give men grounds for hoping that moral action will in fact lead in some sense to the fulfilment of all legitimate human interests or that man will progress in the realization of his freedom. This moral faith, it may be objected, is a self-inspired faith, a faith arising out of one's will to maintain power over one's life and achieve worthiness of happiness. How strong is this stoic will? How much faith can one instil into oneself? Is the faith in the coming realization of the *summum bonum* strong enough for men to dare to act motivated by duty alone? These questions and the insistent presence of a need of finite men for hope force Kantian thought to push on in its efforts to understand the human situation and ask what hopes are credible. This also leads him to examine what religion and the facts of institutionalized religious life have to say.

The question of hope is related to the question of our current motivation. Do men today act really morally, that is, motivated by pure impulses (or rational self-discipline), or do they act morally only apparently, motivated in fact by fear of social consequences, that is by desire to maintain their happiness rather than by desire to protect the freedom and dignity of all men? This leads Kant to seek for empirical generalizations about the current moral condition of man. If it is shown that men in general act only outwardly in conformity to the law, what grounds of hope are left, since we cannot have the confidence that men in fact have a genuine will to progress? The question asked of religion ultimately is whether there is another ground of hope besides that found in the currently prevailing dispositions of men. Can a critical examination of the Christian religion validate the existence of such another ground of hope?

The answers given will indicate not only whether men have a hope or not, but will also characterize the nature of our hope. Must we place our hope in another world, or in future history, or in both? Any description of what lies in store for us in another world may be hard to make, but can we characterize what we may hope for in history? What can men at best expect in history—a peace which is a balance of terror, an equilibrium of contending forces, or a peace shared by friends who are open to each other and trust each other?

The key to the two sets of questions is found in an evaluation of the present condition of human wills, and this issue leads Kant to move beyond the investigation of our moral life into the investigation of our religious life. *Religion* begins with an inquiry into the existential predicament of the human freedom and of the human will in their social and historical dimensions. The assumption is that the area common to moral and religious life manifests the deepest core of the self, and shows light into man's innermost motivations. There we shall discern how much power for good there is in man's will. Or there we shall discern the fullness of the conflict between good and evil, on the results of which depends the only real ground of hope that a worldly thinker can take into his philosophy.

In the ethical writings the will had been examined as to what it ideally is and what it ideally can do. The logic of Kant's philosophy, however, urged him on to look into the actual dynamics of the will, or into the concrete history of the will, its actual predicament in the individual's life and in contemporary society (which is either victory over the obstacles or captivity to them). It was allowed that free beings have the power to misuse their freedom. What in fact do they choose? So Kant had to turn to an historical, social, personal, and religious question: What is the state of my freedom now? He left the realm of metaphysics and questions of right for that of history and questions of fact, not facts of nature but the factual status of freedom or facts of moral attitude. At this point his reflection is forced to become theological as well as historical, because it is forced to look into the dynamics of the lived religious life.

As J.R. Silber put it:

> Kant's ethical statics, to borrow a term from physics, may be found in varying degrees of systematization in most of his post-critical works. Only in the *Religion*, however, do we find what might be called Kant's ethical dynamics. Kant had discussed the nature of the good, the character of imperatives, and the method-

ology of moral inquiry in his earlier works; in the *Religion* he addresses himself to the problem of evil—its nature, its origin, and the possibility of its eradication. In the process he raises questions which necessitate an understanding of the will in its full complexity and dynamic unity. We therefore find, in the *Religion*, in his struggle with the problem of evil, Kant's most explicit and systematic account of the will and of human freedom—an account which, in turn, clarifies his entire system of ethics.[24]

We can now understand the full implications of Kant's statement in the preface to *Religion* that morality "leads ineluctably to religion." The moral man neither needs nor seeks further clarification of his duty than the moral law. He does not require further motive either, but, as moral man, he wants to attain good results in the world; he hopes for happiness to be added to worthiness of happiness, and he inquires into the prospects for the realization of the kind of world the moral law tells him to work for unconditionally. The need for the grounds of hope is heightened by the sense of conflict between the laws of morality and the natural course of things, a sense of conflict which raises the prospect of the laws of morality remaining powerless in this world. As moral man is led by the postulates of pure practical reason to believe in God as moral governor of the world, he is led to ask also whether there are grounds for hoping that divine Providence will further his moral efforts to complete his work and bring about what he perhaps by himself (for whatever reason) cannot realize.

The Rise of the Problem of Evil

Religion is notorious finally for its examination of the problem of evil and its characterization of it as radical. This notoriety was quick: on 7 June 1793, very shortly after its publication, Goethe wrote indignantly to Herder:

Kant, who spent a whole lifetime cleaning his philosophical mantle from all kinds of prejudices which soiled it, has now ignominiously dirtied it again with the shameful spot of radical evil, so that Christians too can feel they ought to kiss the hem of it.[25]

An analysis of the problem of evil follows from the concerns of the moral man who asks himself whether and when his moral efforts will reach their object and sees evil in himself and in others as a constant threat to the fulfilment of his hopes. To raise the problem of evil is also a consequence of any examination of the further implications of Kant's moral philosophy: freedom for Kant receives the law as an obligation; this means therefore that freedom has the power—and perhaps a tendency—to reject the moral obligation. On the question of evil, therefore, just as on the question of the relative power of freedom and the quality of its motivations, we can see the philosophy of religion further the moralist's inquiry by looking into relevant aspects of the religious life. Is not the confession of guilt part of most religious ritual and the access to forgiveness part of the blessings of the religious life? Is not sanctification one of the promises of religion?

On the point of evil, however, the inquiry into the para-ethical problems which make religion of such interest to the moral philosopher, represents not just a deepening and an extension of Kant's philosophy but a fresh orientation and even a change of mind to some extent. Goethe's instinct was sound. The Kantian discussion of radical evil does amount to a repudiation of aspects of his "enlightened" past. I must therefore briefly summarize the history of Kant's handling of the problem of evil.

Borovski narrates that, a correspondent having asked for a copy of Kant's *Considerations on Optimism* (1759), he went to see Kant and requested a copy. Kant earnestly asked him to forget this essay, and should he come across any copy of it, to withdraw it from circulation.[26] The conversation having been interrupted, Borovski never knew why Kant repudiated this essay, the only one of his early works which he seems to have treated in this way. I surmise—as Bruch did[27]—that its treatment of evil and its acceptance of Leibnitian optimism is the cause of this repudiation.

We saw that in the sixties Kant began to encounter increasing difficulties with the unified teleological world view of Leibniz, as he began to be indebted to both Newton and Rousseau. Nevertheless, the optimism of Leibniz seems to have exercised a lasting hold over the mind of the mature Kant. This is shown by the lectures on *Philosophy of Religion* given in the early eighties and published in 1817 by Pölitz. Kant there stated that evil is a mere negation and an instrument of the progress for good.[28] Without a disproportion between happiness and virtue, there would be no opportunity for true virtue.[29] The world is declared to be the best of all possible worlds on the ground that God cannot have a better will than the one he in fact has. Kant referred his students to his *Considerations on Optimism* and concluded that, with Leibniz, we can set aside all objections to divine Providence drawn from the presence of evil.[30] The various essays in the philosophy of history (beginning with the *Idea for Universal History* of 1784) show what appears to be a more realistic grasp of the nature of evil, since it does start from the perceptions that progress (either in the past or in the future) is problematic, that history does tell a record of crimes, stupidity, and misery, and that man is in need of some insight, or some proof, to reconcile himself with his fate and see the goodness of it. At every turn, however, evil is presented as an instrument which is meant (and is necessary) for the realization of a greater good (the development of human faculties) or which can be deflected by human freedom and made to serve a moral end (social rivalry, for instance, being made to serve for the organization of a civil community). Everywhere, then, evil, scandalous though it is, is made a tool, or is seen as a potential tool for human development (both cultural and moral). In *Religion* we find ourselves in a different intellectual universe: we hear there of forces of evil which are to be defeated rather than utilized.

The *Critique of Judgement* (1790) in its treatment of purposefulness in the world and of God's moral sovereignty shows no inclination to repeat the position of the *Considerations of Optimism*, but on the other hand it does not move towards the kind of radical confrontation with the problem of evil that was to come subsequently. Whenever the idea of evil appeared, Kant's thought followed the kind of solution afforded by the philosophy of history.

The decisive turning point appeared in 1791 with the essay *On the Failure of All Attempted Philosophical Theodicies*. There the Leibnitian optimistic solutions are forever set aside and the very choice of theodicy as a topic indicates the conscious confrontation with Leibniz, whose *Théodicée* was commonly accepted as his major achievement. All theodicies attempted until that time are examined and judged as failures; evil, both physical and moral, appeared as something that must be suffered and borne by man, Job-like, in patience and faith, the only response to it that does not lead us into the yet further evils of explaining evil away, lying for God, or despairing and blaspheming.[31] With this essay Kant passed through his turning point in the problem of evil, and finally consciously confronted a problem which was intrinsically present in the process that had begun in the sixties of limiting the validity and the scope of teleological judgements applied to the world as a whole. The various optimistic solutions are all left behind and the only answer given is that of the steadfastness of the good and religious man.

It all happened as if the bond with the Leibnitian tradition having been broken, Kant became free for the thorough investigation of radical evil in 1793. Further evidence of the philosophical transformation occasioned by this new concept of evil is found in the philosophy of history and in the political thought written after 1793. The essay on *Perpetual Peace* (1795) expects progress from divine Providence more than from human endeavour[32] and the same essay declares that political improvement can move ahead somewhat without waiting for moral improvement. The hope for moral perfection or for facilitating moral improvement through reform of political life no longer enters into his political thinking, although the notion of moral evil remains very much part of it. The ideal city is seen as Utopia "ein süsser Traum." Kant at that time lowered his political sights considerably, although he did not abandon his position of reformism.[33]

I conclude therefore that on the question of evil, the deepening of his thought occasioned by the work on *Religion* led to a consolidation of a profound change of mind signalled first by the essay on theodicy. I am quite unwilling to follow the insinuations of Pölitz who pointed out that the lectures on philosophy of religion were delivered under that enlightened monarch Frederick II while the book was published under the ministry of the horrid Wollner, and added that those who really understand the system of the sage of Königsberg will know which of the two treatments of the problem of evil is more faithful to his spirit.[34] The spirit of the Enlightenment instructed Kant to dare to know. And on the problem of evil he preferred to look at the reality of it rather than to repeat the doctrines of the philosophes.

Chapter 8

Religion within the Limits of Reason Alone: The Core of the Doctrine of Religion

The Early Form of the Doctrine of Religion

Following the suggestions of the previous chapter, I shall argue that *Religion* contains a series of interwoven themes, among which we will find repetitions of previous results of Kant's philosophy, applications, clarifications of such previous results, extensions of his thought into new subject matter, and finally, modifications of previous positions. (Only the last two can properly be called fresh departures.)[1] As examples of repetition we can count the definition of religion and the presentation of pure moral faith. Among the applications we should place the doctrine on historical faith. The pages on the church and moral community, and on the parerga are examples of extensions. And the discussion of radical evil (and possibly that of the parerga as well) must be reckoned as a modification.

It may help to sort out the old and the new in *Religion* if we begin by a brief presentation of the early form of the doctrine of religion. I do not mean of course to return to a discussion of God and of faith in God. This belongs to the doctrine of God and its correlate the doctrine of pure religious faith. What I mean to do is to examine early pronouncements on the matter of the religious community, its doctrines and rituals. I realize that such distinction between the doctrine of God and the doctrine of religion (in the sense of interpretation of the life of religious communities and traditions) is somewhat artificial for the earlier period of Kant's life, since it is only late in his life in 1793 that religion in the sense of concrete institutionalized religious life became the object of concerted and disciplined philosophical investigation.

Such pronouncements on religion are found in his *Lectures on Ethics* given between 1775 and 1780, based on a textbook by Baumgarten, and published for the first time in 1924 after the notes of three students. (Ironically these lectures contain much more on church doctrine and ritual than the *Lectures on the Philosophy of Religion* which contain discussion of theologies and a brief overview of the history of world religions.) These lectures present God as requiring from us a moral life, and present the moral life in eudaemonistic terms.

> God wants mankind to be made happy. He wants men to be made happy by men, and if only all men united to promote their own happiness we could make a paradise of Novaya Zemlya. God has set us on the stage where we can make each other happy. It rests with us, and us alone, to do so.[2]

"Of this task men doubtless make a sorry mess"[3] but it is our own fault. God's will is that man should achieve his fullest perfection through his own freedom.[4] Mankind has not progressed very far on this road. Our hope lies "in education, and in nothing else." The state and the princes have contributed nothing, but "the Basedow institutions give us hope, warm even though small."[5]

When it comes to the role of religion in particular, Kant states, "Natural religion is practical. It includes natural knowledge of our duties in respect of the Supreme Being."[6] (The wording here is important for there are "no God-ward activities of religion, whereby we can show God a service.")[7] It is of course not right for religion to try to make us moral by enticing us with the thought of future rewards.[8] "The theology which is to form the basis of natural religion must contain one thing, the condition of moral perfection."[9] "The outstanding characteristic of natural religion is its simplicity."[10] Faith, for natural religion, is trust in God, "trust arising from the use of the reason, which springs from the principle of practical morality," and it is not trust in a revelation.[11] Religion complements morality. "Morality as such is ideal, but religion imbues it with vigour, beauty and reality".[12]

On supernatural religion, Kant repeated the traditional position that "it is not opposed to natural religion but completes it." He added however that we can have a supernatural or revealed theology (referring to doctrines) and yet have at the same time a religion which is natural, that is, which carries only those duties which reason can appreciate naturally (he was referring to the disposition "which can be imputed" to us and by which we render ourselves "worthy to be per-fected").[13] This led him to the distinction between moral belief ("belief in the actuality of virtue") and historical belief ("readiness to give assent to testimony").[14] Polemics against religious deviations fol-low and tend to tip the scales against the religion of revelation. Prayers are devotional exercises "not intended in any way to please God and do Him service, but only to strengthen in us the dispositions of our souls to please God by our actions in our lives." "To wish to converse with God is absurd."[15] Nor can religion provide us with examples or patterns to follow since "in matters of religion no examples are neces-sary." The teacher of the Gospel is praised for demanding above all good dispositions from us,[16] and "only since the time of the Gospel has the full purity and holiness of the moral law been recognized, although it indeed dwells in our own reason."[17] Finally we find themes very common to the Enlightenment: the usual denunciation of *odium theologicum* (the priestly desire to rule men in God's name), of *odium religiosum* (excommunication), and the usual praise of freedom of thought. "Religious truth does not require force for its support. . . . Freedom of investigation is the best means to consolidate the truth."[18]

All this is a moral version of the common, mild deistic position, as initiated by Locke, for whom Jesus is the publisher in history of a rational, eternally valid truth. The position is "mild" because re-vealed religion is given a completional task, although it is hard to see in what this task consists besides "vigour, beauty, and reality." The examination of institutionalized religious life (which is found in a church based upon revelation) is the object of more warnings, re-strictions, and negative statements than affirmations of a positive role. The whole discourse with its eudaemonistic strain is very much in the vein of the philosophes and never departs from the self-confident, en-lightened tone.

Much of this later reappeared in *Religion*. The later work however does not contain the same eudaemonistic premises or the same opti-mistic convictions. Hope arises in the context of more severe disso-nance. The tone changes and there is not the same quality of categori-cal serenity and robust assurance in the simplicity of it all. *Religion*, for instance, shows Kant often seeking to wrest positive meaning out of at first perplexing if not obscure religious doctrine.

The tone of the public lectures (or of the students' notes), how-ever, may be misleading even as to Kant's own position in the late seventies. For a private letter to J. C. Lavater of 28 April 1775 shows another side of Kant's thinking on religion at that time. He does not strike me there as one who has well learned his enlightened lesson and spreads it to the youth in the university. He gives himself as still involved in research, and uses language which strikes me as much more his own (he is no longer following a textbook) and is much more cautious. Three quotations from the letter may make the point clear.

> I distinguish the teachings of Christ from the report we have of those teachings. In order that the former may be seen in their purity, I seek above all to separate out the moral teachings from all the dogmas of the New Testament. These moral teachings are certainly the fundamental doctrine of the Gospels, and the remainder can only serve as an auxiliary to them. Dogmas tell us only what God has done to help us see our frailty in seeking justification before Him, whereas the moral law tells us what we must do to make ourselves worthy of justification.

> Our trust in God is unconditional, that is, it is not accompanied by any inquisitive desire to know how His purpose will be achieved or, still less, by any presumptuous confidence that the soul's salvation will follow from our acceptance of certain Gospel disclosures. That is the meaning of the moral faith that I find in the Gospels, when I seek out the pure, fundamental teachings that underlie the mixture of facts and revelations there. Perhaps, in view of the opposition of Judaism, miracles and revelations were needed, in those days, to promulgate and disseminate a pure religion, one that would do away with all the world's dogmas. And perhaps it was necessary to have many ad hominem arguments, which would have great force in those times. But once the doctrine of the purity of conscience in faith and of the good transformation of our lives has been sufficiently propagated as the only true religion for man's salvation (the faith that God, in a manner we need not at all understand, will provide what our frail natures lack, without our seeking His aid by means of the so-called worship that religious fanaticism always demands)—when this true religious structure has been built up so that it can maintain itself in the world—then the scaffolding must be taken down. I respect the reports of the evangelists and apostles, and I put my

humble trust in that means of reconciliation with God of which they have given us historical tidings—or in any other means that God, in his secret counsels, may have concealed.

When I spoke of New Testament dogmas I meant to include everything of which one could become convinced only through historical reports, and I also had in mind those confessions or ceremonies that are enjoined as a supposed condition of salvation. By "moral faith" I mean the unconditional trust in divine aid, in achieving all the good that, even with our most sincere efforts, lies beyond our power.[19]

The oscillation and ambivalence in these passages is amazing. Pure moral faith is self-sufficient and New Testament reports and historical beliefs are auxiliary. Yet the New Testament miracles may have been real and necessary, yet they are now no longer necessary. Yet the New Testament reports are still to be respected. We must do everything we can to make ourselves worthy of justification, yet we put our humble trust in God's means of reconciliation proclaimed by the apostles. . . . There is much unresolved tension in this letter. Perhaps we can take a cue from the fate of the early insight on evil as the positive opposite of the good and suggest that Kant's broodings over the idea of God being active in Jesus Christ which appear here and are such a departure from his public enlightened position (which is that of all his class of philosophes) remained submerged while he published his critical philosophy and especially his moral philosophy and reappeared only in 1793. (See note 30 of Chapter 7.) At any rate there is plenty of evidence to conclude that not all was clear cut in Kant's mind on the subject of religion in the silent seventies, when most of his efforts were absorbed by the preparation of the *Critique of Pure Reason* (1781).

The Sources of *Religion* as Indicative of the Object and Method

Few have paused to consider the fact that *Religion* contains very few quotations of, and very few references to, the numerous eighteenth century authors, philosophers, and theologians who wrote on religion and its relationship to philosophy. A look at the index in the Harper edition of *Religion* makes the point immediately: the names of Lord Herbert of Cherbury, Hume, Knutzen, Leibniz, Schultz, Semler, Spinoza, Tindal, and Toland are all there, but the references are always to the two introductions written by modern authors. This, coupled with the fact that Kant, no stranger to debate and no man to hesitate at publishing a public refutation of some author (if his time allowed), never entered into any polemical discussion in philosophy of religion, becomes strange indeed. (Of course an answer is found if one holds the view that Kant wanted no trouble and kept his real views to himself in these matters.)

No solution to this can be found in the view that Kant was not fond of name dropping and that the three Critiques proceed very well and very far without learned footnotes discussing the production of other scholars. *Religion* departs from Kantian habits in writing precisely in that it has an abundance of footnotes, long and short, and numerous references to other authors. The other authors, however, besides the customary sprinkling of classic, especially Latin, authors, are people such as Charlevoix, a Jesuit missionary in Canada who left reports on the religion of the Iroquois; Captain Samuel Hearne who gave an account of his travels through the land of the Arthabaskan and Dog Rib Indians; A. Reland, the Dutch orientalist who wrote on Islam; and Father Georgius who wrote on the Mongols and Tibetans. When recent German theological authors are referred to (like Reimarus, for instance), they are more often brought in for their contribution to the investigation of questions of historical facts than to questions of doctrine and ideas.

Kant's book contains a relative wealth of anthropological information on religious behaviour, attitudes, and beliefs across cultures, and a relative paucity of references to recent Western philosophical discussions of religion (relative of course to the average philosophical production in the eighteenth century). Kant documented himself abundantly in all that was available in the area of anthropological information.[20] Most of it was from travellers' reports; these, as P. Gay argued, were "the ancestors of treatises on cultural anthropology and political sociology."[21] His lectures on geography (and their conclusion that the non-theistic religions of the East can be authentic paths to the free and holy life) and the conversation at his table show that there was here on his part both a keen curiosity and a serious academic interest.

This is not to say that *Religion* was not influenced by eighteenth century philosophical and theological debates and investigation in Germany and the rest of Europe. Bohatec showed how wide was Kant's reading in the *Dogmatik*, that is, in the works of German and Swiss university professors of theology, and how decisive their contribution was to the final argument of *Religion*. It can also be pointed out that the work would have been impossible but for the various philosophical contributions to an understanding of religion, starting from Locke's deism (the influence of which we saw in the *Lectures on Ethics*) down to Hume's *Natural History of Religion*. But the contributions of all these authors are assimilated by Kant and enter into his own structure and discourse (although it is at times recognizable enough for the modern interpreter to write a footnote pointing to the source of this particular theme). There are a few exceptions (for instance, the debate between Pfenninger and Lavater and the orthodox theologians who insisted on miracles then but not now is examined) but such exceptions do not require a significant qualification of our general presentation.

The state of affairs, I believe, is indicative of a profound intention of Kant. It is evidence of Kant's deep-seated consciousness of being involved in doing original work (the very start of his discussion with the doctrine of radical evil should by itself make him aware that he is departing from the beaten path). Kant went through a very serious and intense apprenticeship before he wrote *Religion* through his familiarity with the results of a century of theological development and of philosophical results in the discussion of religion. But when he arrived at his own grasp of the problem, his own insights into the nature of it, and his own perspective upon its solution, the scaffolding went down and almost disappeared (to use a metaphor of his, albeit one used in a different context). Kant was not the man to rest content with a contribution of his that would be a further piece to be added to the dossier compiled by littérateurs, essayists, and amateur philosophers. Here again he had to be something of an arbiter who would put an end to the irrational conflict of opinion and would set the inquiry upon a firm new path. He therefore left aside the objectified doctrines of the schools.

If Kant did not write a piece that was in the mainstream of eighteenth century philosophical productions on religion, where is his own crucial redefinition of the issue to be found? The abundance of all the anthropological and *Religionsgeschichtlich* material in *Religion* provides us, I think, with the answer. He turned to as rich an account of historical religious life as he could provide. Such relative abundance of historical material is unprecedented for Kant. The writings on moral philosophy contain no such wealth of reference to the lived concrete elements of moral life or to social history (although the *Observations on the Feeling of the Sublime*, the *Lectures on Ethics*, the *Doctrine of Virtue*, and the *Anthropology* show that his moral philosophy also was capable of turning to psychological observation). The book on religion does not present itself as a discussion of the religious ideas of philosophers, and the Kantian discussion of the various theologies does not even reappear in it. I believe, therefore, that *Religion* represents Kant's access to the concepts of religious phenomena and of religious traditions, and the beginning of a properly philosophical investigation of the problems inherent in the new perspective created by the new concepts. Kant there was no longer discussing primarily the marks of the rational faith in God and the individual's religious attitude, but he did discuss there the nature of the religious community, of its own life, of the conflict between good and evil waged in that community and in all members of it, of the place of revealed doctrine in that community, of the role of the founder of the tradition, and so on. The discussion quickly focuses on the Christian tradition, on Jesus and the history of the Church. The issues of comparative religion however never totally recede. As Troeltsch put it, Kant, like his century, had a limited knowledge of the history of religion, but with little capital made the most of his opportunities.[22] Consistently, therefore, Kant's inquiry bears into religious life as lived in all religious communities in history, and shows interest for theology (rational and revealed) insofar as it seeks to guide and exercise authority over the religious life of the various traditions.[23] Finally Kant's inquiry also bears into the question inherited from the philosophy of history; namely, does the life of religion show evidence of a moral progress on the part of mankind?

I therefore agree with Troeltsch's statement that Kant saw three elements in the inquiry into religion as a social and historical reality:

    1. anthropological study (causal considerations);

    2. systematic arrangement of the material (critical and regulative elements, the search for the norm);

    3. systematic history: the relationship of actual life to the progressive realization in history of the ethical goal.[24]

And to Troeltsch I would add that this kind of investigation into religion, which is admittedly juxtaposed to older elements in *Religion* and thus does not constitute all there is in it, amounts at the same time to a departure from common eighteenth century discussions of the topic and to a departure from a previous Kantian position; we find there the conquest of a concept of religion wider than that implied in the recognition of all duties as divine command. The departure from the eighteenth century tradition means that religion is no longer seen as an objectified body of doctrines, or as a feeling the cause of which may be traced through psychology to human nature (another kind of objectifying process). The departure from the previous Kantian position means the access to a concept of religious community and religious tradition (and its subjection to philosophical investigation), added to the concept of religion as individual religiousness. Religion as individual religiousness had been analysed in the period of Kant's maturity in order to remain true to its rational and moral norm, and the doctrine of pure moral faith or rational faith was the answer. In Kant's old age religious communities and traditions were called upon to heed to a norm intrinsically valid for them and one which would enable them to conform more closely to the grand plan of Providence for the constitution of a moral commonwealth encompassing all men. The doctrine of the true church became the answer.

One more comment. Kant has been called the secular fulfilment of Luther or the secular fulfilment of Calvin and a body of literature sees him as being the final (or the inevitable) philosophical outcome of the Protestant Reformation.[25] There is enough truth in that for the view to endure. However nowhere are Luther and Calvin quoted in *Religion* and neither is the Protestant Reformation presented as a turning point in Kant's history of religious progress. As a matter of fact, it is completely ignored. The next important turning point in the history of religious progress after Jesus is the Enlightenment. Kant would have agreed with Troeltsch's strictures against those who saw in Luther the father of modernity. If *Religion* is undoubtedly the work of a Protestant, it is indebted to the Protestant principle more than to the Protestant ecclesiastical tradition, and Kant felt free to draw upon any aspect of Catholic substance. He repeatedly came closer to Protestant doctrine than to Catholic doctrine, but he also warned that there are "many laudable examples of Protestant Catholics" and "still more examples, and offensive ones, of arch-Catholic Protestants."[26]

The Structure of the Inquiry

If one accepts our two previous conclusions, namely, that Kant was led to an investigation of the religious life because of the problems inherent in the limitations of the power of our freedom (or because of the historicity of freedom) and that *Religion* represents in its new elements a fresh investigation which focuses on the life of religion in its social and historical dimensions, there still remains one more question to be settled. What is the inner source of the vigorous originality of the work on religion, or the spring that gives its energy to the investigation?

Two schools of interpretation clash here. On the one hand some authors see the pivot of the work in the doctrine of radical evil. Our freedom has limited power because evil in us either defeats our impulses or deflects our good intentions, or because evil in others tempts our virtue and destroys our achievements. Religion in this case is relevant because it penetrates to the core of the hearts, achieves there a conversion, a regeneration (or a redemption) that defeats evil at its innermost source. On the other hand some authors find the pivot of the work in the doctrine of the moral community and in the overcoming of the individualistic standpoint found previously in Kant's moral philosophy. Our freedom has limited power in this case because the realities of social life always divert our pure moral intentions into pragmatically necessary arrangements (moral man and immoral society . . .). The individual may strive after the good and act from duty alone but can never realize in groups the ideals of a society of friendship based upon morality alone. All we find in society are coercive controls of evil and balance of power, but no positive encouragement to virtue. Religion in this case is relevant because we find in the religious community a moral association, where the social reality is a support to the virtuous man rather than a perpetual temptation, and where begins a progressive ethicization of all social relations that moves towards the realization of the Kingdom of God on earth.[27]

A look at the structure of the inquiry in *Religion* may settle the claims of each interpretation. At first sight the line of the argument is relatively clear. The four books are organized for the sake of a discussion of a conflict between evil and the good principle and of the ultimate victory of good over evil. The titles of the first three books indicate that. Thus the discussion begins with the notion of radical evil, and goes on with the conflict and with the victory. The progressive line is unbroken until the last book, which discusses service and pseudo-service of God in the church, namely discusses the permanent temptation for moral evil in the very institution, the church, which is the place where the evil principle comes under the sovereignty of the good principle. (Kant seems to be accustomed to such pessimistic last words: the essay on progress in *The Strife of Faculties* demonstrates that we can expect progress and finishes with a conclusion that has a disillusioned tone.)[28] So we can see *Religion* as a work organized for a discussion of the nature of religion through the understanding of the solution provided by religion to the moral conflict created by radical evil, with a last warning against seeing the church as the home of unadulterated good.

A second look, however, will show that the discussion of the conflict between the good principle and the evil principle in the second book consistently speaks of the individual and that the solution of the conflict or the victory of the good principle found in the third book is afforded by the foundation by God of a moral community, the belonging to which is the key to the individual's improvement. Book Four then gives the necessary qualifications by calling attention to the temptations that institutionalized religious life affords to individual motivation and virtue. It seems then that the tension between individual moral life (powerless alone, but freshly tempted in groups) and the life of the moral community offers a better guiding thread to the dialectic of the last three of the four books.

The sequence of the four books, however, far from indicates the whole of the subject matter handled in the work. There is also at the end of each book a "General Observation" on parerga, namely on aspects of religious life and doctrine which religion, when it is kept within the limits of reason alone, cannot integrate, but which it nevertheless cannot ignore. And these four sections create numerous problems of their own. Generally speaking, they discuss works of grace, miracles, mysteries, and means of grace, although none gives a clearly visible title and one hardly finds full and systematic discussions of the topic indicated.[29] None of the four exhibits a close connection to the topic of the book to which it is appended, this being especially true of the second and third one. They all have in common the general fact that they tend to lead to a discussion of what God does, rather than of what we should do to become worthy of his favour and thus draw upon a distinction found much earlier in Kant. They all bear upon doctrines which church theologians tend to consider as the core of the positive or historical faith they teach. Thus they all tend to belong more or less to revealed religion rather than to rational religion, to use the older deistic division. Finally, Kant did not manage by any means to maintain a strict division between the philosophical doctrine of the four books and the doctrine that is beyond the limits of reason alone and is placed in the parerga. (The second book, for instance, contains a lengthy discussion of grace.)

Thus if we follow the indication that Kant's work discusses not the pure religion of reason but a religion remaining within the confines of reason, namely a religion that encompasses more than pure reason while remaining under the regulative influence of reason, then the major problem of the book and its major achievement is to be found in the uneasy balance between the four books on the one hand and the four general observations on the other, and in the unstable distinction they establish between those aspects of religious life and belief which can be shown to agree or disagree with reason, and those aspects of which one cannot say either but which are still worthy of respect and are especially intriguing, since, by speaking of divine providential action, they seem to hold the ultimate key of the answer to the question of hope. Should this be the correct interpretation, then the very unsystematic nature of the "General Observations" becomes awkward and the conclusion is inevitable that the Kantian project is not perfectly carried out.

Further evidence of the technical imperfections exhibited by the structure of the whole work is found in the fact that some extremely important doctrines (such as those on the schematism of analogy, damnation, and the Judgement) find a place for themselves only in long, weighty footnotes.

These facts about the structure of *Religion* indicate that it is complex enough to make the search for the single insight that gives systematic unity of the whole possibly somewhat presumptuous. However, because the work does open with a book on radical evil, and because the confrontation with the problem of evil and the dissolution of all traditional theodicies does seem to have been an intellectual earthquake of some magnitude in the life of Kant,[30] it was, I conclude, the doctrine of radical evil, as the most radical challenge to the idea of our freedom having power to reform the world and as the most radical questioning of all our hopes, that moved Kant to turn to a philosophy of religion in search of solutions to a problem that was exercising him. (And it is also the doctrine that gives most offense to the camp of the Enlightenment.) Conversely, its handling of the problem of evil and its finding of new grounds for hope gives to the religious life, as seen in the community and in history, the most specific core of its originality. Thus we will see in the first three books the main meat of the work, and will tend to see in the fourth book a kind of appendix of application containing practical warnings and advice to the leaders and members of the religious community.

This conclusion does not mean in any way that I minimize the importance of the acquisition by Kant of a concept of moral community. Its cruciality to the doctrine of religion is obvious and its impact upon his view of progress in history indubitable. The idea of moral association as distinct from civil or political association is a profound and important theme in his authorship.

Finally, the place Kant found for the parerga remains an equally decisive foundation stone in Kant's edification of a doctrine of religion. I shall accordingly devote to it a specific chapter in order to try to bring greater clarity to the issue than Kant achieved.

The Nature of Evil

To begin a discussion of religion by an analysis of evil is a common procedure in apologetic theology. Pascal is perhaps the most famous example of the train of thought that begins by portraying man's misery without God.[31] Such a procedure however is rare in philosophical theories of religion, especially those of the eighteenth century. Ruyssen accordingly proposed to see in this starting point a memory of the beliefs of Kant's youth.[32] Kant's letter to Friederich Wilhelm II, protesting the accusation of having deprecated Christianity, also implies the conventional view that the very doctrine of evil in his book makes clear the need for a revealed doctrine.[33] Jaspers however is convinced that only with radical evil does Kant's doctrine of religion reach its true philosophical depth.[34] Even though Kant's notion of moral evil was slow in appearing (the moral philosophy skirted it and the philosophy of history led away from it by maintaining the optimistic emphasis upon the instrumentality of evil to some further subsequent good), I believe we can assume from our previous results that it is no foreign body in Kant's thought, and is not introduced in the spirit of making concessions to any orthodoxy.[35] It is rather the ultimate outcome of Kant's steady disaffection from monistic and metaphysical teleological thinking and of the slow development of a deeper and livelier religious sense characterized by the insight into the split between the world of fact and the world of moral ideas, and by the faith in an ultimate reconciliation of the former with the latter.

The key part of Kant's doctrine of evil is his presentation of the origin of evil. Such origin can be found only in man and in man's freedom.

> Man *himself* must make or have made himself into whatever, in a moral sense, whether good or evil, he is or is to become. Either condition must be an effect of his free choice; for otherwise he could not be held responsible for it and could therefore be *morally* neither good nor evil.[36]

But why should man's will choose evil? Or rather, to use a formulation more directly arising out of the critical method: how is man constituted that moral evil is possible?[37] Kant quickly parted company from the moralists and theologians who see the ground of evil in the drives of man's animal nature.[38] Happiness, as the wholeness of the desires of our sensible nature, is a good. It is a good, however, which must be subordinated to the laws of freedom and the rational desires of pure practical reason. The crossroads of the will is thus a matter of having to choose between two different kinds of good. As Silber put it: "The evil man is one who freely decides to subordinate the demands of the law to the demands of his sensible nature."[39] Or as Krüger put it in a formulation consonant with his interpretation of Kant's metaphysics: good and evil are two modes of being. The good is unconditional opening before God as law-giver, governor, and judge; evil is the closing of the human being to the condition or the place he received. "Both are grounded in the spontaneous submission to an obligation. Man appropriates either the ends of God or the ends of the surrounding world."[40] Note that the latter are good—in their place in the teleological hierarchy. Being a choice among goods, man's evil is free, it is an act of a genuine moral nature and the first such act of a self is not conditioned by predispositions to evil or evil drives. The consequence of such an act is the maiming or negation of the personality of the violator.

To clarify this point one needs to bring out the refinements to his doctrine of freedom added by Kant in *Religion*. Kant had previously distinguished between *Willkür*, will in the sense of power to choose, a faculty which has temporal manifestations, and *Wille* as the pure rational will which, unlike the former, is not free since it prescribes to itself the eternally valid law of freedom. (This will makes us members of the noumenal world.)[41] (The two wills reappear in the *Foundations of the Metaphysics of Morals* as negative freedom—the power to act independently of foreign external causes, that is, spontaneity, and as positive freedom—the property of the will to be a law to itself, that is, autonomy.)[42] When *Willkür* makes the evil choice, that is, chooses to be determined by the inclinations of man's sensible nature rather than by the demand of the moral law or of *Wille*, it makes a heteronomous choice. Nevertheless this act is not the act of a slave. It is a free act, it is an expression of what Silber called "transcendental freedom"[43] as he referred to our autonomous freedom qua noumenal beings. This free act, however, is not a fulfilling realization of our freedom, but an abnegation of it. It is an enslaving act. As an act of absolute freedom it diminishes rather than enhances our relative freedom and as such it denies our personality. As Silber put it:

> Heteronomous and irrational actions involve the denial and misuse of the power of spontaneity, the failure to actualize its potentialities, and, therefore, the destruction of the person as a spontaneous being.[44]

The momentous consequences of moral evil are further brought out by the concept of disposition, a concept which Kant really developed only in *Religion* and which Silber called the most important single contribution of the book to Kant's ethical theory.[45] Disposition accounts for continuity and persistent responsibility in the exercise of *Willkür*. Each act of the free will strengthens a good or evil disposition in us, and a strong disposition becomes the ultimate subjective ground of our decision. Thus our free decisions can stem from our moral character while remaining manifestations of our freedom. The quality of the moral disposition in others is hidden from us and can be only inferred, although God intuits it. Silber summarized the significance of the concept in this way: disposition "is the enduring pattern of intention that can be inferred from the many discrete acts of Willkür and reveals their ultimate motive."[46]

Now we can see in what sense Kant discerned radical evil in human nature. It is not that man's animal nature is the source of evil (although it is frail), it is not that his social being (or the fact that he is existing in a state of culture) is the source of evil (although this is a temptation to impurity in motives), but it is the fact that his moral self, his personality which alone is capable of wickedness, again and again departs from the moral law and thus creates in him upon a free moral basis a real evil moral disposition, or an entrenched propensity to evil.

> . . . the proposition, Man is evil, can mean only, he is conscious of the moral law but has nevertheless adopted into his maxim the (occasional) deviation therefrom. He is evil by nature, means but this, that evil can be predicated of man as a species; not that such a quality can be inferred from the concept of his species (that is, of man in general)—for then it would be necessary; but rather that from what we know of man through experience we cannot judge otherwise of him, or, that we may presuppose evil to be subjectively necessary to every man, even to the best. Now this propensity must itself be considered as morally evil, yet not as a natural predisposition but rather as something that can be imputed to man, and consequently it must consist in maxims of the will which are contrary to the law.[47]

Now we know what it means to be radically evil. The question of fact, however, is still open. Are we evil in this way? The evidence for such a universal, corrupt propensity as rooted in man is twofold. First of all is "the multitude of crying examples which experience of *the actions* of men put before our eyes."[48] And secondly moral introspection shows in ourselves "a certain insidiousness of the human heart." "This dishonesty, by which we humbug ourselves and which thwarts the establishing of a true moral disposition in us, extends itself outwardly also to falsehood and deception of others."[49]

Such account of the origin and nature of moral evil has the advantage of providing a theoretical account of the possibility of the duplicity and ambivalence of human volition and of placing the root of evil in the will itself. But the concepts of radical evil and that of disposition play interesting havoc with the fundamental Kantian dualism between the noumenal world and the phenomenal world.[50] Kant seems to have been aware of it, since he said in his preface to the second edition that the terms noumenon and phenomenon are "used only because of the schools"[51] (a rather interesting *obiter dictum* about the distinction which was presented as the most solid achievement of the first Critique!). The discussion of the will began with such a distinction. *Wille* is noumenal and a-temporal. *Willkür* acts in time and results in actions which are observable in the phenomenal world. But dispositions and the propensity to evil are neither noumenal nor phenomenal realities. They result from the exercise of our freedom and thus must be represented as having a beginning in time, yet being characteristics of our moral character, they as such are not visible in the phenomenal world.

This state of affairs is worthy of notice first of all because it represents one of the original areas of inquiry of *Religion*. Such inquiry —which is neither into our absolute freedom and its categorical imperative nor into the the consequences of our moral action in the phenomenal world, but into our moral character, the power of our will, and our relative freedom—is one of the major further developments which the book on *Religion* represents in Kant's authorship and it goes a long way towards modifying the finality of the two-standpoint theory. If the investigation into the relative aspects of our freedom amounts to yet another bridge between the phenomenal and the noumenal worlds and allows us to state that Kant's two standpoints theory is not his final word, it must be added that this bridge, like those built in the *Critique of Judgement*, is a slim one. As soon as Kant sought to further delineate the significance of the dispositions, he returned to a disjunction that is analogous (although not an exact parallel) to that between the two worlds. On the one hand man's moral dispositions are morally extremely important: they enable us to judge (by inference) a man's character (good or evil); they enable us to discern captivity to the evil principle in even the best of men; they enable us finally to see evil as a real captivity of our relative freedom. On the other hand, the moral dispositions are not morally decisive: however depraved, all men can fight the evil principle and, however enslaved to evil our relative freedom may be, our absolute freedom ultimately remains unaffected. The bridge between the two worlds, in other words, is not wide enough or strong enough to allow our evil dispositions, captive though we may be to them, to destroy our absolute or transcendental freedom. Radically evil though we are, we are not undividedly or absolutely evil.

The same disjunction appears in the case of two other crucial concepts which are brought forward in the first book of the work, namely that of the fall into evil and that of moral conversion. The fall from original innocence into evil and the return from radical evil to the life of virtue are two morally crucial "phenomena" which presuppose an intimate interaction in a temporal moral world between the a-temporal world of noumena on the one hand and the phenomenal world on the other.

The fall into evil had a beginning in time and in the time of each self (or else we could not possibly be responsible for it personally; thus we must always look for it in a previous period of our lives).[52] It is an event, however, which affects our whole moral nature and our worth before God. (It does not merely create an unpleasant consequence in the phenomenal world.) A dilemma now exists because "it is a contradiction to seek the temporal origin of man's moral character,"[53] since our moral character does not depend upon inclinations or other manifestations of the temporal world of sense but upon a decision of our noumenal self.

As a solution Kant accepted "the manner of presentation which the Scriptures use"[54] in Genesis. He did not see in this presentation an explanation but a valid representation, valid because the story of the Fall of Adam can be appropriated by each of us as telling a truth about ourselves. "*Mutato nomine de te fabula narratur.*"[55] The rational origin of evil "remains inscrutable to us,"[56] because evil is contingent and not necessary in any way. But evil cannot be shown to have a phenomenal origin. Contingent though it is, evil came from a moral decision and resulted in a powerful disposition that has moral impact. In other words moral evil cannot be rooted either in the noumenal or the phenomenal world. It can rise or maintain its power only in the in-between bridge of temporal free acts and of the dispositions arising from it. And as such it can only be represented symbolically.

Similar difficulties arise when we try to represent the "reascent from evil to good."[57] On the one hand it seems that virtue can be acquired or reacquired in time only little by little (by a gradual reformation). And the reascent will be a matter of progressive change of practice. But on the other hand, since the core of evil lies in a disposition, what is required is rather a revolution in the disposition, a change of heart, or a kind of rebirth which takes place once and for all. That alone could produce a man who would be morally and not just legally good.[58]

As a solution to this dilemma Kant suggested that in the judgement of men conversion will appear as a gradual reformation, whereas "for him who penetrates to the intelligible ground of the heart" this change can be regarded as a revolution.[59] But what of it in our own judgement? This solution is basically unsatisfactory and fails to bridge the gap between the phenomenal and the noumenal worlds as well as the story of Adam did. Perhaps the answer lies in the fact that for conversion Kant could not find a *fabula* as satisfactory as that found for the Fall. For the story of Adam by presenting us a live moral drama gives an account which, while it is not rational, is not trivial either and shows us both the contingency of evil and its weighty impact upon our moral character, gives us a representation in which the absolute and relative aspects of freedom rather than being split by analysis are welded together in a representative act: the contingent act of a momentous consequence, or the temporal act of eternal significance. As Bruch pointed out, Kant may have been presenting an unorthodox interpretation of the narrative in Genesis, but he could not do without it, and that point can perhaps be extended to his whole attitude to "revealed religion."[60] At any rate I believe that such "representations" can be shown repeatedly to be Kant's solution to dilemmas in his philosophy of religion.[61]

A further dilemma arises because radical evil, being rooted in our will itself, appears to be such that human powers alone cannot defeat it. And yet demands of the moral law make it imperative that we, being free, should be able to overcome it.[62] Our relative freedom may be radically captive to evil but our absolute freedom remains absolute. This, however, leads to the problem of divine assistance and as such belongs to the parerga and thus will be discussed later.[63] At this stage it is important to emphasize that the doctrine of evil, unlike the doctrine of unbelief presented in the context of the discussion of rational moral faith, makes of evil something more than sloth and something less than full-scale rebellion against the good.[64] Wickedness is Kant's favourite term for it. Evil for him is the conscious and willful ignorance of the moral law when it interferes with the natural incentives. But it is not and cannot be a total disowning and definitive rejection of the moral law whose demands remain with even the most evil of men. There is thus no perfectly alienated consciousness for Kant. Silber correctly interpreted Kant on this point:

> Kant tried to explain categorical moral obligation in such a way as to make it consistent with the Christian insight into the dark and irrational depths of human nature and, simultaneously, with platonic confidence that freedom and obligation are both ultimately grounded in reason.[65]

We encounter morality as an obligation not just because we are finite (this is the position of the *Critique of Practical Reason*), but also because we are potentially and actually wicked, that is, disposed to depart from it for contingent and irrational reasons of our own which we willfully judge good reasons or good enough for us. But we cannot surrender totally to unreason and the moral law never deprives us of its insight nor ever of its motivating power.

> Kant, unlike Plato, recognized that men can will evil intentionally. But Kant agrees with Plato by denying that men will evil for its own sake. Both assertions can be made with consistency by Kant because he recognizes the heterogeneity of the good and hence can designate the natural good as the object of volition of the wicked will which is fully conscious that willing that object is morally wrong.[66]

There is thus no manicheism whatsoever in Kant's doctrine of radical evil. Evil is universal, radical, and persistent, and it is a real, positive force in conflict with good.[67] But it cannot erase totally the original goodness or the predisposition to good and the power of the moral law. There was a time and there may be one yet when the sovereignty of the good principle remained undisputed. However dramatic is the current conflict between the two principles, there is no parallelism between them, for one can be ultimately defeated while the other cannot.[68] In the same year, 1793, Kant declared that evil destroys itself while good maintains itself.[69] This leads us to the problem of the conflict of the two principles and it is the topic for the next chapter.

To conclude, Kant's position on radical evil can be called, in spite of all it says about the universal entrenched captivity of our relative freedom, a fundamental optimism or rationalism because it leaves our absolute freedom untouched, and can be said to run counter to orthodox Christian doctrine, and its idea of total depravity. It is certainly true that for Kant there was no invincible ignorance of the law, and no absolutely powerless consciousness of the law. We are not innocent for Kant, but we can struggle against evil. We are radically evil, there is call for the confession of guilt and total unworthiness before God, but there is no call for total despair. This however is no ground for assimilating Kant to the tradition that sees in evil only the privation of good. Kant did manage a synthesis of the Christian and of the Platonic position on evil, two positions which we are more trained to see as incompatible than as reconcilable since we now tend to assimilate the Christian concept of evil with the existentialist one and its premise of irrationalism.

Having emphasized that the self is not totally powerless before evil for Kant, it is only fair to add that while he departed from some Christian doctrines, Kant did recover a prophetic insight the philosophers of his century had forgotten: the heart is crooked beyond all imagination. Kant used the metaphor of men being made out of crooked wood,[70] a metaphor which Augustine and Luther had used before him to characterize the permanence of man's selfish bent.[71] To Kant the metaphor pointed rather to man's shiftiness and duplicity, to man's permanent bent away from honest self-knowledge. The metaphor of the crooked appears in a German proverb:

Je Krümerer Holz, je bessere Krücke
Je ärger Schalck, je grösser Glücke.

This proverb was quoted with some approval by Leibniz in his *Theodicy*.[72] But this optimistic bit of folk wisdom and its claim that something good is bound to come out of one's crookedness (at least for oneself) is to Kant moral alibi and insidious self-deception, a "foul taint in our race,"[73] one of the very evidences of the radical evil in our nature, and it is precisely what Kant left behind. Thus Kant radically broke with all suggestions—and they are numerous—that moral evil is something other than evil.

The Conflict between Good and Evil and the Life of Jesus

Book Two was written a period of time after Book One which had originally been published separately and begins with a summary of Kant's position on evil. It then proceeds to discuss "the legal claim of the good principle to sovereignty over man." A second section of the book examines "the legal claim of the evil principle" and the conflict between the two principles. (In fact the analysis of the conflict appears in both sections.) Consistent with the results of the doctrine of evil, the legal claim of the good principle turns out to be one that is permanently valid, whereas the legal claim of the evil principle turns out to be a claim contracted in time and subsequently broken in principle.

Man in his complete moral perfection is the end of Creation and "the idea of him proceeds from God's very being; hence is no created thing but his only-begotten Son."[74] Kant began his discussion of the legal claim of the good principle *in mediis rebus* with something he found in the Christian tradition, namely the representation of Jesus Christ as morally perfect man and only Son of God, or, as he calls him, as the personified idea of the good principle. The method is worthy of notice: Kant began with a representation available in a religious tradition, although he presented it in terms that show the mark of his own interpretative activity (one that emphasized the moral perfection of Jesus).

> This ideal of a humanity pleasing to God (hence of such moral perfection as is possible to an earthly being who is subject to wants and inclinations) we can represent to ourselves only as the idea of a person who would be willing not merely to discharge all human duties himself and to spread about him goodness as widely as possible by precept and example, but even, though tempted by the greatest allurements, to take upon himself every affliction, up to the most ignominious death, for the good of the world and even for his enemies. For man can frame to himself no concept of the degree and strength of a force like that of a moral disposition except by picturing it as encompassed by obstacles, and yet in the face of the fiercest onslaughts, victorious.[75]

The next point follows directly from Kant's method. What is the objective reality of the Idea? "From the practical point of view this idea is completely real in its own right, for it resides in our morally legislative reason. We *ought* to conform to it."[76] Morally, strictly speaking, we need no such historical example or personification of the good principle for "this idea as an archetype is already present in our reason." Thus the archetype is not a "representation" comparable to the account of the Fall in Genesis. Our absolute freedom is at any time the source of a clear moral law. And should one try to enhance the moral value of the example of Jesus by endowing him with superhuman qualities of holiness, one really deprives him entirely of moral significance, because being so unlike us he could not be represented as an example for our imitation.

A footnote, however, proceeds to undertake a qualification by bringing in the point about the schematism of analogy and stating that only such personification can make moral qualities intelligible to us.

It is indeed a limitation of human reason, and one which is ever inseparable from it, that we can conceive of no considerable moral worth in the actions of a personal being without representing that person, or his manifestation, in human guise. This is not to assert that such worth is in itself (κατ' ἀλήθειαν) so conditioned, but merely that we must always resort to some analogy to natural existences to render supersensible qualities intelligible to ourselves.[77]

The moral import of this personification is clear: man, evil though he is, must and can "make his own disposition like unto" that of Jesus or must appropriate his righteousness by making his disposition "at one with that of the archetype."[78] The victory of good over radical evil is to be found in a change of inner personal disposition. And the picture of the life of Jesus, showing the strength of the good disposition by showing its victory over the evil one, will facilitate this change. In this context, the picture of Jesus becomes a symbolic representation, and begins to be seen to be necessarily such in order to effect the change in our dispositions. Or, in the language Kant used in the first section when he presented the idea as he found it in the tradition (and as he interpreted it): "Man may . . . hope to become acceptable to God (and so be saved) through a practical faith in this Son of God."[79]

Three difficulties however stand in the way of our becoming good again through appropriation of the dispositions or righteousness found in the representation of Jesus. First a good disposition cannot be taken as the equivalent of a good life. The answer to this is that God will consider as essentially well-pleasing a man of good disposition, even though his life-conduct after conversion may remain defective. The second difficulty is that a man of good disposition has not any proof that this good disposition will remain constant. Kant added that too much confidence or not enough in this matter is perilous and may endanger perseverance in the good. In a solution strongly reminiscent of theological discussions of the assurance of salvation, Kant stated that a good and pure disposition "creates in us, though only indirectly, a confidence in its own permanence and stability, and is our Comforter (Paraclete) whenever our lapses make us apprehensive of its constancy."[80] The third difficulty is that radical evil means we have a personal and infinite debt, which cannot be wiped out by a mere change of disposition or even perserverance in good conduct.[81] Where, for one thing, is the punishment? During the change of heart, said Kant, when the old man is crucified. Can one think of the Son of God as bearing as vicarious substitute the guilt of sin, and offering his merit to us, not as something to which we have a legal claim, but out of sheer grace?[82] Kant did not really answer this question but stated that no positive use can be made of such an idea of *justificatio impii*, and much negative results may follow (such as evasions from the real change of heart).

The whole discussion of the conflict between the two principles starts again in the second section on the legal claim of the evil principle and the conflict between the two principles. This discussion is strongly indebted to federal theology, and its ideas of covenants man entered into and is bound to (just as the previous discussion is much indebted to Anselm's handling of the atonement). And in this second section Kant was led to use more openly theological language.

The first example of it is the summary presentation of the history of salvation. Man yielded a dominion over his heart to the evil principle and thus a Kingdom of evil was set up, to which each man again becomes covenanted through his own consent.

> Because of its legal claim to sovereignty over man the good principle did, indeed, secure itself through the establishment (in the Jewish theocracy) of a form of government instituted solely for the public and exclusive veneration of its name.[83]

But this religion, which Kant rather called a government, did not undertake an effective war against evil.

> . . . there suddenly appeared a person whose wisdom was purer even than that of previous philosophers, as pure as though it had descended from heaven. This person proclaimed himself as indeed truly human with respect to his teachings and example, yet also as an envoy from heaven who, through an original innocence, was not involved in the bargain with the evil principle into which, through their representatives, their first parents, the rest of the human race had entered, and "in whom, therefore, the prince of this world had no part." Hereby the sovereignty of this prince was endangered.[84]

The second example of Kant's greater wealth of theological discourse in this section is in the description of the life of Jesus. The devil tried in vain to recruit Jesus into his kingdom.

When this attempt failed he not only took away from this stranger in his house all that could make his earthly life agreeable (to the point of direst poverty), but he also incited against him all the persecutions by means of which evil men can embitter life, [causing him] such sorrows as only the well-disposed can feel deeply, by slandering the pure intent of his teachings in order to deprive him of all following—and finally pursuing him to the most ignominious death. Yet he achieved nothing by this onslaught through the agency of a worthless mob upon his steadfastness and forthrightness in teaching and example for the sake of the good.[85]

This death (the last extremity of human suffering) was . . . a manifestation of the good principle, that is, of humanity in its moral perfection, and an example for everyone to follow. The account of his death ought to have had, and could have had, the greatest influence upon human hearts and minds at that time, and, indeed at all times: for it exhibited the freedom of the children of heaven in most striking contrast to the bondage of the mere Son of Earth.[86]

So the moral outcome of the combat, as regards the hero of this story (up to the time of his death), is really not the *conquering* of the evil principle—for its kingdom still endures, and certainly a new epoch must arrive before it is overthrown—but merely the breaking of its power to hold, against their will, those who have so long needed subjects, because another dominion (for man must be subject to some rule or other), a moral dominion, is now offered them as an asylum where they can find protection for their morality if they wish to forsake the former sovereignty.[87]

Here Kant does seem to have found a dramatic story to show the power of the good principle in its conquest over the evil one, and the power of a good man to act upon and liberate the captive freedom (in the relative sense) of those who are preys of evil. The final paragraph, however, after calling this story so reminiscent of the *Christus Victor* theme in Christian doctrine "a vivid mode of representation," proceeds to divest it of "its mystical veil" and reduce it to this meaning, one that was previously established in the course of Kant's discussion: "There exists absolutely no salvation for man apart from the sincerest adoption of genuinely moral principles into his disposition."[88] The demands of absolute freedom prevail again. One cannot help but feel something of a letdown. The symbol of Christ's conquest over evil as a "symbol for reflection" does not seem to have been one which gave Kant "much to think." The same disappointment is maintained in the "General Observation" which follows and which is a discussion of miracles. In fact this discussion has nothing to do with evil, but is related to the previous discussion only by the fact that the New Testament tells us that Jesus performed miracles. In fact we would want Kant to look more closely into the hypotheses of grace, forgiveness, and substitution, which his book on the conflict between the two principles repeatedly touched upon. This, however, he did not do at this point.[89]

Of all the books in *Religion*, Book Two (with possibly Book Four) is the one that gives the best basis for seeing in the work a public confession of deism (as De Vleeschauwer and Greene do).[90] For in the core of the argument of the book we find the following classical positions of deism (or of a moral version of deism).

1. The major significance of Jesus is that he was the first to teach publicly the moral law which men, however, could have discovered by their unaided reason.

2. The life of Jesus is an exemplification of what reason tells us in the first place.

3. Such exemplification is useful on account of the frailty of people's minds, and the canon of natural religion is accessible to us without the historical vehicle that may have been necessary to our coarser ancestors or to the simpler of our contemporaries.

But I find even in this second book considerable tension and believe I can show that Kant, under the impact of his growing understanding of symbols, either modified each one of these points, or added something to them, which meant that he moved beyond the classical deist position.

1. The novelty of the teaching of Jesus is such for Kant that he does find it meaningful to say that it came from on high and that he is the Son of God. Furthermore the significance of his life is not only what he taught but also that he broke the power of the evil principle over mankind. He thus not only taught the law that issues from our freedom in its absolute sense but also in his own relative freedom conquered the evil principle. Kant here was very cautious, because he was very afraid of naive designations of Jesus as loving Saviour into whose

arms we should flee, but the presentation of Jesus as mere teacher does not account for the full reverence he had for him.[91] Kant here was ambivalent and we find a good insight into his oscillations on this paragraph on Jesus found in the notes which served to the preparation of *Religion*.

> When I see a being, who in possession of the highest bliss submits himself to the deepest misery in order to allow to guilty creatures participation in this bliss, I am inclined to the greatest veneration and gratitude towards him; but as soon as I believe that there is thereby an advantage for me which spares me the need to satisfy eternal justice then I sink again into the lowest ranks of servitude. But when reason tells me that precisely this being must serve me as an example to rise to the same level of morality, and that I must find in myself the disposition to become like him, that so elevates my soul that it animates it and causes the frailty of my nature to disappear.[92]

The issue emerges more clearly. Kant did not want any mercenary devotion to a Saviour, but he did find Jesus to be a liberating figure who exercises saving power over his disciples, and gives fresh power to their freedom in the relative sense in its struggle against the evil principle.

2. Kant indeed was so conscious of our own responsibility to defeat evil in ourselves that he repeatedly stated that we imitate Jesus, we adopt his dispositions in such a way that the initial action is always ours. The demands of absolute freedom forced him to do so. It was an opinion of long standing with him that "imitation has no place in morality and that examples are only for encouragement," for any morality that follows inspiring examples rather than the original law which is in our reason is heteronomous in nature.[93] Yet the example of Jesus is significant because it does assure us that the archetype is realizable in this life and thus a crucial and perhaps decisive kind of encouragement.

In one passage Kant departed from his moral assumption that the dispositions of Jesus are morally significant only if we autonomously make them our own and that imitation is permissible only if we consciously recognize him as personification of a moral law which is in us. By his example (of resistance to the allurements of evil, even to the point of obedience unto death) "he opens the portals of freedom" to mankind and he "gathers together among them a people for his possession."[94] These rare instances of positive verbs to describe the action of Jesus towards us rather than what we do in relationship to him, open the prospect of a permissible influence of his disposition upon ours, thus departing from the usual picture of morally undertaken active imitation on our part. The same point reappeared the next year at the end of the essay on *The End of All Things* (1794) where Christianity is said to promote love for the observance of duty and to elicit such love, because its founder is not one who demands obedience but one "who brings to the heart of his fellowmen their own well-understood wills." Christianity is thus worthy of love and elicits in us love as "the free reception of the will of another person into one's maxim."[95] Such loving salvific influence in this case does not appear to be heteronomy. Theonomy as a matter of fact is the word Tillich coined for it. That Kant in his reflection upon Jesus came to use such description is all the more remarkable because of his earlier insistence upon absolute autonomy. It is for us evidence that unlike most deists he did not simply reduce the significance of Jesus to possibilities inherent in a moral philosophy that puts a strong emphasis upon autonomy.

3. While Kant in Book Two agreed with the deists to give to historical representations only the value of exemplifications necessary on account of our frailty, he departed from most of them in holding that frailty to be one in which he himself as a philosopher participated. Thus he respected such "personifications" and "vivid modes of representation." He did not speak of them with the condescension of most enlightened deists who saw such "fables" as useful for primitive Jews, old women, savages, peasants, and humble pious artisans, but who presumably did perfectly well without them themselves. Kant spoke of these stories with reverence and shared no urge to debunk them in the privacy of his circle of enlightened friends and readers. (Thus, for instance, he was concerned to maintain the moral purity of Jesus and refuted Bahrdt and Reimarus who saw in the story of his death a suicide or a political conspiracy.)[96] It seems that Kant wanted the picture of the life of Jesus to have a positive influence upon our "enlightened" imagination, yet did not want the imagination to run wild. When in a corner, Kant always chose the rationalism of the Enlightenment rather than the unreason of the *Schwärmerei*. (I find him most interesting when he is not backed into this corner.)[97] Hence the strange seesaw effect of the last pages of the book: Kant gave a vivid and moving presentation of the life of Jesus and its victorious struggle against the evil principle and then reduced its meaning to a dry, abstract, minimalist philosophical and rationalistic interpretation.

On all three points, therefore, I believe that Kant even in this book moved beyond the scheme of deism: Jesus gained a victory over evil, he exercised a decisive historical influence and he still exercises an influence on us, and vivid representations are valuable even for philosophers. Yet on each point the restricting doctrines of natural religion as understood by deism exercised a severe control upon Kant's own responsiveness to Christian symbols and the bent of a live Christian piety. But the control is far from being totally victorious.

Tension reappears on the matter of conversion. Kant responded here to a religious presentation of the victorious struggle of the good principle against the evil one that brings great strain to the framework established by his own previous ethical theory, and ultimately bursts through it. Hence the three difficulties he raised and tried to deal with. The notion of conversion which Kant examined amounts after all to a beginning of absolute and eternal significance that begins in time, and that is not a possibility inherent in Kant's concept of time. Everything in Kant's previous doctrine led him to say either that one's essential moral nature (citizenship in the Kingdom of ends) does not change, or that only a good conduct in time can compensate for evil conduct in time. Yet the doctrine of conversion plays havoc with all this by introducing the notion of one's becoming well pleasing to God (and for all eternity, an essential change if there is one) after having been guilty before him, through an inner moral change located at some point in one's biographical development. The doctrine of conversion was to prevail against all difficulties and thanks to solutions which are not always satisfactory. The doctrine also creates moral difficulties (How can a bad will will to become a good will?) and is nevertheless not rejected. That Kant did not solve the problem of conversion is indicated by the fact among others that he did affirm imperfections in the regenerate man but could not in any way account for it (weakness is no answer for the man who had the power to change his will from good to bad). Here again the moral difficulties, weighty as they are, do not lead to the abandonment of such a crucial religious concept.[98]

Another tension—but one with a different outcome—is occasioned by the religiously important idea of forgiveness and justification. Everything in Kant's moral philosophy ruled out the idea of vicarious suffering and gracious forgiveness. Much in the Christian religious tradition leads to such ideas. A head-on collision was inevitable. Silber put it this way: "Even God cannot help the guilty individual without violating the moral law."[99] Here Kant's previous results prevail and the notion of forgiveness is kept at arm's length. The divine attribute of justice prevails over that of goodness and the divine judge in a crunch will always be just rather than good.[100] The debt incurred by sin being moral is not transmissible. The results of sin are not annullable. Thus guilt cannot be forgiven, transferred, or annulled. It must be atoned for by the guilty himself.[101]

The second book of *Religion* thus illustrates the character of the work as a transitional work. It exhibits a transition in two senses. First of all it is still partly within the framework established by the classical doctrine of natural religion for which the philosophical task when confronting any given religious tradition is to see which ones of its doctrines correspond to those of natural religion and which ones do not. But it is also partly within the framework of a new philosophy of religion for which the philosophical task is first of all to understand what a religious tradition says, what it means, and what testimony the members of it give about the nature of their religious life in it, and next examine what normative criteria emerge out of the context of the religious life itself.

Secondly the work is transitional in that some aspect of it obeys the norms established by the older Kantian definition of religion (the recognition of all duties as divine commands) and thus again and again uses pure moral faith as the norm of religious faith (that is, forgiveness is immoral). But at the same time it extends the concept of religion to encompass the whole of the religious life in its socio-historical dimensions and thus begins to conceive of a moral and religious fellowship in which relative freedoms are interrelated and apparently take no offense at the thought of one bearing the burden of the other. We thus gain a glimpse of a fellowship very different from that based merely upon the mutual respect which absolute freedoms have for each other. This leads us to the next section and the third book of the work.

It must be emphasized that the two definitions of transition, while they have in common the new interest in the social and historical dimensions of religious life and in the search for its norms there, are not at all parallel. For the transition away from deism is a move in the philosophy of religion that takes it away from rationalistic dogmatism and takes it to the standpoint of regulative criticism to which Kant had previously arrived in the three Critiques. The second transition begins to move beyond the individualism of the second Critique. Thus in *Religion* Kant at the same time produced a philosophy of religion that catches up with the Critiques and one that points beyond them.

The Victory of the Good Principle and Spread of the Kingdom of God

Book Two analysed the conflict between the good and evil principles in the individual and gave a representation of a successful version of the conflict in Jesus Christ's victorious struggle against evil. Book Three proceeds to look at the struggle between the two principles in society and in history. So at one level the passage from one book to the other is a change of point of view: from the individual to mankind, from the microcosm to the macrocosm, from Jesus as archetype for the individual to imitate to the church as the community in which is found the seed of the future moral perfection of mankind. However Book Two is about the struggle, while Book Three indicates the victory of the good principle as its title. At another level, therefore, the transition between the two books points to two subsequent stages in the progressive defeat of evil. Jesus won the first victory and then the results spread through mankind in space and time.

The second facet of this transition is especially intriguing. Kant repeated his familiar doctrine that social life is fraught with temptations to morality.

> Envy, the lust for power, greed, and the malignant inclinations bound up with these, besiege his nature, contented within itself, *as soon as he is among men*. And it is not even necessary to assume that these men are sunk in evil and examples to lead him astray; it suffices that they are at hand, that they surround him, and that they are men, for them mutually to corrupt each other's dispositions and make one another evil.[102]

One might expect Kant to have continued with the implications of the individual's absolute freedom: it is man's own fault if he yields to temptations, and social contagion is ultimately irrelevant to the growth of vice as well as to the growth of virtue. Such is not at all the case, however, and Kant, following a logic that proceeded from his insights into the nature of man's relative freedom, saw the possibility of defeat of evil only through the availability to the individual of a good moral community to which he can belong.

> . . . the sovereignty of the good principle is attainable, so far as men can work towards it, only through the establishment and spread of a society in accordance with, and for the sake of, the

laws of virtue, a society whose task and duty it is rationally to im-
press these laws in all their scope upon the entire human race.
For only thus can we hope for a victory of the good over the evil
principle. In addition to prescribing laws to each individual,
morally legislative reason also unfurls a banner of virtue as a
rallying point for all who love the good, that they may gather
beneath it and thus at the very start gain the upper hand over the
evil which is attacking them without rest.[103]

Such a passage in Kant which shifts from the point of view that
makes the quality of society dependent upon the moral nature of the
individual to one that makes the individual's own moral life (that of
his "hidden" dispositions) dependent upon the quality of his associations is a novel one indeed, and it led to a profound renovation of many
aspects of Kant's thinking (above all of his hopes for history and of his
views on the ground of hope). However we cannot trust that evil men
will be able to found a good society.

The idea of such a state [i.e. the Kingdom of virtue] possesses a
thoroughly well-grounded objective reality in human reason (in
man's duty to join such a state), even though, subjectively, we
can never hope that man's good will will lead mankind to decide
to work with unanimity towards this goal.[104]

The founding of such a state is morally urgent. To become free
from the bondage to the evil principle is the highest prize.[105] The seven
sections of the first division of Book Three (The Philosophical Account
of the Founding of a Kingdom of God on Earth) proceed to examine
the implications and ramifications of an initial dilemma set in these
terms.

1. The ethical state or Kingdom of virtue is distinct from the
juridico-civil or political state. In the former men are united under
laws of coercion. In the latter "they are united under non-coercive
laws, that is, *laws of virtue* alone."[106] (It follows that no State can
compel its citizens to enter into an ethical commonwealth.) Furthermore, ideally all mankind belongs to such an ethical commonwealth.

2. It is man's duty to leave his "ethical state of nature" (in which
the good principle is continually attacked by evil) to become a member of an ethical commonwealth, dedicated to the spread of the highest
social good. This duty is one distinct from all others "in kind and in
principle"; it is a duty towards the race itself and more importantly

"it involves working towards a whole regarding which we do not know whether, as such, it lies in our power or not."[107] The duty asks us to work not for eternal peace as a balance of power but for a society of perfect friendship. Such duty is a genuine one since it is an aspect of our duty to promote the highest good with all our strength. This duty led Kant to the derivation of a new postulate.

> We can already foresee that this duty will require the presupposition of another idea, namely, that of a higher moral Being through whose universal dispensation the forces of separate individuals, insufficient in themselves, are united for a common end.[108]

3. and 4. The ethical commonwealth, being a non-coercive union of well-disposed men, cannot be gathered by any exterior legislation. Its law-giver can only be the one who knows the hearts. It is therefore a people of God. "To found a moral people of God is therefore a task whose consummation can be worked for not from men but only from God himself."[109] For how can one expect something pure out of impure beings, or "something perfectly straight . . . out of such crooked wood"? But in a familiar oscillation, Kant added that man must not on this account "be idle in this business and . . . let Providence rule." He must proceed "as though everything depended upon him." "But what preparations must they now make that it shall come to pass?"[110]

Kant did not answer the question but proceeded to define a visible church as "the actual union of men into a whole which harmonizes with that ideal."

5. This section is perhaps the most surprising. In a generalization that Kant believed he could illustrate in the world history of religion, he affirmed in his title that "the Constitution of every Church Originates always in some Historical (Revealed) Faith, which we can call Ecclesiastical Faith; and this is best Founded on a Holy Scripture."[111]

Kant's argument here seems to rest more upon observed facts of history than upon results of an analysis of human nature. It appears that a church cannot be established on pure moral faith, but is always based upon "a determining of religion," namely upon acceptance of a historical account of "how God wishes to be honoured (and obeyed)." Only such an historical faith with its statutory legislation can be "propagated among men by tradition or writ" and it only comprises "the means to its furtherance and spread."[112] The thought can even be entertained that such "determination of the form" of religion can "perhaps be a special divine arrangement."[113] The conclusion is clear: "In men's striving towards an ethical commonwealth, ecclesiastical faith thus naturally precedes pure religious faith." (The second edition adds a footnote "Morally, this order ought to be reversed.")[114]

6. If an ecclesiastical faith is to maintain a claim to universality it must have "pure religious faith as its highest interpreter." The authority of the interpreter, however, is no reason for dispensing with the text or tradition to be interpreted. "Some historical ecclesiastical faith or other, usually to be found at hand, must be utilized."[115] Here Kant believed he could discern a pattern common to all "types of faith." Everywhere wise and thoughtful teachers are found who interpret the holy books to find in them a higher meaning than the literal one, or as Kant put it, to bring them "into line with the universal moral dogmas." Scriptural scholarship and the pure religion of reason are thus set up as the expositors of Scripture which is the norm of ecclesiastical faith.

7. When a church has the consciousness that its historical faith is a vehicle,[116] it can be called the true church.

> In the end religion will gradually be freed from all empirical determining grounds and from all statutes which rest on history and which through the agency of ecclesiastical faith provisionally unite men for the requirements of the good; and thus at last the pure religion of reason will rule over all, "so that God may be all in all."[117]

But we are not there yet. We are still at the stage of recognizing the useful influence of ecclesiastical faith as a vehicle. This vehicle in fact in the true church is subordinated to pure moral religion. Pure religion thus has a "public foothold," in which there lies inevitably, "as in a seed which is self-developing and in due time self-fertilizing, the whole, which one day is to illumine and to rule the world."[118]

Division Two then gives a historical account of the gradual establishment of the sovereignty of the good principle on earth and begins by noting that one cannot write a universal history of religion since religion (in the strict meaning of the word) is to be found only in hearts. One can, however, observe ecclesiastical faiths and give a history of types of faith. Such a universal history which focuses on the gradual establishment of the sovereignty of the good principle must put the history of Christianity at its centre, since this is the only "church which contained within itself from its first beginning, the seed and the principles of the objective unity of the true and *universal* religious faith, to which it is gradually brought nearer."[119]

The Jewish faith is said to be a collection of mere statutory laws, and a commonwealth under purely political laws. "Judaism has not allowed its organization to become religious."[120] It failed to suit the requirements of the church universal. The origins of Christianity are "a thoroughgoing revolution in doctrine of faith." The subsequent history of Christendom "might well justify the exclamation: *tantum religio potuit suadere malorum*, did not the fact still shine forth clearly from its founding that Christianity's first intention was really no other than to introduce a pure religious faith." Kant added that his own time was the best in the entire known history of the church, because the seed of true religious faith was allowed to grow in the church.

Wisdom in this juncture of history of the church is "reasonable modesty in pronouncements regarding all that goes by the name of revelation." Hence the most intelligent and most reasonable thing to do is "to use the book already at hand as the basis for ecclesiastical instruction," and at all times interpret the narratives "in the interest of morality."[121] To this Kant added that one should not wait for a new revelation nor pay attention to those who claim they have received one.[122]

The idea of ethical community is obviously one of the guiding threads of the whole discussion. New though the idea was, it had roots in the older writings of Kant: the philosophy of history (dominated by the ethico-juridical tendency) had the idea of a slow progress towards a perfect political unity of the race, of which in the earlier writings it was hard to say whether it was a state of balance of power or a state in which conflict was really overcome. And the first two Critiques (dominated rather by the ethico-religious tendency) had the idea of a *corpus mysticum* of all rational beings: a noumenal reality in the first Critique, life in which was guaranteed by the postulate of immortality in the second Critique. The conception of ethical community found in *Religion* however moves beyond the exteriority of a politically perfect state and moves beyond the individualism of Kant's moral world of juxtaposed ideal interior moral dispositions. For the ethical commonwealth is an interior union of hearts realized in a visible community. It is thus presented as an intra-historical possibility not as an otherworldly one. It must be particularly noted that the moral interdependence of persons in the ethical community is a serious departure from the absolute independence of persons in the Kingdom of ends. The concept of individual autonomy however is not allowed to suffer qualification. The demands of absolute freedom remain imperative there and Kant does not transcend the dichotomy between autonomy and heteronomy in a concept of koinonomy.

It is quite clear that it is a sensitivity to the realities of religious life and to the doctrines of Christianity that led Kant to such a concept of moral community. Bohatec, I believe, proved that it is the reading of theology and the interest in discussions of Christian eschatology that led Kant to deepen and interiorize his notion of beatitude, and thus move from the individualistic eudaemonism of the earlier writings to the notions of shared spiritual joys of the ethical commonwealth in *Religion*.[123] Kant never seems to have believed in a narrowly individual salvation, since the philosophy of history had expressed his reluctance for accepting the thought that the individual could be said to be saved (through his pure moral faith) in a situation when there are not any signs of a progress of mankind as a whole. The notion of an ethical commonwealth, however, goes beyond such a conception, for it presents salvation as occurring in a community and through a community.

The religious sources of the idea of the ethical commonwealth are acknowledged by Kant.

> The Kingdom of God on earth: this is the ultimate vocation of man; Christ led us to it, but one did not understand him and the Kingdom of the priests, not that of God, was set among us.[124]

The religious implications of the idea of ethical commonwealth go beyond the religious implications of the idea of the *summum bonum* presented in the *Critique of Practical Reason*. In the latter God guarantees that the goal is achievable. In the case of the ethical commonwealth, however, it takes an active dispensation of God or of divine Providence for it to become a reality, since one cannot hope that human good will, such as it is now, will in fact work for such an ethical commonwealth, even though such an objective is in principle possible.[125] Fischer was right in his *I. Kant und seine Lehre* (1898) when he saw the originality of *Religion* in that Kant introduced the concept of redemption, a conversion of human freedom that issues from a divine dispensation mediated through the appearance and development of a true church. This notion takes us to the border of what I deem to be the most important of all parerga, namely the doctrine of grace. At this point it must be emphasized that the revaluation of the historical, social, and institutional dimensions of religion goes of a piece with an examination of the notion of redemption. The doctrine of the visible church is not in Kant the occasion for "enlightened" polemics against organized religion, or for confessional polemics against rival organizations. There are polemics of course, but the baby is not thrown out with the bath water. Kant does believe that salvation is to be mediated through the institution of a visible religious and moral association and organized religion in 1793 was for Kant one of the two institutions that effectively work for the moral progress of mankind; the other of course is education.

Service and Pseudo-Service of God in the Church

Kant began Book Four with a summary of his previous results.

We have seen that it is a duty of a peculiar kind (*officium sui generis*) to unite oneself with an ethical commonwealth. . . . We have also seen that such a commonwealth, being a Kingdom of God, can be undertaken by men only through religion, and, finally, in order that this religion be public (and this is requisite to a commonwealth), that it must be represented in the visible form of a church; hence the establishment of a church devolves upon men as a task which is committed to them and can be required of them.

To found a church as a commonwealth under religious laws seems, however, to call for more wisdom (both of insight and of good disposition) than can well be expected of men, especially since it seems necessary to presuppose the presence in them, for this purpose, of the moral goodness which the establishment of such a church has in view.[126]

Such a visible church, founded by God and organized by men, now exists as a whole which harmonizes with the ideal of the Kingdom of God and since the Enlightenment, consciously strives to approximate it always better. As such it is a "public religious faith" and consists of a historical faith regulated by a pure moral faith. These two elements lead to the distinction between genuine service of God and pseudo-service of God: the former subordinates the historical faith and its statutory laws to pure religious faith; the latter presents "allegiance to the historical and statutory element of ecclesiastical faith as alone bringing salvation."[127]

The rest of the book consists of an application of this distinction to the details of life in an organized church and as such the book offers no major new insight and presents no major difficulty.[128]

Pseudo-service is also called by Kant religious illusion (in obvious parallelism with the transcendental illusion). Such illusion arises when one considers observances of ordinances prescribed by statutory faith "as essential to the service of God generally" and when one makes it "the highest condition of the divine approval of man."[129] The subjective ground of such religious illusion is anthropomorphism, namely the conception of God as a being whom we believe we can win over to our advantage and propitiate through various obeisances. Kant makes it clear that anthropomorphism is not to be avoided in the theoretical representation of God but is highly dangerous in "our practical relation to his will"[130] because it makes of God an all too human despot whose will can be swayed. The moral principle of religion is that true service is to be found in obedience to his will, the moral law, and thus proclaims as "a principle requiring no proof" that: "Whatever, over and above good life conduct, man fancies he can do to become well-pleasing to God is mere religious illusion and pseudo-service of God."[131]

Religious faith as lived in the true church will consist in a tension between "religion" which sees in the pure moral disposition the essence of the worship of God and "heathenism," "superstition," or "religious illusion" which find the essence of the worship of God somewhere else. Kant's position does not abolish the tension, but insists on subordinating the second element to the former. The solution here is reminiscent of the solution Kant gave to the problem of our drive for happiness. Our desire for happiness is not to be denied but is to be subordinated to the imperatives of pure practical reason. The solution is also reminiscent of the solution Kant gave to the problem of symbols: they are truly revealing but misleading if taken literally. Thus Kant did not blame the superstitious man for participating in some ritual act prescribed by historical faith, but blamed him for believing that this and this alone will make him well pleasing to God. Reason tells us that God wants to be served by "morally good life-conduct, and especially the pure disposition as the subjective principle." Yet Kant added, in a comment which indicates his respect for symbolic acts:

But perhaps the Supreme Being may wish, in addition, to be served in a manner which cannot become known to us through unassisted reason, namely, by actions wherein, in themselves, we can indeed discover nothing moral, but which we freely undertake, either because He commanded them or else in order to convince Him of our submissiveness to him.[132]

Ritual action may also have the precious consequence of strengthening our dispositions. A religious man wisely will participate in such symbolic action.

Clericalism (*Pfaffentum*) in a visible church will increase the risks of pseudo-service since clergy will tend mistakenly to exalt their function by claiming to be able "to manage . . . the Invisible Power which presides over the destiny of men"[133] and to encourage people to display a godliness which can quickly become divorced from morally good life conduct. Here again Kant returned to the solution of tension between two elements: true godliness is made up of moral virtue (a fear of God, obedience to his law) and piety (a love of God), with virtue as the regulative principle. "Godliness is not a surrogate for virtue, whereby we may dispense with the latter; rather it is virtue's consummation."[134]

Religious illusion may also consist in requiring assent to doctrines arising from historical faith as essential to salvation. In this case superstition runs counter to conscience, which "is a state of consciousness which in itself is duty."[135] Conscience enables us to discriminate between what we are really certain of (by scientific or moral certainty) from what we strongly believe but without perfect certainty. The demands of orthodoxy are immoral when they ask to profess certainty of things of which we could not possibly be certain.

> *The hypocrite regards as a mere nothing* the danger arising from the dishonesty of his profession, *the violation of conscience*, involved in proclaiming even before God that something is certain, when he is aware that, its nature being what it is, it cannot be asserted with unconditional assurance.[136]

Kant then proceeded to denounce the " maxim of security," namely the principle that affirms "it is expedient to believe too much rather than too little." In a shrewd sociological insight, he noted that this maxim is common among those who have not yet progressed in freedom of thought while others feel "the more ennobled the less they need to believe." The former believes that "what we do over and above what we owe will at least do no harm and might even help." The kinship with the servile cast of mind is obvious. In a previous footnote[137] he had noted that this "principle of security" puts the responsibility for what I should believe on the shoulders of my religious teachers. This whole passage contains almost word for word repetitions of a passage in Shaftesbury's *Letter Concerning Enthusiasm*, although the label *argumentum a tuto* is Kant's own.[138] There is little doubt that Kant's praise of honesty and roundness in the expression of one's thoughts and beliefs is indebted to the polemics of English moralists against cant. As might be expected the book on service and pseudo-service concludes with the famous apostrophe to conscience.

In the "General Observation," Kant examined the significance of church ritual (under the general concept of it being a means of grace, hence justifying the placing of this matter in the section reserved to parerga). Of private prayer,[139] public worship, baptism, and communion, Kant says that under no circumstances should one believe that God has attached special favours to the participation in such activity. Positively, private prayer quickens the moral disposition. Public worship is "not only a means to be valued by each *individual* for his own edification, but also a duty directly obligating them as a *group*." Baptism "is a highly significant ceremony which lays a grave obligation either upon the initiate . . . or upon the witnesses." And communion "contains within itself something great, expanding the narrow, selfish, and unsociable cast of mind among men, especially in matters of religion, towards the idea of a cosmopolitan *moral community* and it is a good means of enlivening a community to the moral disposition of brotherly love which it represents."[140]

The last pages repeat a theme which has been the leit-motiv of the whole book, throughout its definition and discussion of fanaticism, superstition, clericalism, and all the forms of pseudo-service.

All such artificial self-deceptions in religious matters have a common basis. Among the three divine moral attributes, holiness, mercy, and justice, man habitually turns directly to the second in order thus to avoid the forbidding condition of conforming to the requirements of the first. It is tedious to be a good *servant* (here one is forever hearing only about one's duties); man would therefore rather be a *favourite*, where much is overlooked or else, when duty has been too grossly violated, everything is atoned for through the agency of some one or other favoured in the highest degree—man, meanwhile, remaining the servile knave he ever was.[141]

The sharpness of the polemics against institutional religion and the zeal with which Kant ferreted out any shadow of an idea that we might be capable of pleasing God through anything other than the doing of our duty gives the impression that in Book Four Kant was returning to the confines of enlightened rationalism and its dislike of any form of religion other than the "natural" one, or that which met the exacting standards of some philosopher's notion of rationality. There is indeed in Book Four no access to major new concepts as in Books One and Three and something like the return to a deistic position noted in Book Two. (The whole oscillation between the opening of new perspectives and the restricting of them by the doctrines of eighteenth century rationalism is representative of Kant's contribution to the philosophy of religion.)

In spite of the negative restricting tone of Book Four, one should not underestimate the consolidation that takes place in it of the major gains of the book on evil and of that on the moral community.

Unlike that of most enlightened deists, Kant's attack on superstition does not denounce primitive savages or mediaeval Christians but bears upon the modern forms of superstition. Pseudo-service of God was not to him a receding phenomenon, but a live one. Kant therefore portrayed and denounced the kind of sanctimonious self-righteousness that characterizes progressive Christians just as much if not more than the obscurantism of mediaeval ones.[142] His view of superstition has thus a more lasting significance than that of Hume and Voltaire.

Then when Kant described organized religious life, he did not present us sermons, admonitions, bible study, and other forms of teaching and morally hortative activities. He focused on liturgical practices in which he saw means to symbolize and cement the life of the moral community. Cultus for Kant does not pass entirely into ethos. There remains a positive meaning for ritual. The minister is no pure teacher of the law, he is also the presider over the celebration of sacramental activities.[143]

Kant's polemics against organized religion while falling equally heavily on Protestant and Roman Catholic churches was not for him the door to a praise of "private" religion. Kant simultaneously made a radical critique of institutional religious life and pressed for the maintenance and purification of the visible church. The same tension is found in the discussion of church government. Kant criticized clericalism but also wanted an organized church with authority given to scriptural scholars, elders, and ministers. Bruch has the key to this duality.[144] Kant had a deep distrust of all clergy and a profound loathing for all enthusiastic illumined laymen and laywomen who claim to have received revelations. He was thus torn between two parties: orthodox clerical authoritarianism and the anarchy of *Schwärmerei*, both of which claim that whoever is not with them is with their enemy. Thus Kant groped for a paternal domestic form of church government.[145] He wanted a strongly organized church but without coercive features, thereby caught in the dilemma created by the fact that religious associations experience a graver conflict between autonomy and heteronomy than most other associations. As an extra safeguard against chaos or tyranny he granted some authority to the state over the church. The state cannot command the beliefs and rituals but can intervene in an internal controversy when there is any "danger to civil harmony."[146]

Finally Kant's anthropological pessimism, that is, his insight into the crookedness of the human heart, led him to see radical evil even within the church, which is the very institution where evil begins to be vanquished by the good principle.[147] His solution is to have the church fight against the poisons it secretes in its own midst and he believed that the fight can be victorious. The hope in religious progress seems to prevail over the religious insight into the roots of evil in the heart itself. Few in the nineteenth century were to remain true in their ecclesiology to the Kantian position: it was easier to idealize the visible church, or, having seen it realistically, to deprive it of its moral and eschatological significance.

Chapter 9

Religion within the Limits of Reason Alone: The Parerga, Revelation, and Grace

Introduction: Miracles and Mysteries

As we saw before,[1] *Religion within the Limits of Reason Alone* contains at the end of each of the four books "General Observations" ostensibly devoted to the discussion of what Kant called parerga. Kant proposed four titles for these sections: "Works of Grace, Miracles, Mysteries, and Means of Grace."[2] However, much of what falls under Kant's definition of parerga is discussed in the body of the books themselves (the concept of grace, for instance, constantly reappears). Then we find also in the body of the book hints about revelation, a concept which also falls apparently under Kant's definition of parerga. Finally the discussions of miracles and mysteries are not particularly crucial. Consequently, I shall in this section rearrange Kant's material and, after a definition of the concept of parerga and a brief summary of Kant's analysis of miracles and mysteries, focus upon the concepts of revelation and grace.[3]

Traditional Christian dogmas may have received a very rough treatment at the hands of Kant but they are nevertheless all, or nearly all, there in his book, analysed and interpreted with a view to securing a positive religious meaning to them. This is due in some cases to the fact that Kant found in some of them the expression of a rational truth (for instance, Jesus as Son of God). And in all other cases it is due to Kant's concept of parerga.[4] Some matters, said Kant, are "parerga to religion within the limits of pure reason; they do not belong within it but border upon it."[5] But to say that they are beyond the bounds set to religion by pure reason is not to say that they are contrary to reason, or even to say that they are a matter of indifference to a reason that would not know at all what to do with them. Reason is very much concerned about them because: "Reason, conscious of her inability to satisfy her moral need, extends herself to higher-flown ideas capable of supplying this lack, without, however, appropriating these ideas as an extension of her domain."[6]

It follows that not all matters which are beyond the bounds set by pure reason are parerga, but only those which satisfy a moral need. Most specifically, only those are parerga which give grounds for hope to moral men as they undertake the reascent from enslavement to the evil principle to a state where the good principle is sovereign over the dispositions. But after affirming the legitimacy of such parerga, Kant immediately issued a two-fold caution about them: what they speak about is possible, but to make of them motives of action is to fall under heteronomy and religious illusion. "Reason does not dispute the possibility or the reality of the objects of these ideas: she simply cannot adopt them into her maxim of thought and action."[7]

To introduce them into the very body or core of religion itself, rather than keep them beyond the borders, is to open the door to fanaticism (the claim to know effects of grace in ourselves),[8] superstition (the claim to know effects of special divine intervention in the world),[9] illumination (the claim to receive direct revelation of mysteries),[10] and thaumaturgy (the illusory attempt to manipulate the supernatural through the use of means of grace).[11]

Miracles were defined by Kant as "events in the world *the operating laws* of whose causes are, and must remain, absolutely unknown to us."[12] This is a middle position between Augustine's position (miracles run counter to known laws of nature) and that which affirms the impossibility of miracles.

> It is wholly conformable to man's ordinary way of thought, though not strictly necessary, for the historical introduction of (a true religion in a context of a religion of mere rites and observances) to be accompanied and, as it were, adorned by miracles, in order to announce the termination of the earlier religion, which without miracles would never have had any authority.
>
> The true religion which in its time needed to be introduced through such expedients, is now here, and from now on is able to maintain itself on rational grounds.[13]

The wise attitude towards miracles is held by "sensible" men: "They believe in *theory* that there are such things as miracles but they do not warrant them *in the affairs of life.*"[14] This is Kant's standard minimal position on parerga in general: they are possible but we should not "count on" them.[15] And we should "combat with might and main" the idea that one must profess belief in them as a way, or as the only way, of pleasing God.[16]

A mystery is defined as "something *holy* which may indeed be *known* by each single individual but cannot be *made known* publicly, that is, shared universally. Being something *holy*, it must be moral."[17] Thus there are two kinds of mysteries,[18] those of pure rational faith which Bruch called metaphysical realities, and those which are looked upon as "divinely-prompted," which Bruch called revealed dogmas.[19] Only the latter are, strictly speaking, parerga. The former are not because all religion including the religion of reason partakes of mysteriousness. First of all, God is never wholly known, and secondly, everywhere in religion we encounter representations and symbols which are valid but are not reducible to the clarity of a pure rational thought. The representation of God as holy Legislator, benevolent Providence, and righteous Judge is one such mystery that belongs to pure rational faith. How the Legislator issues a "divine call' to his creatures, that is, creates them to a free use of their powers, is mysterious. Atonement (how in his goodness the benevolent Providence supplements man's lack of requisite qualifications for righteousness) is likewise mysterious. And so is election.[20] And all these mysteries are found in a religion that remains within the bounds of reason. Among the second kind of mysteries, or among the mysterious revealed dogmas, the one Kant selected is that of the Trinity presented as Father, Son, and Holy Ghost (Kant had just discussed the idea of three-fold attributes of God). The Trinity of the historical Christian faith Kant noted, is distinct from the Trinity revealed to us through our reason in that it presents God as the loving one.[21]

The place Kant gave to mysteries of both kinds is in keeping with his general solution: the doctrine presented as mystery is possible and even useful, but "a bare literal faith in it hurts rather than improves the truly religious disposition."[22]

The whole discussion of mysteries is rather unsatisfactory for, while it broadens the concept to include the mysteriousness of the origin of the moral law and of the God of pure moral faith, it fails to arrive at any satisfactory account of the relationship between this kind of mystery and the mysteries set forward in the dogmas by historical faith.[23]

In discussing miracles and mysteries, Kant examined two topics that were much debated in the eighteenth century and were probably the most tramped-upon battle-ground for the conflict between philosophers and theologians, Christians and Deists. Kant, apparently responding to the "issues" of his day, included a discussion of them in *Religion within the Limits of Reason Alone* even though neither miracles nor mysteries have much to do with the major problems which exercise his mind in the book: the struggle against evil and the founding of the Kingdom of God on earth. Both miracles and mysteries were issues which arose and were debated in an epistemological context that antedates the solutions of *The Critique of Pure Reason*. They are crucial in a debate that opposes rational truths and revealed truths, but the wind is taken out of the sails of this whole debate with the standpoint of criticism. Neither mysteries nor miracles are particularly relevant to a moral interpretation of religion. For all these reasons it is not surprising that Kant found it difficult to relate these two topics to the matter at hand in *Religion within the Limits of Reason Alone*, and offered a somewhat inconclusive discussion.

The issues involved in Kant's concept of parerga therefore really come to a head with his discussion of revelation and grace. While the third and fourth "General Observations" discuss grace, none is specifically devoted to revelation. The idea of revelation, however, appears many times in the work. My first task therefore is to examine Kant's use of the term and show that it does mean raising the kind of issue that he wanted to raise in the discussion of the parerga.[24]

Revelation

The idea of revelation, as commonly understood in the eighteenth century, was the idea of a communication by God at a definite point in history and through a specific event, to a human being or group of human beings, of a certain number of truths which were necessary to attain true knowledge of God and/or salvation. This idea came under philosophical and moral criticism: why would God act in such a decisive way only at one time (why not sooner, why not later), and how can God make such a blessing available only to a few men, since any historical knowledge spreads but slowly and only to a limited distance? Hence arose the discussion of the conflict between necessary truths of reason and contingent truths of history and the sense of scandal involved in such a notion of revelation. The whole debate is well illustrated by Lessing's statement that "accidental truths of history can never become the proof of necessary truths of reason."[25]

Many theologians, however, found some kind of reconciliation. Knutzen, Kant's teacher, arrived along with quite a few others at the following solution: a divine revelation is necessary on account of human evil and guilt. Such revelation, however, must fulfil certain conditions (to be set by reason). Christian revelation alone fulfils these conditions. There are many traces of such a position in Kant. The Christian body of doctrines, we read, "cleansed the moral relation of men to the Supreme Being" and "we can call the promulgation of the doctrines a revelation of the faith which had hitherto remained hidden from men through their own fault."[26] Revelation on this view is the historic publication of a truth essentially accessible to universal reason but in fact obscured through man's weakness and wickedness.

Kant's use of the term "revelation," however, is not consistent and in another theme in *Religion within the Limits of Reason Alone* we find him resisting the definition of revelation that limits it to the idea of a communication to one group at one point in history. Church or biblical theologians may be insistent that their doctrines are based on the specific divine revelation in history and thus proclaim themselves as defenders of a revealed religion, in opposition to rationalists who are exponents "only" of a rational religion. Rationalists may accept the distinction of revealed religion versus rational religion and be quite happy with hanging revelation like an albatross on the neck of church theologians. But Kant does not accept the thought of letting church theologians and their revealed religion have the monopoly of access to divine revelation, because "God has indeed revealed His Will through the moral law enough."[27] Therefore all religion, rational or revealed, is in a sense based upon revelation or divine self-manifestation. The important distinction then is between the revelation through the moral law, and the revelation through a specific divine dispensation at one point of time.

Such I believe is the thrust of the discussion in Book Four where Kant begins with a distinction between natural religion and revealed religion and promptly substitutes to it the distinction between natural and learned religion. A learned religion is a religion "of which one can convince others only through the agency of learning (in and through which they must be guided)."[28] It follows from Kant's new distinction that revelation qua general revelation through the moral law is no parergon at all but is part of religion within the limits of reason alone. What remains a parergon however is the idea of special revelation. The possibility of it is not to be denied, but the use of the idea must be modest.[29]

The stage is now set for the listing of four possible doctrines on the matter of the relationship between so-called "unaided human reason" and "special divine revelation in history."

> He who interprets the natural religion alone as morally necessary, that is, as duty, can be called the *rationalist* (in matters of belief); if he denies the reality of all supernatural divine revelation he is called a *naturalist*; if he recognizes revelation, but asserts that to know and accept it as real is not a necessary requisite to religion, he could be named a *pure rationalist*; but if he holds that belief in it is necessary to universal religion, he could be named the *pure supernaturalist* in matters of faith.[30]

In keeping with his general solution to the problem of the parerga Kant eliminated the positions of rationalism and naturalism which both deny that reason could have a moral interest in such "supernatural" conceptions. There remain only the claims of the pure rationalist and those of the pure supernaturalist. The solution for Kant is to be found with the pure rationalist but he did bring an important qualification by drawing attention to the peculiar predicament of men as historical beings: that is, a natural religion has to be learned by men at a particular moment in history if it is to be or to become the religion of live human beings, and can spread among men only through the vehicle or means of a traditional or historical faith. Kant did not give a label for that specific modification of the position, but we can use that coined by Collins, "pure non-reductive rationalism."[31]

Kant proceeded to describe such a religion in terms that subsequently proved appropriate for Christianity.

> Such a religion, accordingly, can be *natural*, and at the same time *revealed*, when it is so constituted that men *could and ought to have discovered it* of themselves merely through the use of their reason, although they *would* not have come upon it so early, or over so wide an area, as is required. Hence a revelation thereof at a given

time and in a given place might well be wise and very advantageous to the human race, in that, when once religion thus introduced is here, and has been made known publicly, everyone can henceforth by himself and with his own reason convince himself of its truth. In this event the religion is objectively a natural religion, though subjectively one that has been revealed.[32]

We find here the full statement of Kant's position on the subject of "special" revelation: historical revelation is subjectively necessary and historically advantageous; it gives rise to a public institution and thereby to a spread of sound religion; it gives us access to rational truths to which we could not have had access otherwise at that time, but which can now be based, in our minds, primarily or exclusively upon divine revelation to us through the moral law. It is thus Kant's reflections upon the historical and institutional realities which form the context of man's moral and religious life that led him to a dynamic conception of historical revelation. As R. Vancourt put it, "It is the concept of visible church which leads Kant to the concept of revelation."[33] This position is also found as a possible one in a letter to Jacobi of 30 August 1789.

> For one can just as well admit that if the Gospel had not previously instructed us in the universal moral laws, in their total purity, our reason would not yet have discovered them so completely; still, *once we are in possession of them*, we can convince anyone of their correctness and validity using reason alone.[34]

To present this position Bohatec spoke of a synthesis of Platonism and Christianity, since we find Christianity as the powerful historical force to spread the Platonic enduring idea.[35] I prefer to see in the position an echo from Lessing's basic metaphor of a divine education of mankind, presenting God as a pedagogue who through progressive revelations leads his students to a greater maturity and fuller use of reason.

A twofold point of contact can here be established between *Religion* and a philosophy of history. At the time of the Gospels there appears a crucial turning-point in the becoming of mankind. One reason for this is the moral content of the Gospel. As Kant wrote to H. Jung-Stilling (after 1 March 1789):

> It is quite right of you to seek in the Gospels the final satisfaction for the striving of a secure foundation of wisdom and hope, since

that book is an everlasting guide to true wisdom, one that not only agrees with the speculations of a perfected reason but sheds new light on the whole field surveyed by that reason, illuminating what still remains opaque to it.[36]

Secondly, Kant (as our discussion of grace will show) remained fascinated by the Christian idea of a man-transforming, saving activity of God in Christ. So he discerned at the time of the Gospels not just the acquisition of new moral ideas but also the beginning of an actual moral liberation from enslavement to the evil principle. This position however brings about a total reversal of the position on revelation with which the discussion started: at first we found from Knutzen, echoed in Kant, that reason is the judge of the authenticity of an historical revelation. Now we hear that historical revelation is an educator of reason.[37] Thus we find in Kant a transition between two very different views of the relationship between reason and historical revelation (or between reason and history). These two positions may be summarized as follows:

On the one hand Kant seems to have the concept of an absolute reason which can judge what in history is true or false according to final unchanging rational norms. Christianity can be said to be the true religion because it is the only religion measuring up to standards set by reason for divine revelation. Revelation teaches through historical communication what men could have known through reason (again history and reason are two entirely distinct areas), if it were not for some quirk of their own (laziness, stupidity, or what not). So there is a learned religion beside the rational one. In case of tension between the spirit of Christ as known historically and this moral disposition in us, the ultimate criterion or authority lies in the touchstone of our reason. History can merely illustrate. An interpretation of Scripture is authentic when "the God who is in us is the exegete."

> We do not understand anyone, except him who speaks to us through our own understanding and our own reason; and the divinity of a transmitted teaching can, therefore, be recognized by no other means but the concepts of *our* reason.[38]

Of course the pure religious faith must receive representations. Its ideal, its archetype, must be represented as a concrete human being (because of the limitations of human reason which is sensuously affected). So contents are drawn from history to clothe the pure archetype. This is permissible if we recognize we must conceive of the ideal in such and such a guise and do not claim that the ideal is such and such. So besides pure religious faith, we need an historical, ecclesiastical, learned faith to clothe the former with sensual representations. But this is inevitably to degrade religion and to open the door to all kinds of illusions.

> Every ecclesiastical faith, in so far as it presents statutory dogmas as essential religious ones, contains a certain dose of paganism; paganism consists in presenting the exterior (the accidental) of religion as the essential.[39]

In this perspective the church is true in so far as it is an association for mutual improvement and moral striving. As C. C. J. Webb put it:

> The church or Kingdom of God appears not as the natural environment of the religious life wherein it has its origin and its field of exercise, but rather as a voluntary union designed to counteract the evil effects inevitable in the natural intercourse of men with one another.[40]

This is the common interpretation of Kant. Yet it overlooks some rather subtle points present throughout the work for more clear and simple premature generalizations. In *Religion* there are repeated attacks on the disjunction of reason and history, and reason appears not as an a-historical sum of eternal principles but as historically conditioned, dependent on the community of thought and action.[41]

On the other hand therefore, we see a new vision of reason emerging. Reason is never finished and complete; it grows in its capacity to deal rationally with more and more aspects of the world, and it grows under a divine education which orients it to its own true goal. In this case, history does not merely illustrate what reason knows, but educates reason. We can see many indications in Kant after 1790 that this view of historically created reason strengthens itself, comes to the fore, and, for a while, relegates that of unhistorical reason to the background.

1. In *Religion*, the individualistic conception of moral action is undercut. The individual's good will needs a good society to be born and borne. The moral self is historical and dependent on the state of morality in his society in his day and age. The sovereignty of the good principle is possible only in the divinely instituted good society.[42]

2. In contrast to the views which minimize the originality of what happened in the life of Jesus of Nazareth (merely a historical illustration or realization of the eternal moral ideal), Kant emphasized that a

genuine existential breakthrough took place then and there. The hope in the growth of good on earth became a really live hope only in the Son of God.[43] Opposing the intellectualistic views which stress that Jesus brought a teaching we could have found elsewhere anyway if we tried harder, Kant began to insist that in his person, through his work in history, Jesus Christ liberated us from an enslavement from which we could not liberate ourselves.[44] There is an increasing focusing of the attention on the work of Christ in founding the first true church, namely the first historical moral community which approximates the ideal community of persons. And, short of the reality of such a moral community, moral men have no hope to gain victory over the evil principle.

3. This foundation of the true church in history no longer appears as the natural outcome of the development of man, but as the direct result of divine intervention. It is a crisis which questions reason and re-orients it, not a product of reason.[45] This point is made more or less reluctantly. While Kant affirmed that the true religion, or Christianity, now that it is here, can "maintain itself on rational grounds,"[46] he allowed that, in order to introduce it, men legitimately called upon faith in divine intervention and miracles as witnesses to them.

The Kingdom of God has come to us only when the principle of transition to the ethical state on earth has gained somewhere "a public foothold," and that transition to a new order of affairs did not happen automatically; it was not ours to effect, even though once started it is "self-developing."[47]

The vigour with which Kant made this point did not escape Karl Barth who noticed it with apparent surprise in his study on nineteenth century theology. Kant, he wrote:

> . . . suddenly speaks of the Church in its visible form in quite different tone and with a quite different emphasis, surely, from that with which we heard him speak of the parallel notions of positive religion, the Bible, and the historical Christ.[48]

I argue that Barth was not listening very well when he heard Kant speak on the historical Jesus but entirely agree with his statement that in the case of the visible church at least:

> . . . the concretion, the thing, which he otherwise treats above all with suspicion, or at least, as a mere *adiaphoron*, is on principle necessary and . . . is worth the trouble to devote serious thought to it in itself.[49]

Reason is dependent on the contingencies of history and the realities of institutionalization to establish itself and grow as reason. Morality is dependent on divine foundational activity, not just in order to realize itself under empirical conditions, but also in order to arrive at a correct concept of itself. God does not merely give to our wills the power they lack, but also reveals to our reason that which it seeks to understand. Now Kant tends to deny that men have the bare idea of a church but are incapable of realizing it empirically. It turns out that they do not even have the correct idea.

> Christianity . . . enriched philosophy with far more definite and purer conceptions of morality than morality itself could have previously supplied. But once these conceptions are found, they are *freely* approved by reason, which adopts them as conceptions at which it could quite well have arrived itself and which it might and ought to have introduced.[50]

4. The conflict between the faculties of theology and of philosophy, between authoritative exposition of the revealed creed and critical reason, is not a total war, which will stop only with the submission of one to the other. "It is a conflict of two parties united together for one common end (*concordia discors, discordia concors*)."[51] Each faculty is dependent on the other, theology on philosophy in order not to lose sight of the question of truth, philosophy on theology in order to have something to think about, content to criticize, refine, and help to bring to its true intention. As Barth put it, if Kant denied that the reality and the possibility of special revelation can be accounted for by philosophical means, he equally vigorously disputed the philosophers' right to deny revelation because it cannot be accounted for by philosophical means.[52]

5. Rather than prove the truth of the Bible and of Christianity by their conformity with the rational faith, Kant preferred to validate them by their present power to repeat this miracle, to liberate from enslavement to the evil principle, or by their "tested capacity to found religion in human hearts."[53]

The treatise on *The End of All Things* has a long passage on the *moralische Liebenswürdigkeit* of Christianity.[54] Christianity is said to have a durable power to win assent. Contemporary man's relationship to Jesus Christ is understood in terms of personal love. The moral man no longer simply does the same things that Jesus did; he does not imitate but he follows his personal example, by freely taking up, in love, his will into his own maxims. To say that Jesus taught us the moral law is not to do justice to his work. He elicited love for the law of humanity; he reconciled us to it while we were hopelessly hostile to it. He started in history a new visible community, with a new ethical constitution which is worthy of respect and love and which again and again elicits such liberating and reconciling love. Kant added, typically, that thanks to the critical philosopher this gentle spirit which is the essence of Christianity is preserved and fanatics are not allowed to ruin its intention under the pretence of hastening its success through the use of authoritarian measures. The task of philosophy is thus presented as allowing Christianity to manifest its own intrinsic authority.

In conclusion, Kant effected in these aspects of his authorship a transition from a rational theology with a God postulated as condition of the moral law to a historical theology with a God founding on earth the true community where men are at home with each other. Thus Kant truly began the transition between the rationalism of the Enlightenment and the birth of modern theology usually located in Schleiermacher. Turning to history and the community, to the concrete states of the will and the actual degree of freedom in man's life, he witnessed in history the founding of a community which men could not have founded and which can be interpreted only as the result of divine action in history or incarnation. Such divine society is intrinsically necessary for the development of reason and morality. There is no hope for radically evil man unless such divinely founded society is a reality. So the individual, the reason, and the race should be presented as being mysteriously educated by God.[55]

There is nothing intrinsically surprising, therefore, to find Kant entertaining in *Religion* the prospect of a "universal historical account" of ecclesiastical faiths showing how "the *church universal* commences to fashion itself into an ethical state of God and to march towards the consummation of this state under a steadfast principle which is one and the same for all men and for all times."[56] Such examination of the idea of the progress of mankind towards moral perfection through the agency of what we would now call the higher world religions naturally arises out of the joint results of Kant's philosophy of history and of his philosophy of religion.[57] Such a prospect of the progressive education of reason through morally relevant historical movements and traditions (that is, through the higher world religions) is no sudden thought of his but is a result which arises from the slow process of redefinition of the relationship between reason and history which his thought was undergoing. Just as inevitably Kant was also to touch upon what was subsequently labelled the "absolute religion." The Christian tradition, he said, is "that portion of the human race in which the predisposition to the unity of the universal church is already approaching its complete development."[58] An account of ecclesiastical faith, he added, "can have unity" only if it is confined wholly to that famous portion. Kant, however, did not go all the way to the now familiar completely hierarchical presentation of the progress of mankind through all the higher religions to the highest of them. The reason for this is primarily that to him "religion" remained something which is essentially hidden, whereas what we perceive as we make comparisons are ecclesiastical faiths. Thus we can have a universal historical account of ecclesiastical faiths but not of religion.

Kant's position in this matter is basically unfinished. A world historical account of religious progress is impossible, religion being hidden. A world historical account of development of ecclesiastical faiths would be trivial or would become significant only with the introduction of the true church. He nevertheless has the following elements of a ranking of the "world religions":

1. All higher religions have a "general" revelation since they all have the desire of a purer spiritual interpretation of their literal doctrines. Among these higher religions Kant named Greek and Roman religion, Hinduism, Islam, and Christianity (but specifically excludes the Judaism of ancient Israel. He did include what he called later Judaism. Is this a reference to Mendelssohn?).[59]

2. Some higher religions which began as historical movements with definite ecclesiastical faith embodied in a book have a "historical revelation." Among these Kant named Islam and Christianity.[60]

3. Christianity is the most developed religion.

But these elements which are present in *Religion* do not merge to constitute a philosophy of religious progress, or a theology of world religions, to use a term which is now gaining currency. They represent the appearance of points of contact between the philosophy of history and the philosophy of religion, points of contact which would inevitably appear once Kant granted philosophical significance to the historical Jesus. But philosophy of religion and philosophy of history do not coalesce in Kant in, say, a philosophy of the spirit. Is this because Kant did not have time to finish his system? I would rather say that Kant, having accepted a basic tension between that which is visible and historical and that which is religious, that is, interior and intimate, could not arrive at such a synthesis. His failure thus to arrive at a synthesis was not due primarily to an eighteenth century classical opposition between reason and history but a religious insistence that religiousness transcends historical determination.

I must emphasize that the presence of such scattered elements of a philosophy of world religions does not represent Kant's definite and final position in philosophy of religion, since we find the essence of his philosophy of religion not in any fixed result but in a transitional movement between Deism and a new standpoint. After all, it remains true that Kant also said that all religions are under one steadfast principle valid for all men and all times. This view of the moral education of mankind through world religions can only be presented as the extreme end of his transitional movement, or one pole in his oscillation. He had to move towards this extreme after his insight into the radicality of evil deprived him of the hope of seeing man progressing by his own unaided moral and rational resources. And one of the merits of the study of Kant's philosophy of religion in the context of his philosophy of history is to enable the interpreter to discern all elements of Kant's transition away from Deism and its eternally valid rational doctrines.

Grace

We will find in Kant's subtle, painstaking, and even laborious discussion of grace the same solution: divine grace, just as divine historical revelation, is to be postulated if we are to keep any hope in the possibility of man's achieving his moral goals after we have come to see the radicality of evil in mankind.

In the context of his discussion of the gradual transition of ecclesiastical faith to the exclusive sovereignty of pure religious faith, Kant introduced the following definition of saving faith:

> Saving faith involves two elements, upon which hope of salvation is conditioned, the one having reference to what man himself cannot accomplish, namely, undoing lawfully (before a divine judge) actions which he has performed, the other to what he himself can and ought to do, that is, leading a new life conformable to his

duty. The first is the faith in an atonement (reparation for his debt, redemption, reconciliation with God); the second, the faith that we can become well-pleasing to God through a good course of life in the future. Both conditions constitute but one faith and necessarily belong together. Yet we can comprehend the necessity of their union only by assuming that one can be derived from the other, that is, either that the faith in the absolution from the debt resting upon us will bring forth good life-conduct, or else that the genuine and active disposition ever to pursue a good course of life will engender the faith in such absolution according to the law of morally operating causes.[61]

We are now confronted with a familiar Kantian thought form: "a remarkable antinomy of human reason." (Thus the discussion of grace is more fully thematized than that of revelation.) Both thesis and antithesis are easy to disprove. On the one hand, acceptance by the individual of a profferred favour, belief that such acceptance annihilates the individual's guilt, and belief that good life conduct "for which he has hitherto not taken the least pains" will be the inevitable consequence of this acceptance, each of these points contradicts the law of morality. Thus an improved way of life, it appears, must take precedence over historical knowledge of the atonement. On the other hand,

> . . . if men are corrupt by nature, how can a man believe that by himself, try as hard as he will, he can make himself a new man well-pleasing to God, when—conscious of the transgression of which up to the present he has been guilty—he still stands in the power of the evil principle and finds in himself no capacity adequate for future improvement?[62]

While he never used again in *Religion* the technical terminology of "antinomy" Kant pointed to similar contradictions elsewhere in his work. "How it is possible for a naturally evil man to make himself a good man wholly surpasses our comprehension."[63] In a discussion of radical evil he asked: "If a man is corrupt in the very ground of his maxims how can he possibly bring about this revolution by his own powers and of himself become a good man?"[64] The idea of atonement repeatedly leads to the core contradiction. God in his goodness called man into being, and called him to exist as a member of the Kingdom of God. But Man is not morally worthy or qualified for such a membership. So God:

. . . must also have the means of supplementing, out of the full-ness of His own holiness, man's lack of requisite qualifications therefor. But this contradicts spontaneity (which is assumed in all the moral good or evil which a man can have within himself), according to which such a good cannot come from another but must arise from man himself, if it is to be imputable to him.[65]

This antinomy focusing on the question of whether the reascent from evil to good is to be credited to a human or a divine agency is Kant's version of the old problem of the relationship between nature and grace.

Whatever good man is able to do through his own efforts, and the laws of freedom, in contrast to what he can do only with super-natural assistance, can be called *nature*, as distinguished from *grace*. Not that we understand by the former expression a physi-cal property distinguished from freedom; we use it merely be-cause we are at least acquainted with the *laws* of this capacity (laws of *virtue*) and because reason thus possesses a visible and comprehensible clue to it . . .; on the other hand, we remain wholly in the dark as to when, what, or how much, *grace* will accomplish in us, and reason is left, on this score, as with the supernatural in general, without any knowledge of the laws ac-cording to which it might occur.[66]

The latter part of this text provides us with the first element to Kant's "solution" of the antinomy. The antinomy cannot be solved at all and we do not know how the operations of human spontaneity and those of saving Providence can become reconciled. "It is a question wholly transcending the speculative capacity of our reason."[67] The second element of Kant's solution is more useful and arises from practical considerations.[68]

Practically the question arises: what in the use of our free will, comes first (not physically but morally)? Where shall we start, i.e., with the faith in what God has done for our behalf, or with what we ought to do to become worthy of God's assistance (what-ever this may be)? In answering this question we cannot hesitate in deciding for the second alternative.[69]

On this point *Religion* overrules ecclesiastical faith which tends to begin with what God does for our behalf.[70]

Since we cannot count on divine aid, we might as well, some will argue, forget about the idea altogether, and dismiss these representations issuing from ecclesiastical faith and speaking of divine agency preceding our moral efforts. Not so, said Kant, introducing the third element of his solution to the antinomy. For the hope that God will make up our deficiency, if we strive with good dispositions, is essential to the life of the moral man.

> To believe that there may be works of grace [that is, results of divine saving aid] and that these perhaps may even be necessary to supplement the incompleteness of our struggle towards virtue —that is all we can say on the subject.[71]

In the Christian religion it is a basic principle that:

> only when he has not buried his inborn talent (Luke 19:12-16) but has made use of his original predisposition to good in order to become a better man, can he hope that what is not within his power will be supplied through cooperation from above.[72]

Kant's balanced position on the subject of grace (and on that of the parerga in general) can be summarized by the following quotation.

> Hence, apart from the general assumption that grace will effect in us what nature cannot, provided only we have made the maximum use of our own powers, we will not be able to make any further use of this idea, either as to how (beyond a constant striving after a good life) we might draw down to us its cooperation, or how we might determine on what occasions to expect it. This idea is wholly transcendent; and it is even salutary to hold it, as a sacred thing, at a respectful distance, lest, under the illusion of performing miracles ourselves or observing miracles within us, we render ourselves unfit for all use of reason or allow ourselves to fall into the indolence of awaiting from above, in passive leisure, what we should seek within.[73]

Note here that the dangerous ideas are those of works of grace and those of means of grace, that is to say, the claim of being able to observe specific signs of divine aid and of being able to perform specific ritual acts that will win divine aid. These are the objects of faith which may be believed, says Kant, only with a reflective but not with a dogmatic faith.[74] Grace itself however, strictly speaking, like revelation, is no parergon at all and is to be believed in with moral certainty.[75] It is part of religion within the limits of reason alone to hope in grace and trust in divine aid (just as it is part of it to respond to divine revelation) and as such, such grace and revelation are certain objects of a religious faith within the limits of reason. Such completional grace is "a universal dispensation."[76] What cannot enter into such religion within the limits of reason alone is the notion of observable manifestations in time of such grace and of means of securing or hastening such aid. Since man lives in time the last two ideas will inevitably arise out of the first and symbols of such worlds or means of grace will constantly be before our minds. These symbols however must be kept safely beyond the bounds of religion or else all kinds of morally dangerous illusions will be fostered. They may be believed in reflectively but must not be believed dogmatically.

The discussion of miracles and mysteries as parerga did not create any major strain upon Kant's philosophy. Neither parergon created moral difficulties and both in Kant's hands were quickly reduced to a mild form of deism. Such, however, is not at all the case with grace or with revelation. In these two cases there is a real transcendence of the positions of the previous theoretical and practical philosophy of Kant. With Bruch[77] I believe that grace is particularly crucial. The handling of revelation leads to a historicization of reason, and a view of divine education of the human race, but this trend had already begun in the philosophy of history and was not totally absent from the *Critique of Pure Reason* (see the chapter on the "History of Pure Reason"). The handling of grace runs counter to something that for Kant had an absolute kind of significance: the categorical imperatives of pure practical reason. Yet Kant's basic faith that there is—and that there must be—hope for mankind, led him, once he had arrived at the notion of radical evil, to believe that there is hope for mankind only if there is grace, a general providential goodness that supplements our efforts, and only if there is the availability of symbolic presentations of specific aid at given moments of time to bring about our conversions. (The latter of these hopes, however, the hope in the availability of special grace, a hope which is fostered by symbolic representations, belongs to the parerga and cannot enter into a religion within the limits of reason alone. It is, as Kant put it in a new, technical expression of dubious value, the object of a "reflective faith.")[78]

Such trust in grace found in *Religion* is quite different from the faith in God as a guarantee of the possibility of the object of the moral law which is found in the *Critique of Practical Reason*. The transformation of Kant's thought or rather the extension (for Kant did not disown his notion of a moral faith; he rather deepened it) that is involved here can be noted on at least four points:

1. Religious feeling acquires a new quality that differentiates it more sharply from the moral feeling: it is a silent trust, humble and unconditional confidence in what God will do to supplement the weakness of our efforts against evil. The letter to Lavater in 1775 spoke of "the general and undefined trust that we shall partake of the good in some unknown way, if only we do not make ourselves unworthy of our share of it by our conduct."[79] The confidence has not changed, only the ground of hope is found less in the general constitution of the universe and the origin of the moral law and more in divine providential care.

2. Since Kant examined the relative aspects of our freedom and set in better light the crucial importance of our dispositions, the role of hope becomes more crucial than ever to the sustenance of the moral life. The problem of course had been there all along. Consider the *Lectures on Ethics*.

> Self-conceit and dejection are the two rocks on which man is wrecked if he deviates, in the one direction or the other, from the moral law. On the one hand man should not despair, but should believe himself strong enough to follow the moral law, even though he himself is not conformable to it. On the other hand, he ought to avoid self-conceit and an exaggerated notion of his powers.[80]

The problem reappears in the *Critique of Practical Reason* where Kant stated that Christianity is superior to Stoicism in that it destroys the confidence of being wholly adequate to duty.[81] This insight is then radicalized with the discovery of radical evil: despair becomes more than psychologically possible and probable but morally inevitable. The very undertaking of the moral life appears to require moral virtues and resources such as resolve, courage, hope, and determination. Virtue is moral strength,[82] and strength is no daughter to the wish (unless a mysterious second parent is brought into the picture). The religious community and its moral realities, its ritual and its fellowship, appear essential to the strength of the dispositions and that particularly because it nurtures hope and supports motivation. Even the doctrine of atonement has such positive religious and moral effects (in one passage only!): "The courage to stand on one's feet is itself strengthened by the doctrine of atonement" when it follows the ethical doctrine in that it "opens up to man the path to a new mode of life."[83]

3. God appears more in an eschatological light and what God will do is here at least as important and as much a guarantee of the moral enterprise as what he did as Creator and Author of the moral law. God now appears as the one who completes the moral enterprise as well as the one who is found as the ground of it. His justice will be manifested in the end, and also, we hope, will be his mercy. The letter to Lavater had spoken of what God did for us and referred to the life and death of Christ in orthodox Christian terms. The discussion of grace in *Religion* frequently speaks of what God will do. It is true that when this work examines the past, it leaves aside the idea of God having done something for us through the sacrificial death of his Son. The contrast with the letter to Lavater however should not be made too sharp: the memory of Christ's victory over evil is just as important as the hope of God's supplemental activity.

4. While moral theism had a concept of the goodness of God as Providence, it saw this goodness operating through a general governing activity and always submitted it to divine justice. *Religion*, as it gains access to the concept of grace, also sees the contrast between this moral Providence and the traditional Christian understanding of Providence which makes it an active love. On this point Kant's thought was uneasy. Christ is presented as having managed to elicit from us love for as well as obedience to the moral law. "Love God" and "Love your neighbour as yourself" are found to be meaningful precepts. ("They are precepts of *holiness* which we ought to pursue, and the very pursuit of them is called *virtue*.")[84] The thought of God being love still created difficulties for Kant[85] (unless one reduces it to the thought of the goodness of the purpose God had in mind, when he made man the final end of Creation and destined him to a moral commonwealth). The thought of God being love is another one to be held at a very respectful distance, or else religion will degenerate into sentimental effusion and moral alibis. Nevertheless Providence, in the book on religion, appears as a redeeming kind of Providence as well as a sustaining and governing kind. It thus wins the attributes of a more active goodness.

Finally there is one question that remains unanswered in Kant's doctrine of grace: What does it mean to strive to make ourselves worthy of divine aid through our moral life-conduct, when it is our very capacity to have a good life-conduct which is radically questioned and even categorically denied? We should not wait upon God, said Kant; we should proceed as though everything depended on us and we should pray for the coming of the Kingdom. "But what preparation must they now make that it shall come to pass"?[86] Kant, we saw, left this question unanswered in his text.

The answer, I believe, is to be found in the texts on conscience at the end of the essay *On the Failure of all Attempted Philosophical Theodicies* and in Book Four of *Religion*. Subjective honesty, that is, the undistorted and sure knowledge of what we in fact believe, of what we actually feel, of what we know and what we do not know, is the one virtue of which all men are always capable, no matter how corrupt, depraved, and prone to lying they may be. What our own conscience says about our own internal state of mind or state of feeling is something we can always know with certainty and directly, if we only try to be honest with ourselves. It is also something we can always achieve if we but wish to. On this particular point for Kant, the power to do something is daughter to the wish to do it. We can demand subjective honesty, or sincerity, of all. This is the permanent and inalienable basis of conscience and all inner religion.[87] This, I propose, is the one minimum preparation we can always achieve. And, if we can make the Bible speak for Kant: a broken and contrite heart God will not reject.

This answer has considerable merit. It does enable the morally conscientious man to avoid dejection (*accidia*) and self-righteousness. There is one endless and infinitely significant moral task, self-knowledge, which can always be undertaken by all and in which an infinitely valuable degree of success can always be achieved. There is one kind of integrity of which man can never be deprived and this integrity cannot overreach itself in pride since it is integrity in a knowledge that makes us humble. In other words, man for Kant has always the power to know the limits of his power.[88] This answer helps man to find something meaningful to do in all circumstances without allowing the development of a Pelagian faith. Calvin managed to convey such sense of purpose and such incentive to action in history and society without letting us believe that our action would bring the Kingdom of God. But in Calvin the tension between presumptuousness and hope is not fully conscious and certainly not resolved. Consciousness of the tension between the moral task and the religiously realistic perception of man's moral strength appears in the statement by the seventeenth century Calvinist Jurieu that we must "dogmatiser comme Augustin et prêcher comme Pélage."[89] One century later Kant exhibited true kinship with this aspect of the Calvinist tradition; as philosopher of ethics and moral psychologist, he achieved more rigour and more specificity in his analysis of the springs of action and in his guidance to action. "Out of such crooked lumber as man nothing straight can be made."[90] Kant does not allow the man who has reached such lucidity about himself to despair. He tells him how to work to approximate straightness, and gives him a good hope without giving him false hopes. He promises him moral integrity without promising moral perfection. Kant started *Religion* by opposing those enlightened souls who are "interested in education" and who believe (in spite of the evidence, repeated and overwhelming) that man steadily forges from bad to better, to those pessimistic minds who believe that from the Fall on man went from bad to worse.[91] After yielding to the evidence for corruption and without the assumption of steady inevitable progress, he chose to side in his intentions with the well-intentioned, those who try to cultivate the "seed of goodness which perhaps lies in us," even if it were only for the sake of not letting the man who waits upon God fall into despair.

Chapter 10

Religion within the Limits of Reason Alone: Conclusion

The One (True) Religion and the Traditional Faiths

Although we frequently notice in *Religion* a return to the usual Kantian ethical standpoint and a focusing of the religious philosophical discourse upon the statement of what we must—and can—do, we should not overlook the elements of genuine novelty introduced into Kant's philosophy by the results of his philosophy of religion. In *Religion*, unlike the *Critique of Practical Reason*, and unlike the writings on history, the ground of the hope moral men have of achieving their moral objectives is given by a positive religion (admittedly one in a stage of progressive transformation), namely Christianity which was for Kant the observable society which inaugurated the sovereignty of the good principle on earth and which then furthered such sovereignty. In *Religion* the ground of hope is not based solely upon a consideration of the postulates of moral action. The origins of this positive religion are shrouded in mystery. We can only say that our knowledge of human nature and of human hearts is such that we cannot give the credit for the rise of Christianity to unaided human wills. Whatever its origins are, the existence of the enlightened Christian church is a source of hope, and the moral philosopher affirms the validity of this source of moral hope.

Kant's pages on radical evil and on the hope in grace make, however shyly, one suggestion which has far-reaching consequences. Rational free men might after all be in need of specific divine help in history. Rather than endangering the autonomy of men and making them superstitious slaves, this divine help restores autonomy to captive men and thus brings them to free maturity. More precisely, it enables men to make of autonomy not a formal principle governing human thinking, but an effective power governing human relationships. It enables absolute freedom to incarnate itself and give motivation and content to human actions themselves. It thus promotes goodness in the world. Furthermore, such cooperation between divine help and autonomous human wills is not presented as the result of some eternally pre-established harmony willed by the Creator, but as a redeeming divine action which overcomes the results of human evil.[1]

Revelation and redeeming or supplementing grace are thus definitely introduced into Kantian discourse. The grounds of the legitimacy of this innovation is that revelation and grace afford hope.

> Whatever, as the means or the condition of salvation, I can know not through my own reason but only through revelation, and can incorporate into my confession only through the agency of an historical faith, and which, in addition, does not contradict pure moral principles—this I cannot, indeed, believe and profess as certain, but I can as little reject it as being surely false; nevertheless, without determining anything on this score, I may expect that whatever therein is salutary will stand me in good stead so far as I do not render myself unworthy of it through defect of the moral disposition in good life-conduct. In this maxim there is genuine moral certainty, namely, certainty in the eye of conscience (and more than this cannot be required of a man).[2]

As sources of hope and of moral help that do not contradict the moral imperative, revelation and grace complete man's moral endeavour, supplement his moral powerlessness (victim of evil) or change it, and, joined to man's autonomous efforts, work towards the realization of man's moral object, the one to which he is destined by God: the progressive coming on earth of the Kingdom of God. The structure of the argument is similar to the moral proof of the existence of God through the construction of the *summum bonum* and to the derivation of eternal peace as a political duty and historical probability. The rationally based moral objectives must be achievable. There are, however, the following differences.

1. The goal is a moral commonwealth on earth, not a political state of perpetual peace and not a *corpus mysticum*.

2. The hope is for a purification of our dispositions on earth, not for a social curbing of our evil dispositions, and not for an eternal moral progress in immortality.

3. The hope progresses towards realization in a religious moral community, not in an individual moral progress, and not in the establishment of a better yet still coercive juridico-civil state.

4. The hope is grounded in a redeeming divine activity and not merely in the truthfulness of the moral law of which God is the Author and certainly not merely in historically exhibited human patterns.

Having brought out the positive meaning of the concepts of revelation and grace as they are used in the most innovative strain of the argument in *Religion*, I can now make my commentary on the title of Kant's work on religion and on the basic metaphor of two concentric circles which is found in the preface to the second edition. I plan thereby to complete the summary of what I believe to be the essential significance of the work.

Kant did not undertake to discuss merely the religion of pure reason. This was satisfactorily done in his previous discussion of pure moral faith found in the second Critique. Kant undertook to discuss a wider sphere of religion, namely all that can be held within the limits of reason alone.

Regarding the title of this work (for doubts have been expressed about the intention concealed thereunder) I note: that since, after all, *revelation* can certainly embrace the pure religion of reason, while, conversely, the second cannot include what is historical in the first, I shall be able (experimentally) to regard the first as the *wider* sphere of faith, which includes within itself the second, as a *narrower* one (not like two circles external to one another, but like concentric circles). The philosopher, as a teacher of pure reason (from unassisted principles a priori), must confine himself within the narrower circle, and, in so doing, must waive consideration of all experience. From this standpoint I can also make a second experiment, namely, to start from some alleged revelation or other and, leaving out of consideration the pure religion of reason (so far as it constitutes a self-sufficient system), to examine in a fragmentary manner this revelation, as a *historical system*, in the light of moral concepts; and then to see whether it does not lead back to the very same pure *rational system* of religion.[3]

The first experiment has kinship with the method in philosophy of religion which proceeds from what we may call the eighteenth century rationalist premise: the philosopher defines the normative or essential religion, deduces or constructs or somehow establishes the necessity of this concept of religion. This leads to what W. Schultz called the "constructive philosophy of religion" exhibited in German classical idealism.[4] In reference to the diagram shown on page 241 this is the experiment that starts from the centre.

The second experiment has kinship with the method which proceeds from the empiricist's premise: the philosopher observes the empirical variety of religious behaviour and belief, describes them "as they are" and seeks to find some order in it. He may group the phenomena in families, classify them or seek whether the phenomena obey any law. In any case religion is seen as a phenomenon which must be interpreted by itself. This is what W. Schultz called the "phenomenological philosophy of religion."[5] In reference to the diagram given on page 241 this is the experiment which starts from the periphery.

The results of the first experiment are exhibited in Kant's conclusion that "there is only *one* (true) *religion*,"[6] but the data of the second experiment are immediately added when the sentence finishes with: "but there can be *faiths* of several kinds." Ultimately the religiousness of all upright men is somewhere one. In fact the traditions in which they learn and apply their religiousness vary. And the Kantian joint result of the two experiments is found in the thesis (put in classical deist terms) according to which "the nature of the religious vehicle is not indifferent to natural religion."[7] In the terms of the new post-deist philosophy of religion the thesis is put in this way: the concretization of religion in historical religions is the only place where the one true religion can be seen at work.[8]

It is not surprising that the core of Kant's method in philosophy of religion consists in a transcending of the conflict between empty dogmatism on the one hand and blind empiricism on the other, through the method of transcendental deduction, and through the regulation of the manifold of experience by the deduction of the conditions of possibility and the search for pure a priori principles. When applied to the philosophy of religion this doctrine means that the diversity of higher religious faiths while morally offensive is morally legitimate and inevitable at this stage of the education of the human race. All higher faiths are manifestations of religion. All faiths have potentially and some consciously within themselves the regulatory principle which will bring them in the future to a greater purification and to an ultimate convergence in the cosmopolitan religious community, or moral commonwealth, or Kingdom of God on earth.

The following diagram presents Kant's entire delimitation of the field of religion, individual and social, pure and historical (or applied),

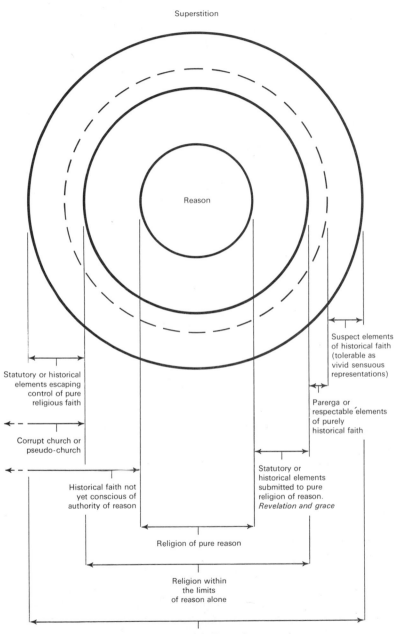

Superstition

Reason

Statutory or historical
elements escaping
control of pure
religious faith

Corrupt church or
pseudo-church

Historical faith not
yet conscious of
authority of reason

Suspect elements
of historical faith
(tolerable as
vivid sensuous
representations)

Parerga or
respectable elements
of purely
historical faith

Statutory or
historical elements
submitted to pure
religion of reason.
Revelation and grace

Religion of pure reason

Religion within
the limits
of reason alone

True church (will narrow its focus as it progresses)

rational and revealed, essential and positive. It gathers the results of his two experiments: the delimitation of the authority of pure reason in religious matters (the experiment that starts from the centre), and the delimitation and evaluation of the various elements found in empirical lived religious systems (the experiment that starts from the periphery). The former arrives at the pure rational faith. The latter at the "reflective faith," namely the faith in which the objects of faith are believed in reflectively, that is, considered as symbols, as bearers of a truth that strengthens hope.

The sea of superstition is endless. Reason is the centre, the focus where man humanizes himself as an end in himself, and learns the pure worship of God as Creator, Legislator, and Judge of free human beings. A true church will encompass the whole field with the exclusion of only superstition. At the periphery it will contain suspicious elements. As the true church progresses in history and more closely approximates the Kingdom of God, it narrows its focus to centre itself more and more on the pure religion of reason.

Kant oscillated on the matter of representation of the source of this purifying process and reforming energy that leads the church to progress. On the one hand he may speak of reason as the focus that draws and attracts. On the other hand he may speak of revelation and grace as the dynamic realities that move man along this progressive path.

The interpreter of course would like to know which one of these two positions is the most faithful expression of Kant's mind. But rather than trying to plumb the depths of this problem, it may be wiser to apply the lesson which M. J. Lasky drew as he wrote on a basic ambiguity in Kant's political philosophy: "It is an ambiguity which illuminates more meanings than most fundamental clarities."[9] This oscillation between the view that sees reason as the educator of history and that which sees history as the educator of reason is the major locus of his transition away from the standpoint of deism, and it led Kant to observe and respond to the life and death of symbols that mysteriously emerge along the course of man's development.[10] In this latter case, religious symbols cease to be concessions made to the frailty of our minds and to our sensuous nature; they become the source of our cultural development, of our increasing rationality, of our moral growth, and the means the divine pedagogue uses to educate mankind.

Kant fully saw the power of symbols in poetry and literature: he was more cautious, however, when it came to symbols in religion. Let us not forget that in the nineties Kant found himself at a time of historic crisis in politics, society, and religion. Old symbols died, new symbols were born. The King was beheaded. Men died and killed for "liberty, equality, and fraternity" and were aroused by the ceremonies of nationalistic republicanism. At this historic juncture Kant became afraid of opening the door to emotionalism and anarchy and, by prudence, for the sake of order, was rather prone to return to rationalism rather than to plunge into enthusiasm. For the sake of civilization as he saw it, reason demanded conservative reflexes in such times of crisis rather than the love of utopia. Kantian reason thus insisted on seeing symbols tested before they received allegiance of the heart.

Whatever we may think of the ultimate Kantian decision which judged the merits of rationalism greater than those of the irrational dynamics of historical movements, it must be emphasized that this position enabled Kant to account for the modern aberrant religious attitudes as well as for the superstitious relics of previous ages. It also kept the borders between the various elements of religion rather fuzzy: the very doctrine of the parerga as religious doctrines of which reason can say nothing very positive and nothing very negative and which are yet still respectable indicates his dislike of hard and fast separations. Furthermore, fuzziness reappears within the limits of religion within the limits of reason alone: the claims of human freedom and of divine Providence are never fully sorted out: Kant did not try to create in his language more clarity than the reality of our growth in moral goodness affords. It must be added, however, that blurred though some details may be, the specificity of reason and of revelation are well brought out, and the work delivers what Kant promised in the draft to his preface: a reunion of reason with revelation that will do honour to the latter and will be achieved with each defending its just and particular rights.[11]

The originality of Kant's philosophy of religion may thus be fully brought out. It consists of a transition between the rationalistic theology of the Enlightenment (deistic or orthodox) and the modern attempt at a descriptive and normative interpretation of mankind's religious life in its totality. The indices of this transition have been neglected by nearly all English-speaking interpreters of Kant. The neglect of these indices is all the more surprising since E. Troeltsch began to draw them to the attention of Kantian scholars in a monumental article in 1904. (C.C.J. Webb made no reference to it.)

Kant, Troeltsch wrote, stands at the point where deism moves into modern research of history of religion. It begins to be assumed that naked reason is not enough, that there is a need for a positive religion, for a vehicle of religious truth, on account of the factual psychological make-up of man.[12] (To this interpretation it should be added that it is also on account of man's historical moral condition, and of his finiteness.) The aim of the Kantian effort was not a religion of pure reason but a religion within the limits of pure reason,[13] and this simple distinction has been too often overlooked. "He does not want a religion of pure reason, but a 'rectification' of positive religion through the religion of reason."[14]

Thus the need for an ecclesiastical Christianity is firmly established. If, like his rationalistic predecessors, Kant toyed with the idea of a new Bible, he always quickly abandoned the idea; his answer was consistently that one should stay with Christianity and get as much good out of it as one can.[15] Although Kant drew a distinction between pure religious faith (defined by critical reason) and an ecclesiastical faith (set forth by confessional authority), these are not mutually exclusive, but in inner mutual relation.[16] Far from offering or suggesting a new religion, a perfect one, the philosopher criticized the best of those already offered to us on the basis of its essential idea, or of its condition of possibility. Kant's method is "transcendental-critical not metaphysical-speculative."[17] In ethics Kant started with a radical separation between the intelligible norm and the psychological fact. But in *Religion* the Ideas of pure reason and the concrete history of the will are put in a dialectical relationship. To their dialectic corresponds another one between the pure religion of reason (valid by a priori necessity) and the historical religions. The former is only a critical canon to reform and refine the empirical religions. Here again the critical principle is meant only to regulate the empirical reality, not to establish it.[18] It is truly critical and not constitutive. It is a canon, not a creative source of the perfect religion.

So if we accept the Kantian dualism between the normative and the anthropological, the a priori and the a posteriori, it is evident that the two stand in mutual need of each other. Thus there was for Kant the possibility of three kinds of theologies:

1. purely scientific theology which deduces the whole of religion from reason alone (the a priori form);

2. purely positive ecclesiastical theology which expounds the dogmas contained in the revealed and inspired Bible (the a posteriori matter) (We should correct Troeltsch to add that such "ecclesiastical theology" is found in all religious traditions and may be described historically as well as expounded authoritatively.);

3. an alliance of the two, in which the latter is given first but then is illumined and regulated by the former.

The first is empty and ineffective; the second alone is superstitious, hypocritical, and fanatical. It is by the use of the third that all higher religions have been guided in the past and that the visible Christian church will be guided towards the ideal church of the future. This solution is consistent with that found in political philosophy where we saw that Kant wanted reform, based on principle, not revolution or conservation. Troeltsch correctly concluded that Kant did not wish revolutionary replacement of historically conditioned theology by a pure theology of reason;[19] the truth of the Christian doctrine of the Kingdom of God and of the church as embodiment of it was recognized;[20] and Kant gave an interpretation drawn out of Christianity's own essential basic ideas, not an allegorization of Christianity in the light of ideas brought from the outside.[21]

It must be noted, however, that the philosophical criticism bears on form only and not on content.[22] The question it asks is whether this or that faith can be held "honestly" and in all integrity by a sincere man. It is not whether or not reason conceives the possibility of the object of this faith.

> I do not say here that in things of religion reason must boldly claim that it is sufficient to itself, but only that, when it is not sufficient to the task, either in insight or judgement or in power, it must expect everything which needs to be added to its capacity, from the supernatural help of heaven, without being capable of knowing in what it may consist.[23]

It may be legitimate therefore to conclude that in this particular strain of Kantian thought (when pursued in its deeper implications), the religion of reason develops itself along with and in dependence upon the positive religions which confess that their development is led by divine interventions and revelations. The correlate of this conclusion is that Kant had a vision of the development of reason itself in history. As his philosophy of history had already shown, human reason is always finite, never absolutely creative or constructive like the *intellectus archetypus*. It is inherently critical and that means receptive, organizing, dependent upon that which is not reason, dependent upon relationships towards which it behaves spontaneously and rationally. It further means that the quality of its criticism depends on that which it criticizes. Reason is a capacity to deal with the arational or the less rational with a view to establishing a society where free men are at home. Its capacity becomes more and more powerful, less and less tentative, as that with which it deals becomes increasingly susceptible to being subsumed by free men in their organization for rational purposes, or increasingly friendly to the interests of man.

Thus we find in Kant's doctrine of reason traces of the idea of the education of the human race that had appeared in the philosophy of history. Reason also is educated and the pedagogue is a God whose purpose is to establish friendship among men. The person of Christ as liberator of moral man becomes in that perspective the surest ground of hope. It is a token of God's determination to inspire and support the efforts of moral men. It is legitimate for men to hope that genuinely moral purposes, if struggled for by mankind, will not be frustrated. Such hope will strengthen the moral disposition of men (without endangering the purity of their motivation) just as Christ strengthened the moral dispositions of those who came in contact with him. Moral men may hope to be rescued by a moral agency other than their own. There is redemption and thus religious faith comes to the rescue of the tenuous hope allowed to those who believe that there will be progress if men will it.

Kant's Philosophy of Religion as Partner for Christian Theology

Kant's philosophy of religion does not end up with a project to abolish religion nor with a disposition to leave it as it is and leave religious life as observed in late eighteenth century German society basically untouched. It concludes with a project of reform based on a religious norm. This result follows directly from the general reformist bent of Kant's thought and, more specifically, from the fact that his philosophy of religion is not reductionist and is not merely descriptive and analytical. It arrives at a norm, which is a norm for action and which emerges from religious life itself and seeks to regulate it towards the realization of its true nature.

Since religious life for Kant has a social and historical dimension and finds its true hope in a community and since Kant believed himself to be a Christian,[24] his philosophy of religion, remote though it may be from the methods and concerns of church theologians entrusted with the leadership of the community, nevertheless ends up giving advice to churchmen and thus claims to have ecclesiastical theological value.

My conclusion will focus on problems in philosophy of religion and thus will not return to specifically Christian problems. In order, however, to bring out the full scope of the Kantian undertaking, I shall examine in this section to what extent Kant—or his interpreters —made good the claim that his philosophy of religion purified the Christian religious tradition—or at least sought to purify it—while remaining essentially faithful to it. I am not asking whether Kant's philosophy of religion successfully "vindicated the claims" of Christianity to be *the* revealed religion, or whether it made Christianity into the absolute, most rational, or most moral or highest religion (and whether it was justified to do so), because I believe I have shown that these were not the questions Kant really undertook to answer, even though they were the questions he inherited from the Christian-Deist debate. The question is rather whether the leadership Kant offered to the Christian church is heretical (that is, whether it totally distorts the truth of which this religious tradition is a bearer), or whether bold and radical though it may be, it emerged from bases that had been present all along in the tradition.[25]

To answer this question one should begin by noting that in Kant's philosophy of religion, philosophy and religion both keep an integrity and an autonomy of their own. Philosophers have their "worldly" man-centred questions and their rational methods for examining evidence, and the philosophy of religion does not compromise in any way this fundamental nature of philosophy. Religious life keeps a coherence and integrity of its own, and is not systematically reduced to the fate of appearing to be pseudo-philosophy, pre-philosophy, or something defined only by virtue of its being something less than philosophy.[26] The relationship between theology and philosophy is complex in Kant as is well indicated by his further remark after his acknowledgement that philosophy may be called the servant of theology: Does the servant walk before the mistress holding a torch, or behind her carrying the train?[27] Each, however, is allowed to have dynamics of its own and to follow the logic of its attitudes for a while without being censored by the other. This point was well brought out by J. Collins in his description of Kant's position as standing between Zoroaster and Job. The philosopher of religion is embodied by Zoroaster; he is the wise man, or the seeker after wisdom. He remains distinct from Job the religious man, who strives after holiness. The philosopher of religion does not technically need to be a religious man, although he will have to be capable of sympathetic understanding, and the philosopher of religion cannot take the place of or abolish the religious man.[28]

To this can be added that the philosopher, while he cannot make anything out of what he does not understand and will tend to pronounce such mysteries useless to the further humanization of man, is not thereby imprisoned in a circle. What remains incomprehensible is not necessarily to be pronounced impossible. The function of the parerga is to keep the borders of religion within the limits of reason alone open to further light. Likewise, while the religious man remains always sensitive to his conscience and thus has a touchstone in himself he dares not contradict, he nevertheless is open to the word emanating from God. "In Job's conduct, we hear the invitation to enter in dialogue with God himself, and not with our own moral reason."[29] But in such an invitation, the accent is different from that of the philosopher who insists that only our reason can decide whether it is God himself who has spoken, or rather, to be as precise as the text is, who insists that our reason is in a position to decide that some "revelation" does not come from God, if it contradicts rational moral certainty.[30]

It can be concluded, therefore, that the style of Kant's philosophy of religion does not prohibit it from becoming a partner to the undertaking of the church theologian. But if this is granted it still remains to be seen whether what this particular philosophy of religion proposed is in fact of any value to its partner and can be recognized as being true to the Christian tradition in any sense.

One instance will suffice to focus my argument. A positive contribution may be found in Kant's handling of the doctrine of justification. While Kant specifically stated that he could not see what positive use could be made in religion of the idea of justification of a guilty individual,[31] it seems that he nevertheless achieved a restatement of the doctrine of justification by grace through faith. For, after all, the entire doctrine of *Religion within the Limits of Reason Alone* on the subject of our salvation, or our reascent from evil to good, moves between two poles beyond which Kant never trespassed: on the one hand we cannot exercise any influence on God or do anything that will win us favours; on the other hand we are moral beings by his own decree, and cannot remain like putty in his hands. As moral beings we must strive to obey the moral law. As honest moral beings we must acknowledge we cannot achieve purity in virtue and may hope with moral certainty that God will supplement our efforts in some way or other. But what is this if not a restatement of the position according to which we are justified by grace alone and confess our spiritual poverty?

Kant's position follows directly from the sovereignty of God. God is Lord; one cannot work on him or conjure up divine assistance by magic or ritual. Man, however, is not a passive animal. Man is finite and rational, he is spontaneity-in-relation; he sets his own ends and it is his essence always to work towards a purpose. Since man cannot work on God, all he can do when it comes to religion is to work on himself, namely to strive to bring himself in conformity with the will of God, to endeavour to be well-pleasing to him.[32] And since he cannot bring himself into full conformity with the will of God, all he can do in the end is acknowledge the extent of his failure in an act of moral honesty. If religious faith were to ask of man to avoid doing even that, as his *quod in se est*, it would ask him to stop being a human being. Kant is often said to have limited true religion to morality. It is not so; he limited man's preparation to true religion, and man's contribution to the encounter between God and man, to moral preparation or morality.

Furthermore, since man cannot be passive, religious grace must be owned by an individual or appropriated. For Kant, since the individual is active, this amounts to an active interpretation, a re-orientation of the will. Only the "moral service of God (*officium liberum*) is directly well-pleasing to God."[33] Morality, or life under the moral law, is the only part which man can play both in preparation and in response. Its two alternatives (effort to win God's favour or act on him, or quietism) are negations of the very form of humanity: to be free and strive after goals of one's own.

Conscience is an absolute which no revelation or no grace in the world or out of the world can violate. To make us morally better at the cost of a violation of conscience would be to make us into non-human beings, that is to say, not moral at all. This does not mean that man dogmatically decides what revelation can or cannot be. Conscience does not predetermine the what but only the how. Revelation or grace can be accepted by the individual only when it is related to the nexus of experiences, involvements, and objectives in which he exists, or when it becomes appropriated by man's good will and enters into the strengthening and orientation of it. So the treatise on religion concludes that conscience is the only guide in matters of faith. The consciousness of man is problematic; there is no whole undivided possession of truth, no unconditional unambiguous assurance. "Lord, I believe, help thou my unbelief" is man's predicament.[34] But there is a wholeness in intention, a firmness in moral determination, there is a good will and this is an unconditional state of mind. No religious faith can be allowed to be held at the cost of insincerity, doublemindedness, or deception. A faith is valid only if it is held by the conscience with integrity and, properly, Kant concluded with a praise of sincerity.

Kant's doctrine of justification stresses our constant responsibility for conscientious activity and thus does not include Luther's point about accepting to be passive and accepting to lose control since the petty control we have upon our smaller sins only magnifies our self-righteousness. This, however, makes Kant's doctrine only more like that of Calvin who believed that man never forfeits the task of self-government. This is not surprising since Kant's interest for those theologians who gave a moral interpretation of religion led him to read Calvinist ones, especially Stapfer.

Kant's doctrine, however, differs from that of both Luther and Calvin (and the Council of Trent too, for that matter) in that it is not held within the framework of traditional supernaturalism, with a God who is offended, deliberates with himself, fastens upon the scheme of salvation that will reconcile his justice and his mercy, sends his Son, accepts his sacrifice, and administers the resulting extra merits by decisive applications of grace to various individuals at various times. All these representations fall under Kant's strictures against literally taken anthropormorphisms that have moral implications. Kant also abandoned the thought of the church as administrator through the word and the sacraments of the substantial gifts of divine mercy. All these doctrines in Kant are victims of the rationalism of the Enlightenment and of his standpoint as a moral philosopher.

But the doctrine of justification does not lose its reference to transcendence for all that. Grace remains both free and divine. Kant, did not move all the way to the existentialist subjectivism of Feuerbach for whom feeling is both Holy Spirit and faith, and for whom justification by faith means that we are justified if we feel justified.[35] There is no such thoroughgoing immanentization in Kant. But he could see two barriers beyond which religious faith cannot go: it cannot admit either immanent grace or heteronomous man.

Kant could propound simultaneously that the corrupt man, "try as hard as he will," cannot "make himself a new man well-pleasing to God," and that "a reasonable man" cannot accept atonement "in order to regard his guilt as annihilated" and must first "improve his way of life."[36] The grace which brings our moral nature to its fulfilment or completion is not immanent. It is not a natural effect of the constitution of the world or the striving of our will. We cannot take it for granted. It is genuinely transcendent, given by God in his unbounded freedom and creating a possibility not inherent in the situation of man. Not being immanent, grace is not within the grasp of reason, and cannot be understood, even though we may trust it will supplement our earnest efforts.[37]

Anxious to avoid heteronomy for man and immanence for grace, Kant had a very perilous balance to maintain. To keep it, he repeatedly returned to his key solution: we cannot achieve our end; the grace of God may help; we may hope for it but we cannot count on it; we must rather keep on proceeding as if everything depended upon us. Not to require moral striving while waiting upon God is to ask man to abandon his humanity and make himself a slave or a mercenary before God, a knave with duplicity.

No hope, only the moral law, should determine the direction of our will. To act on a hope would be heteronomy (to be determined by a material state). But this is not to deny us the possibility of acting with hope. For Kant, to be a servant of God rules out being a favourite but is compatible with being his son.[38] The Christian faith is natural (in the sense that it requires no infraction of the moral law and no intellectual sacrifice), but it is not naturalistic because it does not deny that God can help us to reach our destination. Kant is no naturalist and divine forgiveness constantly stands on the edge of his discourse. Autonomous man and transcendent grace strive to be reconciled. When Kant concludes that "the right course is not to go from grace to virtue but rather to progress from virtue to pardoning grace,"[39] he speaks of the course of man's doing, which remains a striving begun by him and brought to its end by an agency other than his own. In the order of being, or in the course originating not from man but from God, things go from grace to virtue. Nothing in Kant denies this possibility and much points to it.

The doctrine of justification is crucial enough to allow us the conclusion that Kant offered a system of thought which remains true to one of the basic norms of the Christian tradition. It is true that Kant undertook on philosophical grounds to discriminate among the doctrines and rituals of Christianity and this philosophical trespassing should not be obscured. Nevertheless Kant, unlike Hume and Goethe, can be said to have criticized the Christian tradition (and even to have objected to many of its doctrines) from the inside. The authority of the Founder is real and some lessons of the tradition are learned. His philosophy of religion thus in its final moments (when it undertakes to interpret what Christianity is all about) could be presented as a Christian philosophy, namely a philosophy which has learned from the Christian tradition. The best evidence for that is the permanent distance maintained between God and man, while at the same time the divine will to bridge that gap is maintained in a way that is conducive to the humanization of man rather than the demonization of human existence. The moral law, not the incarnation, was for Kant the logos, but such reinterpretation of the logos doctrine maintains some of the results of Nicaea and Chalcedon: man remains man and God remains God. Ultimately he has presented us with a worldly philosophy which affirms the dignity of man and his limitations and that is neither Promethean nor despondent. Furthermore his philosophy forever remains at the school of reality, thus maintaining an attitude akin to some kind of piety. Kant is "respectful of reality in all its forms. He does not try either to reduce it or to deduce it."[40] Our powers to conceive and understand reality are never allowed to assume idolatrous proportions. Kant's may be the first philosophy to have achieved at that deep epistemological level a synthesis between Greek philosophical consciousness and Semitic religious consciousness, and perhaps that could have been done only in the context of European modernity rather than in that of the Roman Empire (at any rate this is what Hegel thought). We can perhaps understand now J. Lacroix's judgement that Kant's thought, in spite of the fact that it does not claim to be a Christian philosophy, or rather precisely because it does not claim it, is the one philosophy that best approximates it.[41]

The Historic Position of Kant's Philosophy of Religion

I have established, I believe, that Kant's philosophy of religion, while it seeks to introduce a radical reform within the Christian tradition, is nevertheless a thought which proceeds from within the

Christian tradition. It must be emphasized however that Kant offered a "Religionslehre," a philosophy of religion, not a Christian philosophy or a theology. He thus treated a relatively new subject matter that had appeared only recently in the intellectual history of the West: religion. Many factors went into the appearance of religion as a subject matter offered to the consideration of philosophers. The knowledge of cultures other than the Christian one, and the appearance of a split in Western culture between the modern scientific world view and the traditional one which became labelled religious are, in short, the two most important factors. By seeking to handle philosophically that new subject matter Kant responded to an intellectual challenge proper to his day. I would like in this section to examine how well he rose to this challenge. I will hopefully establish whether Kant's philosophy of religion passes a second test: not whether it is faithful to the Christian tradition or downright heretical, but whether it is an intelligent handling of the problems created by the attempt of religious men to find a style of life and thought in the context of post-enlightenment culture.

I must emphasize first the size of the challenge. The eighteenth century saw an attack on traditional metaphysics as well as on all traditions of society. Religious faith in the eyes of some was just another one of the traditions which would be left behind. The Newtonian revolution especially, having redefined the concepts of nature, of law, and of order in the universe, and having led to a natural science that was reaping unprecedented successes in the control of the physical world, inevitably created a serious intellectual challenge for those who undertook to formulate the meaning of religious faith. We saw that this intellectual revolution in many cases ruined metaphysics by giving currency to the notion that natural science was the only possible science of beings and being, thereby reducing being to extended beings.[42] Thus the old alliance between Christian religious faith and metaphysical theism or ontology was endangered since one party was losing its authority. In many cases the Newtonian revolution threatened also to ruin religious feeling by objectifying it and making of it one more causally explainable phenomenon in a mechanical world.

Part of the stature of Kant comes from the fact that he sensed the importance of the intellectual transformations represented by such phenomena of his century as the success of Newtonian science, the first steps in the understanding of foreign cultures, and the French revolution, but did not add to such sensitivity an unthinking urge to join the new schools and leave the old ones. He sensed the enormous significance of what is called the Enlightenment, but did not simply board the new wagon. Rather he sought to understand precisely the implications of one school of thought (or one style of life) prevailing over another, indicating thereby one of the important differences between a philosopher and an ideologue. In times of intellectual turmoil—we would call it cultural change now—he sought to reach afresh for the foundations, foundations which perhaps may be grasped only when the systems begin to totter and reveal the gaps in man's knowledge and the contradictions in his wisdom. As L. W. Beck pointed out, Kant did not radically change his Weltanschauung at any point, but:

> ... when he found that the Leibnizian metaphysics could not be supported "as a science" ..., his technical philosophy underwent a profound revolution, a revolution which, if successful, would provide a foundation for the Weltanschauung which had become almost second nature to him. The Weltanschauung remained; but it was given a new foundation.[43]

Beck thus emphasized the conservative character of Kant's philosophy. The key affirmations of the old metaphysics remain but, while their old foundations have crumbled, they receive a new, more solid foundation, rooted in the very nature of man as a finite rational being. These key affirmations, Beck added, "are at least as old as Christian Aristotelianism."[44]

I do not wish to quarrel with this broad characterization but must add that when it comes to this new, vast subject matter for philosophers, religion, the awareness that the times in the cultural history of the West which called for radical rethinking led not just to a reaffirmation of a new philosophical basis of older affirmations but led also to a vast amount of destructive work and to an opening of a new path both for the philosophy of religion as an academic discipline and for the reorientation of religious life and institutions as an existential concern of all cultured men. James Collins correctly emphasized that: "It is Kant's critical office to unsettle the new harmonization proposed between religious faith, theism, and the Newtonian mechanistic universe."[45]

This new harmonization was primarily the work of the deists who were not without roots in the Renaissance, and who added a solid dash of enlightened views to their blend of wonder, cosmological arguments, and praise for a unified world system. But orthodox theologians also welcomed the Newtonian revolution, praised the divine

Mechanic, forgot the old metaphysics, and accepted most of the ontological implications of the new science. As long as each dogma—or at least some of them—could be made safe one way or the other, it escaped them that such an apologetic operation reified their faith into a belief system from which the life of religion quickly became absent.

We saw that Kant destroyed the compromise worked out by the deists, and that, unlike them, he did not undertake to argue for a new religion, a natural one, and a minimum set of rational beliefs. He looked at positive religion, at the concrete lived and institutionalized religious traditions, and he looked at their dogmas in this experiential context. He thus came to contrast faith and belief. Unlike the rationalist theologians who were involved in the rescuing of that part of traditional dogmas which they thought could be rescued, he asked the radical question of a philosophical anthropology: What is religious man, and what norms ought to govern his religious life?

I must therefore at this stage emphasize the radical novelty of Kant's philosophy of religion; it is anthropocentric, experiential, critical, and has no ostensible apologetic concern. Most importantly, it undertakes to examine mankind's religious life without in principle hastening to metaphysical conclusions about God. It is thus no longer dependent upon an accommodation between the Christian faith and philosophy that was at least as old as the Renaissance. This is not to say that all of Kant's philosophy of religion is a radical founding of a new intellectual discipline with new criteria and with a new object. We saw that the lessons taught by Knutzen and his religious rationalism influence a good deal of *Religion*. This is not to say either that what is new in Kant had no antecedents; the role of the pietists and of the Calvinist moral theologians in the development of Kant's notion of moral faith is too obvious for that. And some figures of the Enlightenment had begun to gather documentation on the varieties of religious experience. But it is to say that whereas Kant could find an old Weltanschauung worth founding a new basis for (and for which he could in good faith find a new basis that could claim to be a scientific one) he could not find an old philosophy of religion that existed and was worth re-establishing. Metaphysics and ontology, theism, theodicy, Christian piety, Church history, the anthropological investigation of religious man, the body of thought on the role of religion in history, the speculation on the nature and source of religious feeling, all this did not form a coherent whole when Kant appeared on the scene. Different parts had developed in the defense of different intellectual interests. Theodicy for example was worked out by orthodox minds. Church history was a battle ground for erudite clergy and witty critics, for obscurantists and nasty-minded sceptics. And interpretation of religious feeling, with the help of Lucretius, was a fond subject for all anticlericals and atheists. Kant of course did not leave a "finished" philosophy of religion that put all these elements together. But he did do a good deal of the work. That Kant's work could enable future thinkers, starting with Schleiermacher and Hegel, to see and to realize the possibility of a philosophy of religion that would bring all this body of hostile and unrelated thought into a coherent whole centred upon the philosophical interpretation of what it means to be a religious being is no small measure of the novelty and size of his achievement.

Having thus brought together the main argument of this book, namely that Kant's philosophy of religion approximates a systematic whole, is innovative, and founds a new branch of philosophy, one must be careful to state precisely the extent of the innovation. The end of this section will try to set limits to this affirmation of novelty and modernity. Limits after all, should be expected in the light of the conservative character of Kant's philosophy. This I shall do by means of three questions: Is Kant's philosophy of religion entirely secularized, non-religious, or pagan? Is it accompanied by metaphysical liberalism? And is it alienated from the past?

The matter of paganism first. Peter Gay recently interpreted the Enlightenment as the rise of modern paganism. The philosophes, he argued, systematically turned to the pagan world of Greek and Roman wisdom, and especially to the sceptics and atheists among them, to find a "classical" alternative philosophy of life, distinct from the mediaeval Christian one and occasionally opposed to it. Gay opened the presentation of his case by referring to Kant's quote of Horace: "*Sapere aude*,"[46] and finished with Hume, "the complete modern pagan."

> Without drama but with the sober eloquence one would expect from an accomplished classicist, Hume makes plain that since God is silent, man is his own master; he must live in a disenchanted world, submit everything to criticism, and make his own way.[47]

It is tempting to see Kant in this light. Kant argued that reason should look critically into everything, that man should become autonomous, and he quoted the classics frequently in *Religion within the Limits of Reason Alone*. Gay's case is brilliantly made and there is no doubt that with the Enlightenment the opportunity existed, perhaps for the first time, for a philosopher to offer a philosophy of religion that would be non-Christian, non-religious, pagan, or secular (or that could be at least one or two of these things).

But while Gay's interpretation does justice to much of the French and English Enlightenment, the German Enlightenment can hardly be interpreted as a systematic turning away from Christian roots. That Kant's philosophy of religion is resolutely man-centred is beyond doubt. It is also clear that it harbours little fear of worldly and ecclesiastical authorities, and that it addresses itself to a bold man who has come of age and who will make his own way. But God is hardly silent and Kant did not quite live in a disenchanted world. God speaks in the moral law and man, autonomous though he is, finds his autonomy is respectful obedience to a moral law that is the object of awe. When Gay stated that mediaeval philosophy subordinated rationality to higher things, while for the Enlightenment "philosophy was autonomous and omnipotent, or it was nothing,"[48] he formulated an alternative between two positions neither of which can be said to be Kant's. For Kant, philosophy is autonomous, and any curtailment of its self-ascribed freedom will be its death. But philosophy is not omnipotent, it does not dispose of truth. Man, if not philosophy, is for Kant subordinated to—or dependent upon—higher things as the moral law and the need for hope constantly remind us. Kant is worldly in the sense that his philosophy educates us for living within this world, but he is not worldly as Gibbon for instance is worldly, for whom this world is the only world. We must conclude therefore that Kant's philosophy of religion is not quite modern, if to be modern is to seek to abolish every trace of the Christian Aristotelian synthesis. We saw that it is not a philosophy of religion that seeks to abolish religion or to replace it. And as it seeks to reform religion, Kant was willing to draw upon classical Greek or Roman sources but nowhere used them as an alternative superior to Christian views. He specifically found fault with the Stoics, who were probably to him the best antiquity had to offer. Rather, the significance of Kant's philosophy of religion lies precisely in the fact that it is worldly and man-centred without being a secularizing influence bent upon banishing God and religion from the horizon of man, and without claiming to be rooted in a rival to Christianity.

Similar, metaphysically conservative features will appear if we examine the question of whether Kant was a thoroughgoing liberal. I define liberalism as George Grant did:

. . . a set of beliefs which proceed from the central assumption that man's essence is his freedom and therefore that what chiefly concerns man in this life is to shape the world as we want it.[49]

Leo Strauss formulated in what sense Locke may be said to be the leading liberal:

From now on, nature furnishes only the worthless materials as in themselves; the forms are supplied by man, by man's free creation. For there are no natural forms, no intelligible "essences": the "abstract ideas" are "the inventions and creatures of the understanding, made by it for its own use.[50]

Here more than in the case of enlightened paganism, it is tempting to assume as self-evident that Kant, who invented formalism in ethics, is to be counted among the liberals and the moderns. Man according to him is wrenched from the bosom of nature to make himself; of all beings he is the only one free to choose his own ends. Since his autonomous freedom is the human form and must be preserved at all costs, why hesitate before the conclusion that freedom is man's essence and that nature is nothing but material to man's form? Kant's politics furthermore were liberal. He assumed that in the free clash of opinions truth in the end would prevail. He even specifically stated that history is the result of the clash of human purposes as men choose them. Further evidence of the similarity between Kant and the liberal view is the fact that for both, as for most of Europe since the seventeenth century, philosophy became militant, or became an instrument of political amelioration. It sought to direct and activate man's striving after purposes relating to his welfare on earth rather than to guide his thinking about his condition. At any rate many of the moderns list Kant among their mentors when they accept the liberal account of the human situation: "An unlimited freedom to make the world as we want in a universe indifferent to what purposes we choose."[51]

Even though Kant was being a good liberal when he stated that mankind will progress in the future if and only if men work at it, it is highly misleading to place him squarely in the liberal mainstream. Kant remained with the old distinction between reason and will. Man is free to strive after purposes of his own choosing, but only those purposes are moral which reason in us dictates rather than our mere will chooses. The moral law may be presented as our autonomous creation, but only with the rather radical qualification that it is the creation of our reason rather than of our will, or in Kantian terms of *Wille* rather than *Willkür*. And this reason has an absolute authority. It is "pure," Kant would have said, and it is not a pragmatic utilitarian instrument for the furtherance of the greatest good for the greatest number, or for the furtherance of one's interest as one sees it. Furthermore the positive role of teleology in the Kantian system allows for the feeling of continuity with nature and the legitimacy of placing man, as a free being, in a teleological development originating in an authority higher than his own and enveloping all that is. Kant's man is modern in that he is not imprisoned in a teleological system, but he is not modern if to be modern is to be cut off from nature and all that is, in splendid, free spiritual isolation. The moral law calls for a pure religious faith that roots the rational moral law in the holy will of the Creator. Within the context of his ethical formalism he could not affirm more clearly that the moral law is rooted not in the fiat of a historical reason but in the very nature of things.[52] So on each count Kant is in continuity with the older metaphysics and its insistence upon the ultimately higher authority of that which is good over that which is freely chosen.[53]

Finally the question may be asked as to whether Kant's philosophy of religion is alienated from the past and from past religious history. Kant, again being typical of his century, is among the first Christians for whom Jesus threatens to become a remote and alien historical figure. Kant began to feel an enormous historical distance between himself and the founder and central figure of his religious tradition. Many factors entered into the making of such a situation. Not least among them was the first major public presentation of an offensive account of the historical Jesus, namely Reimarus's presentation of Jesus and his disciples as unfortunate schemers making of Jesus a pathetic and possibly dishonest figure. The authority of scientific historical criticism could be adduced to support this account. But the conflict of Christian interpretations of Jesus, from enthusiastic sects through pietism to strictest orthodoxy, would also have gone into the making of a situation in which Jesus began to appear as an incomprehensible, and, what is perhaps even worse, ungraspable figure from the past. Thus Kant was at the beginning of a series of thinkers for whom it became clear that Jesus must either be reinterpreted or lost. The case has been made that by settling for an account of Jesus as teacher of a moral law which reason itself teaches, Kant ended up with the palest possible Jesus and a Jesus so radically reinterpreted as to be more an invention of the eighteenth century deism than a presence from the past.

I disposed of such an interpretation by showing how important to Kant was his account of the life of the historical Jesus.[54] It is not necessary to make the case here again. But it is important to the argument of this chapter to note that, while Kant was threatened by a feeling of alienation from his past, he was able to conserve much from that past that was of meaning to him. This is true of him both as a Christian and as a philosopher. On the one hand, he spoke in a vein very close to the extreme enlightened way, and presented the whole of church history (with the exception of Jesus) as a shameful past to turn away from, and saw in all previous metaphysics a record of successive failures, and yet, on the other hand, he seems well read in the theological classics and made good use of them, borrowed from Plato the noumenon-phenomenon distinction at the crucial stage of the elaboration of the critical philosophy, and strove mightily to find a sense in which teleological judgements, that major piece of the Aristotelian heritage, can be said to be true. And in politics, we saw him flirting with Rousseau's attempt to start everything de novo and ending up trying to reform the old.

The question now before us is inescapable: How can the old and the new be reconciled in Kant's philosophy of religion? Were they reconciled in his own mind or is his philosophy of religion a hodgepodge of juxtaposed elements: a natural history of religion, and a divine plan for the education of the human race, in brief, a new anthropology and an old metaphysics? Or is there some unifying concept, which, while allowing for that which is incomplete and not entirely worked out, will enable us to see why all these observations on Lapps and Mongols, these comments on superstitious and enthusiastic Westerners, these debates on biblical exegesis, and these examinations of the traditional proofs of the existence of God, may end up forming a whole which may be called a philosophy of religion? There is such a unifying concept, I believe, and I suggest that all these anthropological, philosophical, and theological elements coalesce into a reasoned discourse on religion as a whole because everywhere Kant saw—or perhaps sensed or began to see—symbols. We saw earlier that Kant was aware of the symbolic nature of our knowledge of God and that he began the determination of the religious world as being a world of symbols.[55] It is there, I believe, that we can find the key to the historic position of Kant's philosophy of religion. It is because of his theory of symbols and his actual art of interpreting symbols that he could in-novate, create a philosophy of religion as a new, vaster, man-centred field, and say new, intelligent things about religion in the post-enlightened world. It is also because of his view of symbols that he could conserve much of the well-consecrated affirmations of Western metaphysics.

Of course there are, in Kant, only the beginnings of a systematic theory of symbols.[56] But such beginnings are, in my opinion, decisive because it is the interpretation of the religious world as a world of symbols—not literal truths—that can cleanse the modern religious world of the defects of mediaeval supernaturalism. And the interpre-tation of the religious world as made of symbols—not illusions—is done in the context of a philosophy that can discriminate among these sym-bols and can validate some of them. Kant's interpretation of religious faith as being expressed in and strengthened by symbols but focused on a core of pure rational faith makes of the religious world an intrinsic part of man's cultural life and of his search for a culture that will do justice to his nature. Remember that genuine religious symbols are seen as supports that provide the kind of hope moral men need and the kind of moral hope that does not deter them from their moral task. Such symbols of hope for Kant are legitimate, they are rooted in reality; they make men at home in the world, and no more and no less at home than God wanted them to be. Thus religious faith, as inter-preted by Kant, can mediate to modern enlightened man what can still be mediated truthfully of the affirmations of traditional meta-physics that had brought so much light and wisdom to Western man in the past and had helped bridge the gap between culture and nature, between what men do and "all that is."

Kant's doctrine of transcendent grace especially, which is free from the metaphysics of supernaturalism yet points to a transcendent world of higher authority, may well be a necessary part of any theistic faith in the post-enlightenment world and of any attempt to mediate the affirmations of traditional metaphysics. After man was proclaimed to be the measure of all things, the Aristotelian doctrine of Nature undertook to provide the measure for man, and offer thereby self-knowledge, self-control, and wisdom as civilizing influences upon the demonism of human wills. At the time of Kant, however, rationality and an account of human excellence could no longer be mediated through the doctrine of Nature only. First of all Aristotle's Nature had been replaced by Newton's and little moral wisdom emanated from the latter. Secondly man had perceived himself as a historical being constrained to make himself and to invent his culture. Nature from that point on could only appear as antithetical to freedom and the source of heteronomous norms. Through God as the Author of the moral law who also complements what we cannot fulfil as we undertake the burden of this modern kind of freedom, Kant sought to provide a new, non-coercive, persuasive measure for man and to close the door to enthusiasm and savagery, and to the doctrine according to which private feeling can and will provide the supreme consecration to our existence. In this sense Kant can be presented as having sought to rescue the meaning of theistic faith for autonomous man with a historical consciousness, a service philosophers of religion might wish to acknowledge gratefully.[57]

Chapter 11

The Results of the Philosophy of Religion as Extensions of the Results of the Philosophy of History: The Meaning of the Kantian Faith in God and Man

Divine Education and Redemptive Providence

My conclusion will attempt to present in a synthesis, as it were, Kant's views on the development of mankind as they appear in his political thought, his philosophy of history, his ethical theory, and his philosophy of religion.

"Man," wrote Kant in a typically man-centred formulation, "is an animal which, if it lives among others of its kind, requires a master."[1] Similar ideas often lead others to recommend or accept tyrannical policies. In Kant this starting point led to a search for the authority which will educate man and guide him to a state of free maturity. The master Kant was looking for is a pedagogue not a tamer. "Man can only become man by education." "The greatest and most difficult problem to which man can devote himself is the problem of education."[2] The very question asked prevents our giving to it an individualistic answer. Man's individualistic reason and whatever solitary rational insights he may have, his cogitative powers, are as much in need of discipline and education as his instincts or his imagination. Only hard individual and corporate wrestling with his limits will bring to man insight into his own nature. Work, the measuring of oneself against obstacles, appeared to Kant to be the source of objectivity and rationality because it is the school of discipline. Without work all is dreaming innocence.[3] Man's reason may be said to be the answer to man's search only if reason is to be made into a working process with social and historical dimensions.[4] Kant proposed to see in the human race as a whole such a pedagogue for each one of its individual parts. But who then will be the educator of the race? Or can we make the race as a whole the depository of all wisdom?

The philosophy of history supplies one kind of answer. This answer extends to the experience of the whole life of the individual and the whole experience of the race the experience of education at the hands of a teacher. Nature at times is presented as the school and the teacher: nature shows unity of design, says the *Critique of Pure Reason* and this serves as a model for the activities of our mind. "Without it there would be no school for reason."[5] Teleological unity as unveiled by the philosophy of history shows the process of history to be a better school yet. Man is led by the hardships of existence to the development of all faculties and is challenged with the establishment of order and peace, a challenge in which his survival, not to mention his happiness, is at stake. When Kant used the metaphor of education, he had in mind not a doctrinaire and authoritarian kind of education but the eighteenth century progressive conception of education which aims at developing the potentialities of the pupil and at issuing forth in the pupil's autonomous and virtuous activity.[6] The education of the race so far has led to a stage of maturity, where man begins to be responsible for his own fate; now he must learn how to act. And the time of action is also the time of orientation towards the future, namely the time of faith and of hope. (The time of passive obedience and purely emotional motivations is in Kant the time of credulity and superstition.) The efforts of man in time rest upon faith in man's future and the possibility of that future as a future of justice: such faith is also a faith in God. Evil present in man and in society makes education (of individuals and of the race) difficult, but not impossible.[7] Difficulty, as Tillich pointed out, is not a philosophical concept.

The book on *Anthropology* summarizes under the heading "The Character of the Species" the various implications of the usage of this key metaphor of education and distinguishes between self-education, education by other men, education by the experience of the whole race, and education by God.[8] Man starts as an animal capable of reason and can make of himself a rational animal. He will do so by a historical education. The development of technical, pragmatic, and moral faculties will enable him to reach his end, which will be reached only by the species. Through association with others, man is destined to cultivate, civilize, and moralize himself through arts and sciences. Man thus needs a social education. However, since all the race is caught up in frailty, mutual oppression, and wickedness, the problem of education appears to be without an ultimate moral solution. Historical education promises a more rational civilization but cannot promise the abolition of moral evil. Such redemptive education of the race as a whole can be expected only from Providence, namely a wisdom that works at the preservation and teleological development of the race with a moral purpose in view.[9]

The philosophy of religion arrives at a different kind of answer to the search for the "master." The educational process is interiorized. In the philosophy of history, mankind learns by trial and error and the hard schooling of cruel facts, until man acquires wisdom, a notion which has at first pragmatic overtones. Wars, for instance, are instruments of this pedagogy. In the philosophy of religion the educational process must reform, change the interior dispositions of man's heart, and that takes a more delicate hand than the blows of fortune and the mechanisms of power among men. At the same time, evil being more deeply entrenched in man, being entrenched actually in his very heart, the dependence upon Providence increases and becomes radical. The lectures on anthropology say that one can deem something that is very difficult to do to be "impossible for all practical purposes" or "subjectively undoable."[10] Such seems to be the case with the human victory over human evil. To stretch the metaphor, mankind does not seem to need so much the rough kind of school for normal kids but that more hypothetical reality: a remedial school for sick adolescents who have an unusual need for loving guidance.

The historical faith of Christianity does not hesitate to state that it can mediate such healing power and that God is love and has revealed redemptive concern. This representation however clashes with Kant's insistence upon human spontaneity, autonomy, and responsibility—three anchors which he cannot let go since his alternative to them is unreason and anarchy. There appears thus the threat of an estrangement between Stoic natural religiousness (God put us in a garden where we must fend for ourselves, and he will see that we learn, although we will have to learn our way, namely the hard way) and Christian revelational faith (God succors his children when they turn to him in need). Kant offered his non-reductive rationalism as a way to prevent such mutual estrangement between the two kinds of faith. He corrected the Stoic interpretation of natural religion to include hope in God's grace and he purified Christian piety to tolerate only those prayers to God which stem from moral need (and reject those which come from purely emotional or pathological need). Revelation, being an abiding revelation of God in the moral law, plays a role in the process of concretization and humanization of man's moral life;[11] grace, also an abiding attribute of divine ruling Providence, will complete what our moral efforts are insufficient to achieve.[12] We can thus see God as being eternally concerned for the redemption of all, although not the one who keeps picking up his favourite children when they keep falling into holes. "*Gott regiert als Monarch aber nicht als Despot.*"[13] A despot whose principles of action systematically authorize him to depart from law in order to do favours for his friends or even for his whole people is just as immoral as one who departs from law occasionally to torture his enemies or tyrannize his whole people.

The transformation of Kant's faith in God as Creator, Legislator, and Judge into a faith in redeeming Providence is made possible because the idea of God issuing a call, that is, creating free creatures, giving them an ultimate end, and challenging them to an autonomous teleological development, was paradoxical and incomprehensible in the first place: either God creates puppets or he creates free beings who then have subsequently no obligation or bond to him. But Kant had come to say that mysterious though this divine creation of free beings may be, such is precisely what divine creative power does.[14] To give to divine providential power the capacity to redeem a free though captive human being without realienating his alienated freedom was a mere extension of the mystery and not the introduction of a fresh scandal.

The faith in redeeming Providence is accompanied by three doctrines that contradict previous results in Kant's moral philosophy: radical evil contradicts autonomy of the will, conversion contradicts the ideality of time, and the theory of the moral community contradicts the previous individualism. This faith also led Kant to present a more dramatic view of the becoming of mankind, with falls and salvations, although the really dramatic view belongs rather to the ecclesiastical faith pure, since in religion within the limits of reason alone, revelation and grace are continuous divine activities. Finally the hope for moral progress is not founded so much on the fact that the blows of fate and the consequences of our stupidity and wickedness force us sooner or later to come to ourselves and discover the interior law within us (for what good is it to find the interior law if one finds the interior evil as well?), but is based on the fact that a true church exists, namely an association where true virtue is the only ultimate norm and is a reality in the process of realization.

Kant in his philosophy of religion brought all these modifications to the view of education that emerged from the philosophy of history without compromising the core of self-education. To do what lies in our power remains forever what is to be done first.

The affirmation of the tenability of the faith in a gracious Providence, as final result of Kant's philosophy of religion, corresponds deeply to his own religiousness. This faith in a gracious God manifested by his late writings (the essay on theodicy in 1791, *Religion* in 1793, and *Perpetual Peace* in 1795) represents a deepening and on some points a modification of Kant's religiousness as I characterized it earlier[15] by drawing from writings stretching from 1755 to 1790.

Kant's philosophical hypothesis of a mankind progressively educated in history by a divine pedagogue builds upon a religious feeling: namely the readiness to be educated by God, or the readiness to obey and respect a higher moral authority than our own current insights and those of mankind. This religious feeling that is prepared to see a foundational authority (namely an authority on which the whole undertaking of civilization is based and which we shall obey if we can discern it and to which we shall always remain open) that is transcendent and is beyond ourselves and mankind is but a restatement of the earlier characterization of religious feeling as respect for the higher authority of a moral order, a sense Kant believed he could discern in all forms of religiousness.

In Kant's own piety and religiousness this feeling becomes further characterized as a sense of the holiness of God. The God who is an educator of mankind is presented as a rational idea and as a necessary postulate. This should not obscure the fact that for Kant he is also—and he is primarily—the highest reality before which all knees bend. The Sovereignty, Majesty, and Righteousness of this Master of which mankind is in need are not for Kant the faded conceptualizations produced by an intellectual theological exercise; they are objects of awe and elicit worship and obedience.[16]

The sense of the holiness of God not only characterizes what Kant meant by religion but also lies at the core of his understanding of man. That God is holy means that there is an unconditional border between the human and the divine. Here Kant clearly has sensibilities similar to those of the Old Testament. But that God is holy means also that his overwhelming omnipotence is not demonic and is not destructive of humanity, provided, that is, that humanity remains within its limits. W. Schultz was quite right to derive from the sense of the holiness of God Kant's profound sense of the limits and of the freedom of man.[17]

On the one hand, that God is holy means that there are before man barriers which he may not and cannot transgress. The sense of the holiness of God maps out the human area as an area of finitude; God cannot be known by us in his nature; we cannot prove his existence. Man's mind has limits in what it can know, his will must prescribe limits to itself, and there are limits to what he may hope. The life of man is a life of search, not a life of possession. This crucial core element of Kant's philosophy results from a sense of the holiness of God that balks at any implication of anything divine in us. Thus the task of the philosopher lies in the definition of our limits not in the attempt to transcend them. This leads to a task of radical criticism of ourselves, of the world we believe we know and we in fact organize, and to a philosophy which more often presents itself as preventing error than as discovering truth, since truth in itself forever remains beyond our grasp.

On the other hand this severe tracing of the implication of man's finitude is united to an equally radical understanding of man's freedom. Through his moral actions, man may transform the prison of his finitude into a home for human beings. Here an absolute is to be found: that of the task which human beings must set before themselves and which they may undertake. From the transcendence that we cannot reach comes a call through the moral law: the call to know ourselves through honesty and conscientiousness and to practise justice (not to become holy).

The attempts of Kant to differentiate religion from servile superstition and to relate religious faith and pure rational faith (or moral faith) represent a quite consistent deepening of the early position: namely, religion raises man above the beast without making him into a god, or religion consists of awe before the authority of an order which is not our own, which is moral in essence and which is entirely legitimate. The religious self experiences a tension between two worlds, neither of which he fully belongs to. The holy remains beyond his reach and the phenomenal world cannot make man entirely his own. The self that experiences this tension is not destroyed by it and lives in a world of his own: the human world, a world defined by historical, social, and cultural characteristics. This human world however is not without openings beyond itself (it is centred but not rounded, one might suggest). The development of Kant's philosophy of religion remains consistently concerned with the mapping out of religion as an area of autonomy (hence the polemics against various heteronomous pseudo-faiths) in which the autonomous man is not closed in upon himself in a self-prescribed and illusory independence but is open to that which has authority and has not its origin in himself. The mature form of Kant's understanding of religion emphasizes the finitude of our faculties, the moral maturity of religious man, and his confidence in a gracious Providence. The philosophy of religion thus integrates into Kant's understanding of religion the results of the three Critiques, namely the conclusions regarding the limits of our knowledge, the laws of our practical reason, and the truth and value of symbols. The implications of the freedom of man are shown to their last ramifications. The implications of the holiness of God are stretched to the representation of an eternal redeeming activity. But as each one of these two poles is deepened and modified the unity between them is not broken. The religious man remains a man and he is related to the wholly Other, or better the religious man becomes a man as he relates to the wholly Other, a relationship which can become the story of his humanization but never the story of his divinization.

Systematic Answer to the Question: What May I Hope?

The Kantian insight into the finitude of man led him to the formulation of three questions: What can I know? What must I do? and What may I hope? The answers, by determining the nature and location of the limits and the extent of what man rationally can do within them, give us knowledge of man or self-knowledge.[18]

The third question is particularly poignant because it includes awareness of time. What is the future of such a finite and precarious being as man, and what may I hope for in the future, when I know for certain that my future includes death and terminates with it in a very radical sense and perhaps absolutely? The problem became particularly sharp for Kant when, under the impact of Newtonian science and the knowledge of the mechanical laws of nature and of Rousseau and his knowledge of man's oppressed moral nature, Kant abandoned the Leibnitian conception of the world as perfect, or at least as the best of all possible, and came to have a vivid sense of the wrongness of things. Is my own life to end on such a note of wrongness? Is it going to be deemed worthless in the end? Can it achieve a perfection of some kind? What exactly may I hope?

Practically all writings of Kant touch upon this problem of hope. The question of hope is necessitated by the entire system, writes Bohatec.[19] The problem may be subdivided into two aspects: What are the grounds of our hope: the nature of man, Nature, the moral law, a Providential God? And what is the nature of our legitimate hope: individual immortality, immortality of the race, individual moral progress, progress of the race towards durable peace, moral progress of the race? A good deal of the intellectual and spiritual travail of the eighteenth century was focusing precisely on the question of the grounds of hope (the progress of science, of the arts, and of education being a very powerful new ground in the eyes of many) and on that of the nature of our hope. Peter Gay aptly speaks of the age of Enlightenment as an age of recovery of nerve.[20] The affirmation of worldly hopes for more happiness for mankind in the future is a large part of such recovery. Worldly and otherworldly hopes thus came to be put in a fresh contrast. Diderot, as was often the case with him, put his finger on it: "What posterity is for the philosopher, the other world is for the religious man."[21]

Kant inevitably participated in this redefinition of the nature of hope, a question so crucial to his century. In three places Kant's works undertake to deal with the question in its two aspects: in the *Critique of Practical Reason* (following here lines already set in the first Critique), in the philosophy of history, and in the philosophy of religion. In each treatment a different kind of answer appears. Each answer, however, is a modification of the basic Kantian positions: de jure man is promised to a brilliant future, he is capable of reason, he is nature's final end, he knows the moral law; de facto the worst may be feared, man has demonstrated his capacity for unreason, he is free to negate his original good predisposition, he can disobey the moral law and very often does. This is why hope is a problem; man is not unconscious of his great possibilities, and neither does he have proof of being doomed to a tragic fate. Hope is possible. But man does bring a tragic fate upon himself, he does show himself unwilling or unable to realize his great possibilities. Thus the question of hope has to be raised: What hopes will in fact be realized?

This, however, is not the whole question. What does it mean for a hope to be realized? Does it bear much resemblance to what happens when an anticipation is met, or an expectation fulfilled? To return to Diderot's question: Is posterity (or future time) or heaven (or eternity) to be the locus of realization of human hopes? Much of the secularization of the Western mind that took place in the eighteenth century consisted in a temporalization of eternity, posterity became the deity that rewards virtue, punishes vice, and wipes tears. In each of Kant's treatments of the question of hope we see him wrestling with the very question of secularization of hope and seeking to reinterpret the meaning of that which is called an immortal hope by the religious man.

The question of hope is raised in the *Critique of Practical Reason* by means of the question of the relationship between the *bonum supremum* and the *summum bonum*. Every moral man can now, right away or in the very near future, achieve one good: the consciousness of having done one's duty. However the one who did the virtuous thing, obeyed duty for duty's sake, satisfied his conscience, and so to speak cast his bread upon the waters, will not fail to ask what will be the consequences of this moral deed woven into the fabric of events? He would be less than moral if he were not concerned about the furtherance of the good in the world. He will not act from hope of success, his action is done for duty's sake, but he does act with a hope of some kind.[22] Will the wickedness of men or of the gods frustrate this good deed (the doer having done his duty is in a sense beyond frustration) and prevent it from doing its bit towards the realization of the good on earth (the *summum bonum*)? Or will the natural cooperativeness of man and the providential design of God respond to good with good and thus bring closer the day when all men will live in harmony? Kant did not see such cooperativeness at work in the world now: evil is often returned for good, the combination of virtue with happiness, or the combination of upright effort with historical success is not "derivable from experience." Yet it is "a priori necessary to bring forth the highest good through the freedom of the will."[23]

The prospect for worldly hopes thus does not appear to be very good in the second Critique. The *Critique of Practical Reason* however raises the question in a fundamentally a-historical way. It speaks of joining happiness to virtue, not historical success to moral effort.

Its answers are likewise a-historical. The postulate of the immortality of the soul, the postulate of the existence of God, and the practical faith in God as Author of a truthful moral law and of the world as well, guarantee that the *summum bonum* is possible. An "infinitely enduring existence," that is, immortality, gives us time to grow morally until our intentions are completely fit to the moral law.[24] And the existence of God, as cause of nature and of the moral law gives us the assurance that the highest good is possible in the world, and thus enables us to accept the duty of working towards its realization. Our hope is thus twofold: we can hope to have time to achieve individual moral perfection in ourselves and we can have hope that the highest good will be realized in the world.

A look at the history of the interpretation of the second Critique shows that its doctrine of immortality had much more impact than its doctrine of the perfectibility of the world. This is not surprising. The ground of hope here is totally a-temporal: it is God and the truthfulness of the moral law of which he is the Author. The hope, furthermore, is an individual one (I have the hope that the moral law does not cheat me and does not tell me to roll the rock of Sisyphus). It is to be expected therefore that the representation of the hope resulting from it will be primarily individualistic and a-temporal. (Kant did present immortality as duration—a representation he was to question subsequently in the essay on *The End of All Things*—but duration beyond death in a *corpus mysticum* has little or nothing in common with historical time.) The hope thus is presented as part of an individual moral faith: no matter what are the results apparent in my life or in the world so far, I can hope that I will, in the end, in the very end, be found worthy. For if there is no possibility of this accomplishment, the whole moral endeavour is futile, and if the probability of the accomplishment is uncertain the moral effort is weakened. To go ahead with our moral projects in the confidence that we shall somehow and in some sense succeed amounts to practical faith in God.[25]

> Thus without a God or without a world invisible to us now but hoped for, the glorious ideas of morality are indeed objects of approval and admiration, but not springs of purpose and action.[26]

Faith in God makes the difference between moral effort as asinine folly and as *kalos kindunos*.

Such an answer has its weaknesses and its strengths. The strength is that the ground of hope is beyond the reach of historical and personal contingencies and casualties. I may again and again find myself powerless in the fight against evil. I may repeatedly fail to purify my motives and have to declare myself guilty. I may repeatedly fail to do anything useful or good in the midst of the chaos and conflicts of society and have to declare myself ineffective. But as long as I keep trying to heed the moral law, hope is not robbed from me because it is anchored in a transcendent source. The weakness is that it opens the prospect for an individualistic private morality that cultivates one's own inner treasure of innocence and breaks the bond between the self and mankind of which the self is a part. What kind of salvation is there for me, if it is achieved for me (and a few of my friends) alone? Or if it is achieved while mankind as a whole is still heading towards disaster on account of the grip which moral evil maintains over it?

The notion of the perfectibility of the world found in this solution to the problem of hope effects the transition to the second solution, that of the philosophy of history. For Kant replaced the Leibnitian conception of the world as the best of all possible by the Idea of the World as Creation, as caused by God, and containing within itself a hidden ethical teleology object of practical faith, which does not make it perfect in any way, but does make it perfectible, because this ethical teleology leads to our action under the laws of practical reason, and guarantees the possibility of successful free moral action in the world.

The philosophy of history, however, does not take its departure from the connecting link found in the idea of the perfectible world, but from a current issue much debated in the eighteenth century: namely that of progress. Getting into the problem of hope in this case from the other end, namely from an area where empirical evidence could conceivably exist, the analysis takes a slightly different turn. For one thing the question is very much whether the race as a whole has a hope. (It did not have to be so, for the question could very well have been whether the young individual—or the underprivileged group— has a hope in the social structure to achieve his reasonable goals during his lifetime, which is another possible and interesting formulation of the question of hope, and becomes particularly acute when class consciousness arises.) Then the question is raised in a very historical way: the question is of the future of the race in this world. Finally the question focuses upon such "material" things as: Will wars stop? Will happiness increase?

We know the answer the question of progress received in the end.

Little by little, those that have power will use less violence, and obedience to the laws will increase. There will arise in the body politic perhaps more charity and less strife in law suits, more reliability in keeping one's word, etcetera, partly out of love of honour, partly out of well understood self-interest. And eventually this will also extend to nations in their external relations towards one another up to the realization of the cosmopolitan society, without the moral foundation of mankind having to be enlarged in the least; for that, a kind of new creation (supernatural influence) would be necessary.[27]

Such progress is strictly juridical and political. Coercive laws still remain the lot of mankind. Earlier versions of the philosophy of history held the hope of a moral progress linked up with such political improvement (the disjunction between a future consisting of a perpetual peace as political achievement and the ethical commonwealth result of a religious and moral transformation arises after the impact of the philosophy of religion has been felt).

The ground of such hope in progress of the race is Nature. "Nature inexorably wills that the right shall finally triumph."[28] Nature was the term preferred in the early writings and although in the 1790s Kant was more prone to confess reliance upon a supernatural Providence, the term is again given favour in matters pertaining to theory of history.

The use of the word "nature" is more fitting to the limits of human reason and more modest than an expression indicating a providence unknown to us. This is especially true when we are dealing with questions of theory and not of religion.[29]

Note, however, that in this writing Kant limited himself to the question of political progress.

The philosophy of history ultimately lands upon the same guarantee of hope as the second Critique, namely a teleologically organized history, in which the ends pursued by Nature and the ends pursued by men conspire to work towards the ends which Nature, good and wise, had in the first place. Kant's doctrine of progress, cautious though it is and full of warning against human evil though it may be, is a historically stretched version of the doctrine of the perfectibility of the world with which he replaced Leibniz's best of all possible worlds.[30] Such a perfectible world can ultimately be rooted only (for Kant) in an intelligent Author and, prudent though Kant may have been, his metaphysical conception of Nature was bound to find a theistic basis. The causes for the caution are twofold. First Kant was wary of theological providentialism as held by theologians expounding on history: Secondly he was aware that philosophy of history speaks of a juridical progress and not of a moral progress; the Nature which guarantees such progress is a nonmoral one and should not be graced with the name of God or Providence, names that must keep moral and religious implications.

The kind of answer found in the philosophy of history has strengths as well as weaknesses. It gives us hope for something tangible and tangible hopes may be the greatest spur to our motivations, even though they are the source of all their impurities. And the goods hoped for are cultural achievements, not "merely" material ones: the eradication of violence is not a project to be spurned by sensitive moralists on the grounds that such a thing can be achieved by better coercive laws and neither needs a transformation of the heart nor brings about one. Finally the grounds of such hope are also found in ponderables: Did mankind lose some of its roughness? Did it gain greater control over nature and over its own passions?

The weakness, of course, was that on which Dostoevski and Renouvier based their case against belief in progress. How much comfort is there for the "sacrificed individuals" and "sacrificed generations" in the hope that posterity may reap the benefits of their blood and tears? Kant had denied even to God the right to use man merely as a means.[31] Did he then make of history a Moloch that devours some of its creatures for the sake of a greater good to be enjoyed by other creatures (a Moloch incidentally to whom more victims were sacrificed in the last century than ever were to its eponym)? Kant was aware of the problem as early as his first major essay in the philosophy of history. "It remains strange that the earlier generations appear to carry through their toilsome labour only for the sake of the later."[32]

Thus neither answer to the problem of hope is by itself entirely satisfactory. The first answer is dependent on the ethico-religious tendency, the second on the ethico-juridical one. Kant's problem at the completion of his philosophy of history and of his moral philosophy may be presented by looking at the problematic relationship between the two tendencies, which differ in their presentation of the end which man must work for and may hope for.

On the one hand, the end is conceived as the arrival to maturity of the Kantian person, as a free personality. This is the ethico-religious tendency as apparent in the second Critique. It is the individual who is saved. He finds his salvation when his will is strictly determined by the moral law, when he is of perfectly good will, no matter how powerless the good will is on the course of the world. Eschatology is extrahistorical (history being understood in its racial sense). The individual can reach the *bonum supremum* now and is saved even when the world is still at war. And the individual will reach the *summum bonum* in immortality, outside of history. The kingdom of ends is a noumenal reality in which the person participates no matter what empirical commonwealth he lives in.

On the other hand, the end is conceived as the arrival of the commonwealth of nations, the state of perpetual peace between individuals and nations. This is the ethico-juridical tendency. It may take long to come and many individuals will die unfulfilled, but the race's destiny will ultimately be realized in a perfectly rational empirical society. Eschatology, or rather progress, is intra-historical (again racially speaking, for the individual now the *summum bonum* always lies in the future). The kingdom of ends will be realized or approximated on earth.[33]

The thrust of the ethico-religious tendency is that man is already a noumenal perfection by his capacity to set ends before himself knowingly. The weight lies on the side of the absolute meaning of freedom. Men know that they should treat each other as ends in themselves and begin to deal (or to mean to deal) with each other not as mere instruments but also as ends. They have a right to and already are citizens of the kingdom of ends. But the perfection of the kingdom has to be realized in history: this is the thrust of the ethico-juridical tendency. Men still have to take possession of their kingdom and learn in their hearts to treat each other as ends and not as instruments.

It may be possible to solve the tension between the two tendencies by saying that they are complementary and correct each other. By keeping the balance between the two tendencies, and between the two meanings of freedom, it could be argued, Kant affirmed both man's possession of himself and his control over history (a power over himself which is unique in all creation and makes him an end in himself) and man's enduring incapacity to transcend history or absolutely control it. Man's dignity is affirmed, whatever he and his fellow men choose to do, and an endless task is set before those who will live up to that dignity. In this case Kant's achievement is that he found meaning both in modern secular notions of progress and in traditional Christian other-worldly eschatology. There is meaning in history, but one cannot find ultimate meaning in it. Man has a stake in history but ultimately transcends it. Man's relationship to the transcendent is no ground for an a-historical consciousness but rather gives him a mandate for work in history.

There is wisdom in that position and it could well be Kant's final position. One difficulty, however, stands in the way of such a conclusion. The philosophy of religion as found in *Religion within the Limits of Reason Alone* seems to attempt in 1793 a merging of the two tendencies or at least the working of a more subtle relationship between the two tendencies. It does so by presenting the notion of the Kingdom of God, or ethical community, as future visible intra-historical community. Apparently responding to the apocalyptic representations of a thousand year reign of the saints on earth (which Kant universalized of course), he examined and allowed us the hope—rooted in divine providential care—of a moral progress and of a morally perfect society realized on earth. We saw how this changed his view of the ground of hope to a more actively providential and redeeming God. What matters here is that Kant thereby having disjuncted his presentation of the nature of our inner-historical hope into political and moral progress, allowed us to hope in both, allowed God to guarantee both, and thus entertained Utopian expectations as well as "realistic" political ones. (The earlier hope, dating from before the doctrine of radical evil, for a progress in which the moral and political dimensions are not so sharply differentiated, cannot be properly called Utopian since it does not rest upon a moral revolution.) The complete picture of Kant's doctrine of hope could then be summarized by the following diagram.

NATURE OF HOPE	GROUND OF HOPE
Political progress (historical) institutional and exterior	Nature and man
Individual moral progress (eschatological) hidden and personal	God of moral theism and man
Moral progress of the race (historical) institutional and personal	Redeeming God and man

Man, of course, must be included among all the grounds of hope since at every stage Kant restated that we must do everything as if it depended on us alone. Such a progression would be quite in keeping with Kant's progression towards increasingly sophisticated conceptions of God and increasingly subtle investigations of our morality, all under the impact of the Gospels and the subsequent ideas they introduced.[34]

I do not believe, however, that we can accept this picture of three kinds of hope as the final state of Kant's mind. When he returned to the philosophy of history after 1793, the only wing of his disjunction between political and moral progress was the pessimistic one: Kant was looking for the kind of political progress of which even devils are capable. One would argue that a philosophy of history would have to bear upon externals only and thus could not admit the notion of moral progress within itself. This is correct. But Kant never returned after 1793 to the notion of the philosophy of the history of religion, that is, a philosophy of history that encompasses religious and moral progress. And that prospect which makes the church a source of hope for the individual and for the race once shyly opened had been shaken by the final discussion of the permanence of evil in the true church itself. We see therefore in the notion of a philosophy of history of religion a prospect which Kant opened, but on which he did not build and which did not gain enough sway over his mind to lead to a thoroughgoing revision of all his philosophy and to an overcoming of the tension between exterior relations of persons and inner realities.[35] Perhaps Kant recoiled before the thought that there is now among us an institution with political and moral power that works infallibly for moral progress. At any rate the thought so well expressed by F. Y. Congar that "we cannot know which of the forces of history ultimately works in behalf of the Kingdom" is an honourable one.[36]

Thus we must conclude that the tension between the ethico-religious and the ethico-juridical tendency is more firmly rooted in Kant than the synthesis that holds before us the hope of worldly moral and religious progress. The tension between the two tendencies corresponds more accurately to his sense of the duality and tragic dimension of our predicament of being caught between two worlds. The two tendencies are complementary, although each relativizes the other. A purely individual and eschatological salvation or a purely social and historical salvation is really no salvation at all. I have hope even if I keep failing historically, but mankind as a whole has hope only if it does not forever fail historically. Not only do I have hope but I need hope because action fails to bring about the states of affairs which the man of action projects as he undertakes to pursue his purposes. As Hannah Arendt pointed out in her penetrating essay "The Concept of History," Kant at the end of his moral philosophy (and also at the end of a modern development expecting the achievement of human dignity through action) found out that "action fulfilled neither of the two hopes the modern age was bound to expect from it." The life of action does not lead to a purification of our motivations and the achievement of an inner purity. It rather manifests passions and private aims. And the life of action almost never fulfils its original intention since "projected into a web of relationships where many and opposing ends are pursued" it is almost always inevitably deflected and thus fails to deliver the peace, happiness, or order which it aimed at. Kant thus saw the moral deficiencies of the life of action and the incapacity of action to overcome the ambiguity of the human predicament and rid us of evil.[37] Where the Greeks offered contemplation as the answer to the incompleteness of the historically active life, Kant offered hope and faith. His philosophy of history ends with a statement of faith that has a religious quality because Kant could not stop with an enlightened affirmation of progress or with a pessimistic affirmation of the permanent ambiguity of human affairs. After what Pieper correctly called a "typical inner debate," and a lengthy one I would add, Kant spoke of a hope of a measure of fulfilment within history as well as of an a-historical fulfilment. In the words of Pieper, he attempted, "in spite of principled rationalism, to keep the superrational dimension of existence at least within sight."[38] Kant succeeded in this attempt, I believe, because of his constant sensitivity to counter-arguments which destroy any simple presentation of political historical hopes and of individualistic religious a-historical hopes without entirely destroying the boldness of hope. Faith for him thus has both the quality of courage of moral men who persevere under tragic conditions and the quality of grand hope of religious men who believe that life will not always have to be lived under tragic conditions. Kant's faith was that evil will not have the last word either in one's own heart or in history. Such is the most consistent and simple answer Kant gave to the problem of hope.

That the ethico-juridical and the ethico-religious tendencies do not merge in a systematic and total view of human development means thus that the Kantian sense of conflict between the two worlds remains a conflict which for him was in the core of religion itself. It means also that hope keeps a live quality. The dialectic of hope prevents the concretized historical expectation to stand for hope and thus rob it of its dreamlike boldness. It also prevents the interior yearning to stand for hope and thus rob it of its bold demand for corporate incarnation. In this way also the realization of hope will always remain something of a surprise or of a grace.[39] But it also means that neither philosophy of history nor philosophy of religion ever became for Kant a prefectly unified whole, nor did they both ever become part of an even grander thing, such as a philosophy of the spirit for instance. Kant did not provide us with a complete solution to what we may hope and to what are the grounds for such a hope. The summary I gave above was negative in formulation: "Evil will not have the last word either in one's own heart or in history." This is not fortuitous. The positive affirmations of the ethico-juridical and of the ethico-religious tendencies are each negated by the other. Hope is kept as something which transcends current anticipations or yearnings. A system of hope appears to be a contradiction in terms.

That there may be a (non-systematic) philosophy of hope only if philosophy of history and philosophy of religion remain in tension with each other may be illustrated by drawing attention to a remarkable feature of Greek civilization. On the one hand the Greeks had a historiography which contained an implicit philosophy of history and a political science. Mistakes in the conduct of human affairs can be discerned and rules made for the maintenance or perhaps even restoration of the health of the city. On the other hand the Greeks had tragedy, a literary form closer to the religious sources, where fate was more cruel and guilt more sharp, where the estimate of what man can learn from experience was more pessimistic, but where maturing and purification was nevertheless made available to the individual. Much of subsequent philosophy of history—the mention of Augustine and Hegel will here suffice—represents an effort, under biblical influence, to merge the wisdom afforded by Greek historiography and that afforded by Greek tragedy, to show that tragedies can have beneficial world historical consequences and to integrate the tragic vision within the broad developmental one. The Kantian position is a refusal to merge the values of tragic maturing and those of political experience. Kantian formalism is largely responsible for this refusal. History qua story of human freedom cannot have a material goal.[40] Fulfilment of history qua reaching of a goal cannot alone be a meaningful fulfilment.

Meaning in history is to be found not only in the reaching of a goal, but also in the preservation of a form: the human form of man qua moral being.[41] The presentation of the preservation of this form will always remain disjuncted between two kinds of hope: the hope for preservation of civil freedom in the city and the hope for preservation of teachability and honesty in the individual. In his philosophy of history Kant drew out the juridical and political ramifications of the struggle for freedom. His philosophy of religion climaxes with his presentation of Job. Kantian formalism, biblical exegesis, and tragic wisdom converge to present Job as the broken, honest, and teachable individual who is robbed of everything history has to offer but is not robbed of his integrity. The answers of any philosophy of history are impostures to Job, and the answer Job has, such as it is, has few historical implications. Thus for any philosopher thinking in the Kantian tradition there will always be a disjunction between two kinds of hope: the political hope for freedom and order for the society of men as they are, and the religious hope of being like Job and achieving maturity and integrity, no matter what.

We have seen hope as a problem that must be critically investigated and must receive a rational answer. In another sense, however, hope was always a fundamental fact in Kant. As we find Kant searching his way among possible representations of our future, possible representations of God, and possible doctrines of evil, Christ, grace, and revelation, there is all along one kind of guiding thread on the basis of which some doctrines are accepted as necessary or meaningful and some as meaningless or dangerous. This thread is the faith and hope that moral striving will not be meaningless and that it will not be forever robbed of reaching its object. Teleological organization of history remains a faith and a task. It is a faith and a task, however numerous and legitimate the representations that tell us we must think as if it were there before us in the first place. (Such results of the *Critique of Judgement* were not in any way altered, although further legitimate representations were added.) At every stage and every turn Kant found his direction from this basic orientation: it must be possible for our moral efforts to meet ultimately a fate other than tragic, and it must be true that whatever in their object is beyond our strength will be somehow supplemented. As Kant probed into the heart, saw the radicality of evil, he saw the necessity for a hope in grace. He thus moved somewhat beyond the doctrine of God found in his moral theism. But he made these further moves on the basis of the same kind of reasoning that led to the moral proof. Ultimately, therefore, all Kant's philosophy of religion hangs upon this "proof." He refused to yield any part of his moral interest. This refusal was the source of his hope. He let himself be directed by this stubbornness and found his hope a good guide in the philosophy of religion, as well as in ethics and in the philosophy of history.[42]

Kant: On the Failure of All Attempted Philosophical Theodicies (1791)

TRANSLATED BY MICHEL DESPLAND

By theodicies, one means defences of the highest wisdom of the Creator against the complaints which reason makes by pointing to the existence of things in the world which contradict the wise purpose. One calls such defence a "plea for God's cause." (Ultimately however, as we shall see, this can be nothing more than a plea for a reason which presumptuously ignores its own limits in these matters.) This cause is not the easiest to defend. It can be legitimately attempted, however, in so far as man as a rational creature has the right, without being presumptuous of course, to test before accepting it, every opinion and every doctrine which asks for his respect, in order that this respect may be sincere and not simulated.

To win the case, the so-called advocate of God must prove one of three things: either that what one deems contrary to purposefulness in the world is not so; *or* that while it is indeed contrary to purposefulness it must be considered not as a positive fact but as an inevitable consequence of the nature of things; *or* finally that, while a positive fact, it is not the work of the supreme Creator of things, but of some other responsible being, such as man or superior spirits, good or evil.

The author of the theodicy agrees that the case be tried before the tribunal of reason, and agrees to be an attorney who will defend the case of his client under attack by formal refutation of all the complaints of the adversary. Therefore, he may not during the course of the process declare arbitrarily that the tribunal of human reason is incompetent (*exceptionem fori*). In other words, he must not use the fact that the adversary willingly concedes that the Creator has supreme wisdom to state then that all doubts raised against it must be immediately set aside without further examination as completely groundless. Rather, he must listen to the complaints, and since they do not attack the concept of supreme wisdom,[1] he must make this highest wisdom intelligible through illumination of its ways and elimination of the objections.

However, there is a task which our attorney does not need to undertake, that is to prove the highest wisdom of God by what is learned from experience in the world. This he could not do at all, for it requires omniscience to recognize in any given world (as known in experience) such perfection that one could say of it with certainty that there could not be any greater in the creation and government of the world.

There are three kinds of contradictions to purposefulness in the world out of which objections could be made to the wisdom of its Creator.

1. That which is absolutely contrary to purposefulness, which wisdom cannot allow nor desire, neither as an end nor as a means.

2. That which is conditionally contrary to purposefulness, which cannot coincide with the wise will as a goal, but can as a means.

The *first* is that which morally runs against purpose, evil properly speaking (sin). The *second* is that which physically runs against purpose, evil as pain. Furthermore, there is also a purposeful relationship in the connection between physical evil and moral evil, for an existing pain sometimes cannot or should not be stopped on account of moral considerations. This means there is a relationship between physical evil or pain (as punishment) and moral evil (as crime). The purpose-

---

1. Strictly conceived, *wisdom* consists only in the ability of the will to coincide with the highest good as the ultimate goal of all things. *Art*, in contrast, lies in the capacity to find the appropriate means for the ends that one likes. However, when art shows itself capable of achievements the possibility of which lie beyond all human reason, for instance, when ends and means bring each other out reciprocally, like in organic bodies, this *divine art* may not without reason be also called wisdom. Nevertheless, to avoid confusion we shall call this kind of wisdom the Creator's *artistic wisdom*, to keep it distinct from his *moral wisdom*, Teleology (physical theology) finds in experience abundant proof of the former. But from that we cannot conclude that the Creator is morally wise too, since natural law and moral law rest upon completely different principles. The proof of the moral wisdom of God is completely a priori and cannot at all be based upon experience of what happens in the world. In order to have a religious value (the only value it needs to have, since it is not needed for the explanation of nature from a speculative standpoint) the concept of God must be the concept of a moral being. And this concept cannot be based either on experience or on the purely transcendental concept of an absolutely necessary being who is for us completely inaccessible. It is then clear enough that the proof for the existence for such a being cannot be other than a moral one.

fulness in the world is also questioned when one asks whether everyone in this world, in fact, receives his moral due. This leads us to see our *third* kind of opposition to purpose.

3. The contradiction to purposefulness in the world which lies in the disproportion of crime and punishment.

The attributes of the supreme wisdom of the Creator against which each kind of contradiction to purposefulness raises complaints are also threefold.

First, the *holiness* of the Creator as *legislator* contrasts with moral evil in the world.

Secondly, the *goodness* of the Creator as *governor* (or sustainer) contrasts with the countless woes and sufferings of rational beings.

Thirdly, the *justice* of the Creator as *judge* contrasts with the scandal which seems to be brought into the world by the unbecoming disproportion between the impunity of the guilty and the gravity of their crimes.[2]

2. These three attributes cannot be reduced to each other—justice, for instance, cannot be reduced to goodness—and therefore cannot be brought down to a lower number. Together they constitute the moral concept of God. One cannot alter the order of these attributes (and make goodness, for instance, the highest end of creation, and subordinate the holiness of the legislator to it) without doing harm to religion which is based on this moral notion. Our own reason, pure as well as practical, determines this order, since legislation would lose all its dignity if it were to be inspired by goodness and would also lose any firm concept of duty. It is true that man first of all wishes to be happy; but he sees and accepts (although often reluctantly) that the worthiness to be happy (i.e. the agreement between the use of his freedom and the holy laws) is by decree of the Creator the pre-condition of human goodness and therefore must precede it. For the wish to be happy, which rests on the subjective end (self-love), cannot determine the objective end (determined by wisdom); the objective end is prescribed by the law which gives the rule unconditionally to the will. Likewise, in the exercise of justice, punishment exists not as a mere means, but as an end of the legislative wisdom. Transgression brings about woe, not in order to bring about another good, but because this connection is good in itself and morally necessary. Justice, it is true, presupposes the goodness of the legislator, for if his will was not concerned about the well-being of his subjects the latter could not be obligated to obey it. But justice is not goodness. It is distinct from it although it is also contained in the over-all concept of wisdom. Therefore, in the charge about the lack of justice found in the distribution of men's lot here on earth, the complaint is not that the good ones are not well but that the evil ones are not in woe (although to add the first statement to the second increases the scandal even more). For in a government of things established by God, the best man cannot make his wish for happiness rest upon divine justice but only upon his own goodness; and he who does all his duty cannot have any rightful claim upon divine benevolence.

These three complaints will each receive an answer by using either one of the three types of plea listed above. The value of each answer will have to be examined individually.

1. To the complaint against the holiness of the divine will on account of the moral evil found in the world which is his work, the following answers justifying God are advanced.

a. Such absolute opposition to purpose which we take to be a transgression of the pure laws of our reason does not exist at all. There are only stumbling blocks which are so only in the eyes of our human wisdom. Divine wisdom judges according to entirely different rules, which are inconceivable to us. That which we find objectionable in the eyes of our practical reason and its dictates of what is right may be, in the eyes of supreme wisdom and with reference to divine purposes, the best means to achieve both our individual good and that of the universe. The ways of the Almighty are not our ways (*sunt superis sua iura*) and we err when we make a law valid only relatively for men in this life into an absolute law, so that we hold that what, in our consideration from our lowly observation point, appears unsuitable must be so also from the highest observation point. This plea in which the response is worse than the charge needs no reply. It can safely be left to the reprobation of any man who has the slightest sense of morality.

b. The second justification, while admitting the reality of moral evil in the world, holds the Creator to be innocent of it, by saying that this evil is inevitable since it rests on the limitations of the nature of men as finite beings. But thereby evil itself would receive a justification; and, since guilt for it cannot be attributed to me, we should stop calling it a moral evil.

c. The third reply states that in the case of the evil we call moral we find a fault of man, and that God cannot be made responsible for it. God on wise grounds tolerates it, but does not approve of it in any way, does not will it, and does not bring it about himself. I do not find any objection to this concept of a mere *permission* allowed by God who is the absolute and only creator of the world. I point out, however, that it has the following similarity with answer (*b*) above; since it was impossible for God to prevent this evil without contradicting other higher moral ends, the ground of this misfortune (for this is how it must properly be called) must be sought in the nature of things, in the necessary limits of humanity as finite being, and thereby mankind cannot really be made responsible for it.

2. Similarly to the charge made against divine goodness because of the woes, namely sufferings, which are found in the world, the following three replies can be made.

a. It is false to hold that in man's fate there is an excess of woes in comparison with the agreeable things enjoyed in life. However unhappy one may be, everyone prefers life to death. Even those who chose death admitted the enjoyableness of life as long as they postponed death. When in the end they were mad enough to commit suicide, they moved right away to a state of insensibility in which no pain can be felt. To reply to these sophistries, it is enough to turn to the sentiments of any man of sound understanding who has lived long and has thought enough about the worth of life, so that he can pass judgement. Suppose that one asks him whether he would be disposed to play once again right through the whole game of life, not in the same conditions of the first time but in any other condition that would please him better (provided, of course, that it would not be in some fairy world but in this earthly world of ours)?

b. The excess of painful feelings over pleasurable ones is inherent to an animal nature such as the human one. (This is more or less what Count Veri contended in his book on the *Nature of Pleasure*.) To this I reply: if such is the case, another question arises; why has the Author of our existence called us into this life when this life, rightly evaluated, is not desirable? Our dissatisfaction with this life would be like that of the Indian woman who told Genghis Khan (when the latter stated that he would neither give her satisfaction for damages suffered nor would he promise her future security): "If you do not want to protect us, why then have you conquered us?"

c. The third way of untying our knot is this: God, for the sake of a future bliss, that is out of goodness, has placed us in this world. However, it is necessary that this hoped for, superabundant blessedness be preceded by the toil and sorrow of this life, so that we can become worthy of the future joy by a struggle against adversities. That this time of trial (in which many succumb and with which even the best are not satisfied) could be considered by the supreme wisdom as the absolute condition of the joy to come, and that it was impossible to see to it that the creature could be satisfied with every period of his life, is a position which can be stated. It is not a position which can be understood. By referring in this way to the supreme wisdom, one can cut the knot; one does not untie it, which was what theodicies promised in the first place.

3. To the last complaint, that against the justice of the universal judge,[3] the following replies are given:

a. The statement that unjust men go unpunished in the world has no foundation whatsoever. Every crime by its nature carries with itself its proportionate punishment. The inner reproaches of conscience plague vicious men more relentlessly than the Furies. This answer rests upon an obvious misunderstanding. The virtuous man lends to the vicious one his own character: he supposes that the vicious man has a fully-developed conscience which cries against the least oversight of the moral law, all the more vigorously the more the man is virtuous. But in cases where this way of thinking and the attending conscience are absent, the punisher for the crimes committed is absent also. As long as he can escape public punishments for his crimes, the vicious man laughs at the fear of those inner reproaches which plague honest people. The small reproaches which he may make to himself from time to time either do not come from his conscience, or indicate that he still has some conscience left. In the latter case, this remorse is set aside and largely compensated for by the pleasure of his senses, the only pleasures for which he cares.

b. The charge can also be answered in this way. One cannot deny that there is no just relation between guilt and punishment in this world. One must unfortunately admit that one finds in the world lives which are lived in horrible injustice and remain happy to the end. But this lies in the nature of things, and no one willed it to be so. It is not therefore morally objectionable. It is the essence of moral virtue moreover to contend against odds. And the pain which the virtuous must suffer when they compare their own happiness with the misery of the vicious is one of these odds. Thus pain only serves to heighten the worth of virtue and thereby the dissonance created in the ear of reason by the undeserved woes in life resolves itself in the most beautiful moral harmony. There are objections to such solutions. Although the

---

3. It is remarkable that among all the difficulties found in the attempt to reconcile the course of the world with the divinity of its Creator, none are so pressing to the mind as those which arise out of the seeming lack of *justice* in the course of events. If it happens (and it happens rarely) that an unjust man, especially a man with unusual powers for evil, does not die unpunished, then the impartial observer has a sigh of relief and is reconciled with heaven. No purposefulness in nature will bring to him such wonder and will convince him as powerfully that the hand of God is at work. Why? Because he discovers there a moral purposefulness and this is the only kind of instance in which he can hope ever to see it at work in this world.

woes which *precede* or accompany virtue can be considered as having some real moral relationship to it (since they sharpen virtue), it still remains expected that life at its end gives the crown to virtue and punishes evil. But when this end runs counter to common sense, as we have many examples in experience, then the sufferings of the virtuous seem to befall him not at all because his virtue could thereby become purer but because his virtue was pure and did not pay attention to the rules of prudent self-love. Thus, things happen in direct opposition to justice as man can conceive it. And when we consider the possibility that the end of this earthly life is not perhaps the end of all life, this in no way amounts to a *justification* of providence; it is rather a sovereign sentence passed by rational moral faith which can advise patience to the doubter but does not give him satisfaction.

c. There is a third way to try to explain the discordance between the moral worth of man and the lot which befalls him. In this world, it is said, all welfare and woe must be estimated proportionally as the result, according to the rules of nature, of the use made by man of his capacities, that is, must be estimated by reference to the ingenuity and the intelligence which men have used together with the circumstances in which they found themselves. They must not be estimated by reference to supersensible purposes. In the future world however, another order of affairs will prevail, and everybody will have the fate which he deserves, in the light of a moral evaluation of his deeds here below. This hypothesis is quite gratuitous. Furthermore, there is another objection. When reason does not pass a sovereign sentence in her capacity as moral legislator, reason must rest only on the rules of theoretical knowledge. According to these rules, it is likely that human destinies in the future world would still be ordered by the natural course of the world just as they are now. What guide can be used by reason in its theoretical capacity except the law of nature? Even when reason is told, as in (*b*), that it can draw patience from the hope of a better world, how can it really expect that the course of things according to the laws of nature, which is not wise here below, would, while following the same laws, become wise in the future world? Thus reason cannot find any conceivable relation between the inner determination of the grounds of the will following the laws of freedom (the moral law) and the causes of our welfare (which are for the most part exterior). We can presume, therefore, that an agreement between human destinies and the divine justice as we conceive it is not to be expected in the future world any more than here.

The result of this trial before the tribunal of philosophy is that no theodicy proposed so far has kept its promise; none has managed to justify the moral wisdom at work in the government of the world against the doubts which arise out of our experience of the world. It is also true, I must add, that, in the light of the limits of our reason, these doubts cannot disprove such moral wisdom either. Will it be possible in time to find better grounds of justification so that the supreme wisdom under attack will not be simply absolved on lack of evidence but will be positively vindicated? This question remains undecided, since we cannot demonstrate with certainty that reason is completely powerless when it comes to determining the *relationship between this world, as we know it through experience* and *the supreme wisdom*. However, as long as the power of reason in these matters is not demonstrated either, all further attempts of "human wisdom" to fathom the ways of divine wisdom must be abandoned.

But we are capable at least of a negative wisdom. We can understand the necessary limits of our reflections on the subjects which are beyond our reach. This can easily be demonstrated and will put an end *once and for all* to the trial.

We have in fact a concept of an *artistic wisdom* manifested in the arrangement of the world. The objective reality of this knowledge is adequate and our speculative reason can develop a physical theology. The moral ideal of our practical reason gives us also the concept of a *moral wisdom* which could be realized in a world created by a perfect Creator, but we have no concept—and cannot hope to obtain one—of a unity and agreement between artistic and moral wisdom in a world of experience. To be a creature, and as such obeying the laws of its Creator, and yet to be also a freely acting being (who has a will independent of exterior influences and who can resist in many cases the will of the Creator); to be responsible, and yet to consider one's actions as the operations of a Superior Being—the unity between these two sets of concepts is a unity which we must postulate in the idea of a world that would be the highest good. But it is a unity which can be understood only by the one who has obtained a knowledge of the supersensible (intelligible) world and has seen how this world lies at the basis of the world of experience. On this knowledge only can be based the proof of the moral wisdom of the Creator of the world—no mortal man however can attain to this knowledge.

All theodicy must be an interpretation of nature and must show how God manifests the intentions of his will through it. Such exposition of the manifest will of the legislator can be either doctrinal or authentic. The first kind of exposition interprets the expressions used by the legislator in the light of his intentions known from other sources. The second kind is made by the legislator himself.

As a work of God, the world can be considered as being a divine manifestation of the *intentions* of his will. In this regard the world is often a closed book. It is always a closed book when we want to read the ultimate intention of God (which is always a moral one) from a world which is only an object of experience. Philosophical interpretations of this kind are doctrinal and they constitute a theodicy in the traditional sense, which we can call doctrinal theodicy. But we must also give the name theodicy to the simple rejection of all reproaches addressed to divine wisdom when this rejection rests on a divine *sovereign sentence*, on a sentence of that very reason which gives us necessarily before all experience the concept of God as a moral and wise being. In this latter case God, through our reason, becomes the interpreter of his will as manifested in creation. And this interpretation we can call authentic theodicy. This is not an interpretation set forth by *ratiocinating* (speculative) reason but by an *authoritative* practical reason, which having in itself authority to legislate can be considered to be the immediate expositor and voice of God in charge of the interpretation of the book of creation. Such an authentic interpretation I find expressed allegorically in an old scripture.

Job is represented as a man who lived in the best circumstances that one can imagine for the enjoyment of life. He was healthy, rich, free; he had authority over other men whom he could make happy; he lived in a happy family, had good friends, and above all (this is the most important) he was at peace with himself and had a good conscience. All these blessings, except the last one, were taken away from him by a terrible fate sent to try him. When he gathered again his senses after the stupor caused by the unexpected reversal, he complained about his ill fate. Soon a dispute arose between him and his friends (who had come to comfort him). Each side proposed his own theodicy for the moral explanation of this bad luck, each according to his opinion (or rather according to his station). The friends of Job accepted the doctrine which explains all woes in the world by reference to divine justice; they are punishments for crimes committed. Although they were not able to name any crime with which to charge the unfortunate man, they nevertheless believed they could judge a priori that Job must have committed such a crime, or else divine justice would not have allowed him to become so unhappy. In contrast, Job confidently asserted that the conscience of all his life did not reproach him; as for his inevitable human frailties, he added that God himself would note that he made him a frail creature. He therefore accepted the doctrine of *unconditioned divine decree*. "God is unique," he said, "and does what he wills."[4]

The ratiocinations which both sides produced either for or against are not remarkable. But the character which the men exhibited while they reasoned is more worthy of attention. Job spoke as he thought, as he felt, and as every man in his position would feel. His friends, however, spoke as if they were overheard by the Almighty whose behaviour they were judging, and as if they cared more for winning his favours by passing the right judgement than for saying the truth. The dishonesty with which they affirmed things of which they should have confessed that they had no knowledge and with which they feigned convictions which in fact they did not have, contrasts with Job's free and sincere outspokenness, which is so removed from lying flattery that it almost borders on temerity. This contrast puts the friends in an unfavourable light: "Do you want," asked Job, "to defend God with unjust arguments? Do you want to make considerations for his person? Is it really his cause that you want to plead? He will punish you if you make considerations for persons! No hypocrite can stand before him."[5]

The denouement authenticates this last statement of Job's; for God honoured Job by showing him the wisdom of his creation and its unfathomable nature. He let him see the beautiful side of creation, where man can see in an indubitable light (and understand) the purposes of the Creator and his wise providence. But he also showed the horrible side, by naming the products of his might, among which there are harmful and terrible things. These things by themselves can serve some purpose but in relationship to other beings and especially to man, they are destructive, run against all purposes, and do not seem to agree with the idea of a plan established with wisdom and goodness. Even through these things, God showed to Job an ordering of the whole

4. Job 23:13.
5. Job 23:7–11, 16.

which manifests a wise Creator, although his ways remain inscrutable for us, already in the physical ordering of things but even more in the connection between this order and the moral one (which is even more unfathomable to our reason). The conclusion is this: Job confessed not that he had spoken sacrilegiously for he was sure of his good faith, but only that he had spoken unwisely about things that were above his reach and which he did not understand. But while Job confessed that, God made the condemnation fall upon his friends, because, considered from the standpoint of conscience, they had not spoken of God as well as his servant Job did. If one examines now the theories set forth by both sides, that of the friends would probably appear more reasonable to speculative reason and would seem to exhibit more pious humility. If Job were to appear before some tribunal of dogmatic theologians, some senate or inquisition, some worthy presbytery or some high consistory of today (with the exception of one), he probably would have met with a worse fate. Thus, only the uprightness of the heart, not the merit of one's insights, the sincere and undisguised confessions of one's doubts, and the avoidance of feigned convictions which one does not really feel (especially before God, where dissemblance would never work), these are the qualities which caused the upright man Job to be preferred in the eyes of the divine judge to the pious flatterers.

The faith which arose out of such unusual answers to his doubts, that is, which arose simply out of the conviction of his ignorance, could arise only in the soul of a man who in the midst of his most serious doubts could say, "Until the hour of my death, I will hold fast to my piety." (27, 5-6) With this resolution Job proved that he did not base his morality on his faith but his faith upon his morality. In this case, faith, however weak it may become, is a truer and purer one; this kind of faith is not found in a religion that cultivates self-interest and seeks favours, but in a religion of good behaviour.

Concluding Remark

As we have just seen, theodicy is not a task of science but is a matter of faith. The authentic theodicy has taught us that what matters in such affairs is not reasoning but honesty in the avowal of the power-lessness of our reason and sincerity in the expression of our thoughts (a sincerity that never lends itself to a lie, however pious it might be). This leads me to a brief consideration of a very important matter: the opposition between sincerity as the main requirement in matters of faith and the disposition to falseness and deception as the main vice found in human nature. One cannot guarantee that everything one says to one's self or to others is *true* (for one can err) but one can and must always guarantee that what one says is *sincere*, for of this every-body can be immediately certain. In the first case, one's expression can be confronted with the object through the logical judgements of the understanding; in the second case, however, as soon as one states a conviction, one confronts this statement immediately with the subject and the conscience. If one states that something is true without check-ing that one is convinced of it, then one lies, because one expresses something other than what one is certain of. That such impurity is found in the human heart has been noticed a long time ago. Job re-marked about it. And yet, one is tempted to believe that those who teach ethics and religion are only beginning to notice it. It is difficult for man to purify his intentions, especially if he means to act according to duty; but our teachers pay little attention to that and do not seem to take notice of man's duplicity. One can call sincerity the *formal conscience*. Material conscience consists of the concern never to say something which is wrong. The formal conscience consists in the consciousness of having maintained this concern in a given case. Moralists speak of an erroneous conscience but this is an absurdity. If there were such an erroneous conscience man could never be certain of having done right, since the last resort judge too could make mis-takes. I can err when I believe a judgement to be right; this judgement however belongs to the understanding which alone can judge objec-tively (and in fact judges rightly or wrongly); but *whether I really believe* I am right or merely feign to believe it, in this inner conscious-ness I cannot at all err, for this judgement, or rather this sentence, merely says that I deem something to be the case.

The formal conscience, which is the ground of all truthfulness, consists in the care that makes sure of what one believes and what one does not believe, and in the care never to state a conviction when one is not really certain of it. He who says to himself (or to God; in matters of religion this amounts to the same thing) that he *believes* something, without having perhaps given a single look at himself to ascertain whether he is indeed certain, or certain up to a point, of this conviction,[6] tells a *lie*, and his lie is not only the most stupid one before the One who searches the heart, but it is also the most criminal one because it cuts under the ground of sincerity, the basis of every virtue.

It is easy to see how such blind and exterior *confessions* (easily accompanied by an equally untrue inner confession) can bring about progressively, especially if they are a source of worldly advantages, a certain duplicity in everyone's way of thinking. Since the free expression of one's thoughts will, in all likelihood, become the rule only in the distant future (when, in the age of freedom of thought, it will become a general principle of upbringing and education), we must now still further examine the vice of insincerity which seems so profoundly rooted in human hearts.

6. The oath (*tortura spiritualis*) as the means to force witnesses to say the truth is not only allowed by human tribunals but is even held to be indispensable; a sad proof of the little honour which men have for truth, even when they are in the temple of public justice, where the mere idea of justice should inspire them with the greatest awe! But men can lie to themselves in their own self-examination about their convictions, or at least about the strength of them. As this insincerity (which can progressively grow into a state of real persuasion) can have harmful consequences, the oath can be used as a means of obtaining sincerity and can shake up (if not do away with) the audacity of bold affirmations which sounded credible at first. (I refer of course only to the inner oath, the test that sees whether a conviction survives the inner self-examination which the witness makes as he becomes under *oath*.) All that the human tribunal can require of a conscience under oath is a declaration that this man will answer for the truth of his testimony before the Supreme Judge if such a God and such a future life exist. But the tribunal does not need to require the confession that there is a Supreme Judge. If the first attestation cannot prevent a lie, a second false one will not be any more successful. Let us suppose that after having taken the first oath the man asks himself: "Are you willing, in the name of all that is dear and holy to you, to give yourself as pledge of the truth of the existence of the Supreme Judge or any other equally important article of faith?" Of such a question the conscience is frightened, because it fears to advance more than it can claim with certainty, and the conviction is about an object which is not at all accessible to knowledge in its theoretical aspect. It is right indeed to admit the existence of this object (for only thereby can the principles of practical reason agree with those of the theoretical knowledge of nature, and only thus can reason be reconciled with itself); but while it is recommendable to admit the existence of the Supreme Judge, such confession is always free.

Confessions of faith which have a historical source should even more be submitted to a trial by fire of sincerity before people in authority instruct others in these beliefs, because here an impure conviction would be spread further among the multitude; the guilt in this case falls upon the shoulder of the one who gives himself as the guarantee of the conscience of others, since most men are passive in their relationship with their consciences.

There is something moving and edifying to the soul in the example of an upright character who has no trace of duplicity and dissimulation. And yet, especially in frank conversation, honesty is nothing but mere simplicity and straightforwardness in one's way of thought. It is the least that one can ask from a man with a good character. It is hard to see then why this quality should receive such admiration. It must be that of all qualities, honesty is the one which is furthest removed from human nature; sad observation, since all other qualities can have true worth only if they rest on this one! A contemplative misanthrope (someone who wishes no ill to any man but is inclined to believe the worst of all) finds it hard to decide whether men deserve *hatred* or *contempt*. The properties which make men hateful are those which make them positively harmful. The property which makes them contemptible cannot be any other than a disposition which is not morally evil in itself and harms no one; a disposition to things which serve no purpose and which are objectively good for nothing. The first evil is nothing other than enmity (or, to use a euphemism, lack of charity). The second evil cannot be any other than the *inclination to lie* (the falsity which has no intention to harm). The first inclination may have an intention which in some cases can be used and may even be good, as for instance the hostility against incorrigible disturbers of the peace. The second inclination is to the use of a means, the lie, which is good for nothing, whatever may be the intention behind it, because this means is in itself evil and objectionable. In the makeup of the first man, there is *malice*, an evil which can be used in certain circumstances for good purposes; it sins only in the choice of means (which, however, are not condemnable in all cases). The evil of the second kind of man is *worthlessness*, an evil which completely ruins the character of the man. I insist here especially on this duplicity which lies hidden in the depths of the heart, because man manages to falsify his innermost sentiments before his own conscience. It is one more reason for not being too surprised at his inclination for exterior lies. If this inner duplicity were not universal, one would have to admit that men go on keeping false currency in circulation, in spite of that fact that each one fully knows that the currency with which he trades is false.

I remember reading in M. Deluc's *Letters on Mountains, the History of the Earth and of Man*, that his travels undertaken partly for anthropological reasons had arrived at the following results: this friend of mankind started out with the presupposition of the original goodness of our race, and tried to verify it in those places where the luxury of cities could not have exercised any influence yet in corrupting the hearts. He travelled in the Alps from Switzerland to the Hartz. After his belief in man's selfless inclination to help the fellow man had been shaken by experience, he came to the conclusion that man, when it comes to benevolence, is good enough (little wonder! for this rests on an innate inclination of which God is the author), but there exists in him a disposition to subtle duplicity! (This also should cause no wonder, for the repression of the vice rests upon the human character, which man himself must build.) A result which every inquirer could reach without having to travel through mountains; it is enough to observe one's neighbours, or even—closer to home—to look in one's own breast.

Notes

NOTE ON CITATIONS

I have indicated the titles of Kant's works in English. If very long, and if used frequently, these titles have been abbreviated. The abbreviations used are found in the bibliography. I have referred to Kant's works in the authoritative edition of the *Gesammelte Schriften* (abbreviated G.S.) published by the Prussian Royal Academy. In order to follow common usage, exception to this rule has been made for the *Critique of Pure Reason*, where reference is made to the page numbers of the first and second editions. Also indicated, in parentheses, is a page reference to the standard English translation, whenever available, without repeating the title of the work when it is the same as the one indicated at the beginning of the reference. Information on these translations appears in the bibliography, but not in the footnotes.

In the case of books and articles by authors other than Kant, an abbreviated title is often used after the first reference.

INTRODUCTION

1. Kant's writings on religion are difficult, not because they are very technical, but because they are very subtle and imply many delicate problems of interpretation.

2. S. Korner, *Kant*, pp. 168–71.

3. C.C.J. Webb, *Kant's Philosophy of Religion*, p. 17. F. Copleston makes no departure from this traditional interpretation in his *History of Philosophy*, Vol. 6, *Modern Philosophy*, Part II, *Kant*.

4. It is very significant to note the shift of meaning between the familiar quotation and the actual sentence out of which it is lifted. M. Arnold wrote: "The true meaning of religion thus is not simply morality, but morality touched with emotion" (*Literature and Dogma*, paragraph 2). As we shall see a similar fate overtook Kant's philosophy of religion: summaries of it entirely left out important and perhaps decisive qualifications.

5. E. Troeltsch, "Das Historische in Kants Religionsphilosophie," *Kant Studien* 9 (1904).

6. A. Schweitzer, *The Essence of Faith, Philosophy of Religion*. Schweitzer seemed to limit Kant's philosophy of religion to an examination of the problem of God.

7. C.C.J. Webb referred to Otto as exemplifying a dangerous tendency to overemphasize the irrational in religion and contrasted Otto's views with a view he attributed to Kant: "that of the implicit rationality of religion" (*Philosophy of Religion*, p. 202). Characteristically, Webb placed himself halfway between the two extremes.

8. J. Bohatec, *Die Religionsphilosophie Kants*, p. 16.

9. While these post-neo-Kantian developments in the German interpretation of the *Critique of Pure Reason* found relatively little echo in Kant studies published in English, French scholarship developed in closer contact with the German authors; J.L. Bruch's

La Philosophie religieuse de Kant is a superb culmination of a generation of French Kantian studies.

10. I. Kant, *Critique of Pure Reason*, B–XIII (p. 20).

11. This is a widely accepted thesis. See for instance Karl Löwith, *Meaning in History*; Carl L. Becker, *The Heavenly City of the Eighteenth Century Philosophers*, and E. L. Tuveson, *Millenium and Utopia*. Peter Gay's more recent *The Enlightenment: An Interpretation* which has much to say against Becker does not disagree with him on this point.

12. K. Weyand, *Kants Geschichtsphilosophie: Ihre Entwicklung und ihr Verhältnis zur Aufklärung*, p. 8.

13. For the purposes of this study the most important writings of Kant are:
On history
   1784 *Idea for a Universal History*
       What is Enlightenment?
   1785 *Reviews of Herder*
   1786 *Conjectural Beginnings of Human History*
       What Does It Mean to Orient Oneself in Thought?
   1791 *On the Failure of All Attempted Philosophical Theodicies*
   1793 *On the Common Saying: This May Be True in Theory but not in Practice*
   1794 *The End of all Things*
   1795 *Perpetual Peace*
   1798 *The Strife of Faculties* (2nd part)
On religion
   1793 *Religion within the Limits of Reason Alone*
   1798 *The Strife of Faculties* (1st part)
       Passages from *On the Failure of all Attempted Philosophical Theodicies* and
       The End of all Things
I will be proposing a clear distinction between Kant's writings on religion and his discussion of the problem of God (a discussion consisting mainly of the examination of the proofs in the first Critique).

14. For the origin of evil see *Religion within the Limits of Reason Alone*, G.S. 6, pp. 39–44 (pp. 34–39). On the end of history see ibid., G.S. 6, pp. 115–24 and pp. 134–36 (pp. 105–14 and 124–28). The whole of Book Three treats of the victory of the good over the evil principle. The question of the divine "tolerance" of moral evil is handled by showing the "Original Predisposition to Good in Human Nature," G.S. 6, pp. 26–28 (pp. 21–23) and showing the root of the propensity to moral evil in freedom itself, G.S. 6, pp. 28–32 (pp. 23–27). At the basis of this distinction lies the view that God wants man to make himself, in a moral sense, good or evil, G.S. 6, p. 44 (p. 40).

15. This point is tellingly brought forth by L. W. Beck's introduction to a translation of some of Kant's writings on history. See I. Kant, *On History*, trans. L. W. Beck, R. E. Anchor, and E. L. Fackenheim, pp. xxi-xxii.

16. This is the sense of Nature which Lovejoy, in his famous essay on "Nature as Aesthetic Norm," defines as "nature in general: the cosmical order as a whole, or a half-personified power (*natura naturans*)." *Essays in the History of Ideas*, p. 72.

17. See Emil Fackenheim, "Kant's Concept of History," in *Kant Studien* 48 (1956–57). I. Kant, *On History* (L. W. Beck, editor). Klaus Weyand, *Kants Geschichtsphilosophie*.

18. Here also a new trend seems to be arising. French Kantian scholarship for instance has recently paid much interest to Kant's political philosophy and this meant a study almost exclusively of the minor writings. Kantian scholarship in general has come increasingly to emphasize the continuity of Kantian thought with its eighteenth century context. See L. W. Beck, *Kant Studies Today*, pp. 2, 10, 12. This alone would create fresh interest in the minor writings where this continuity is most apparent.

19. Fackenheim, "Concept of History," p. 387.

20. E. Cassirer, *The Philosophy of the Enlightenment* and many subsequent authors disposed of that opinion, which goes back to the Romantics' depreciation of the age that preceded them. To complement E. Cassirer see S. Toulmin and J. Goodfield, *The Discovery of Time*, a study which focuses on the history of scientific ideas, and the monumental two volumes by P. Gay, *The Enlightenment : An Interpretation*.

21. E. Troeltsch: "Das Historische," F. Medicus, "Kant's Philosophie der Geschichte," *Kant Studien* 7, 1902; V. Delbos, *La Philosophie pratique de Kant*.

22. Quoted in Weyand, *Geschichtsphilosophie*, p. 28.

23. *Critique of Pure Reason*, A 707-8, B 735-36 (pp. 573-74).

24. See Fackenheim, "Concept of History," p. 382. See also David W. Tarbet, "The Fabric of Metaphor in Kant's Critique of Pure Reason," *Journal of the History of Philosophy*, Vol. 6, 1968, for interesting observations on Kant's use of metaphors. Tarbet's article, limiting itself to the first Critique, makes a good case for the powerful and revealing use of metaphor in Kant who never made of metaphor a surrogate for argument. The point should be extended to the minor essays, which are of course much richer in metaphors.

25. See L. W. Beck's statement: "Remember that Kant in 1784 . . . was sixty years old (and felt much older); that the working out of his system was a challenge he feared he might not live to meet; and that he and his disciples were then involved in disagreeable polemics that showed him that he had not yet succeeded in making his new philosophy intelligible and acceptable, so that work already done had to be done again. Is it not more likely, then, that this busy and hurried man saw his writings on history in some more intimate connection with the main body of his life work than many of his interpreters have found?" *On History*, p. viii.

26. The term is used in an unpublished prize essay, "The Progress of Metaphysics in Germany since Leibniz and Wolff," G.S. 20, p. 307.

27. Fackenheim, "Concept of History," p. 382.

28. I. Kant, *On History*, p. xv.

29. It is divided into four books which were not all published at once. The first book appeared in 1792 in the *Berlinische Monatschrifft*, after having been cleared by the censorship established by Wöllner. The second book submitted soon afterward for publication in the same magazine did not receive the necessary imprimatur. Kant later submitted successfully the last three books to another censoring body (the philosophical faculty at Jena) and published the four books together in one volume in 1793. That the whole book was at first meant to be serialized does not severely diminish the quality of the overall composition. *Religion within the Limits of Reason Alone* bears no resemblance in this respect to the three articles somewhat artificially put together in *The Strife of Faculties*.

30. That the three Critiques make up the systematic core of Kantian philosophy is a view which should be qualified. Kant did state three times that the task of philosophy

lies in the answering of three questions "What can I know? What must I do? What may I hope?" *Critique of Pure Reason*, A 805, B 833 (p. 635), *Logic*, G.S. 9, p. 25, and letter to C. F. Stäudlin, 4 May 1793, G.S. 11, p. 429 (trans. A. Zweig in Kant, *Philosophical Correspondence 1759-1799*, p. 205). In the last two of these texts, Kant added a fourth question which he put somewhat apart: "What is man?". While the first two Critiques exhaust Kant's views on the first two questions, the third Critique fails notoriously to deal directly with the third. Moreover in his letter to Stäudlin Kant specifically stated that the answer to the third is to be given by religion. Where do we find the core of Kant's system? In the actual results of his three major writings, or in his statement of his systematic purpose? If we start with the latter, we must conclude that the answer to the third question is found in the writings on history and on religion. This problem is one of the major unresolved tensions in the whole of Kantian thought. On the subject of system in Kant, see Jaspers, *Kant*, pp. 144-45. Jaspers concluded that we find in Kant not a fully articulated system but different layers of systematization. This view I have found to be the most useful hypothesis.

CHAPTER I

1. This is particularly brilliantly illustrated by the lectures of C. L. Becker, *The Heavenly City of The Eighteenth Century Philosophers*. See also Chapters 6, 7, and 8 of A. O. Lovejoy, *The Great Chain of Being*. Such teleological reading of the order of nature and history is no invention of the eighteenth century. It had started with Greek philosophy. See R. A. Nisbet, *Social Change and History*, pp. 15ff.

2. In a similar manner his critical epistemology was developed in a context of opinion which accepted Newtonian physics as the model of scientific knowledge. H. J. Paton's case for the strength of the teleological strain in Kant is found in pp. 17, 109, and 150 of *The Categorical Imperative*. Kant's deep-seated favour for expressions of teleological belief is perhaps best highlighted by reference to his statement that of all arguments for the existence of God, the one from design, or physico-teleological one, "always deserves to be mentioned with respect," *Critique of Pure Reason*, A 623, B 651 (p. 520). For a discussion of this see J. Collins, *The Emergence of Philosophy of Religion*, pp. 109ff, and L. W. Beck, *A Commentary on Kant's Critique of Practical Reason*, p. 272. E. Troeltsch stated that Kant's thinking was more teleological than most admit and emphasized that Kant made ample use of faith in Providence, "Das Historische," p. 90.

3. Kant, *Universal Natural History and Theory of the Heavens*, G.S. 1, p. 321 (pp. 155-56).

4. The term "optimism" was a neologism of the eighteenth century and was first used in 1737 by a French Jesuit who was describing the doctrine of Leibniz's *Theodicy*. The term became popular with Voltaire's *Candide ou l'Optimisme* (1759).

5. G.S. 2, p. 34.

6. Ibid., G.S. 2, p. 35.

7. Ibid., G.S. 2, p. 34.

8. *Observations on the Feeling of the Beautiful and Sublime*, G.S. 2, p. 217 (p. 60).

9. G.S. 20, pp. 58-59. The text of the remark is found in P. A. Schilpp, *Kant's Precritical Ethics*, pp. 47-48.

10. *The Universal History of Nature and Theory of the Heavens* already shows the impact of Newtonian science since Kant formulated in it a hypothesis that would account for the formation of the solar system in entirely mechanical terms. This kind of thinking however did not at that time displace in the least his teleological modes of thought. Kant was aware that such hypothesis might appear to be irreligious, but he sought to provide his reader with ample reassurance, G.S. 1, pp. 221ff. (pp. 18ff.).

11. G.S. 20, pp. 58-59. See also Schilpp, *Pre-Critical Ethics*, p. 48.

12. Schilpp, *Pre-Critical Ethics*, p. 46. Krüger spoke of a "moral conversion," *Philosophie und Moral in der Kantischen Kritik*, p. 59.

13. Schilpp, *Pre-Critical Ethics*, p. 49.

14. The interested reader will read Chapters 4 and 5 of Schilpp. On Kant and Rousseau see also E. Cassirer, *Rousseau, Kant and Goethe*.

15. The idea reappears in 1788 in the essay *Concerning the Use of Teleological Principles on Philosophy*.

16. *On the Different Races of Men*, G.S. 2, p. 434.

17. G. Vlachos, *La pensée politique de Kant*, p. 142.

18. Vlachos considered Kant's thinking on race a good door into the deepest motivations of his thought (*Pensée politique*, p. 137). He found there the basis of a philosophy of history which reconciled natural evolution with the practical postulates of political reformism (p. 143), thereby breaking a fresh path between the philosophy of organic continuity (or automatic teleological development) characteristic of conservativism on the one hand (a philosophy that denies that man has any crucial role to play—initiating development or progress for instance—in history), and the voluntaristic social contract revolutionary reconstructionist philosophy of Rousseau on the other hand (a philosophy which sees history as having to be made out of human will and resolve). My interpretation of Kant's teleological thinking as reconciliation of Providence and freedom (see pp. 73, 47-51, 86) is in systematic unity with Vlachos' interpretation of his political philosophy (with the exception of his rejection of theism).

19. G.S. 8, pp. 9-14.

20. Ibid., p. 13.

21. *Idea*, G.S. 8, p. 30 (*On History*, p. 25).

22. Ibid., G.S. 8, p. 17 (p. 11).

23. Ibid., G.S. 8, pp. 17-18 (p. 12).

24. Ibid., G.S. 8, pp. 18-19 (pp. 12-13).

25. Ibid., G.S. 8, pp. 18-19 (pp. 12-13). As Beck summarized it, "History is the recounting of the movement of man from the state of being a mere part of the mechanisms of nature to the state of being the creator of and citizen of the world of culture, where he can eventually come to know and perform his duties and realize his moral ends." "Editor's Introduction," in I. Kant, *On History*, p. xviii.

26. *The Concept of Race*, G.S. 8, pp. 98-99.

27. *Deutsche Merkur*, Oct.-Nov. 1896, pp. 57-86, 150-66.

28. G.S. 8, pp. 182-83.

29. G.S. 8, p. 180.

30. For a full treatment of the question, see the valuable study of J. D. McFarland, *Kant's Concept of Teleology*. He examined fully Kant's mind on the question of organisms which in some way form an exception to the general mechanical treatment of nature.

31. See pp. 171-72.

32. G.S. 8, pp. 307-12.

33. G.S. 8 (*On History*, p. 109).

34. *Anthropology*, G.S. 7, pp. 321-30.

35. Walter Frost, "Kant's Teleologie," *Kant Studien* 9 (1906), p. 335.

36. *Critique of Pure Reason*, A 405, B 432ff., (pp. 384ff.)

37. F. Alquié, *La Critique kantienne de la métaphysique*, p. 67.

38. Ibid., pp. 71-72.

39. We laugh at Kant's ideas about driftwood today, but we have learned by experience through technological progress how to live in the Arctic without driftwood. Are we ready, however, to rule out all teleological statements that confirm our faith in the human possibility of living the moral and cosmopolitan life on this earth?

CHAPTER 2

1. Note that this third element is the last of the famous three questions: What can I know? What must I do? What may I hope? The answer to the third question given in the philosophy of history is, however, not the whole Kantian answer to the problem of hope.

2. "Editor's Introduction" to *On History*, p. xxi. The order past-present-future may have the disadvantage of encouraging the reader to think of Kant's view of history as consisting of a series of stages, while it is in fact a view of a process which is oriented by an end. I have tried to guard against such a misunderstanding in my exposition. The "plan of Nature" seems for Kant to be one and consistent throughout the process.

3. This essay was apparently prompted by Kant's reading of Herder's commentary on the first chapters of *Genesis* found in his *Idea for a Philosophy of the History of Mankind*. Kant found the essay full of too many gratuitous representations of the imagination. He reviewed the two volumes of Herder and expressed interest for the undertaking and numerous objections to the execution.

4. *Conjectural Beginnings*, G.S. 8, p. 111 (*On History*, p. 55).

5. Ibid.

6. *Critique of Judgement*, G.S. 5, p. 431 (II, p. 94).

7. *Conjectural Beginnings*, G.S. 8, p. 112 (*On History*, p. 56).

8. Ibid., G.S. 8, pp. 114-15 (p. 59).

9. Jaspers put it this way: "There is—hence Kant agreed with Rousseau—an inevitable conflict between culture and nature. But it is obviously through this conflict that man develops all his powers and faculties and progresses towards rational freedom. Kant therefore held that Rousseau was wrong in demanding a return to nature. Calamity, vice, evil spur man to improve himself." Jaspers, *Kant*, pp. 104-5.

Rousseau was not so naive, except in a few unhappy phrases, as to demand such a return. And Kant knew it very well. "Ultimately what Rousseau wanted was not the return of man to the state of nature; he wanted, however, man to look back upon that state from where he is now." *Anthropology*, G.S. 7, pp. 326-27.

10. *Conjectural Beginnings*, G.S. 8, p. 123 (*On History*, p. 68).

11. *Idea*, G.S. 8, p. 20 (*On History*, p. 15). *The Conjectural Beginnings* of 1786 also attempt to show that the birth of reason was a legitimate occurrence, necessary for the achievement of a long-range goal. See G.S. 8, pp. 120-23 (*On History*, pp. 66-68).

12. This concept has numerous antecedents. Leibniz spoke of *Concordia discors* and Mandeville's *Fable of the Bees* developed the idea of anti-social sociability as he showed that private vice leads to public benefit. Mandeville, however, used the idea to unveil the functioning of society, not its dynamic development. He had no historical perspective. For the source of the whole tradition, we must go back to Augustine. "There is nothing so social by nature, so anti-social by sin, as man." *De Civ. Dei*, XII, 26.

13. *Idea*, G.S. 8, p. 21 (*On History*, p. 15). The similarity with passages in Rousseau is striking: see *Du contrat social*, Book I, Chapter 8: "The passage from the state of nature to the civil state produces a very remarkable change in man by substituting in his conduct justice for instinct, and giving his actions the moral quality they had lacked before."

14. Ibid., G.S. 8, p. 21 (p. 16).

15. Ibid., G.S. 8, p. 22 (p. 17).

16. Did Kant praise war? Did he introduce this virus into the German philosophical tradition? The nature of his interest in peace makes the answers clear. See for instance the famous tirade in the *Conjectural Beginnings*: "Undoubtedly war is the greatest source of the evils which oppress civilized nations . . .," G.S. 8, p. 121 (*On History*, p. 66). Nevertheless a whole contentious dossier exists on the matter. Indications on it can be found in C. J. Friedrich, *Inevitable Peace*, p. 60. See also Hans Saner, *Kants Weg vom Krieg zum Frieden*, Vol. 1, *Widerstreit und Einheit*.

17. *Anthropology*, G.S. 7, p. 268.

18. *The Metaphysical Elements of Justice*, G.S. 6, p. 306 (p. 70).

19. See for instance *Anthropology*, G.S. 7, p. 151.

20. In his introduction to the *Metaphysical Elements of Justice*, John Ladd defined the main function of the civil state according to Kant as: "To maintain the rule of law, to guarantee and protect the rights of its subjects." This Kant called "the juridical condition of society, the state of public justice, legal justice," p. xxi.

21. *Perpetual Peace* describes this process. G.S. 8, pp. 365–66 (*On History*, p. 111).

22. *What Does It Mean to Orient Oneself in Thought?*, G.S. 8, p. 145.

23. In his erudite study, *Théorie et praxis dans la pensée morale et politique de Kant et de Fichte en 1793*, A. Philonenko demonstrated that, whereas Kant saw the moral and political problems as an indivisible whole in 1784 (the date of the *Idea*), he came to separate rather sharply the moral and the political problems in 1795 in his essay on *Perpetual Peace*, where it is affirmed that a sound state may be organized even if demons were to be its only citizens. Since Philonenko did not handle the problem of history as such, he did not address himself to the question of the chronological sequence between the two stages, although it is clear that a sound political republic is susceptible to realization in history before the moral commonwealth.

24. *What Does It Mean to Orient Oneself in Thought?*, G.S. 8, p. 144.

25. *What Does It Mean to Orient Oneself in Thought?* gives further detail on the dialectic of man's intellectual life. Three stages are given leading to a definitive fourth: (*a*) the genius or enthusiasm. The mind enjoys and gets lost in the audacity of its representations; it yields to the mystery of what is called with awe a transcendent intuition and refuses the guidance and control of reason in the name of revelation to the inner sense. What it really means is that the mind indulges its own fancies. (*b*) Since each man follows his genius and his inner revelations, the discourse of each becomes unintelligible. To restore order, some will suggest to canonize some series of events, to consider them as exterior revelation, and to make them the basis of all orientation in

thought. This is religious positivism. (*c*) Reason revolts against the authority of imposed canons and wants to accept only its own proofs. However, intoxicated by the affirmation of its independence, reason too will become arrogant and will consider itself capable of giving dogmatic proof for everything true. Like the two previous misguided mentalities, even rationalism will become authoritarian and will try to use the political authority to reduce adversaries to silence. (*d*) Finally the Critique will put an end to dogmatic rationalism also, and thus to all wars between minds, first by insisting on absolute freedom of thought, and then by a free common effort at giving a strict formal definition of the limits of what man can know, what he should do, and what he may hope. Thus it will pass the "eternal sentence" which will ensure peace. It is in this way that peace emerges out of war, rationality progressively out of irrationality, and a more perfect freedom out of the states of violence and coercion which followed the deterministic states of nature.

In *Progress of Metaphysics* (1793) three stages are mentioned: dogmatic, sceptical, and critical. G.S. 20, p. 264.

26. "The homage which each state pays (at least in words) to the concept of law proves that there is slumbering in man an even greater disposition to become master of the evil principle in himself." *Perpetual Peace*, G.S. 8, p. 355 (On *History*, p. 99). "Subjection to lawful constraint" and "rational freedom" are identified in a passage from the same essay. "When we see the attachment of savages to their lawless freedom, preferring ceaseless combat to subjection to a lawful constraint which they might establish, and thus preferring senseless freedom to rational freedom, we regard it with deep contempt as barbarity, rudeness, and a brutish degradation of humanity." Ibid. G.S. 8, p. 354 (p. 98).

27. *The Metaphysical Elements of Justice*, G.S. 6, p. 354 (p. 128).

28. *What is Enlightenment?*, G.S. 8, p. 40 (*On History*, p. 8).

29. Ibid., G.S. 8, pp. 41–42 (p. 10).

30. *Idea*, G.S. 8, p. 30 (*On History*, p. 25).

31. *The Strife of Faculties*, G.S. 7, p. 79 (*On History*, p. 137). The question is also discussed in *Theory and Practice*, G.S. 8, p. 307 and *Progress of Metaphysics*, G.S. 20, p. 307.

32. *The Strife of Faculties*, G.S. 7, pp. 79–80 (*On History*, p. 137).

33. Ibid., G.S. 7, p. 82 (p. 140).

34. The reference to Sisyphus is in *Theory and Practice*, G.S. 8, p. 307.

35. *The Strife of Faculties*, G.S. 7, p. 83 (*On History*, p. 142).

36. Quoted in *Theory and Practice*, G.S. 8, p. 307.

37. Ibid., G.S. 8, p. 309.

38. *Progress of Metaphysics*, G.S. 20, p. 307.

39. *Theory and Practice*, G.S. 8, pp. 309–10.

40. This may look like buttressing a doubtful statement by an even more doubtful one. Kant at least endeavoured to give a clear meaning to such faith in Nature and Providence. See pp. 85–90.

41. *Theory and Practice*, G.S. 8, p. 310. Such a guarantee of progress in Nature or Providence is affirmed in *Perpetual Peace*, G.S. 8, p. 368 (*On History*, p. 114), *Religion within the Limits of Reason Alone*, G.S. 6, p. 123 (pp. 113–14) and in *The Strife of Faculties*, G.S. 7, p. 93 (*On History*, p. 153).

42. Weyand in a comprehensive analysis found that Kant in his search for examples of general moral improvement listed on various occasions a total of six of them: States

pay interest to their internal cultural development, civil liberties improve, and so does freedom of religion; States begin to see that civil liberties contribute to public peace; States see the advantages in arbitration of conflict; and the idea of a League of Nations is making its way into people's minds. Weyand, *Geschichtsphilosophie*, pp. 100–1.

43. Kant had a long argument to show that a Republican constitution reduces the risk of war, whereas the policies of the dynasties increased them. *Perpetual Peace*, G.S. 8, pp. 349–57 (*On History*, pp. 92–102).

44. *Opus Postumum*, G.S. 22, pp. 622–23.

45. *The Strife of Faculties*, G.S. 7, p. 88 (*On History*, p. 147).

46. *The Metaphysical Elements of Justice*, G.S. 6, p. 352 (p. 125).

47. *Perpetual Peace*, G.S. 8, p. 357 (*On History*, p. 101). Kant's path to such a definitive and just order in the relations among states is given full and precise treatment in the essay on *Perpetual Peace* (1790). The path requires political reform in each state, especially republican government and what he called elsewhere "a constitution in harmony with the natural right of man." *The Strife of Faculties*, G.S. 7, p. 90 (*On History*, p. 150).

48. Fackenheim, "Concept of History," p. 397.

49. As we saw earlier, from 1793 on Kant made a sharp distinction between political progress and moral progress, two problems which were seen in a single glance in the *Idea* of 1784. It is very clear from this point on that the League of Nations is not the Kingdom of God yet. The reason for this zeal in making the distinction was satisfactorily accounted for by Philonenko. Ever since the period of the Terror, elements of the politically conservative opinion, Rehberg in particular, had argued that the permanence of evil made revolutions incapable of keeping their promises and that revolutions only substituted fresh and fierce evils for old and domesticated ones. Kant did not diminish in any way the power of evil, but he did not want this moral consideration to become the ground for reactionary politics. Philonenko, *Théorie et praxis*, p. 29.

50. *The End of All Things*, G.S. 8, pp. 330–31 (*On History*, pp. 72–73).

51. *The Failure of All Theodicies*, G.S. 8, p. 263.

52. Ibid., G.S. 8, p. 267.

53. The expression is borrowed from Fackenheim, "Concept of History," p. 388.

54. *Critique of Judgement*, G.S. 5, p. 431 (II, p. 94).

55. Ibid., G.S. 5, p. 433 (II, p. 96).

56. Ibid., G.S. 5, p. 433 (II, p. 97).

57. Ibid., G.S. 5, pp. 433–34 (II, p. 97).

58. Kant used the concept of *Mündigkeit* in *What is Enlightenment?*, G.S. 8, p. 35 (*On History*, p. 3).

59. *Critique of Judgement*, G.S. 5, p. 433 (II, p. 96).

60. This summary is indebted to that made by Troeltsch, "Das Historische," pp. 123–27. Troeltsch however indicated four stages. His third stage, which he called the moral one, corresponds to my stages three and four. I arrive at five stages in order to bring out the difference between the political conditions before and after political reform.

As the quotations show, these stages can also be found in the paragraph in the third *Critique* where Kant gave a summary of his philosophy of history.

Note that this outline of history gives contemporary man a twofold orientation for his hope: there is a disjunction between the hope for political and cultural improvement and that for moral or even religious improvement. History in this outline has a twofold telos. The first one (stage 4) is indubitably a worldly telos. Whether stage 5 will ever be realized in worldly conditions is something else again.

Finally for the sake of completeness it should be noted that the ethical writings, by speaking of the noumenal self, of his belonging in a Kingdom of ends, and by arriving at postulating the immortality of the soul, give to the self a third orientation for its hopes: an entirely otherworldly one this time. (See pp. 91-92, the discussion of the distinction between the ethico-juridical and the ethico-religious tendencies in Kant.)

61. Such interpretation of his philosophy of history does draw upon a neighbouring but distinct part of his philosophy, namely his political philosophy, and its investigation of law, the state etc.

62. See Nisbet, *Social Change and History*, pp. 119, 149, 166, and following.

63. Delbos, *Philosophie pratique*, p. 269.

64. This means however that there are no absolute proofs that history will ever reach its telos. There is even a proof that such things can never be proved: a history of freedom, by definition, cannot follow necessary laws of development. The future stages described in the grand outline are possible and perhaps probable. They are certainly what is to be hoped for and worked for. But things could always go wrong.

The strength and originality of Kant does not lie so much in the affirmation of the unknown quality of the future. It lies in the emphasis that it would be immoral to have things otherwise. Any idea of inevitable progress was for Kant an offense to the practical power of reason, and the free responsibility of human beings. It is interesting to note that the one French philosopher who in the nineteenth century criticized the philosophy of history found, for instance, in Auguste Comte, was the neo-Kantian Renouvier, who reiterated the Kantian control of the philosophy of history by the practical demands of morality.

65. Delbos, *Philosophie pratique*, p. 270. Delbos emphasized that the major part of the philosophy of history was either published or conceived before the publication in 1785 of the *Foundations of the Metaphysics of Morals* (see p. 295). The *Critique of Practical Reason* came in 1788.

66. Fackenheim, "Concept of History," p. 396.

67. *Idea*, G.S. 8, p. 19 (*On History*, p. 13).

68. Ibid., G.S. 8, p. 25 (p. 20).

69. Ibid., G.S. 8, pp. 29-31 (pp. 23-26).

70. This point was well brought out by Jean Lacroix in his essay on Kant's philosophy of history in *Histoire et mystère* when he emphasized that it is up to morality to choose and determine the meaning of history. He credited Kant with having saved the idea of progress by purifying it, i.e. by making it clear that it is immorality itself to count on the progress of laws to make men perfectly moral. Thus Kant achieved a philosophy of history which gave a sense to history while keeping unharmed the specificity and significance of moral action. See *Histoire et mystère*, pp. 20, 30-31, 55.

71. *Idea*, G.S. 8, p. 22 (*On History*, p. 16).

72. The oscillation between references to "Nature" and references to "Providence" are examined later. See pp. 57, 73, 90-95, 274.

73. *Perpetual Peace*, G.S. 8, p. 362 (*On History*, p. 107). Note that the author of the plan in this late text is Providence, not Nature. Kant was less afraid of speaking of determinative power when speaking of Providence than when speaking of Nature.

74. Friedrich, *Inevitable Peace*, p. 51.

75. Vlachos, *Pensée politique*, p. 180. See also p. 242: "The moral interpretations of Kantian thought which are exclusively wedded to the idea of a strict opposition between *is* and *ought*, between nature and freedom, appear narrow if not entirely erroneous."

The study of what Kant meant by "orientation" would lead to a similar result, namely to indications that an absolute split cannot be found between what is given to man and what man does. To orient oneself is to find bearings in what surrounds one, and to choose a direction in which to head. See Eric Weil, *Problèmes kantiens*, p. 91 and, of course, the whole essay *What Does It Mean to Orient Oneself in Thought?*, G.S. 8, pp. 131–48. This remarkable essay that is not as well-known as it deserves is the most convenient source for showing that human existence for Kant is fundamentally a being-in-the-world, or a spontaneity-in-receptivity. A full historical and philosophical introduction by A. Philonenko is available in the French translation of the essay *Qu'est-ce que s'orienter dans la pensée?*, pp. 7–74.

76. Vlachos, *Pensée politique*, pp. 160–61.

77. Ibid., p. 518.

78. Marginal Notes on the *Observations*, G.S. 20, p. 14. Quoted in Vlachos, *Pensée politique*, p. 92.

79. Pragmatic knowledge of man is knowledge of what "man, as a freely acting being, makes or can and must make of himself." *Anthropology*, G.S. 7, p. 119. History is given as a source for such "anthropology, from the pragmatic point of view," p. 121.

80. Troeltsch, "Das Historische," p. 51.

81. Delbos, *Philosophie pratique*, p. 290.

82. *Reviews of Herder's Ideas*, G.S. 8, p. 43 (*On History*, p. 27). The reviews of Herder do not add much to the content of Kant's philosophy of history, but by using Herder's approach as a foil they indicate how Kant thought one should go about writing a philosophy of history.

83. Ibid., G.S. 8, p. 55 (*On History*, p. 39).

84. *Perpetual Peace*, G.S. 8, p. 367 (*On History*, p. 113).

85. *Idea*, G.S. 8, p. 29 (*On History*, p. 24).

86. *Reviews of Herder's Ideas*, G.S. 8, p. 64 (*On History*, p. 49).

CHAPTER 3

1. *Idea*, G.S. 8, p. 17 (*On History*, p. 11).

2. C. F. Von Weizsäcker, *History of Nature* (Chicago, University of Chicago Press, 1959), p. 134.

3. This is another indication that the split between nature and history cannot be considered as final for Kant.

4. "Outline of Courses for Winter 1765–66," G.S. 2, p. 312. The best available text of these lectures is found in H. von Glasenapp, *Kant und die Religionen des Ostens*. A treatment of Kant's work in geography is found in J. A. May, *Kant's Concept of Geography*.

5. See Weyand, *Geschichtsphilosophie*, pp. 25–26 for evidence of the "catastrophic" state of historical studies at the University of Königsberg.

6. *Critique of Pure Reason*, A 642, B 670 (p. 532).

7. Ibid., A 644, B 672 (p. 533). The article by Stanley French, "Kant's Constitutive-Regulative Distinction" in L. W. Beck, ed., *Kant Studies Today*, shows that much in contemporary analytic philosophy is focusing on the problem Kant handled with his distinction.

8. *Critique of Pure Reason*, A 866-67, B 714-15 (p. 560).

9. Ibid., A 681, B 709 (p. 557).

10. The *Critique of Pure Reason* illustrates the regulative employment of the Ideas by means of yet another Idea: that of the systematic unity of Nature, A 648-68, B 678-96 (pp. 536-49). Another example of such Ideas is found in the political philosophy, in the Idea of an original social contract. Kant specifically denied that the original social contract was a fact of history. He had too much respect for the rules of historical evidence to present an account of what had taken place in the organization of society as a piece of history. To deny that the social contract was a fact of history is not, however, to relegate the idea to the realm of useless fictions. The Idea of a social contract as an Idea plays an important regulative role in Kant's political philosophy.

11. *Critique of Pure Reason*, A 668, B 696 (p. 549).

12. Ibid., A 689, B 717; A 693, B 721 (pp. 561-64).

13. Ibid., A 697, B 725 (p. 566).

14. Ibid., A 698, B 726 (p. 567).

15. Ibid., A 699, B 727 (p. 567).

16. Ibid., A 681, B 710 (p. 557).

17. The handling of this question is made difficult by Kant's terminological inconsistency. The philosophy of history speaks of Nature or Providence. The *Critique of Pure Reason* speaks of the Idea of the world, and of different meanings of nature. See A 405, B 432ff. (p. 384ff.) The metaphor of the home is found there too. A 707, B 735 (p. 573). As is often the case with Kant, terminological inconsistency exists here because he did not always gather in one place for systematic treatment a variety of ultimately coherent solutions that came as he dealt with various problems in various places in his authorship.

18. Troeltsch, "Das Historische," p. 50.

19. "Not entirely" is an important qualification. Nature and its plan do not undergo change, but our hopes for the future, an important part of the philosophy of history, may depend on what men actually do.

20. *Foundations of the Metaphysics of Morals*, G.S. 4, p. 436 (H. J. Paton, *The Moral Law* [London: Hutchinson University Library, 1948], p. 98).

21. Ibid.

22. See Delbos, *Philosophie pratique*, p. 264.

23. *Foundations of the Metaphysics of Morals*, G.S. 4, pp. 395-96 (pp. 11-12). Paragraph 84 in Part Two of the *Critique of Judgement* is Kant's final treatment of this point.

24. Paton, *Categorical Imperative*, p. 17.

25. Ibid., p. 164. See also p. 45. L. W. Beck fully agrees with Paton on this point. See *Commentary*, p. 128, note 4.

All those who see Kantian ethics as exclusively duty-centred repeat the error of C. Garve who thought that Kant maintained that the observation of the moral law without any attention to happiness was the only ultimate end and that one had to see in it the only end the Creator had in mind. In *Theory and Practice* Kant protested against this misinterpretation. "According to my theory it is not man's morality in itself nor happiness in itself, but the highest possible good in the world (i.e. the union and accord of the two) which is the Creator's only end," *Theory and Practice*, G.S. 8, p. 279.

On Kant's concept of the good and its relationship to the will see J. R. Silber, "The Copernican Revolution in Ethics: the Good Reexamined." *Kant Studien* 51 (1959), reprinted in R. P. Wolff, *I. Kant: A Collection of Critical Essays*.

26. *Critique of Practical Reason*, G.S. 5, p. 59 (p. 61).

27. Beck, *Commentary*, p. 128, note 4.

28. *Critique of Practical Reason*, G.S. 5, pp. 62–63 (p. 65).

29. Ibid., G.S. 5, p. 57 (p. 59).

30. The concept of the *summum bonum* is one of the most controversial aspects of Kantian ethics. It contains obscurities and inconsistencies. Beck has an excellent discussion of the problems it creates. See *Commentary*, pp. 239–58, especially pp. 242–45.

31. To reintroduce in this way the notion of happiness, by the back door so to speak, is not too satisfactory, as Paton pointed out. Paton adds quite correctly that what matters really here is whether our good volitions can or cannot be successful in realizing their aims. *Categorical Imperative*, p. 43.

32. *Critique of Practical Reason*, G.S. 5, p. 114 (p. 118). There is an excellent discussion of Kant's "moral proof" for the existence of God in Allen W. Wood, *Kant's Moral Religion*. See especially on pp. 25–34 the discussion of the passage just cited on the moral law being "inherently false" if God were not to exist and if the highest good were to be impossible of attainment. Wood's discussion has the merit of showing that "the moral arguments aim at justifying not simply the assent to certain speculative propositions, but more fundamentally the adoption of an outlook on the moral action."

I have nothing to add to Wood's discussion except to point out the bases for Kant's position in Christian doctrine. In the New Testament we find Jesus promising to his disciples that the Holy Spirit will come to their help and will give them the power to do that which they ought to do (Mt. 10:19–20). We also hear Paul teach that God, being faithful, will not cause men to be tempted beyond their strength (I Cor. 10:13). It has been a frequent insistence in Christian theology that God being truthful does not mislead men or expect from them the impossible. Luther in his turn insisted that God's promises in the Gospel are not false and must be taken at their word. To suspect God of being a liar is the one thing incompatible with faith. Commentary on *Romans* 4:18–25, *Vorlesung über den Römerbrief 1515–1516*, ed. J. Ficker (Leipzig: Dieterich, 1925), pp. 42–44. The doctrine of Providence, which had more impact upon philosophers, commonly taught that God sees to it that men are not left without the possibility of doing what they ought to do. It also assured that human moral striving was not to be undertaken in a world that condemns it to absurdity. The doctrine that the divine commands were not false was thus a common place in apologetics. Savonarola, *Triumphus Crucis* 4, 6, "God never gives anything an end without giving it also the means to reach it."

All this does not diminish the originality of Kant's argument which uses the idea of the truthfulness of the rational moral law to serve as the basis for a faith in the kind of world we are in and in God as the Creator of it. But these antecedents constitute elements out of which Kant organized his argument. Both sets of views conceive man (religious man or moral man) as living in a tried condition where questions as to the justice of fate may rightly be asked and both invite to a faith that such a condition is not ultimately unjust, tragic, or absurd.

33. *Critique of Practical Reason*, G.S. 5, p. 134 (p. 139).

34. Beck, *Commentary*, p. 245.

35. See *Critique of Pure Reason*, A 811, B 839 (p. 639).

36. Beck, *Commentary*, p. 245.

37. This opens up the delicate question of the relationship between the first two Critiques, a problem handled very satisfactorily by Beck (*Commentary*, pp. 13ff.). In summary then, the second Critique is not a continuation of the first and was not at all

envisaged at the time of the writing of even the second edition of the first Critique. It does maintain contact with the results of the first. It amounts to a fresh beginning in another realm of experience, the moral one, while the first Critique focused on the problems of cognition. It does coordinate with the first but is not another wing in the system. (This does fit with our general hypothesis of many fresh starts in the Kantian opus.) Its main original result is a stronger affirmation of the reality of the three traditional ideas of metaphysics: freedom, the immortality of the soul, and God. As G. Martin concluded, basing himself upon the *Critique of Practical Reason*, Book II, Chapter II, Section 7, G.S. 5, pp. 134-41 (pp. 139-47), its result is "an extension of speculation." G. Martin, *Kant's Metaphysics and Theory of Science*, p. 148.

38. Paton, *Categorical Imperative*, p. 256.

39. Beck, *Commentary*, p. 250.

40. Ibid., p. 254.

41. *Critique of Practical Reason*, G.S. 5, p. 143 (p. 148).

42. *Critique of Judgement*, G.S. 5, pp. 445-46 (II, pp. 112-13).

43. What Kant meant when he stated that finite men need qua moral men to believe in the possibility of the *summum bonum* may also be brought out by drawing upon the third Critique. It returned to a question parallel to that of the *summum bonum* by asking whether nature harmonizes with our moral end. The parallelism between the two inquiries is obvious: Is the world of nature such as to make possible—or even to encourage—the human pursuit of moral ends? In an important article, W. T. Jones, asking why such harmonization is necessary in Kant's eyes, concluded that the moral purpose coming from pure practical reason does not require the existence of nature as a whole as a purposive system. This is to restate that the moral law does not require proof of—or even belief in—the realizability of its purposes to have authority. Yet, pursued Jones, Kant insisted on some connection between the world of morality and the world of nature, because in the absence of any verification of the impact of the supersensible world upon the sensible world, or of any proof of the harmony—or harmonizability—between the two, there would arise "a sceptical attitude towards morality." Undoubtedly in such a situation the mind would be tempted to consider the moral law as sheer folly. Such connection is found (in the third Critique) in teleologically conceived organisms, which embody spontaneity in observable phenomena. Such organisms serve to Kant "as an illustration, an embodiment in physical nature, of that supersensible moral activity." Thus signs—if not proofs—are available to defeat the sceptical temptations in our minds, confirm the authority of the moral law in a tangible way, and strengthen our moral dispositions. These signs testify—to our relief—that the laws of morality and those of the physical world are not forever doomed to work at cross-purposes, or to seek to defeat each other, but may come to cooperate to bring about the highest good, or the moral commonwealth realized under the conditions of this world. See W. T. Jones, "Purpose, Nature, and the Moral Law" in G. T. Whitney and D. F. Bowers, eds., *The Heritage of Kant*, pp. 241 and 242. This notion of "sign" will receive fresh significance in the philosophy of religion. See pp. 151, 190-91, 197-98, 261.

A. W. Wood also put his finger on the need of the human moral spirit for sources of strength when he wrote that "failure, suffering, and the evils of the world do not so much refute hope as *exhaust* it," *Kant's Moral Religion*, p. 160.

44. *Progress of Metaphysics*, G.S. 20, p. 305. The right to affirm faith in God is, interestingly enough, related to man's right to create a cultural world as he develops in history. We shall return to this point. See pp. 92-93.

45. The particular weakness of this problematic of virtue and happiness over that of the feasibility of successful moral action is well shown by W.H. Walsh, "Kant's Moral Theology," *Proceedings of the British Academy*, Vol. 49.

46. *Critique of Practical Reason*, G.S. 5, p. 143 (p. 149).

47. Ibid., G.S. 5, pp. 150–61 (pp. 155–65). The same distinction reappeared in *Religion*, G.S. 6, p. 156 (p. 144).

48. Delbos, *Philosophie pratique*, p. 296.

49. Ibid., pp. 518ff.

50. Since the length of the first introduction (which was found in manuscript form by Dilthey in 1889 and published in 1914) appears to have been its only fault, it shall be considered as part of the work.

51. Problems related to those found in the philosophy of history appear in the conclusion of the third Critique. We find here another indication of the centrality of the philosophy of history in Kant's eyes.

52. *Critique of Judgement*, G.S. 5, p. 175 (I, p. 14). Examining this problem of compatibility between the world of nature and that of man in his answer to Eberhard, Kant noted the similarity of his solution with the preestablished harmony which Leibniz found between the realm of nature and the realm of grace. *On a Discovery*, G.S. 8, pp. 249–51.

53. *Critique of Judgement*, G.S. 5, p. 170 (I, p. 7). The next major published work is *Religion within the Limits of Reason Alone* (1793) closely preceded and followed by three important essays in philosophy of history: *The Failure of All Theodicies* (1791), *The End of All Things* (1794), and *Perpetual Peace* (1795). What I called the second strain of Kantian philosophy (philosophy of history and philosophy of religion) even under the pressure of time could not yield to the first one, namely that emerging from the three Critiques and which should have directed Kant at this time to the doctrinal part of his work.

54. I will thus leave entirely aside—for want of place—the first half of the Critique, the examination of aesthetic judgement. It too provides evidences, or traces, of a benevolent disposition of Nature since our own mental faculties are constituted in such a way as to produce a possible teleological unity among them that culminates in the feeling of the beautiful and of the sublime. There is thus in our own mental constitution and mental activities evidence of teleological organization, of subjective teleological organization to be precise. This first part contains also a theory of symbol to which we shall return.

55. *Critique of Judgement*, G.S. 5, p. 387 (II, p. 37).

56. Ibid., G.S. 5, p. 183 (pp. 21–22).

57. It does not even rule out the need for a deterministic social science: we could foresee a man's future behaviour if all internal incentives and external occasions were known. *Critique of Practical Reason*, G.S. 5, p. 99 (pp. 102–3).

58. First "Introduction" to *The Critique of Judgement*, G.S. 20, pp. 242–43.

59. This step is particularly bold since it involves what the *Critique of Pure Reason* warned against: a transcendental use of concepts. Kant was perfectly aware of this boldness. First "Introduction," G.S. 20, pp. 234–35.

60. See B. Rousset, *La Doctrine kantienne de l'objectivité*, pp. 461–62.

61. *Critique of Judgement*, G.S. 5, p. 392 (II, p. 44).

62. Ibid., paragraph 73, especially G.S. 5, p. 395 (II, p. 47).

63. Ibid., G.S. 5, p. 410 (II, p. 67).

64. According to G. Martin, Kant was the first to use the idea of "theoretical model" without which no modern scientific investigation would be possible, in physics, in biology, or in sociology. Martin, *Kant's Metaphysics*, pp. 94–95.

65. Troeltsch, "Das Historische," p. 147.

66. In the *Foundations of the Metaphysics of Morals* Kant used a metaphor that does justice to his understanding of Nature, calling it a stepmother, G.S. 4, p. 394 (p. 10). Leibniz had previously used this metaphor. *Theodicy*, p. 130. The metaphor ultimately goes back to Pliny. In the Kantian understanding of Nature, this cruel stepmother weans her children and deprives them of the fullness of a mother's love for the sake of enabling them to reach maturity.

67. *Critique of Judgement*, G.S. 5, p. 433 (II, p. 96).

68. Ibid., G.S. 5, p. 433 (II, p. 97).

69. Ibid., G.S. 5, p. 378 (II, p. 27).

70. The two German terms are: "der letzte Zweck" and "der Endzweck." "Ultimate" thus might be best replaced by "last" to emphasize that Nature while having an end at the top of its systems of ends does not have an end of properly metaphysical significance. Only Creation, as Creation of a good God, can be said to encompass man as the bearer of the really final end, or of the only metaphysically significant end.

71. *Critique of Judgement*, G.S. 5, p. 436 (II, p. 100).

72. Ibid., G.S. 5, p. 431 (II, p. 94).

73. See Delbos, *Philosophie pratique*, pp. 594–95, Beck, *Commentary*, p. 273, and Schweitzer, *Essence of Faith*, p. 118.

74. On this see Krüger, *Philosophie und Moral*, pp. 145, 170–71, 211, and Martin, *Kant's Metaphysics*, pp. 201ff.

75. *Critique of Pure Reason*, A 801, B 829 (pp. 632–33).

76. *Idea*, G.S. 8, p. 30 (*On History*, p. 25).

77. *Conjectural Beginnings*, G.S. 8, pp. 120–21 (*On History*, p. 66).

78. Thus I believe we can dismiss Collingwood's position: "In the true style of the Enlightenment, he regards past history as a spectacle of human irrationality and looks forward to a Utopia of rational life." *The Idea of History*, p. 93. Kant does not take over uncritically the beliefs of the Enlightenment in matters of history any more than he does in his philosophy of criticism.

79. Rousset, *Doctrine kantienne de l'objectivité*, p. 577.

80. *Critique of Judgement*, G.S. 5, p. 474 (II, p. 149).

81. *Critique of Practical Reason*, G.S. 5, p. 153 (p. 157).

82. Ibid., G.S. 5, p. 160 (p. 165).

83. *On Education* specifically draws parallels between the education of the individual and that of the race. G.S. 9, pp. 441–50 (pp. 1–14).

84. For a study of the two Kantian meanings of freedom see pp. 165–67.

85. I have taken seriously the warnings of the contemporary interpreters of Kant who insist that however full of tension the Kantian position is, it is a coherent and stable one susceptible of being held to by an intelligent man for a long period of time. Thus I am ready to deride those Kantian interpreters who imitate Fichte and do not hesitate to tell us what kind of post-Kantian Kant would have become had he only lived longer or had he not become senile quite so soon. In the case of the philosophy of history and philosophy of religion however, I believe I can make an exception to my general principle and show how Kant pointed beyond himself. But this does not insinuate that Kant would have followed any of his "disciples" who "followed" the trail he opened.

86. *What is Enlightenment?* clearly states that we do not live in an enlightened age but in an age of enlightenment. G.S. 8, p. 40 (*On History*, p. 8).

87. A defense of Kant's limited use of teleological judgement in the writing of a philosophy of history may be found in B. T. Wilkins, "Teleology in Kant's Philosophy of History," *History and Theory* 5, 1966. Wilkins in particular pointed out that should Kant's application of teleology be found inadequate, the principle of teleology remains intact.

88. *The Strife of Faculties*, G.S. 7, p. 92 (*On History*, p. 151).

89. *The End of All Things*, G.S. 8, p. 330 (*On History*, p. 72).

90. Ibid., pp. 332–33 (pp. 75–76). Such practical considerations which in this essay led Kant to reject universal salvation led him in his lectures on the philosophy of religion to reject the idea of divine decree and double predestination (see *Religionslehre*, p. 198). The reason is clear, both positions in Kant's eyes rob moral effort of its significance.

91. Kant's knowledgeability of the great traditional metaphysics and his ontological concerns have been demonstrated by G. Martin's book, *Kant's Metaphysics and Theory of Science*.

92. The idea of God as Architect of Nature is said by Kant to be *vermessen*, extravagant or presumptuous, devoid of any sense of limits. *Critique of Judgement*, G.S. 5, p. 383 (II, p. 34).

93. If the first theme affirms Kant's continuity with Greek ontology, the second places him in the Christian tradition.

94. Recall that this strain really comes to the fore only in the late writings on history. The *Idea for a Universal History* does not really contain it and sins on the side of optimism.

95. Kant probably read *Candide* and seems to have developed his picture of Job as the answer to the problem of theodicy in contrast with the statement found in *Candide*. See G.S. 19, p. 626.

96. See also *The End of All Things*.

97. Beck, *Commentary*, p. 258. See also the famous pages in the *Critique of Practical Reason*, G.S. 5, pp. 146–48 (pp. 152–53) in which Kant argued that should God and His Majesty always be before our eyes we would be puppets with predictable behaviour and thus "be a mechanism," totally deprived of life and truly moral character.

98. *What Does It Mean to Orient Onself in Thought?*, G.S. 8, p. 145.

99. *Critique of Pure Reason*, A 850, B 878 (p. 664).

100. Kant's very a priori approach centring upon the imperatives of the moral law, would for instance make a crucial contribution to any theory of meaning in history. For Kant, the condition of possibility of meaning lies in the fact that we live in concern and in effort, and have a will which can make a difference, bring us to our destination, or fail to. There is meaning in the world, because there is in it a striving man who decides on ends and works to approximate them. If we could somehow conceive of a state where the will would have no work to do, no duality between what is and what ought to be, then our lives would be entirely devoid of meaning. We would have no purpose to set before ourselves; there would be no need to do anything and everything would be supremely indifferent.

In other words, "meaning" is a notion of practical import. It has significance only for a finite being, and for a being who struggles to reach its purpose. What is meaningless is what is entirely irrelevant to it. We know that there would be no satisfaction in a world without want. Yet meaning is not that which satisfies (the animal in his process of goal-attainment finds satisfaction). Meaning serves a moral interest not a physical one. That is meaningful which enables us to be free. R. Aron's major book is entitled *Introduction à la philosophie de l'histoire: Essai sur les limites de l'objectivité historique* (Paris: Gallimard, 1948).

CHAPTER 4

1. One of the occasional notes that evidences Kant's interest and knowledgeability in the field of comparative religion gives a list of the various metaphors used by "wise men" who wanted to convey the sentiment that the world on the earth was a nasty place to be in: thus it has been compared to a messy inn, a prison, a place of trial and purification, a madhouse, and a latrine. See *The End of All Things*, G.S. 8, p. 331 (*On History*, pp. 73–74).

2. Leibniz, *Theodicy*, p. 42.

3. *The End of All Things*, G.S. 8, p. 332 (*On History*, p. 75), Leibniz, *Theodicy*, p. 38, Horace, *Odes* 3, 2.

4. Krüger put the concept of "Creation" at the centre of his interpretation of Kant (*Philosophie und Moral*, pp. 145, 170). Martin also put this idea at the centre of his interpretation of Kant's ontology (*Kant's Metaphysics*, pp. 197ff.).

5. Man is the ultimate end of Nature as a teleological system (paragraph 83). Moral man, or man who gives ends to himself in a way that is consonant with his being an end in himself, is the final end of Creation itself (paragraph 81). Thus the ends of Nature and those of Creation are distinguished.

6. The expression *"grosse Weltbühne"* appears in the *Idea*, G.S. 8, p. 17 (*On History*, p. 12).

7. This expression is E. Weil's in *Problèmes kantiens*, p. 67. E. Weil fully agreed with the emphasis upon the unique significance of these pages at the end of the *Critique of Judgement*. (He even presented the third Critique as the second revolution in Kant's thought, a rather extreme expression.) Although he wrote of the rediscovery of the world as "cosmos" rather than Creation (*Problèmes kantiens*, p. 107) he did agree that the significance of those pages is that they present a divine created world which is a place where human purposes and natural laws are not condemned to clash.

8. It is clear that for Kant man, free and adult, does not belong to himself: "Human beings are sentinels on earth and may not leave their posts until relieved by another beneficient hand." *Eine Vorlesung über Ethik*, p. 193 (*Lectures on Ethics*, p. 154). The consideration of man as a divine possession however does not enter at all into the grounds for the prohibition of suicide. There are no moral duties towards God in Kant. That religion can never dictate to morality is not, however, to make religion meaningless and morally irrelevant.

9. This is the conclusion of Heidegger's analysis of Kant's anthropology: Man is spontaneity-in-receptivity.

10. *Critique of Pure Reason*, A 686, B 714 (p. 560). This idea of an ordered world in the first Critique was split in the third into the idea of a teleologically organized world of nature and of creation in which the idea of the natural world is synthesized with that of the moral world.

11. *Critique of Pure Reason*, A 700, B 701 (p. 568).

12. See Philonenko, *Théorie et praxis*, p. 40. Here again Hegel was to build—extravagantly a Kantian would say—on a Kantian basis.

13. "Suggest something feasible—that means suggest what is already being done." Such is Fichte's taunt to Rehberg. See Philonenko, *Théorie et praxis*, p. 103.

14. See Peter Gay, *The Enlightenment* II, p. 95 and pp. 529ff.

15. Nisbet, *Social Change and History*, p. 81.

16. Leo Strauss, *Natural Right and History*, p. 317. Kant's formal method in ethics may be taken as a vigorous restatement of this position.

17. Vlachos made such a case in *Pensée politique*, pp. 176, 194-244. I do not believe we should seek to refute those Kantian interpreters (like G. Rousset) who tend to silence or set aside the Kantian theistic affirmations as being due to family atavism, prudent fear of censorship, or the atmosphere of the age. Ultimately none of these interpretations are any more serious than the misleading witticisms of Heinrich Heine on the first two Critiques in *Philosophy and Religion in Germany*, pp. 118-19. I cannot see Kant's theism as an island of historically conditioned thinking in a sea of eternally valid rationalism.

18. See *Perpetual Peace*, G.S. 8, p. 361 (*On History*, p. 107).

19. J. Moltmann stated that in Kant one has more of an eschatology of history than a philosophy of history. He quoted H. Urs von Balthazar to the effect that Kant leads us to "practical realization of eschatological existence." *Theology of Hope*, pp. 46, 47, 261-64. In his essay *Histoire et mystère*, p. 9, Lacroix drew the interesting conclusion that "the major virtue of Kant is to have tried to reconcile progress and eschatology."

20. The reflections on anthropology of the old Kant restate that the study of history leads to contempt of the human race which is wicked and yet quick to take offense. The conclusion is spontaneous: "We are completely mad." Vlachos, *Pensée politique*, p. 206.

21. This rebirth of teleological faith after its death is best illustrated in *Perpetual Peace*, G.S. 8, pp. 372-80 (*On History*, pp. 119-28).

22. This very basic and illuminating distinction was first made by Delbos, *Philosophie pratique*, pp. 297-98.

23. See *Perpetual Peace*, G.S. 8, pp. 361-62 (*On History*, pp. 106-7). Providence founds, rules or governs, and directs. See pp. 265-67. E. Troeltsch and K. Weyand concur with our judgement. *Das Historische*, p. 150, *Geschichtsphilosophie*, pp. 183-85.

24. Philonenko, *Théorie et praxis*, p. 128.

25. "Beliefful realism" (Tillich's phrase) does not shine with a steady glow in Kant but wavers between fits of "faith" and fits of "realism."

26. Using the terms employed by the third Critique we cannot prove that the world is a Creation, or that the Author of all teleology is moral as well as intelligent.

27. Already in 1775 a letter of Kant shows his interest in the figure of Job. Job appears as a model of candor and of refusal to flatter God. Kant to Lavater 28 April 1775, G.S. 10, p. 176 (*Philosophical Correspondence*, p. 80).

28. The figure of Jesus cannot be placed on quite the same level as that of Adam and Job. For one thing he is something more of a historical figure, and Kant, no biblical literalist, was conscious of that. Furthermore Kant stated that the moral law which he taught is one which we could have found on our own by a purely rational process (thus restating the deistic view of Jesus as historic publisher of an eternal teaching) and this is not apparently true of the insights Adam and Job give us (Adam and Job are figures

or models for our existential self-interpretation). As we shall see later however, such presentation of the figure of Jesus is not the whole picture and Kant was able to see in Jesus more than the doctrine he taught.

29. *Critique of Practical Reason*, G.S. 5, p. 86 (p. 89).

30. Ibid., G.S. 5, p. 128 (p. 132).

31. *Critique of Judgement*, G.S. 5, p. 314 (I, pp. 175–76). This role of symbols, pictures, or signs is explored in Part II.

Part Two

INTRODUCTION

1. For a brief resumé of the state of the church and of the religious debate in Germany, see Peter Gay, *The Enlightenment: An Interpretation*, Vol. 1, pp. 328ff. and 347ff. For the state of the philosophical schools see Part III of L. W. Beck's *Early German Philosophy: Kant and his Predecessors* (Cambridge: Harvard University Press, 1969).

CHAPTER 5

2. *I. Kant, Sein Leben in Darstellung von Zeitgenossen*, p. 13.

3. Quoted by Jachmann in his "I. Kant, Geschildert in Briefen an einem Freund," in *I. Kant, Sein Leben*, p. 62.

4. Willibald Klinke, *Kant for Everyman*, p. 13.

5. Kant's best friend seems to have been an English merchant settled in Königsberg. Kant met him in memorable circumstances: during a conversation Kant defended the American colonists and blamed England who made war against them; Green then heatedly stepped forward and asked for reparation. Witnesses intervened, cooler heads prevailed, Kant agued his point quietly and, according to Jachmann, the friendship began. *I. Kant, Sein Leben*, p. 153.

6. Borowski's affirmation that Kant "never touched theological researches of any kind" thus must be criticized and is too sweeping. *I. Kant, Sein Leben*, p. 79. Borowski, however, was right when he stated that Kant knew little of Semler and the new biblical exegesis.

7. This particular edition of the *Prussian Catechism* (which had Luther's *Smaller Catechism* in the appendix) is totally lost although there are hopes that a copy might be found in some library in Kaliningrad.

8. These *Lectures on Philosophy of Religion (Religionslehre)* published in 1817 by Pölitz will be shortly available in Volume 28, Part II of the Akademie edition.

9. Indicated by Jachmann. See *I. Kant, Sein Leben*, p. 134.

10. Schmalenbach's book *Kant's Religion* was a turning point of some sort in Kantian studies. It tried to grasp not Kant's philosophy of religion but his own religiousness, to discern it as manifested by Kant's own convictions and affirmations and to analyse its

contents. It finds it in the experience of the sublime and the infinite (and uses the pages on the sublime in the *Critique of Judgement* to present that) as well as in the sense of the holiness of God and of his will.

11. Kant to Friedrich Wilhelm II, after 12 October 1794, G.S. 11, pp. 527-30 (*Philosophical Correspondence, 1759-1799*, pp. 217ff.).

12. Troeltsch, "Das Historische," pp. 38, 86, 131, 134.

13. For a discussion of the issues see the "Preface" by T. M. Greene in *Religion within the Limits of Reason Alone*, pp. xxxiiff. See also Borowski in *I. Kant Sein Leben*, pp. 59ff.

14. Bruch, *Philosophie religieuse*, p. 186.

15. Kant to M. Mendelssohn, 8 April 1766. G.S. 10, pp. 69-73 (*Philosophical Correspondence*, p. 54).

16. *Critique of Practical Reason*, G.S. 5, p. 86 (p. 89).

17. *Religion*, G.S. 6, p. 190 (p. 178).

18. Borowski in *I. Kant, Sein Leben*, pp. 47 and 90. This last statement should be balanced by Jachmann's statement that he had great respect for Jesus and the influence of his teaching on the improvement and education of the people. Ibid., p. 170.

19. *I. Kant, Sein Leben*, p. 14.

20. The statement is already found in 1763 in the "Essay to Introduce in Philosophy the Concept of Negative Size," G.S. 2.

21. Collins, *Emergence of Philosophy of Religion*, p. 88.

22. I am here much indebted to W. C. Smith's book *The Meaning and End of Religion* and the insights it affords into the history of the word.

23. *Critique of Practical Reason*, G.S. 5, p. 130 (p. 134). See also *Critique of Judgement*, G.S. 5, p. 481 (II, p. 158). The definition appears in *Religion within the Limits of Reason Alone*, G.S. 6, p. 153 (p. 142) with an added parenthesis emphasizing that it speaks of religion "subjectively regarded." The second Critique states that "divine command" does not mean "ordinances of a foreign will" but "essential laws of any free will as such." The definition may also be found in *The Doctrine of Virtue*, G.S. 6, pp. 440, 487 (pp. 106, 162-63).

24. *Religion*, G.S. 6, pp. 107-8 (pp. 98-99). The point reappears in a major footnote in *Perpetual Peace* which contrasts religion to "different kinds of historical faiths," G.S. 8, p. 367 (*On History*, p. 113). The point was briefly made in an earlier section of *Religion within the Limits of Reason Alone* and contrasted religion to cult (cultus), G.S. 6, p. 13 (p. 11).

25. H. Fielding, *Tom Jones*.

26. *Religion*, G.S. 6, p. 84 (p. 79).

27. The very fact that Kant was involved in a major shift in terminology makes his thought hard to understand and interpret for, as we shall see, occasionally his discussion owes more to the old school than to the new one which he was in the process of founding. Furthermore many interpreters are more familiar with the old views.

28. Beck, *Commentary*, p. 280.

29. Collins, *Emergence of Philosophy of Religion*, p. 149. Collins also proposed the definition of religion for Kant as "man's practical bond with God through belief and action," ibid., p. 98.

30. *Critique of Pure Reason*, A 819, B 847 (p. 644).

31. See Collins, *Emergence of Philosophy of Religion*, p. 140.

32. See Bohatec, *Die Religionsphilosophie*, p. 46.

33. See pp. 18–19.

34. *Universal Natural History and Theory of the Heavens*, G.S. 1, p. 306 (p. 135).

35. *Religionslehre* (Pölitz edition), p. 128.

36. G.S. Vol. 27, 1, p. 175.

37. Von Glasenapp, *Kant und die Religionen des Ostens*, p. 153. Von Glasenapp (p. 134) also pointed out that Kant seems to have had greater sympathy for the religion of India than for that of China. The stock of India was beginning to go up at the end of the eighteenth century (China of course had been praised much earlier), but there may be here an appreciation by Kant of the dualistic thrust of Indian thought.

38. Von Glasenapp, *Religionen des Ostens*, p. 152.

39. *Critique of Practical Reason*, G.S. 5, pp. 161–62 (p. 166).

40. Ibid.

41. "Man was not born to build eternal huts on this stage, which is a stage of vanities," *History and Natural Description of the Earthquakes of 1755*, G.S. 1, p. 460.

42. *Religion*, G.S. 6, pp. 197–98 (pp. 185–86). In the light of this text, the Kantian reticence in religious matters may come not from shyness but from a sense of the impotence of words.

43. *Religion*, G.S. 6, p. 195 (p. 183).

44. R. Vancourt concluded that the feeling of the sublime and the religious feeling overlap for Kant to a large extent. See "Kant et la solution rationaliste au problème des religions" in *Mélanges de Sciences Religieuses* 22, p. 172.

45. *Critique of Judgement*, G.S. 5, p. 482 (II, p. 159).

46. Krüger, *Philosophie und Moral*, p. 225.

47. *Critique of Judgement*, G.S. 5, p. 482 (II, p. 159).

48. *Critique of Judgement*, G.S. 5, p. 264 (I, p. 114). See also *Theory and Practice*, G.S. 8, p. 287 on the "sacred shudder" we feel before the grandeur and sublimity of our disposition when we become conscious of the divine origin of our moral nature.

49. See W. Schultz, *Kant als Philosoph des Protestantismus*, p. 78.

50. *Critique of Judgement*, G.S. 5, pp. 445–46 (II, pp. 112–13).

51. First draft of *The Strife of Faculties*, G.S. 23, p. 440.

52. *Religion*, G.S. 6, p. 183 (p. 172). See Schultz, *Kant als Philosoph des Protestantismus*, pp. 66ff.

53. This link between religion and morality is specifically called "godliness" in *Religion*, G.S.6, p. 201 (p. 189). Godliness is said to be the "true religious disposition" and consists of virtue combined with piety. This text is perhaps the most convenient evidence for the Kantian distinction between the moral and the religious dispositions.

54. *Opus Postumum*, G.S. 21, p. 81.

55. *The Doctrine of Virtue*, G.S. 6, p. 439 (p. 105).

56. Ibid., G.S. 6, p. 441 (p. 107). When Kant discussed the role of biblical religion in the development of our notions of morality he referred to Jesus and the Gospels who taught us "purer notions" of morality. In the light of his frequent references to the notion of God who searches the hearts it seems that some credit should also be paid to the Scriptures of the Old Testament.

57. *Critique of Judgement*, G.S. 5, p. 472 (II, p. 91).

58. See p. 239.

59. G.S. 20, p. 427.

60. Bohatec, *Religionsphilosophie*, p. 60. The terms "positive" and "natural" religion could also be listed among the contenders for terminological expression of the distinction Kant arrived at. But to my knowledge, Kant never used these terms and the

expression "positive religion" seems to have been used only in the nineteenth century. Until the eighteenth century the distinction was employed for a discussion of law (see Hooker, *Of the Laws of Ecclesiastical Polity*, I, 15 and Hobbes, *Leviathan*, II, 26).

61. *The Doctrine of Virtue*, G.S. 6, p. 491 (p. 167).

62. The parallel with law is drawn in *Religion*, G.S. 6, p. 10 (p. 9).

63. See K. Barth, *Protestant Thought from Rousseau to Ritschl*, pp. 192–96.

64. The *loci classici* for this distinction are *Religion*, G.S. 6, pp. 109–14 (pp. 100–5), and *The Strife of Faculties*, G.S. 7, p. 66.

65. *The Strife of Faculties*, G.S. 7, p. 66.

66. G.S. 20, p. 428.

67. On the nature of the conflict see Collins, *Emergence of Philosophy of Religion*, p. 190 and Bruch, *Philosophie religieuse*, pp. 96ff.

68. Collins, *Emergence of Philosophy of Religion*. We are very much indebted to this impressive study which focuses its inquiry on Hume, Kant, and Hegel as the "three classical thinkers" for modern philosophy of religion. It is noteworthy that Collins came to write this book after seeing the insufficiencies of a book on the problem of God in modern philosophy.

69. Troeltsch, "Das Historische," pp. 41–42.

70. Ibid., p. 40.

71. This is the title of one of the three essays translated in P. Tillich, *What is Religion?* This paragraph follows loosely Tillich's interpretation of the significance of Kant's critical period.

72. Tillich, *What is Religion?*, p. 128.

73. This rise to consciousness of the concept of religion (which may be systematically subdivided into religiousness and religious traditions) is related to the rise of secularization and the cultural discovery of the other continents, both phenomena which became part of public, educated consciousness only in the eighteenth century. To call oneself religious (in a sense other than being a member of a religious order) is a phenomenon which appeared in Europe only as a European minority called itself non-religious.

74. Cassirer, *Philosophy of the Enlightenment*, Chapter 5. See especially pp. 197–99.

75. Bruch stated that *Religion within the Limits of Reason Alone* offers a theory of religious beliefs and institutions, and that pure moral religion, that which we called religiousness is at the basis of the work but is hardly its object. *Philosophie religieuse de Kant*, p. 14.

76. Collins, *Emergence of Philosophy of Religion*, p. 155.

77. *Prolegomena*, G.S. 4, p. 373 (p. 150).

78. Collins said that the theory of religion has a substitutional function, namely that it is elaborated by men in the absence of a metaphysical theory of God. *Emergence of Philosophy of Religion*, p. 106.

79. Ibid., p. 95.

80. Ibid., p. 93.

CHAPTER 6

1. I have already referred the reader to the works of Martin and Krüger. To these names I should now add Heinz Heimsoeth, whose fundamental article "Metaphysical Motives in the Development of Critical Idealism" is now available in English in M. S. Gram, *Kant: Disputed Questions*. M. Heidegger's *Kant and the Problem of Metaphysics*

can also be mentioned, although this book, important though it is in its own right, rightly remains somewhat marginal in Kant studies. Among the French authors Ferdinand Alquié, *La Critique kantienne de la métaphysique* has numerous merits and finds, rightly I believe, the expression of Kant's metaphysical concerns in the transcendental dialectic of the *Critique of Pure Reason.* The three lengthy articles of E. Weil gathered in *Problèmes kantiens* are models of clarity and accuracy, and philosophical classics in their own right besides major contributions to Kant studies.

2. *Prolegomena*, G.S. 4, pp. 382–83 (p. 162).

3. Ibid., G.S. 4, p. 377 (pp. 154–55).

4. Ibid., G.S. 4, p. 351 (p. 121).

5. Ibid., G.S. 4, p. 352 (p. 122).

6. Ibid., G.S. 4, p. 353 (p. 124).

7. Ibid., G.S. 4, p. 262 (p. 9). These passages are taken from the *Prolegomena*, but the same message comes from the second preface of the *Critique of Pure Reason.* The first preface having given such a negative tone as to the task of metaphysics that some readers believed Kant had undertaken a turn toward empiricism, the second edition was given a new preface which emphasizes that the task of the work is to find a solution to the problem of metaphysics which had been until then a mere battleground for random groping. *Critique of Pure Reason*, B XV (p. 21). Ignorant armies should no longer clash by night, nor do they need to.

8. *Prolegomena*, G.S. 4, p. 354 (p. 125). See also p. 361 (p. 133). Beyond the border, "we can conceive form of things, but not things themselves." Is this a hint of the role of symbols?

9. *Critique of Pure Reason*, B XXII (p. 25).

10. *Prolegomena*, G.S. 4, p. 367 (p. 142).

11. Ibid., G.S. 4, pp. 380–81 (p. 160).

12. Ibid., G.S. 4, p. 363 (p. 137).

13. Ibid., G.S. 4, p. 383 (p. 163).

14. *Critique of Pure Reason*, B XXIV (p. 26).

15. Ibid., B II (p. 4).

16. Ibid., A 837, B 654 (p. 657).

17. *Prolegomena*, G.S. 4, p. 271 (p. 20).

18. Krüger, *Philosophie und Moral*, p. 230.

19. E. Coreth, *Metaphysics*, p. 24.

20. Ibid., p. 21.

21. *Critique of Practical Reason*, G.S. 5, pp. 3–4, 134–38 (pp. 3–4, 139–42). See also Beck, *Commentary*, pp. 27–28 and Martin, *Kant's Metaphysics*, pp. 146ff.

22. For Kant's notes see G.S. 18, pp. 155, 512. For Eberhard's book see ibid., pp. 513ff.

23. In his commentary upon this passage J. Collins rightly suggested that this kind of natural history of religion "is based upon (an) analytic correlation between the cognitive operations of human nature and the dominant religious attitudes at any stage in human history." *Emergence of Philosophy of Religion*, p. 131.

24. The basic text here is the lectures on *Religionslehre*, pp. 11–13.

25. Ectypa are called "imperfect copies" in *Critique of Pure Reason*, A 578, B 606 (p. 492).

26. This whole view of the natural history of religion and of the progressive regulation of empirical theology by rational theology implies a historical view of reason, progressively emerging and growing throughout history.

27. The sources for Kant's systematic view of rational theology are first of all the *Critique of Pure Reason*, A 631–32, B 659–60 (pp. 525–26). The lectures on *Religionslehre*, pp. 11–12, and the notes in G.S. 17, pp. 421, 595; 18, pp. 196–97. Collins' diagram is found on p. 102 of *The Emergence of Philosophy of Religion*. Collins also pointed out some of the terminological inconsistencies found in Kant's designation of the various kinds of theologies, the most important of which is that by speculative theology Kant may mean "a dogmatic uncritical study of God" or, as in the above diagram "a reformed critical study of Him made in full awareness of the regulative limits of human experience."

28. Lectures on *Religionslehre*, pp. 33ff.

29. *Critique of Pure Reason*, A 631, B659 (p. 525).

30. Ibid., A 675, B703 (p. 553).

31. Lectures on *Religionslehre*, p. 71.

32. Ibid., pp. 89ff.

33. *Critique of Pure Reason*, A 632, B 660 (pp. 525–26).

34. Lectures on *Religionslehre*, p. 113.

35. Ibid., pp. 127ff.

36. Ibid., p. 128.

37. Ibid., p. 130. Kant also brings in, among others, Brahma, Vishnu, and Shiva; Osiris, Isis, and Horus; Odin, Frega, and Thor. Practically everyone is there except Father, Son, and Holy Ghost. See Lectures on *Religionslehre*, p. 133. Obviously Kant was more impressed by *L'Esprit des lois* than by the *De Trinitate* (if he ever read it, which is very improbable).

38. Collins, *Emergence of Philosophy of Religion*, p. 111.

39. Ibid., p. 363.

40. Ibid., p. 129. A disciple of Coreth or of Martin would rather speak of an ontological radication of religion.

41. Note that we are not concerned to retrace the steps whereby Kant arrived at his moral proof of God and his moral conception of God. This can be found at pp. 62–63. See also p. 139 for a discussion of the moral attributes of God. I am rather trying to discern what made moral theism uniquely significant to Kant.

42. *Critique of Pure Reason*, Preface, 2nd edition, B XXX (p. 29).

43. Ibid., A 828–29, B 856–57 (p. 650).

44. *Progress in Metaphysics*, G.S. 20, p. 298. Note that this "moral" need is built upon the basic religious insight: namely the tension between the world as it should be and the world as it is.

45. Ibid. Kant's "proof for the existence of God" is a defense of faith, not an attempt to make of faith in God something other than faith. As Wood put it, the "defense of faith cannot substitute for faith itself," *Kant's Moral Religion*, pp. 32–33. He who freely and conscientiously adopts the life of obedience to the moral law has already subjectively the faith which can be shown by Kant to entail rationally faith in God.

46. Weil, *Problèmes kantiens*, p. 94.

47. Collins, *Emergence of Philosophy of Religion*, p. 113. Collins added, "This does not mean that the speculative investigation becomes a servile instrument, however, pandering to a set of religious prejudgements."

48. Beck, *Commentary*, p. 277.

49. *Prolegomena*, G.S. 4, p. 356 (p. 128).

50. E. Weil, *Problèmes kantiens*, p. 31. Both J. Lacroix, *Kant et le kantisme* and F. Alquié, *La Critique kantienne de la métaphysique* are ultimately dependent upon this point of Weil.

51. Ibid., pp. 39-49, 95.

52. Lacroix rightly found the term postulate unfortunate since it might imply that one arrives at the concept of God through a mere logical operation. He proposed to see in the postulates a "metaphysical experience." This term is clear for those who know their Descartes; however, it is hardly satisfactory since it gives to the term experience a meaning totally different from the Kantian one (Lacroix, *Kant et le kantisme*, p. 70, p. 104).

53. Weil pointed out that his usage on this point is not always consistent. *Problèmes kantiens*, p. 22.

54. *Critique of Judgement*, G.S. 5, pp. 471-73 (II, pp. 145-47).

55. *Critique of Pure Reason*, A 673, B 701 (p. 551).

56. *Critique of Judgement*, G.S. 5, p. 353 (I, p. 223).

57. G.S. 18, p. 714.

58. *Prolegomena*, G.S. 4, p. 359 (p. 131).

59. See the discussion of the holy will in the *Critique of Practical Reason*, G.S. 5, p. 82 (p. 84).

60. The basic discussion of this problem is in *Critique of Pure Reason*, A 697-701, B 725-29 (pp. 566-69), *Religion within the Limits of Reason Alone*, G.S. 6, pp. 64-65, 168-69 (pp. 58-59, 156-57), *Prolegomena*, G.S. 4, pp. 354-57 (pp. 125-29).

61. I of course mean philosophers-theologians, although Kant would have argued that the simplest religious man, provided he is not superstitious, would have enough religious sense to sense that his representations are not entirely adequate to the God to whom he is turning.

62. *Prolegomena*, G.S. 4, p. 357 (p. 129).

63. *Critique of Pure Reason*, A 140, B 180 (p. 182).

64. See *Critique of Pure Reason*, A 137, B 176ff (pp. 180ff). See also J. Hartnack, *Kant's Theory of Knowledge*, pp. 59ff.

65. For a discussion of the schematism of analogy see also Paton, *Categorical Imperative*, p. 157, and Collins, *Emergence of Philosophy of Religion*, pp. 117ff and 411. Collins pointed out that besides the way of analogy, Kant also used the traditional ways of negation and eminence to arrive at his attributes of God, p. 123.

66. See pp. 86, 139.

67. *Critique of Judgement*, G.S. 5, p. 351 (I, p. 221).

68. Ibid., G.S. 5, p. 352 (I, p. 223). The *Critique of Judgement* gives the following further examples of symbols: the thought of a monarchical state as a living body, or as a mere machine, and such terms as "ground" or "to depend."

69. This book shall subsequently be referred to as *Religion*.

70. See his essay, "Leibniz on Eternal Punishments" (1773), discussed in H. E. Allison, *Lessing and the Enlightenment*, pp. 86ff.

71. Troeltsch, "Das Historische," p. 40.

72. *On a Lordly Tone*, G.S. 8, pp. 405-6.

73. *Critique of Judgement*, G.S. 5, pp. 314-19 (I, pp. 175-82).

74. Ibid., G.S. 5, p. 314 (I, p. 175).

75. Ibid., G.S. 5, p. 315 (I, p. 177).

76. *Religionslehre*, pp. 9-10.

77. Ibid., p. 28.

78. *Critique of Judgement*, G.S. 5, p. 481 (II, p. 158). See also *Religionslehre*, p. 147.

79. *Critique of Judgement*, G.S. 5, p. 482 (II, p. 159).

80. See Delbos, *Philosophie pratique*, p. 589. See Book Four of *Religion* concerning service and pseudo-service of God.

81. Tillich, "On the Idea of a Theology of Culture" in *What is Religion?*, p. 157.

82. Tillich, "The Conquest of the Concept of Religion in the Philosophy of Religion" in *What is Religion?*, p. 124.

83. Tillich, "The Philosophy of Religion" in *What is Religion?*, p. 121.

CHAPTER 7

1. See p. 69.

2. Kant to Stäudlin, 4 May 1793, G.S. 11, p. 429 (*Philosophical Correspondence*, p. 205).

3. *Critique of Practical Reason*, G.S. 5, p. 130 (p. 134).

4. Schweitzer, *Essence of Faith*, p. 79.

5. Ibid., p. 79, 120.

6. L. Goldmann, *La Communauté humaine et l'univers chez Kant*, p. xvi. This point is also recognized by Schweitzer, *Essence of Faith*, p. 123.

7. This point has been well brought out by Bruch, *Philosophie religieuse*, pp. 14-16. See also, p. 247.

8. *Religion*, G.S. 6, p. 67 (p. 61).

9. I do not consider the discussion of the *summum bonum* in the second Critique such a serious discussion, because of the strong affirmation of the belonging of man qua noumenon in the noumenal world. That moral progress is postulated as taking place through immortality, rather than through historical development, shows how superficial and merely "phenomenal" is the temporality of the moral man as presented in the second Critique.

10. This is true even if we should—and I don't believe we need to—restrict the question What may I hope? to be a question of what all men at all times may hope rather than also to ask what I may hope at this juncture of history (e.g. the terroristic turn of the French Revolution).

11. Lacroix, *Kant et le kantisme*, pp. 100, 106.

12. *The Strife of Faculties*, G.S. 7, p. 70.

13. *Critique of Judgement*, G.S. 5, p. 430 (II, p. 93).

14. *Religion*, G.S. 6, p. 44 (p. 40).

15. G. E. Lessing, *Werke* (Salzburg/Stuttgart: Bergland, n.d.), pp. 1067-68.

16. A discussion of Kant's formalism is beyond the scope of this study but we can mention that the sharp cleavage between form and content is perhaps the issue on which Kant has been most criticized. On the one hand Kant is blamed for giving a merely formal ethic, saying *how* one should act but being of no help whatever when it comes to *what* one should do. Thus he seems to advocate a free man whose freedom is completely void and formal, unable to commit itself to any historical idea, to any content whatever. This criticism however lacks a proper understanding of what Kant tried to do. Kant pointed out very clearly the differences between principles which are formal and · maxims which are material. Principles are only meant to discriminate among maxims which are not deduced from the principles but come from another source. The Königsberg's prisoners' desire to sing and Kant's desire to study undisturbed, all

historical factors, are an endless source of maxims setting ends before men. They are all historically and sensuously determined and seek to give content to life, fulfil its needs, and, when acted on, do so. Principles do not attempt to give content to life or define its historical objectives; they are only given in order to determine moral life, namely the art of decision-making.

17. *Theory and Practice*, G.S. 8, p. 290.

18. *What is Enlightenment?*, G.S. 8, p. 35 (*On History*, p. 3).

19. *Critique of Judgement*, G.S. 5, p. 294 (I, p. 152). Schilpp's interpretation is very satisfactory on this point. "Morality is a constructive process temporally extended." (Schilpp, *Pre-Critical Ethics*, pp. 96 ff. and pp. 168ff.). Ancient modes of conduct prove oppressive, no longer emotionally or morally satisfying; man blindly gropes for new objectives. Practical reason comes in as the method capable of coping successfully with the emergencies of human experience and the needs of moral obligation. Among the chaos of constantly arising new proximate objectives, it selects according to its formal procedure those which will prove in closest approximation to or agreement with man's final objective: to grow, to open to oneself new possibilities, to make one's freedom more real, more active, and to extend the range of its actual capacities. All experimenting and exploring under the resources of the imagination are permissible provided one does not give up freedom in one's search for freedom.

20. For Kant only a formal ethic keeps man's future open. Any ethic of the good, of values, is inherently conservative; it closes the door to progress, since it defines the end of man in terms of the values that it knows, and these are by necessity values previously achieved and already established. One does not know the future achievements of man, but one knows the form humanity should ever take: freedom, spontaneity-in-reference-to. So we know what is right. The core of ethical philosophy lies in the presentation of the method whereby human life is kept human, and not in the definition of goods which men should strive to acquire. One cannot have an absolute system, a hierarchy of goods, and include morality in it. This would be to eclipse man's moral dignity, because it would negate his freedom. As Schelling quickly saw, in his *Letters on Dogmatism and Criticism*, 1795, quoted in Richard Kroner, *Kant's Weltanschauung*, pp. 93–94, if we do not know the good—or the supersensible world—or the content of life at the end of history—, it is not because our reason is weak, but because it is strong, because our will is free. We cannot know such objects, because our freedom is still in the process of making them and has not finished them yet.

21. *Opus Postumum*, G.S. 21, p. 462.

22. This was ably shown by M. J. Gregor in her preface to her *Laws of Freedom*.

23. *The Doctrine of Virtue*, G.S. 6, pp. 390–94 (pp. 49–54).

24. J. R. Silber in introduction to Kant, *Religion*, p. lxxx. The philosophy of history also addresses itself to the question of ethical dynamics.

25. Goethe to Herder, 7 June 1793, *Goethes Briefe*, Vol. IV, p. 23 (Berlin 1903).

26. *I. Kant, Sein Leben*, p. 29.

27. Bruch, *Philosophie religieuse*, p. 48.

28. *Religionslehre*, p. 139.

29. Ibid., p. 144.

30. Ibid., p. 169. The position of those lectures is all the more surprising since Kant in 1763 (*Essay to Introduce in Philosophy the Concept of Negative Size*) had analysed the concept of negative size, briefly suggested its applicability to the notion of evil, and thus made a break with Leibniz by seeing evil as a positive force. This analysis however was

to be forgotten in the major writings on moral philosophy and reappears only in *Religion*, G.S. 6, p. 22 (p. 18). For another view see O. Reboul *Kant et le problème du mal*. Reboul argues that the essay of 1763 determined the subsequent development of Kant's moral philosophy.

31. See pp. 292–93.
32. *Perpetual Peace*, G.S. 8, p. 368 (*On History*, p. 114).
33. See Philonenko, *Théorie et praxis*, pp. 69–74.
34. *Religionslehre*, p. 11.

CHAPTER 8

1. See Schweitzer, *Essence of Faith*, *Religion* is in a different field of investigation from that of the first two Critiques.
2. *Eine Vorlesung über Ethik*, p. 66 (*Lectures on Ethics*, pp. 54–55).
3. Ibid., p. 182 (p. 145).
4. Ibid., p. 137 (p. 252).
5. Ibid., pp. 317–19 (pp. 252–53).
6. Ibid., pp. 98–99 (p. 79).
7. Ibid., pp. 130–31 (p. 105).
8. Ibid., p. 63 (p. 52).
9. Ibid., p. 99 (p. 79).
10. Ibid., p. 101 (p. 81).
11. Ibid., p. 100 (p. 80).
12. Ibid., p. 101 (p. 81).
13. Ibid., pp. 104–5 (pp. 83–84).
14. Ibid., p. 112 (p. 90).
15. Ibid., pp. 131, 123 (pp. 105, 99).
16. Ibid., p. 90 (p. 72).
17. Ibid., p. 80 (p. 66).
18. Ibid., pp. 296–97 (pp. 234–35).
19. Kant to Lavater, 28 April 1775. G.S. 10, pp. 175–79 (*Philosophical Correspondence*, p. 80).
20. The point was acknowledged by Collins, *Emergence of Philosophy of Religion*, pp. 90, 193 and Bruch, *Philosophie religieuse*, p. 35.
21. Peter Gay, *The Enlightenment*, Vol. 2, p. 319.
22. Troeltsch, "Das Historische," p. 36.
23. Both similarities and differences from Hume's *Natural History of Religion* are apparent. The interest is in the facts of religions as they are really lived in society. The search, however, is not for the psychological cause, or for regularities of development as can be expected by analogy to all natural history, but for the normative basis of religious life. Kant of course did not write a natural history, but searched for a regulative principle.
24. Troeltsch, "Das Historische," p. 117.
25. For the literature see C. J. Friedrich, *Inevitable Peace*, p. 33. See also Bruch, *Philosophie religieuse*, p. 176.
26. *Religion*, G.S. 6, p. 109 (p. 100).

27. The first view is represented by J. L. Bruch; the second by A. Schweitzer and L. Goldmann.

28. *The Strife of Faculties*, G.S. 7, p. 93 (*On History*, p. 153).

29. Kant indicated these titles in the body of the second edition of *Religion*, G.S. 6, p. 52 (p. 47).

30. See pp. 71–72.

31. Note however that there is a world of difference between Pascal and Kant. The former has a dramatic presentation that consciously uses the art of rhetoric and aims at moving the emotions. Then he invites man convinced of his helplessness to accept the Christian scheme of salvation and revealed doctrine wholesale. On the two points Kant differs. His discussion of evil is analytic and is not presented as instrumental to any other purpose, and he certainly reserves the right to discriminate among revealed doctrines.

32. T. H. Ruyssen, "Kant est-il pessimiste?" *Revue de métaphysique et de morale*, 1904, p. 544.

33. Kant to Friedrich Wilhelm II after 12 October 1794, G.S. 11, p. 528 (*Philosophical Correspondence*, p. 218).

34. Karl Jaspers, "Das radikale Böse bei Kant" in *Rechenschaft und Ausblick*.

35. See E. Fackenheim, "Kant and Radical Evil," *University of Toronto Quarterly*, Vol. 23, 1953–54.

36. *Religion*, G.S. 6, p. 44 (p. 40).

37. P. Ricoeur rightly drew attention to Kant's pages on radical evil as the first radical attempt to find the conditions of possibility of moral evil. See *Finitude et culpabilité*, Vol. I, *L'homme faillible*, p. 15, and *Le conflit des interprétations*, pp. 298ff.

38. The philosophy of religion of the Enlightenment, with its intellectualistic emphasis, carried over the Orphic overtones making the body's motions the origin of evil. Even Leibniz, with his strong monistic pathos, tended to identify individuality with imperfection and sin. For Kant evil is emphatically not a concomitant or inevitable consequence of finitude. To be a being who is sensuously affected does not as such give a propensity to evil, though it makes man fallible. "Natural inclinations, *considered in themselves*, are *good*, that is, not a matter of reproach, and it is not only futile to want to extirpate them but to do so would also be harmful and blameworthy," *Religion*, G.S. 6, p. 58 (p. 51). "The source of evil cannot lie in an object determining the will through inclination, nor yet in a natural impulse. It can only lie in a rule made by the will, for the use of its freedom," *Religion*, G.S. 6, p. 21 (p. 17).

There is in *Religion* no Manichean dualism and the rejection of it is even more consistent than in Augustine or Calvin. Evil lies in man's choice, not in his constitution. It is a spiritual act, not a bodily determination. Fallen man's propensity to evil lies not in his physical nature but in his moral nature (which is "an expression of freedom"), namely in the habits or dispositions resulting from a repeated use of evil maxims; it lies in "the subjective ground of the exercise of man's freedom in general." *Religion*, G.S. 6, pp. 20–21 (pp. 16–17).

39. Silber, "The Ethical Significance of Kant's Religion" in *Religion*, p. cxiv.

40. Krüger, *Philosophie und Moral*, pp. 210–11.

41. The classic discussion of these two meanings of will is in Beck's *Commentary*, pp. 176ff.

42. *Foundations of the Metaphysics of Morals*, G.S. 4, p. 446 (p. 65).

43. J. Silber, "The Ethical Significance of Kant's Religion" in *Religion*, p. xc.

44. Ibid., p. xcii.

45. Ibid., p. xcv.

46. Ibid., p. cxvii.

47. *Religion*, G.S. 6, p. 32 (p. 27).

48. Ibid., G.S. 6, p. 33 (p. 28).

49. Ibid., G.S. 6, p. 38 (p. 33).

50. For a discussion of and a solution to the difficulties involved in Kant's position that man qua moral being is part of the a-temporal noumenal world while not denying that the moral life is lived in time, see Silber, "The Ethical Significance of Kant's Religion" in *Religion*, pp. xcvii–ciii.

51. *Religion*, G.S. 6, p. 14 (p. 13).

52. Ibid., G.S. 6, p. 42 (p. 38).

53. Ibid., G.S. 6, p. 40 (p. 35).

54. Ibid., G.S. 6, p. 41 (p. 36).

55. Horace, *Satires*, I, 1. Quoted in *Religion*, G.S. 6, p. 42 (p. 37).

56. *Religion*, G.S. 6, p. 43 (p. 38).

57. Ibid., G.S. 6, p. 45 (p. 40).

58. Ibid., G.S. 6, p. 47 (pp. 42–43).

59. Ibid., G.S. 6, p. 48 (p. 43).

60. Bruch, *Philosophie religieuse*, p. 75.

61. Such a solution of the problem of the two standpoints on the role of myth seems to me preferable to Silber's solution which proposes to consider ultimately noumenal acts as "morally phenomenal acts of inner sense which are not publicly observable." The whole issue arises of course because Kant, although it seems that he saw the issue, did not provide a solution. Neither did Paton incidentally (see *Categorical Imperative*, p. 247). My solution which uses Silber's concept of a temporal moral world seems to have the advantage of not radically altering the solutions given in the first two Critiques with their two standpoints theory, and of using Kant's profound observations on the schematism of analogy and the role of symbols. As Rousset put it, the stream that conceives the moral law as a-temporal and the stream that sees that moral decision-making must be represented chronologically get nearer in *Religion* and each becomes more aware of the other. But the two do not merge in a philosophical doctrine. As in the *Critique of Judgement*, the merging takes place in symbols, symbols, however, which do follow a legality. *Doctrine kantienne de l'objectivité*, p. 567.

62. *Religion*, G.S. 6, p. 37 (p. 32).

63. See pp. 226–36.

64. Silber convincingly pointed out that Kant, while he moved beyond the Socratic view of evil as ignorance, did not move all the way to the existentialist view of evil as irrational rebellion, and Silber blamed him for that. "The Ethical Significance of Kant's Religion," *Religion*, pp. cxxix ff.

65. Ibid., p. lxxxi.

66. Ibid., p. cxxiv, fn. 114.

67. Kant said that the peculiarity and unique characteristic of Christian ethics is that it places an immeasurable gulf between good and evil, and opposes them like Heaven and Hell and does not allow the thought of gradations between them (as between Heaven and Earth), *Religion*, G.S. 6, p. 59 (p. 53). And one of the weaknesses of Stoicism, the one philosophical ethic that comes closest to Kant's, is that it calls out wisdom to fight against folly while the real enemy is wickedness. Ibid., G.S. 6, p. 59 (p. 51).

68. See Bruch, *Philosophie religieuse*, pp. 63, 71, 122.

69. *Theory and Practice*, G.S. 8, p. 312.
70. *Religion*, G.S. 6, p. 100 (p. 92).
71. Philonenko, *Théorie et praxis*, p. 28.
72. Leibniz, *Theodicy*, p. 38.
73. *Religion*, G.S. 6, p. 38 (p. 34).
74. Ibid., G.S. 6, p. 60 (p. 54).
75. Ibid., G.S. 6, p. 61 (p. 55).
76. Ibid.
77. Ibid., G.S. 6, pp. 64–65 (p. 58).
78. Ibid., G.S. 6, p. 66 (pp. 59–60).
79. Ibid., G.S. 6, p. 62 (p. 55).
80. Ibid., G.S. 6, p. 71 (p. 65).
81. Ibid., G.S. 6, pp. 71–72 (pp. 65–66).
82. Ibid., G.S. 6, pp. 74–75 (pp. 69–70).
83. Ibid., G.S. 6, p. 79 (p. 74).
84. Ibid., G.S. 6, p. 80 (pp. 74–75).
85. Ibid., G.S. 6, p. 81 (pp. 75–76).
86. Ibid., G.S. 6, p. 82 (p. 77).
87. Ibid.
88. Ibid., G.S. 6, p. 83 (p. 78).
89. Such a discussion is found in Book Three, G.S. 6, pp. 116–24 (pp. 107–14) but not in the "General Observation."
90. De Vleeschauwer, *The Development of Kantian Thought*, p. 177. T. M. Greene, "The Historical Context and Religious Significance of Kant's Religion" in Kant, *Religion*, p. lxxvii.
91. Book Two focuses on the life of Jesus. The presentation of Jesus as teacher of a pure religion appears in Book Four, G.S. 6, pp. 158–63 (pp. 146–51) in the context of a discussion of the problem of reason and revelation, a standard discussion of deism.
92. G.S. 23, p. 108.
93. *Foundations of the Metaphysics of Morals*, G.S. 4, p. 409 (p. 25).
94. *Religion*, G.S. 6, p. 82 (p. 77).
95. *The End of All Things*, G.S. 8, pp. 337–39 (*On History*, pp. 81–83).
96. *Religion*, G.S. 6, p. 81 (p. 76). Kant had no sympathy for Reimarus' presentation of the Bible as historically untrustworthy and morally harmful, two points on which the integrity of Kant was extremely sensitive.
97. In this light, the *Critique of Judgement* is perhaps his most interesting achievement since it systematically avoids being backed into this corner.
98. For an excellent and complete discussion of conversion see the chapter on it in Bruch, *Philosophie religieuse*, pp. 79–94.
99. "Ethical Significance of Kant's Religion" in *Religion*, p. cxxxi.
100. See fn. 2 in the essay on the *Failure of All Theodicies* and footnote on pp. 145–46 (pp. 136–37) of *Religion*.
101. For a fuller discussion see Bruch, *Philosophie religieuse*, pp. 95–128.
102. *Religion*, G.S. 6, pp. 93–94 (p. 85).
103. Ibid., G.S. 6, p. 94 (p. 86).
104. Ibid., G.S. 6, pp. 94–95 (p. 86).
105. Ibid., G.S. 6, p. 93 (p. 85).
106. Ibid., G.S. 6, p. 95 (p. 87).

107. Ibid., G.S. 6, pp. 97-98 (p. 89). See also *Critique of Practical Reason*, G.S. 5, pp. 142-43 (p. 148).

108. *Religion*, G.S. 6, p. 98 (p. 89).

109. Ibid., G.S. 6, p. 100 (p. 92).

110. Ibid., G.S. 6, p. 101 (p. 92).

111. Ibid., G.S. 6, p. 102 (p. 94).

112. Ibid., G.S. 6, p. 104 (p. 95).

113. Ibid., G.S. 6, p. 105 (p. 96).

114. Ibid., G.S. 6, p. 106 (p. 97). Besides the evidence of history, there is also a theoretical case for taking seriously the determinate form of religion. As J. Collins put it, the visible church, the historical nature of religion etc. "constitute an essential step in the analytical study of the meaning of religion. For they mark the specific points at which the concretizing process is carried on and the revelational form of religion is made directly pertinent to our moral life. Just as the analysis of scientific judgements and moral judgements must be made sufficiently determinate to characterize the human conditions and limitations in these areas, so also must the philosophical theory of religion reach into the determinate modalities of our religious assent and action." Collins, *Emergence of Philosophy of Religion*, p. 167.

115. *Religion*, G.S. 6, p. 109 (p. 100).

116. Ibid., G.S. 6, p. 115 (p. 106). This is Kant's formulation of the Protestant principle.

117. Ibid., G.S. 6, p. 121 (p. 112).

118. Ibid., G.S. 6, p. 122 (p. 113). Section VII contains also a long discussion of "saving faith" which includes a return to the problems of grace and atonement. I shall examine this very important passage, G.S. 6, pp. 116-21 (pp. 106-11), in my chapter on the parerga.

119. *Religion*, G.S. 6, pp. 124-25 (pp. 115-16). This affirmation of Christianity as the true or truest type of faith departs from the statement on p. 11 where Kant spoke of making an experiment and examining "some alleged revelation or other." The letter to the King also spoke of Christianity as being presented in the book as "the mere idea of a conceivable revelation." G.S. 11, pp. 528-29 (*Philosophical Correspondence*, p. 218). These two texts clearly imply that Kant thought he could have proceeded with the analysis of any historical faith whatsoever.

Furthermore, in a footnote in *Religion* Kant seems to have believed that Islam, like Christianity, did what Judaism could not do: i.e., move to the ideal of universal church. G.S. 6, pp. 136-37 (p. 127). Another footnote in the same work credits the ruin of idol-worship and the renewal of "the concept of God's unity and of his supersensible nature" in early Islam to God and not to Muhammad. G.S. 6, p. 184 (p. 172).

120. *Religion*, G.S. 6, p. 125 (p. 116).

121. Ibid., G.S. 6, p. 132 (pp. 122-23). This "wise attitude" is an accurate description of Kant's own.

122. Feeling cannot be "a touchstone for the genuineness of a revelation, for it teaches absolutely nothing." *Religion*, G.S. 6, p. 114 (p. 105). Kant's idea of a touchstone seems to be a moral-historical one: a revelation may be genuine if it issues forth in the establishment of a true Church.

123. See Bohatec, *Religionsphilosophie*, pp. 627-30. It should be added that this transition passes through a period in which the emphasis lies upon an individualistic stoicism.

124. "Reflection 1396," G.S. 15, p. 608.

125. *Religion*, G.S. 6, p. 94 (p. 86). See quote above, p. 204.

126. *Religion*, G.S. 6, pp. 151-52 (p. 139).

127. Ibid., G.S. 6, p. 153 (p. 141).

128. The structure of the book is particularly unsatisfactory. Part One discusses the concepts of natural and revealed religion which are quickly transformed into concepts of natural and learned religion. G.S. 6, pp. 153-57 (pp. 142-45). References will be made to this section in my next chapter which examines Kant's handling of the problem of revelation. It then proceeds to examine the Christian religion as a natural religion by giving a summary of Christ's teaching, which follows mainly the Gospel of Matthew and shows it to consist of the universal religion of reason, G.S. 6, pp. 157-63 (pp. 146-51) and of a learned religion, G.S. 6, pp. 163-67 (pp. 151-55).

Another flaw in the structure comes from the fact that ecclesiastical ritual is discussed in the "General Observation." I have included it, however, in my discussion of Book Four.

129. *Religion*, G.S. 6, p. 168 (p. 156).

130. Ibid., G.S. 6, pp. 168-69 (pp. 156-58).

131. Ibid., G.S. 6, p. 170 (p. 158).

132. Ibid., G.S. 6, p. 177 (p. 165).

133. Ibid., G.S. 6, p. 176 (p. 164).

134. Ibid., G.S. 6, p. 185 (p. 173). See also p. 201 (p. 189).

135. Ibid., G.S. 6, p. 185 (p. 173).

136. Ibid., G.S. 6, pp. 188-89 (p. 177).

137. Ibid., G.S. 6, p. 132 (p. 123).

138. See Shaftesbury's, *Characteristics of Men, Manners, Opinions, Times, etc.*, p. 26. Kant gave no reference to his source. The use of this author however does give a hint as to how well-read Kant was as he undertook to write *Religion*, not to mention the question of how many books he had by his elbow as he wrote. The same letter on enthusiasm contains also a praise of Job in terms very close to those of Kant. The indebtedness there, too, is inescapable (p. 25).

139. An unpublished long note on prayer is found in G.S. 19, pp. 637-38.

140. *Religion*, G.S. 6, pp. 198-200 (pp. 186-88).

141. Ibid., G.S. 6, p. 200 (p. 188).

142. Ibid., G.S. 6, pp. 178-79 and 188 (pp. 166 and 176).

143. See Tillich, "The Philosophy of Religion" in *What is Religion?*, pp. 112-13.

144. See Bruch, *Philosophie religieuse*, p. 212.

145. *Religion*, G.S. 6, p. 102 (p. 93).

146. *Metaphysical Elements of Justice*, G.S. 6, p. 327 (p. 95).

147. Bruch called the religious illusion the original sin of the Church. *Philosophie religieuse*, p. 191.

CHAPTER 9

1. See pp. 83-84.

2. *Religion*, G.S. 6, p. 52 (p. 47).

3. Thus of all the commentaries upon *Religion within the Limits of Reason Alone*, this is the one in which I claim for myself the greatest scope of interpretive freedom.

4. The term *parergon* is used by Plato to refer to something which "is somewhat aside from the subject we had proposed for ourselves." *The Statesman* 302B.

5. *Religion*, G.S. 6, p. 52 (p. 47).

6. Ibid., G.S. p. 52 (pp. 47-48).

7. Ibid., G.S. 6, p. 52 (p. 48).

8. Ibid., G.S. 6, pp. 53, 174 (pp. 48, 162).

9. Ibid., G.S. 6, p. 53 (p. 48). On p. 174 (p. 162), superstition is defined as the illusion of being able to justify ourselves before God through ritual acts. Kant used the term also in the widest sense to designate anything contrary to pure religion.

10. Ibid., G.S. 6, p. 53 (p. 48).

11. Ibid., G.S. 6, p. 53 (p. 48). This is called sorcery or fetishism on p. 177 (p. 165) in the course of a discussion of the attempt to achieve supernatural ends through natural means.

12. Ibid., G.S. 6, p. 86 (p. 81).

13. Ibid., G.S. 6, p. 84 (p. 79). This is also the position of the letter to Fichte on 2 February 1792. G.S. 11, pp. 321-22 (*Philosophical Correspondence*, pp. 186-87).

14. *Religion*, G.S. 6, p. 85 (p. 80).

15. Ibid., G.S. 6, p. 87 (p. 82).

16. Ibid., G.S. 6, pp. 84-85 (p. 79). A lengthy unpublished essay examined the notion of the theoretical impossibility of miracles and settled somewhat uneasily against the demonstration of their impossibility. See G.S. 18, pp. 320-22. See also Bruch, *Philosophie religieuse*, pp. 145ff.

17. *Religion*, G.S. 6, p. 137 (p. 129).

18. Thus Kant departed from Wolff who saw in mysteries doctrines which are "above reason."

19. Bruch, *Philosophie religieuse*, p. 133.

20. *Religion*, G.S. 6, pp. 142-43 (pp. 133-34).

21. Ibid., G.S. 6, p. 145 (p. 136). The two concepts of Trinity which Kant discussed are very much at odds with each other, and Kant seems to have known it.

22. Ibid., G.S. 6, p. 147 (p. 138). See Bruch, *Philosophie religieuse*, pp. 129-56.

23. This is particularly well-illustrated by his tension between the two kinds of concepts of the Trinity which he presents. Kant's rational Trinity is a theocentric one and one based upon the idea of a three-fold function of one person. The Christian Trinity, as he presented it, is a Trinity of three persons. Kant did not reconcile one to the other in any way. As a historian he was perspicacious enough not to reduce the Christian Trinity to the one that made sense to him. And his systematic subjection of Divine goodness to Divine justice shows how little impact his knowledge of the Christian doctrine of the Trinity had upon his own thought.

24. On this point I believe we can discern the motive of prudence in Kant. By his own admission, church theologians operate within the framework of the faith in revelation. To make a frontal direct philosophical investigation of the idea of revelation would not be conducive to the peace Kant hoped to see between the two kinds of theologians. There were enough possibilities of offense in Kant's doing his own work, without his trespassing upon the core concept at the basis of the work he had allotted to the other theologians. Kant however could hardly refrain from examining, indirectly at least, the nature of the distinction between reason and revelation, distinction in which he had found the basis for his division of the labour between philosophers of religion and theologians. See *Religion*, G.S. 6, pp. 152-53 (pp. 144-45).

25. "On the Proof of the Spirit and of Power" in Lessing's *Theological Writings*,

(California: Stanford University Press, 1947). For a full discussion of Lessing's handling of this question, see Allison, *Lessing and the Enlightenment*.

26. *Religion*, G.S. 6, p. 141 (p. 132).

27. *Religion*, G.S. 6, p. 144 (p. 135).

28. *Religion*, G.S. 6, p. 155 (p. 143).

29. *Religion*, G.S. 6, p. 145 (p. 136).

30. *Religion*, G.S. 6, pp. 154–55 (p. 143).

31. Collins, *Emergence of Philosophy of Religion*, p. 159. Collins opposed pure non-reductive rationalism to naturalism (Holbach), mere or reductive rationalism (Voltaire), reductive supernaturalism, and irrationalism.

32. *Religion*, G.S. 6, pp. 155–56 (pp. 143–44).

33. Raymond Vancourt, "Kant et la solution rationaliste du problème des religions," *Mélanges de Sciences Religieuses*, Vol. 22, p. 180. The second half of this perceptive article is found in Vol. 25.

34. Kant to Jacobi, 30 August 1789, G.S. 11, p. 76 (*Philosophical Correspondence*, p. 158).

35. Bohatec, *Religionsphilosophie*, p. 636.

36. Kant to Jung-Stilling, after 1 March 1789, G.S. 11, p. 10 (*Philosophical Correspondence*, p. 131).

37. See Collins, *Emergence of Philosophy of Religion*, p. 400. Kant did not concentrate "the philosophy of religion upon a closed system of moral theism without any reference to the revealing and saving God, beyond what is necessarily entailed by moral theism." Divine initiative is the "source of a further openness of the human spirit."

38. *The Strife of Faculties*, G.S. 7, p. 48.

39. Ibid., G.S. 7, p. 50.

40. Webb, *Kant's Philosophy of Religion*, p. 209.

41. Lessing opened the door to such an approach by setting forth the concept "of a divine revelation, which does not descend upon man ready made from without, but achieves realization in man through the development of his religious capacity, and which for that very reason has at every point a divine and a human aspect, and is never wholly without truth, yet never quite a whole truth." (Pfleiderer, quoted by T. M. Greene in "The Historical Context and Religious Significance of Kant's Religion" in Kant, *Religion*, p. xx.)

42. *Religion*, G.S. 6, p. 94 (p. 86).

43. *The Strife of Faculties*, G.S. 7, p. 43.

44. *Religion*, G.S. 6, pp. 82–83 (pp. 77–78).

45. As a crisis in the life of reason, the dawn of the sovereignty of the good principle can be compared to the other leaps in the history of the human race, to the awakening of the imagination and of reason, and to the moment when the need for rational self-discipline became conscious of itself.

46. *Religion*, G.S. 6, p. 84 (p. 79).

47. Ibid., G.S. 6, p. 122 (p. 113).

48. Barth, *Protestant Thought from Rousseau to Ritschl*, p. 175.

49. Ibid., p. 175.

50. *Critique of Judgement*, G.S. 5, p. 472 (II, p. 146).

51. *The Strife of Faculties*, G.S. 7, p. 35.

52. Barth, *Protestant Thought from Rousseau to Ritschl*, pp. 193–94.

53. Ibid., p. 64.

54. *The End of All Things*, G.S. 8, pp. 337-39 (*On History*, pp. 81-84).

55. To what extent Kant thought that reason itself is historically conditioned and will go on being involved in a historical development after it reached its current stage remains a delicate matter. (That he believes reason developed in the past is obvious.) On this see the article by Gerhard Lehmann, "System und Geschichte in Kant's Philosophie," reprinted in his *Beitrage zur Geschichte und Interpretation der Philosophie Kants*. Lehmann brought out the fact that Kant knew that history relativizes systems but did not take this into his own system. System and history were connected in his mind because he thought of both teleologically. I hesitate to follow Lehmann, however, when he argues that Kant's use of teleology indicates that his whole philosophy has biological presuppositions.

56. *Religion*, G.S. 6, p. 124 (p. 115).

57. The idea of religious progress was in the air. Hume's *Natural History of Religion* is after all a kind of sociology of religious development from a universal point of view (see P. Gay, *The Enlightenment*, Vol. 1, p. 411). Hume, however, very pointedly denied that the development towards monotheism was any progress. Primitive polytheism, for instance, was definitely more tolerant. Hume also stated that men in a movement of flux will return to polytheism. Kant would have objected to Hume, first that there is potential for moral purification within monotheistic faith, and second that purified monotheistic faith has gained a public foothold. But he certainly would have agreed with Hume that ecclesiastical faiths present to the philosopher a sorry spectacle.

58. Ibid., G.S. 6, p. 124 (p. 115).

59. Ibid., G.S. 6, pp. 110-11 (pp. 101-2).

60. See p. 000.

61. *Religion*, G.S. 6, p. 116 (pp. 106-7).

62. Ibid., G.S. 6, p. 117 (p. 108). Already in his letter to Lavater of 28 April 1775, Kant had stated that the crucial distinction in the New Testament is that "between my duty and that which God has done for me." G.S. 10, p. 178 (*Philosophical Correspondence*, p. 83).

63. *Religion*, G.S. 6, p. 44 (p. 40).

64. Ibid., G.S. 6, p. 47 (p. 43).

65. Ibid., G.S. 6, p. 143 (p. 134), in "General Observation" on mysteries.

66. Ibid., G.S. 6, p. 190 (p. 179). See also p. 174 (p. 162).

67. Ibid., G.S. 6, p. 118 (p. 108).

68. As Kant put it, the knot is cut and not disentangled. See *Religion*, G.S. 6, p. 119 (p. 109).

69. *Religion*, G.S. 6, p. 118 (p. 108).

70. Ibid., G.S. 6, p. 118 (p. 109).

71. Ibid., G.S. 6, p. 174 (p. 162).

72. Ibid., G.S. 6, p. 52 (p. 47). See also p. 171 (p. 159). Man "may hope that what is not in his power will be supplied by the supreme Wisdom *in some way or other*." "This aid may be so mysterious that God can reveal it to us at best in a symbolic representation in which only what is practical is comprehensible to us."

73. *Religion*, G.S. 6, p. 191 (pp. 178-79).

74. Ibid., G.S. 6, p. 52 (p. 48).

75. Ibid., G.S. 6, p. 189 (p. 177).

76. Ibid., G.S. 6, p. 98 (p. 89).

77. Bruch, *Philosophie religieuse*, pp. 134, 251.

78. The expression appears in the context of a discussion of the parerga, and especially of the idea of divine redeeming grace. *Religion*, G.S. 6, p. 52 (p. 48). Reason, Kant said, shall believe in "the possibility of this supernatural complement" with a faith which "might be called reflective." Such faith is opposed to a dogmatic one. The context does not make it immediately clear why the term reflective. Perhaps because the idea of such a supernatural complement results from our reflection upon our duty to pursue the highest good, our inability to reach it, and our rational faith that it must be reachable. Perhaps also reflective faith, like reflective judgement, is to have only a regulative and not a constitutive use.

79. Kant to Lavater, 28 April 1775, G.S. 10, p. 178 (*Philosophical Correspondence*, pp. 82–83).

80. *Eine Vorlesung über Ethik*, p. 160 (*Lectures on Ethics*, p. 128).

81. *Critique of Practical Reason*, G.S. 5, pp. 127–28 (p. 132).

82. *Anthropology*, G.S. 7, p. 147.

83. *Religion*, G.S. 6, p. 183 (p. 172).

84. Ibid., G.S. 6, p. 161 (p. 148).

85. Ibid., G.S. 6, p. 145 (p. 136).

86. Ibid., G.S. 6, p. 101 (p. 92).

87. Ibid., G.S. 6, pp. 185–90 (pp. 173–78).

88. What about circumstances of torture, we might wish to ask.

89. Quoted in D. P. Walker, *The Decline of Hell* (Chicago: University of Chicago Press, 1964).

90. *Religion*, G.S. 6, p. 100 (p. 92).

91. Ibid., G.S. 6, p. 19 (p. 15).

CHAPTER 10

1. See Weyand, *Geschichtsphilosophie*, pp. 179ff.

2. *Religion*, G.S. 6, p. 189 (p. 177).

3. Ibid., G.S. 6, p. 12 (p. 11).

4. Schultz, *Kant als Philosoph des Protestantismus*, p. 11.

5. Ibid., p. 12.

6. *Religion*, G.S. 6, p. 107 (p. 98). The results of the first experiment are also exhibited by such definitions as, "Religion is the recognition of all duties as divine command" (see p. 108), or, "Faith, in the plain acceptance of the term, is a confidence of attaining a purpose the furthering of which is a duty, but whose achievement is a thing of which we are unable to *perceive* the possibility—or, consequently, the possibility of what we can alone conceive to be its conditions" (*Critique of Judgement*, G.S. 5, p. 472 [II, p. 146]).

7. These are the terms of G. Vancourt, "Kant et la solution rationaliste du problème des religions (Suite)," *Mélanges de Sciences Religieuses* 25, 1968.

8. It is the merit of Collins' work to have systematically struggled for such a new formulation of the Kantian thesis. See *Emergence of Philosophy of Religion*, pp. 197ff.

9. Melvin J. Lasky, "The Sweet Dream: Kant and the Revolutionary Hope for Utopia" in *Encounter*, XXXIII, 4 October 1969, p. 17.

10. Incidentally this oscillation also makes of Kant's philosophy a constant corrective to the Hegelian impulse to identify reason and history.

11. G.S. 20, p. 438.

12. Troeltsch, "Das Historische," p. 137.

13. Ibid., p. 141.

14. Ibid., p. 130.

15. Ibid., p. 137.

16. Ibid., p. 151.

17. Ibid., p. 42.

18. Ibid., pp. 145–46.

19. Ibid., p. 70.

20. Ibid., p. 75.

21. Ibid., p. 78. It is still a mystery to me how Troeltsch could arrive at such a fundamentally sound interpretation while holding that *Religion* is a work of compromise and prudence. (See pp. 59–62).

22. Ibid., p. 40.

23. Kant to M. Reuss, May 1793, G.S. 11, p. 431.

24. I do not agree with Goldmann that Kant called himself a Christian only when he wanted to differentiate himself from the Epicureans and the Stoics, although I agree that he did do that when he called himself a Christian. See Goldmann, *Communauté humaine*, p. 233.

25. R. Vancourt concluded that Kant asked Christianity to become a natural religion. See "Solution rationaliste," *Mélanges de Sciences Religieuses* 25, 1968, p. 105. Kant, according to Vancourt, would thus be offering an heretical option. What we have to examine is whether Vancourt who allowed that Christianity needs purification was right in concluding that for Kant Christianity ought to abolish itself.

26. I refer of course to religious life, and not to superstition.

27. *The Strife of Faculties*, G.S. 7, p. 28.

28. Collins, *Emergence of Philosophy of Religion*, pp. 207ff.

29. Ibid., p. 209.

30. *The Strife of Faculties*, G.S. 7, p. 63. *Religion*, G.S. 6, p. 87 (p. 82).

31. *Religion*, G.S. 6, p. 76 (p. 70).

32. Kant had a Calvinistic conception of the impassibility of God and of the foolishness of praying for divine favours. "God cannot be diverted (to our present advantage) from the plan of his wisdom." *Religion*, G.S. 6, p. 196 (p. 184).

33. *Religion*, G.S. 6, p. 177 (p. 165).

34. Mark 9 :24, quoted in *Religion*, G.S. 6, p. 190 (p. 178).

35. Ludwig Feuerbach, *The Essence of Christianity*. Passim and especially pp. 120ff.

36. *Religion*, G.S. 6, p. 117 (pp. 107–8).

37. Ibid., G.S. 6, p. 144 (p. 135).

38. *The Strife of Faculties*, G.S. 7, pp. 44–45.

39. *Religion*, G.S. 6, p. 202 (p. 190).

40. Bruch, *Philosophie religieuse*, p. 262.

41. Lacroix, *Kant et le kantisme*, p. 125.

42. See pp. 25–26.

43. L. W. Beck, *Early German Philosophy*, p. 430. Kant did found a new school but it was a philosophical school, not an ideological faction.

44. Ibid., p. 429.

45. Collins, "A Kantian Critique of the God Is Dead Theme" in Beck, ed., *Kant Studies Today*.

46. See Gay, *The Enlightenment*, Vol. 1, pp. 3ff.

47. Ibid., p. 419.

48. Ibid., p. 236.

49. G. Grant, *Technology and Empire*, p. 114.

50. L. Strauss, *Natural Right and History*, p. 249.

51. Grant, *Technology and Empire*, p. 138. Grant adds: "But if our situation is such, then we do not have a system of meaning" because "human excellence cannot be appropriated by those who think of it as sustained simply in the human will, but only by those who have glimpsed that it is sustained by.all that is." Ibid., p. 133.

52. This matter of the ontological basis of the moral law for Kant has been the object of considerable debate. H. J. Paton argued for the following position: "If a man believes that the supreme value in life, the one which claims priority above all others, is to do his duty; if he believes also that it is his supreme duty to live, so far as he may, as a free citizen of an ideal community, and to seek its realization; if, further, he not only believes this, but strives to act on this belief; then he will find that he is not merely accepting the world as the environment in which he must act, but is obeying moral laws *as if* they were the principles on which the universe is governed." H. J. Paton, *The Modern Predicament*, p. 334.

This position however seems to me to reflect Vahinger's "als-ob Philosophie" more than Kant's own position. In the light of what Kant said about religious feeling, rational faith, and moral and aesthetic awe, it seems more correct to say that the ontological ground of moral laws was for Kant a conviction rather than a wager. John McQuarrie's position is thus perhaps a better reflection of the Kantian results. "Faith thus implies the conviction that there is a context of meaning and value prior to the meanings and values that we create; and, for ethics, this implies that moral obligation is rooted not merely in human convention but ontologically. In terms of the Bible, these convictions of faith first find expression in the doctrine of the Creation." John McQuarrie, *Three Issues in Ethics*.

G. Krüger very carefully pointed out that the Kantian doctrine of God governing the world is not at all a doctrine of universal causation issuing from a first cause, thanks to Kant's understanding of analogy, and that the doctrine of man appropriating the ends of Creation is not at all that of man submitting his will to the laws of nature or accepting the inevitable. See *Philosophie und Moral*, pp. 103–7, 145, 167. (Beck, *Commentary*, pp. 205–7).

53. In other words I restate that Kantian formalism or ethics of the right is a methodology. It states how we should decide in order to become worthy of that which is good. It does not make the good derivative, utilitarian, or a result of our free choice.

54. See pp. 197–201.

55. See pp. 148–53.

56. Ernst Cassirer proposed half a century ago that Kant's doctrine of schematism is the root of systematic unity in his work and suggested that the development from the doctrine of transcendental schematism in the first Critique to the doctrine of symbols in the third is the focal point of constructive thought in Kant during the critical period. And Cassirer based his entire philosophy of symbolic forms on the basis he had discerned in Kant. See E. Cassirer, *The Philosophy of Symbolic Forms*, 3 vols. (New Haven: Yale University Press, 1953–57).

57. In another sense Kant could be presented not as having restated metaphysical theism under fresh pressures and thus rescuing a worthy and ancient Greek tradition, but rather as finally having brought along Christian theism to the full results implicit in biblical Covenant theology. For Kant looked into the conflicts within moral consciousness and focused upon the bond between the free God and the free human agent, and gave the last answer to a personal trust, not to the wisdom of insight. "Our trust in God is unconditional, that is, it is not accompanied by any inquisitive desire to know how his purposes will be achieved," he wrote to Lavater on 28 April 1775, G.S. 10, pp. 175-79 (*Philosophical Correspondence*, p. 80). Note, however, that such unconditional trust is that of a moral man in a moral God. It is not the position of existentialism and is subject to rational control.

CHAPTER 11

1. *Idea*, G.S. 8, p. 23 (*On History*, p. 17).
2. *Education*, G.S. 9, pp. 443 and 446 (pp. 6 and 11).
3. See Philonenko's Preface to Kant, *Réflexions sur l' éducation*, pp. 37-38.
4. See pp. 35-36.
5. *Critique of Pure Reason*, A 817, B 845, (p. 643).
6. For Kant's position among eighteenth century educators see the erudite Preface by Philonenko to Kant, *Réflexions sur l'éducation*. For a more general survey of the eighteenth century approach to education see Gay, *The Enlightenment*, Vol. 2, pp. 497ff.
7. See Preface by Philonenko, in Kant, *Réflexions sur l'éducation*, p. 34.
8. *Anthropology*, G.S. 7, pp. 321-30.
9. *Anthropology* was published in 1798, albeit from older notes. Thus the themes proper to the philosophy of history remain in Kant even after the development of the philosophy of religion, although with a sharper sense of evil and a clearer trust in Providence.
10. *Anthropology*, G.S. 7, p. 147.
11. See Collins, *Emergence of Philosophy of Religion*, p. 163.
12. I do not bring in the parerga, since they are not part of religion within the limits of reason alone.
13. *Religionslehre*, p. 195.
14. See *Religion*, G.S. 6, pp. 142-43 (p. 133).
15. See pp. 116-18.
16. Schultz, *Kant als Philosoph des Protestantismus*, p. 83.
17. Ibid., pp. 23, 88. That both the concept of limits and the concept of freedom derive from Kant's sense of the holy indicates that it is not wise to divorce Kant's philosophy from his religion, as many of the neo-Kantians did.
18. See M. Heidegger, *Kant and the Problem of Metaphysics*.
19. Bohatec, *Religionsphilosophie*, p. 591.
20. Gay, *The Enlightenment*, Vol. 2, pp. 3-8.
21. Quoted in Gay, *The Enlightenment*, Vol. 1, p. 90.
22. *Foundations of the Metaphysics of Morals*, G.S. 4, p. 413. Moral man does not act from pathological interest but with practical interest.

23. *Critique of Practical Reason*, G.S. 5, p. 113 (p. 117).

24. Ibid., G.S. 5, p. 122 (p. 127).

25. W.H. Walsh, "Kant's Moral Theology," pp. 271, 273.

26. *Critique of Pure Reason*, A 813, B 841 (p. 640).

27. *The Strife of Faculties*, G.S. 7, pp. 91-92 (*On History*, p. 151).

28. *Perpetual Peace*, G.S. 8, p. 367 (*On History*, p. 113).

29. Ibid., G.S. 8, p. 362 (p. 108).

30. Once we remember that Leibniz believed the world is the best of all possible and not perfect, and once we add the Kantian premise that such a world for moral reasons has to include a radical freedom with suicidal potential (human freedom for Kant cannot alienate itself absolutely but it can kill the man and deny him the fulfilment of his moral potential), then we can wonder indeed if there is any difference left between Kant's perfectible world and Leibniz's best of all possible worlds. Ultimately the difference may be only between practical and theoretical reason. Leibniz allowed himself to acquire the reputation of having argued that one can show that the world is the best of all possible while Kant underlined that we can perfect it if we but choose to work at it.

31. *Critique of Practical Reason*, G.S. 5, p. 131 (p. 136).

32. *Idea*, G.S. 8, p. 20 (*On History*, p. 14).

33. See Troeltsch, "Das Historische," p. 129, and Delbos, *Philosophie pratique*, pp. 297-98.

34. I find an autobiographical significance as well to the passage: "We find, in the history of human reason, that until the concepts were sufficiently purified and determined, and until the systematic unity of their ends was understood in accordance with these concepts and from necessary principles, the knowledge of nature, and even a quite considerable development of reason in many other sciences, could give rise only to crude and incoherent concepts of the Deity.... A greater preoccupation with moral ideas, which was rendered necessary by the extraordinary pure moral laws of our religion, made reason more acutely aware of its object, through the interest which it was compelled to take in it." *Critique of Pure Reason*, A 817, B 845 (p. 643).

35. Bruch was even more negative than I am and denied that Kant really had a notion of philosophy of the history of religion. See *Philosophie religieuse*, pp. 217ff.

36. Quoted in J. Pieper, *Hope and History*.

37. See Hannah Arendt, "The Concept of History," *Between Past and Future: Six Exercises in Political Thought*, p. 84.

38. Pieper, *Hope and History*, p. 47. I agree with Pieper that Kant's conception of the historical future contains "nearly all the elements of the great traditional eschatology" (ibid., p. 51). Pieper referred of course to Christian eschatology and emphasized the difference on this point between Kant and Hegel's immanentization of divine Providence. I cannot, however, agree unqualifiedly with Pieper's view that "the comprehensive intellectual structure" which could hold together history and eschatology has in Kant "lost its organizing force" (ibid., p. 52). For one thing I do not know where to find such a satisfactory comprehensive intellectual structure.

39. Jacques Ellul noted shrewdly that in the bourgeois philosophy of progress, progress is never gratuitous but always deserved. *Métamorphoses du bourgeois*, pp. 107-8.

40. See p. 162.

41. See E. Kahler, *The Meaning of History*, pp. 19, 50, 210.

42. Collins, *Emergence of Philosophy of Religion*, p. 385.

Bibliography

Unless otherwise noted, citations of Kant refer to the edition of his complete works first published by the Prussian Royal Academy: *Gesammelte Schriften*, 28 vols. Berlin: Walter de Gruyter, 1902–68 (abbreviation G.S.

Some of the lectures are not yet available in this edition and other texts must be used:

Eine Vorlesung über Ethik. Edited by Paul Menzer, Berlin: Pan Verlag Rolf Heise, 1924. *Vorlesungen über die philosophische Religionslehre*. Edited by K. Pölitz, Leipzig: Franz, 1817 (abbreviation *Religionslehre*).

Citations may also refer, after the reference to the German text, to English translations. Such references are always indicated in parentheses.

Critique of Judgement. Translated by J. Creed Meredith. London: Oxford University Press, 1952.

Critique of Practical Reason. Translated by L. W. Beck. New York: Bobbs-Merrill, 1956.

Critique of Pure Reason. Translated by N. Kemp Smith. New York: MacMillan & Co., 1958.

The Doctrine of Virtue, Part II of *The Metaphysic of Morals*. Translated by M. J. Gregor. New York: Harper and Row, 1964.

Education. Translated by A. Churton. Ann Arbor, Michigan: The University of Michigan Press, 1960.

Foundations of the Metaphysics of Morals and *What is Enlightenment?* Translated by L. W. Beck. New York: Bobbs Merrill, 1959. Another translation of the *Foundations* is also found with an analysis in H. J. Paton. *The Moral Law: Kant's Groundwork of the Metaphysics of Morals*. London: Hutchinson University Library, 1948.

Introduction to Logic. Translated by T. K. Abbott. London: Vision Press, 1963.

Lectures on Ethics. Translated by L. Infield. New York: Harper and Row, 1963.

The Metaphysical Elements of Justice, Part I of *The Metaphysic of Morals*. Translated by J. Ladd. New York: Bobbs-Merrill, 1965.

Observations on the Feeling of the Beautiful and Sublime. Translated by John T. Goldthwait. Berkeley and Los Angeles: University of California Press, 1960.

On History. Translated by L. W. Beck, R. E. Anchor, E. L. Fackenheim. New York: Bobbs-Merrill, 1963. This collection contains *What is Enlightenment?*, *Idea for a Universal History from a Cosmopolitan Point of View* (abbreviated *Idea*), *Conjectural Beginnings of Human History*, *The End of All Things*, *Perpetual Peace*, and *An Old Question Raised Again: Is the Human Race Constantly Progressing?* (Part II of *The Strife of Faculties*).

Philosophical Correspondence 1759–99. Translated by A. Zweig. Chicago: The University of Chicago Press, 1967.

Political Writings. Translated by H. Reiss. Cambridge: Cambridge University Press, 1970. Contains among others *On the Common Saying: 'This may be true in Theory, but It Does not Apply in Practice'*.

Prolegomena to any Further Metaphysics. Translated by P. Carus. La Salle, Ill.: The Open Court Publishing Co., 1955.
Religion within the Limits of Reason Alone. Translated by T. M. Greene and H. H. Hudson. New York: Harper Bros, 1960 (abbreviation *Religion*).
Universal Natural History and Theory of the Heavens. Translated by W. Hastie. Ann Arbor, Michigan: The University of Michigan Press, 1969.

The following French translations contain excellent introductions and notes: *Qu'est-ce que s'orienter dans la pensée?* Translated by A. Philonenko. Paris: Vrin, 1959. *Réflexions sur l'éducation.* Translated by A. Philonenko. Paris: Vrin, 1966.

Sources on Kant

Books

ALQUIÉ, FERDINAND. *La Critique kantienne de la métaphysique.* Paris: PUF, 1968.
BECK, LEWIS WHITE. *A Commentary on Kant's Critique of Practical Reason.* Chicago: The University of Chicago Press, 1961.
———. (Ed.) *Kant Studies Today.* La Salle, Illinois: Open Court Library of Philosophy, 1969.
BEYER, KURT. *Untersuchungen zu Kants Vorlesungen über die philosophische Religionslehre.* Halle: Klinz, 1937.
BOHATEC, JOSEF. *Die Religionsphilosophie Kants in der "Religion innerhalb der Grenzen der blossen Vernunft"* Hildesheim: Georg Olms, 1966.
BOUTROUX, EMILE. *La Philosophie de Kant.* Paris: Vrin, 1968.
BRUCH, JEAN-LOUIS. *La Philosophie religieuse de Kant.* Paris: Aubier, 1968.
CASSIRER, ERNST. *Rousseau, Kant and Goethe.* New York: Harper & Row, Harper Torchbooks, 1963.
COPLESTON, FREDERICK. *A History of Philosophy,* Volume 6, *Modern Philosophy,* Part II, *Kant.* Garden City: Doubleday & Co., Image Book, 1964.
DELBOS, VICTOR. *La Philosophie pratique de Kant.* Paris: F. Alcan, 1905.
DELEKAT, FRIEDRICH. *Immanuel Kant: Historisch-Kritische Interpretation der Hauptschriften.* Heidelberg: Quelle & Meyer, 1963.
DELEUZE, GILLES. *La Philosophie critique de Kant.* Paris: PUF, 1967.
DE VLEESCHAUER, H. J. *The Development of Kantian Thought.* London: Nelson, 1962.
FRIEDRICH, CARL JOACHIM. *Inevitable Peace.* Cambridge, Mass.: Harvard University Press, 1948.
GOLDMANN, LUCIEN. *La Communauté humaine et l'univers chez Kant.* Paris: PUF, 1948. Republished as: *Introduction à philosophie de Kant.* Paris: NRF, 1967.
GRAM, MOLTKE S. *Kant: Disputed Questions.* Chicago: Quadrangle Books, 1967.
———. *Kant, Ontology, and the A Priori.* Evanston: Northwestern University Press, 1968.
GREGOR, MARY J. *Laws of Freedom.* Oxford: Basil Blackwell, 1963.
HARTNACK, JUSTUS. *Kant's Theory of Knowledge.* New York: Harcourt, Brace & World, 1967.
HEIDEGGER, MARTIN. *Kant and the Problem of Metaphysics.* Bloomington: Indiana University Press, 1962.

I. Kant: Sein Leben in Darstellung von Zeitgenossen. Berlin: Deutsche Bibliothek, n.d. (contains lives by Borowski, Jachmann, and Wasianski).

JASPERS, KARL. *Kant*. New York: Harcourt, Brace & World, A Harvest Book, 1962.

KAFTAN, JULIUS. *Kant, der Philosoph des Protestantismus*. Berlin. 1904.

KLINKE, WILLIBALD. *Kant for Everyman*. New York: Collier Books, 1962.

KÖRNER, S. *Kant*. Baltimore, Md.: Penguin Books, 1955.

KRONER, RICHARD. *Kant's Weltanschauung*. Chicago: University of Chicago Press, 1956.

KRÜGER, GERHARD. *Philosophie und Moral in der Kantischen Kritik*. Tübingen: J.C.B. Mohr, 1931.

LEBRUN, GÉRARD. *Kant et la fin de la métaphysique*. Paris: Armand Colin, 1970.

LACROIX, JEAN. *Kant et le kantisme*. Paris: PUF, 1967.

LEHMANN, GERHARD. *Beitrage zur Geschichte und Interpretation der Philosophie Kants*. Berlin: Walter de Gruyter, 1969.

LENFERS, DIETMAR. *Kants Weg von der Teleologie zur Theologie: Interpretationen zu Kants Kritik der Urteilskraft*. Ph.D. dissertation, University of Cologne, 1965.

MARTIN, GOTTFRIED. *Kant's Metaphysics and Theory of Science*. Manchester: Manchester University Press, 1955.

MAY, J. A. *Kant's Concept of Geography and Its Relation to Recent Geographical Thought*. Toronto: University of Toronto Press, 1970.

MCFARLAND, J. D. *Kant's Concept of Teleology*. Edinburgh: Edinburgh University Press, 1970

PATON, H. J. *The Categorical Imperative: A Study in Kant's Moral Philosophy*. New York: Harper & Row, 1967.

PHILONENKO, A. *Théorie et praxis dans la pensée morale et politique de Kant et de Fichte en 1793*. Paris: Vrin, 1968.

REBOUL, OLIVIER. *Kant et le problème du mal*. Montréal: Presses de l'université de Montréal, 1971.

ROUSSET, BERNARD. *La Doctrine kantienne de l'objectivité: l'autonomie comme devoir et devenir*. Paris: Vrin, 1967.

SANER, HANS. *Widerstreit und Einheit: Wege zu Kants Politischem Denken*. Munich: R. Piper & Co., 1967.

SCHILPP, P. A. *Kant's Pre-Critical Ethic*. Evanston: Northwestern University Press, 1960.

SCHMALENBACH, HERMANN. *Kant's Religion*. Berlin: Junker und Dünnhaupt, 1929.

SCHULTZ, WERNER. *Kant als Philosoph des Protestantismus*. Hamburg Bergstedt: Herbert Reich, 1960.

SCHWEITZER, ALBERT. *The Essence of Faith: Philosophy of Religion*. New York: Philosophical Library, 1966.

VIALATOUX, JOSEPH. *La Morale de Kant*. Paris: PUF, 1956.

VLACHOS, GEORGES. *La Pensée politique de Kant*. Paris: PUF, 1962.

VON GLASENAPP, HELMUTH. *Kant und die Religionen des Ostens*. Kitzingen: Holzner Verlag, 1954.

VON WEIZSÄCKER, CARL FRIEDRICH. *History of Nature*. Chicago: University of Chicago Press, 1949.

WEBB, C. C. J. *Kant's Philosophy of Religion*. Oxford: Oxford University Press, 1926.

WEIL, E., RUYSSEN, T., VILLEY, M., HASSNER, P., BOBBIO, N., BECK, L. W., FRIEDRICH, C. J., POLIN, R. *La Philosophie politique de Kant*. Paris: PUF, 1962.

WEIL, ERIC. *Problèmes kantiens.* Paris: Vrin, 1963.
WEYAND, KLAUS. *Kants Geschichtsphilosophie: Ihre Entwicklung und ihr Verhaltnis zur Aufklärung.* Cologne: Kölneruniversitäts-Verlag, 1964.
WHITNEY, GEORGE TAPLEY and BOWERS, DAVID F. *The Heritage of Kant.* New York: Russel and Russel, 1962.
WOOD, ALLEN W. *Kant's Moral Religion.* Ithaca: Cornell University Press, 1970.
WOLFF, ROBERT P. *I. Kant: A Collection of Critical Essays.* Garden City: Doubleday & Company, 1967.

Articles

FACKENHEIM, EMIL. "Kant and Radical Evil." *University of Toronto Quarterly* 23 (1953-54).
———. "Kant's Concept of History," *Kantstudien* 48 (1956-57).
FROST, WALTER. "Kants Teleologie." *Kantstudien* 11 (1906).
GREENE, THEODORE M. "The Historical Context and Religious Significance of Kant's *Religion*" in Kant. *Religion within the Limits of Reason Alone.* New York: Harper Bros, 1960.
JASPERS, KARL. "Das radikale Böse bei Kant." *Rechenschaft und Ausblick.* Munich: Piper, 1951.
JONES, W. T. "Purpose, Nature and the Moral Law" in Whitney, G. T. and Bowers, P. F. *The Heritage of Kant.* New York: Russel and Russel, 1962.
MARTY, FRANÇOIS. "La notion de symbole chez Kant." *Sociétés de philosophie de langue française.* Actes du XIII ème Congrès. Neuchâtel, A la Baconnière, 1966.
MELVIN, J. LASKY. "The Sweet Dream: Kant and the Revolutionary Hope for Utopia." *Encounter* (October 1969).
MEDICUS, FRITZ. "Kants Philosophie der Geschichte." *Kantstudien* 7 (1902).
NABERT, JEAN. "Note sur l'idee du mal chez Kant" in *Essai sur le Mal.* Paris: PUF, 1955.
PAULSEN, FRIEDRICH. "Kant, der Philosoph des Protestantismus." *Kantstudien* 4 (1900).
REBOUL, OLIVIER. "Kant et la religion." *Revue d'histoire et de philosophie religieuses* 50 (1970).
RUYSSEN, T.H. "Kant est-il pessimiste?" *Revue de métaphysique et de morale* 12 (1904).
SILBER, JOHN R. "The Copernican Revolution in Ethics: The Good Reexamined." *Kantstudien* 51 (1959).
———. "The Ethical Significance of Kant's *Religion*" in Kant. *Religion within the Limits of Reason Alone.* New York: Harper Bros, 1960.
TARBET, DAVID W. "The Fabric of Metaphor in Kant's *Critique of Pure Reason.*" *Journal of the History of Philosophy* 6 (1968).
TROELTSCH, ERNST. "Das Historische in Kants Religionsphilosophie." *Kantstudien* 9 (1904).
VANCOURT, RAYMOND. "Kant et la solution rationaliste du problème des religions." *Mélanges de sciences religieuses* 22 (1965); 25 (1968).
WALSH, W. H. "Kant's Moral Theology." *Proceedings of the British Academy* 49. London: Oxford University Press, 1964.

WILKINS, B. T. "Teleology in Kant's Philosophy of History." *History and Theory* 5 (1966).

Other Sources

ALLISON, H. E. *Lessing and the Enlightenment*. Ann Arbor: University of Michigan Press, 1966.
ARENDT, HANNAH. *Between Past and Future: Six Exercises in Political Thought*. Cleveland: The World Publishing Company, Meridian Books, 1963.
BARTH, KARL. *Protestant Thought from Rousseau to Ritschl*. London: SCM Press, 1959.
BECK, LEWIS WHITE. *Early German Philosophy: Kant and His Predecessors*. Cambridge, Mass.: Harvard University Press, 1969.
BECKER, CARL L. *The Heavenly City of the Eighteenth Century Philosophers*. New Haven: Yale University Press, 1932.
BREDVOLD, LOUIS I. *The Brave New World of the Enlightenment*. Ann Arbor, Michigan: The University of Michigan Press, 1961.
CASSIRER, ERNST. *The Philosophy of the Enlightenment*. Boston: Beacon Press, 1955.
CHADWICK, HENRY. *Lessing's Theological Writings*. Stanford, Calif.: Stanford University Press, 1957.
COLLINGWOOD, R. G. *The Idea of History*. New York: Oxford University Press, Galaxy Book, 1957.
COLLINS, JAMES. *The Emergence of Philosophy of Religion*. New Haven: Yale University Press, 1967.
CORETH, E. *Metaphysics*. New York: Herder and Herder, 1968.
ELLUL, JACQUES. *Métamorphoses du bourgeois*. Paris: Calmann-Lévy, 1967.
FEUERBACH, LUDWIG. *The Essence of Christianity*. New York: Harper & Row, 1957.
GAY, PETER. *The Enlightenment: An Interpretation*. 2 vols. New York: A. Knopf, 1967 and 1969.
GLASS, B., TEMKIN, O., and STRAUS JR., W. J. (eds.). *Forerunners of Darwin: 1745–1859*. Baltimore, Md.: The John Hopkins Press, 1968.
GRANT, GEORGE. *Technology and Empire*. Toronto: House of Anansi, 1969.
HEINE, HEINRICH. *Philosophy and Religion in Germany*. Boston: Beacon Press, 1959.
KAHLER, ERICH. *The Meaning of History*. Cleveland: The World Publishing Company, Meridian Books, 1968.
LACROIX, JEAN. *Histoire et mystère*. Tournai: Casterman, 1962.
LEIBNIZ, GOTTFRIED WILHELM. *Theodicy* (Abridged). Edited by C. J. Gerhardt. Translated by E. M. Huggard. New York: Bobbs-Merrill, 1966.
LOVEJOY, ARTHUR O. *The Great Chain of Being: A Study of the History of an Idea*. Cambridge, Mass.: Harvard University Press, 1936.
———. *Essays in the History of Ideas*. New York: G. P. Putnam, Capricorn Books, 1960.
LÖWITH, KARL. *Meaning in History*. Chicago: University of Chicago Press, 1957.
MCQUARRIE, JOHN. *Three Issues in Ethics*. New York: Harper and Row, 1970.
MOLTMANN, JÜRGEN. *Theology of Hope*. London: SCM Press, 1967.
NISBET, ROBERT A. *Social Change and History: Aspects of the Western Theory of Development*. New York: Oxford University Press, 1970.
PATON, H. J. *The Modern Predicament*. London: Allen and Unwin, 1955.
PIEPER, JOSEF. *Hope and History*. New York: Herder and Herder, 1969.

346 Kant on History and Religion

RICOEUR, PAUL. *Le Conflit des interprétations. Essais d'herméneutique.* Paris: Editions de Seuil, 1969.
———. *Finitude et culpabilité.* Vol. 1. *L'Homme faillible.* Paris: Aubier, 1960.
SAMPSON, R. V. *Progress in the Age of Reason.* Cambridge, Mass.: Harvard University Press, 1956.
SHAFTESBURY, ANTHONY ASHLEY COOPER, EARL OF. *Characteristics of Men, Manners, Opinions, Times etc.* Gloucester, Mass.: Peter Smith, 1963.
SMITH, WILFRED CANTWELL. *The Meaning and End of Religion.* New York: The MacMillan Co., 1963.
STRAUSS, LEO. *Natural Right and History.* Chicago: The University of Chicago Press, Pheonix Books, 1953.
TILLICH, PAUL. *What is Religion?* New York: Harper and Row, 1969.
TOULMIN, S. and GOODFIELD, G. *The Discovery of Time.* New York: Harper and Row, 1965.
TUVESON, ERNEST LEE. *Millennium and Utopia.* New York: Harper & Row, Harper Torchbook, 1964.
WILLEY, BASIL. *The Eighteenth Century Background: Studies on the Idea of Nature in the Thought of the Period.* Boston: Beacon Press, 1961.

General Index

Index of Names